ENIALE & DEWIELA

KAMOME SHIRAHAMA

1

INDEX

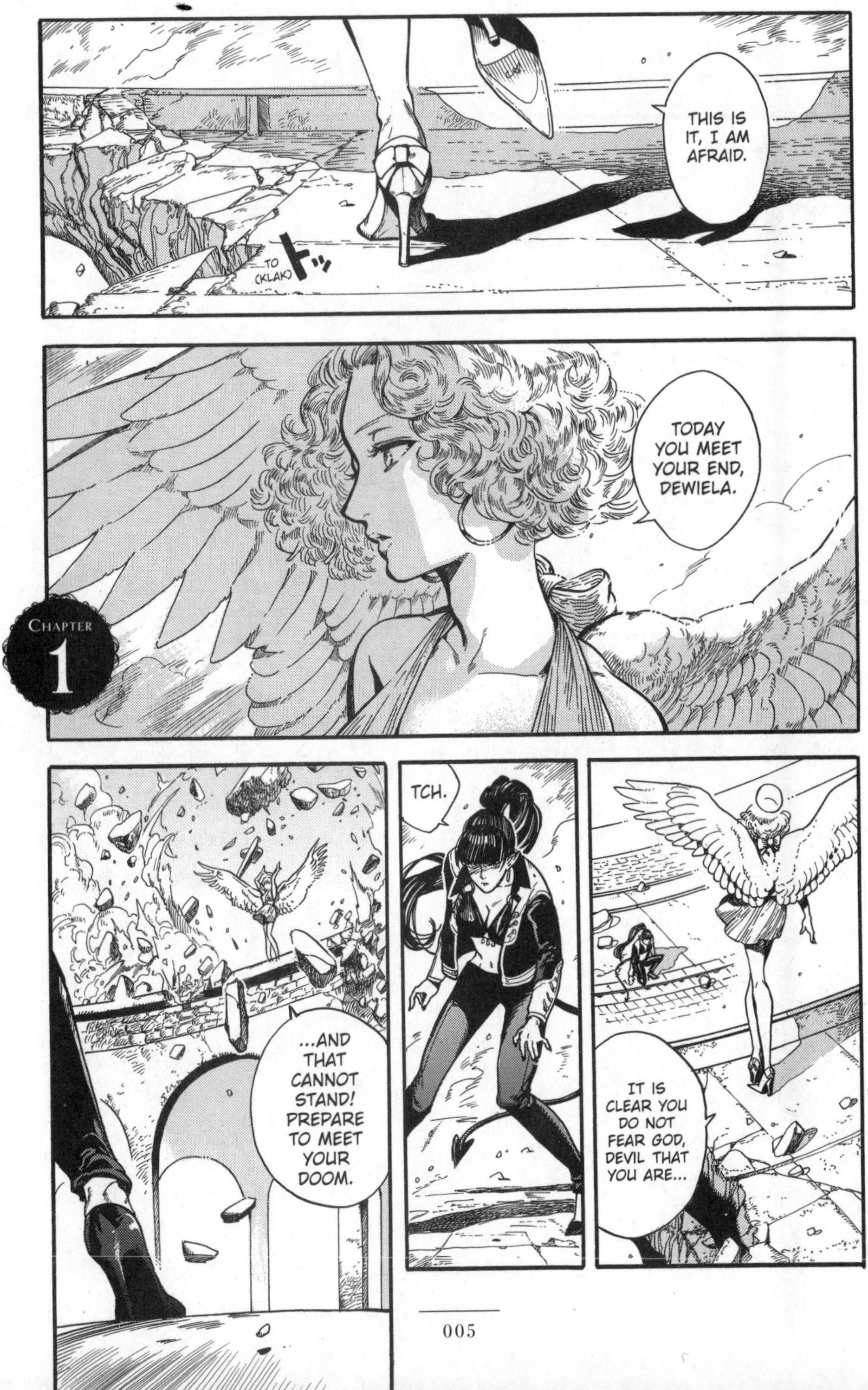
THIS IS IT, I AM AFRAID.
TO (KLAK)
ドッ
TODAY YOU MEET YOUR END, DEWIELA.
CHAPTER 1
IT IS CLEAR YOU DO NOT FEAR GOD, DEVIL THAT YOU ARE...
TCH.
...AND THAT CANNOT STAND! PREPARE TO MEET YOUR DOOM.

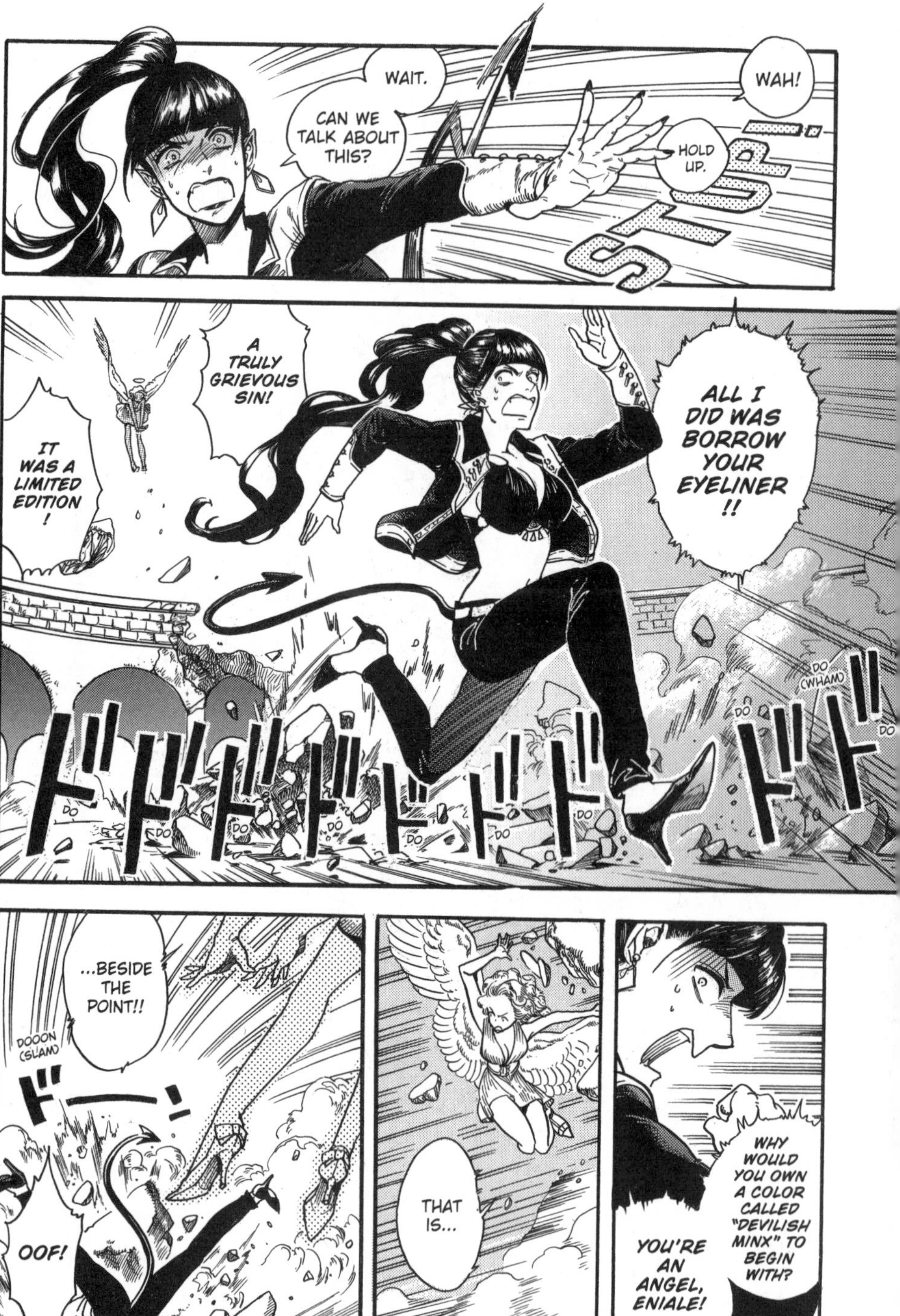
WAH!
HOLD UP.
STOP!
WAIT.
CAN WE TALK ABOUT THIS?
ALL I DID WAS BORROW YOUR EYELINER!!
A TRULY GRIEVOUS SIN!
IT WAS A LIMITED EDITION!
DO (WHAM)
WHY WOULD YOU OWN A COLOR CALLED "DEVILISH MINX" TO BEGIN WITH?
YOU'RE AN ANGEL, ENIALE!
THAT IS...
...BESIDE THE POINT!!
DOOON (SLAM)
OOF!

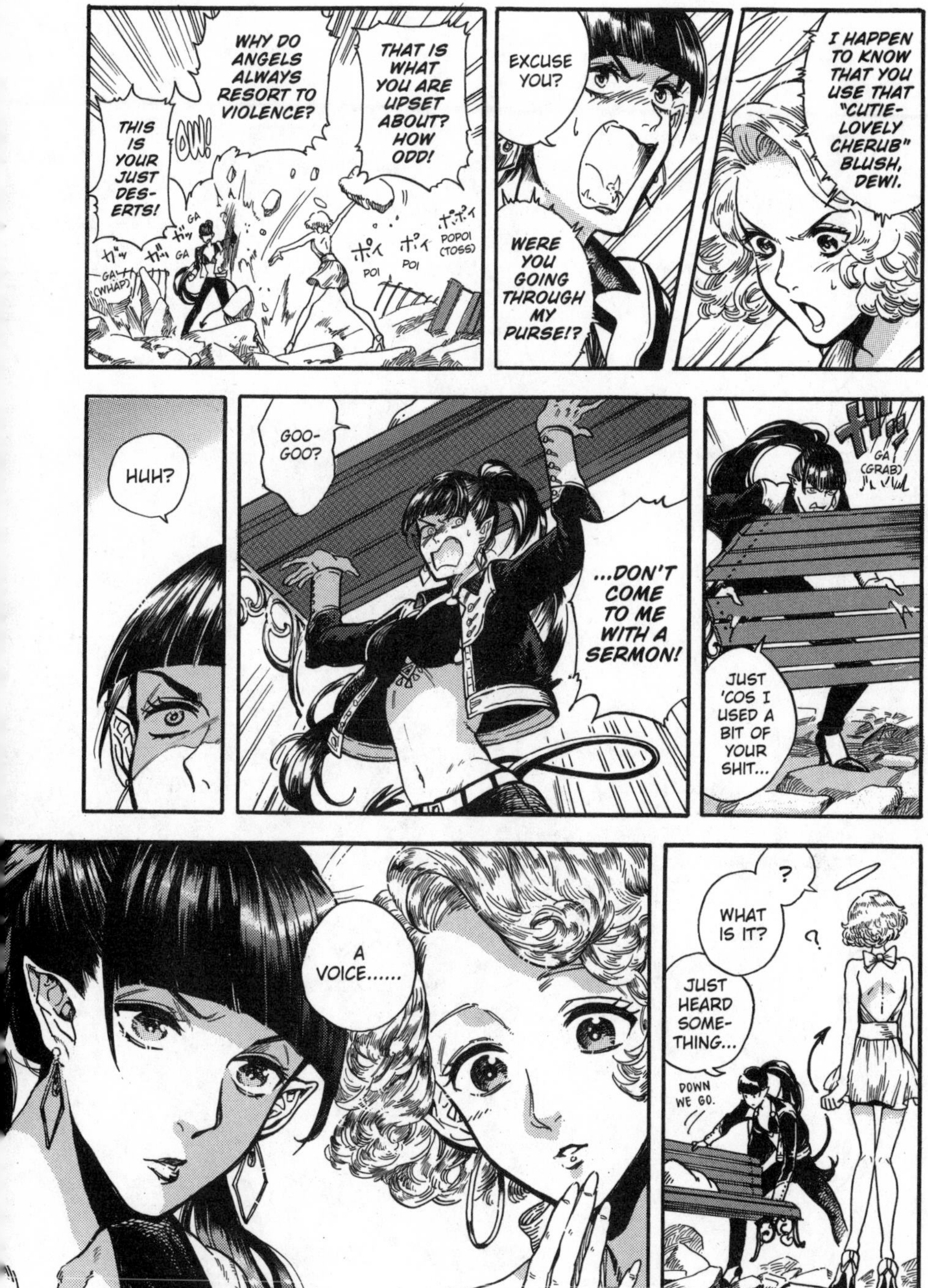
I HAPPEN TO KNOW THAT YOU USE THAT "CUTIE-LOVELY CHERUB" BLUSH, DEWI.
EXCUSE YOU?
WERE YOU GOING THROUGH MY PURSE!?
THAT IS WHAT YOU ARE UPSET ABOUT? HOW ODD!
WHY DO ANGELS ALWAYS RESORT TO VIOLENCE?
OW!
THIS IS YOUR JUST DES-ERTS!
ポポイ POPOI (TOSS)
ポイ POI
ポイ POI
ガッ GA
ガッ GA
ガッ GA (WHAP)
GA (GRAB)
JUST 'COS I USED A BIT OF YOUR SHIT...
GOO-GOO?
...DON'T COME TO ME WITH A SERMON!
HUH?
?
WHAT IS IT?
?
JUST HEARD SOME-THING...
DOWN WE GO.
A VOICE......

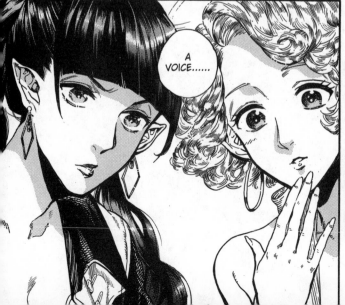

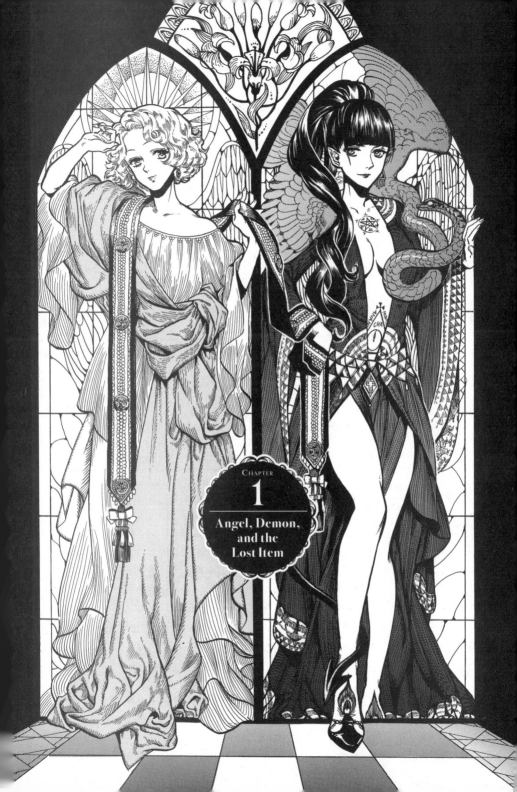

CHAPTER

1

Angel, Demon,
and the
Lost Item

WOULD YOU LOOK AT THAT!

FUNI

TOO YOUNG TO BE DOING THE LOSING, DON'T YOU THINK?

WHY'S IT HERE ALL ALONE?

FUNI

FUNI

IT SEEMS WE HAVE FOUND AN ADORABLE BABY.

FUNI

DID YOU LOSE YOUR MOTHER, LITTLE ONE?

FUNI (SKWOOSH)

OH.

AAAAH, I COULD DO THIS ALL DAY!

ふに ふに ふに ふに ふに
FUNI FUNI FUNI FUNI FUNI
ふに ふに ふに ふに ふに
FUNI FUNI FUNI FUNI FUNI
ふに ふに ふに ふに ふに
FUNI FUNI FUNI FUNI FUNI
ふに ふに ふに ふに ふに
FUNI FUNI FUNI
ふに ふに ふに ふに ふに
FUNI FUNI FUNI
ふに ふに ふに ふに
ふに ふに ふに ふに ふに
FUNI FUNI FUNI FUNI
ふに ふに ふに ふに
FUNI FUNI FUNI FU

ふに ふに ふに ふに ふに
FUNI FUNI FUNI FUNI FUNI

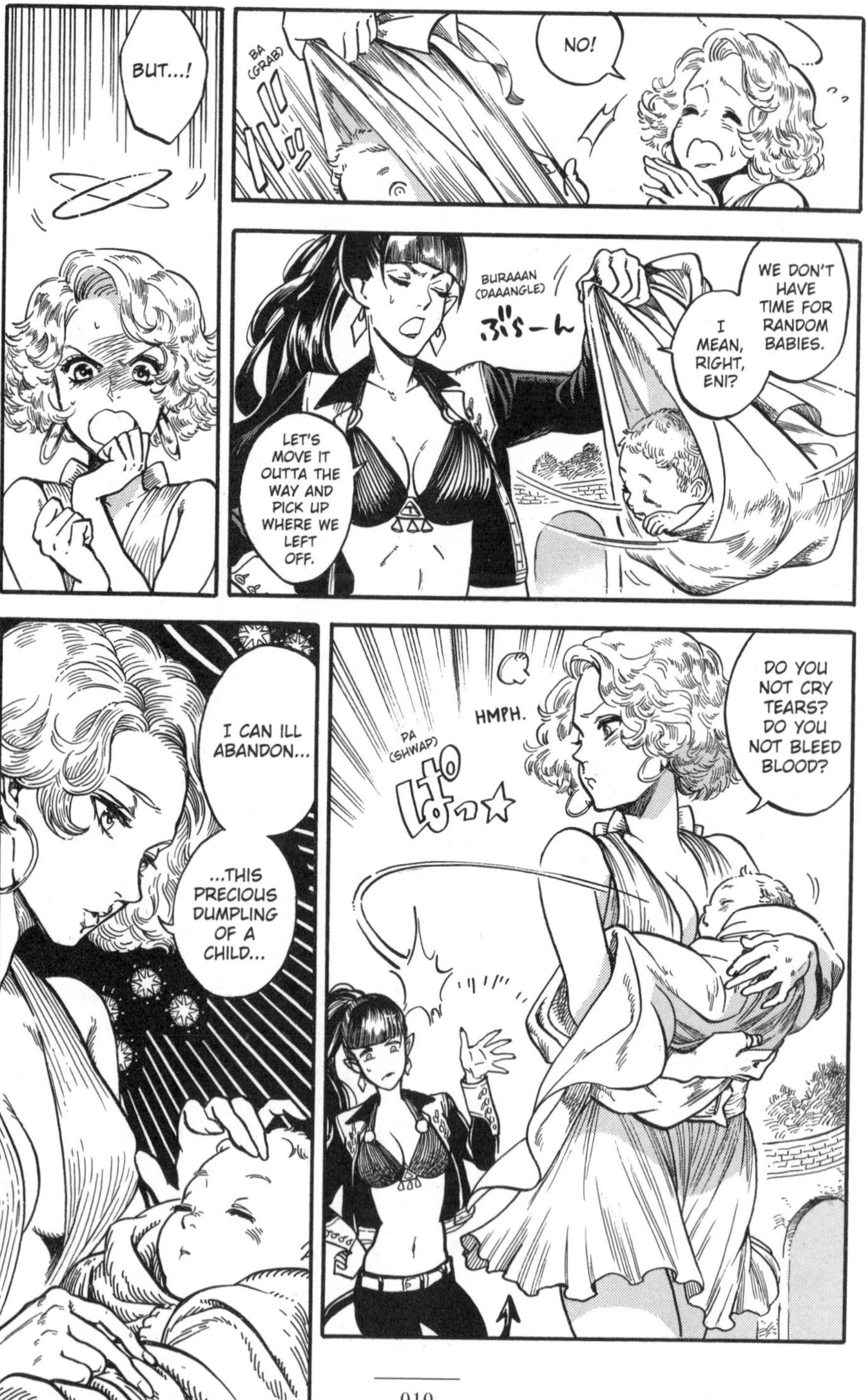
NO!
BA (GRAB)
WE DON'T HAVE TIME FOR RANDOM BABIES.
I MEAN, RIGHT, ENI?
BURAAAN (DAAANGLE)
ぶらーん
LET'S MOVE IT OUTTA THE WAY AND PICK UP WHERE WE LEFT OFF.
BUT...!
DO YOU NOT CRY TEARS? DO YOU NOT BLEED BLOOD?
HMPH.
PA (SHWAP)
ぱっ☆
I CAN ILL ABANDON...
...THIS PRECIOUS DUMPLING OF A CHILD...

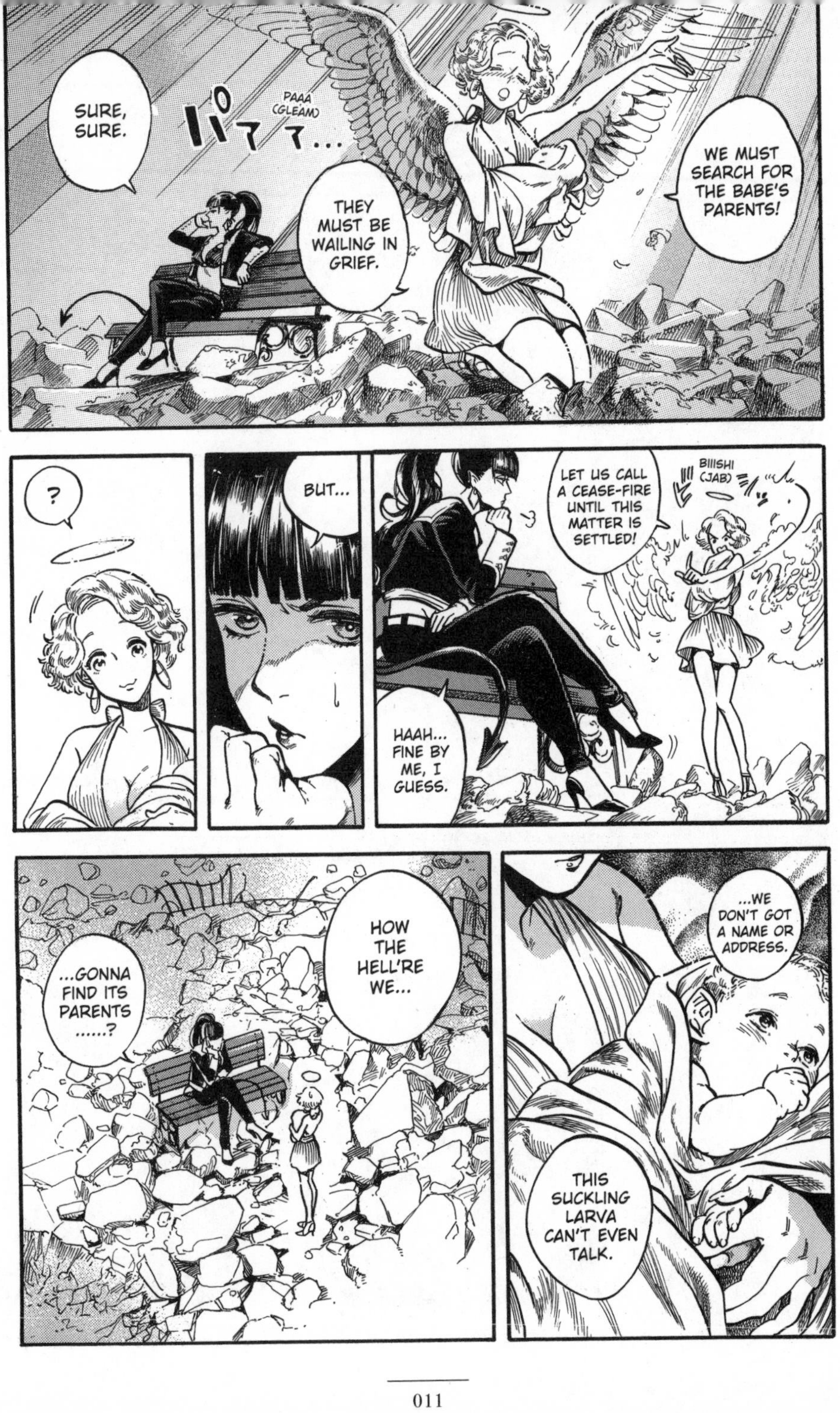
WE MUST SEARCH FOR THE BABE'S PARENTS!
THEY MUST BE WAILING IN GRIEF.
パァァ...
PAAA (GLEAM)
SURE, SURE.
BIIISHI (JAB)
LET US CALL A CEASE-FIRE UNTIL THIS MATTER IS SETTLED!
HAAH... FINE BY ME, I GUESS.
BUT...
?
...WE DON'T GOT A NAME OR ADDRESS.
THIS SUCKLING LARVA CAN'T EVEN TALK.
HOW THE HELL'RE WE...
...GONNA FIND ITS PARENTS ......?

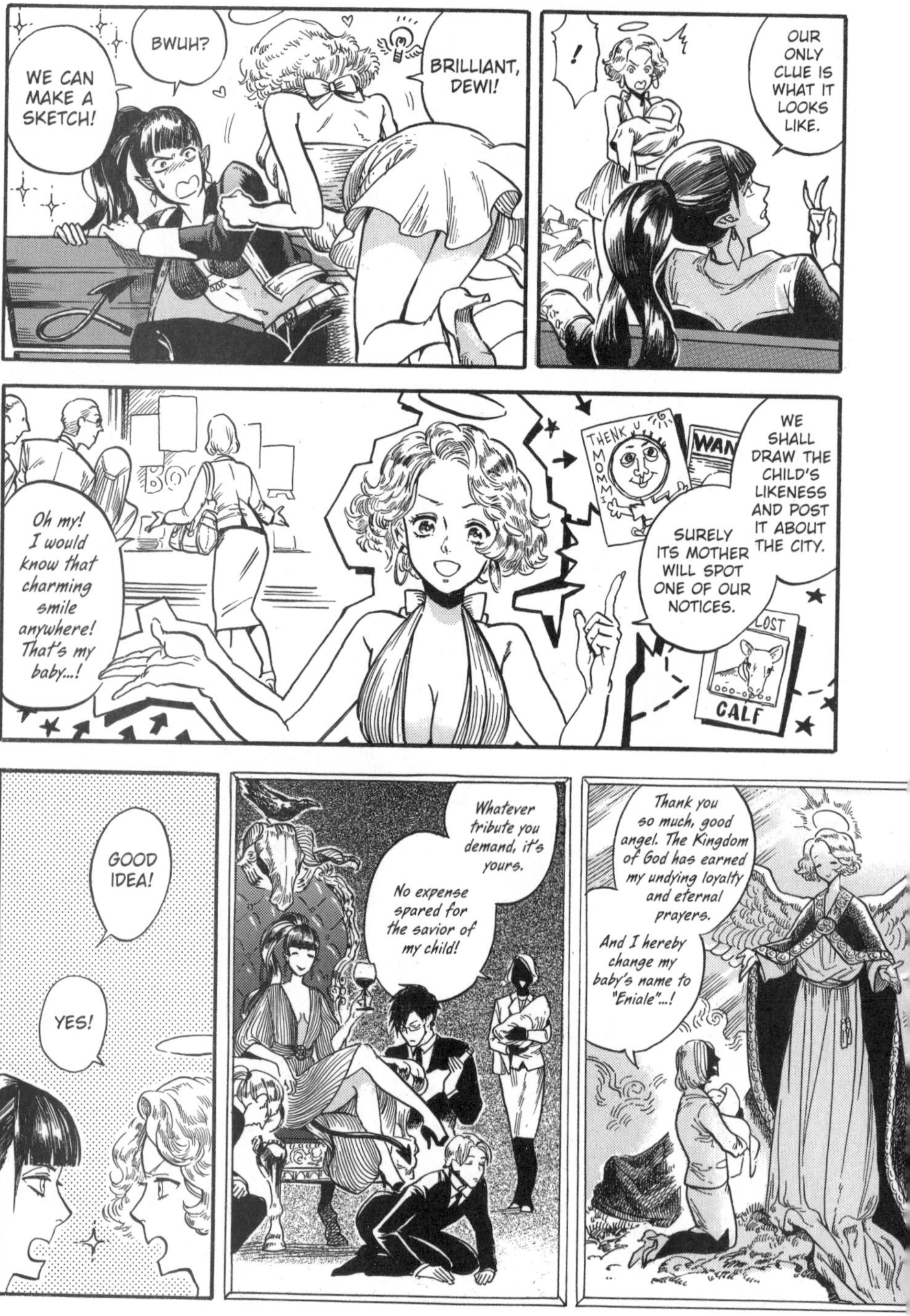
!
OUR ONLY CLUE IS WHAT IT LOOKS LIKE.
BRILLIANT, DEWI!
BWUH?
WE CAN MAKE A SKETCH!
WE SHALL DRAW THE CHILD'S LIKENESS AND POST IT ABOUT THE CITY.
SURELY ITS MOTHER WILL SPOT ONE OF OUR NOTICES.
LOST
CALF
THENK U MOMMI
Oh my! I would know that charming smile anywhere! That's my baby...!
Thank you so much, good angel. The Kingdom of God has earned my undying loyalty and eternal prayers.
And I hereby change my baby's name to "Eniale"...!
Whatever tribute you demand, it's yours.
No expense spared for the savior of my child!
GOOD IDEA!
YES!

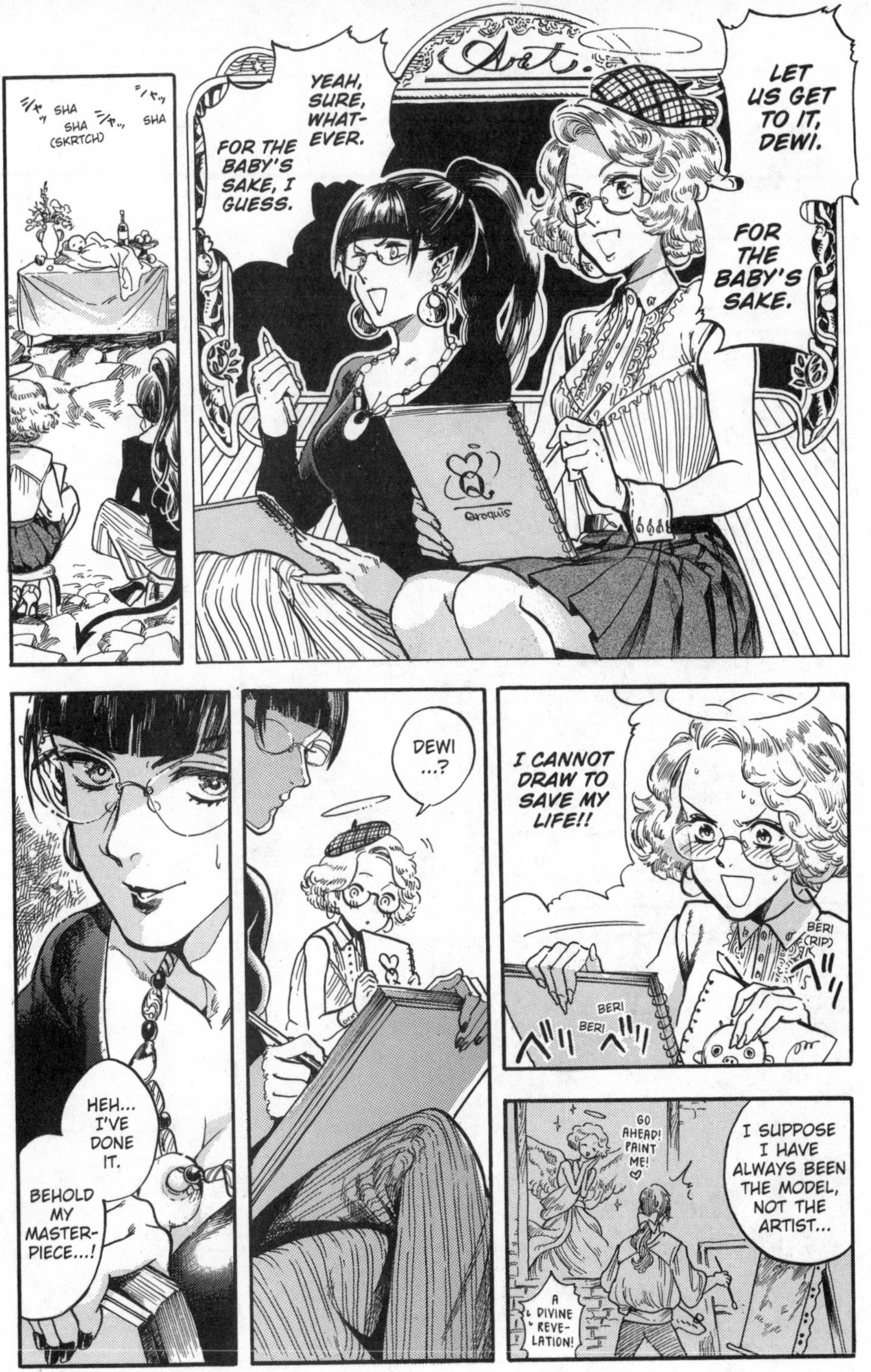
LET US GET TO IT, DEWI.
FOR THE BABY'S SAKE.
YEAH, SURE, WHATEVER.
FOR THE BABY'S SAKE, I GUESS.
シャッ SHA
シャッ SHA
シャッ SHA (SKRTCH)
I CANNOT DRAW TO SAVE MY LIFE!!
BERI (RIP)
BERI BERI
I SUPPOSE I HAVE ALWAYS BEEN THE MODEL, NOT THE ARTIST...
GO AHEAD! PAINT ME! ♥
A DIVINE REVELATION!
DEWI ...?
HEH... I'VE DONE IT.
BEHOLD MY MASTERPIECE...!

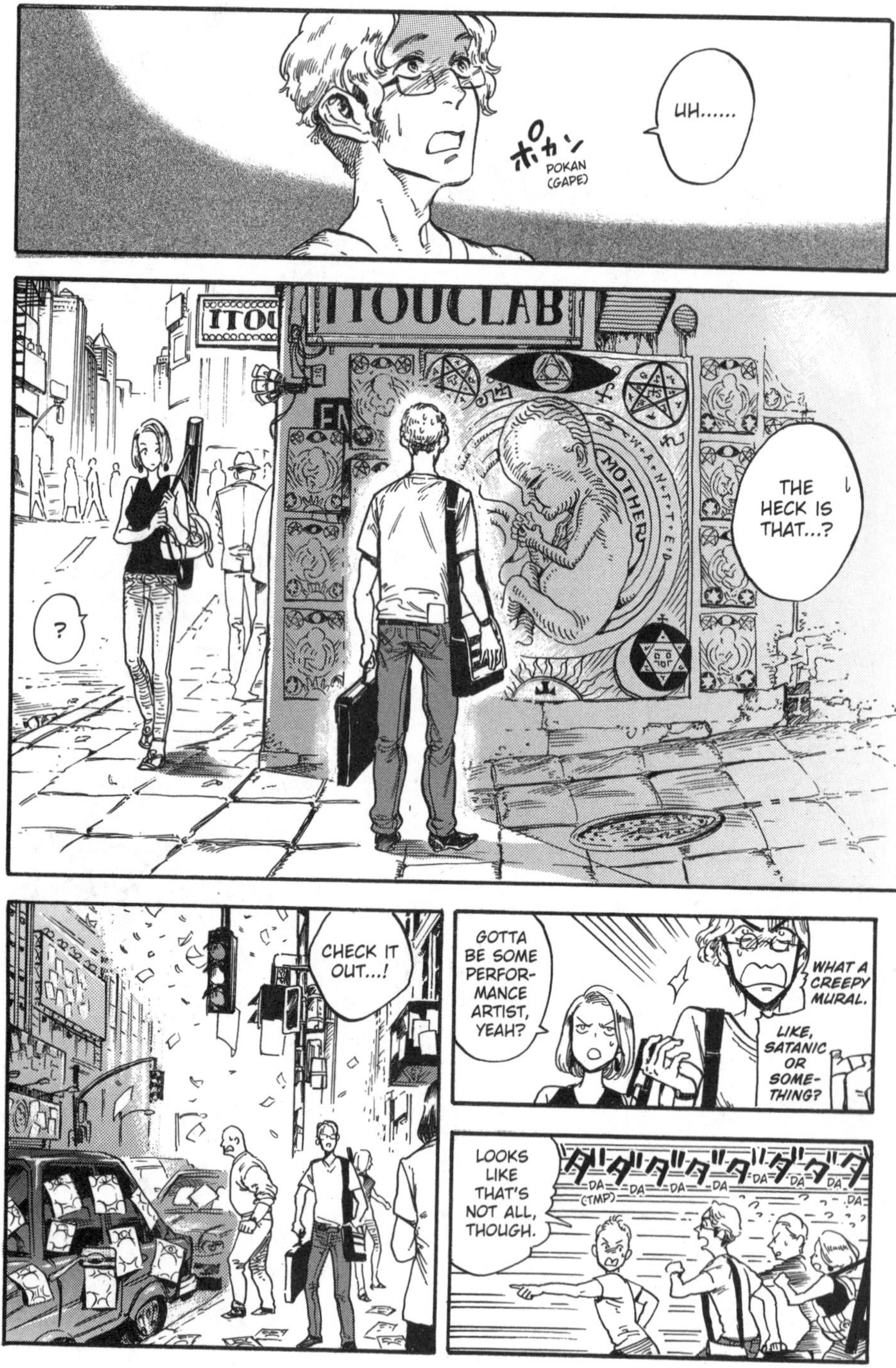
UH......
ポカン
POKAN (GAPE)
THE HECK IS THAT...?
?
WHAT A CREEPY MURAL.
LIKE, SATANIC OR SOMETHING?
GOTTA BE SOME PERFORMANCE ARTIST, YEAH?
ダダダダダダダダ
DA (TMP) DA DA DA DA DA DA DA
LOOKS LIKE THAT'S NOT ALL, THOUGH.
CHECK IT OUT...!

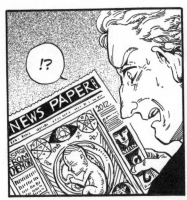

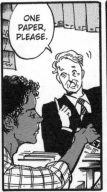

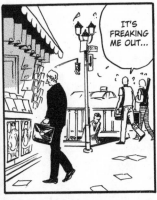

IT'S FREAKING ME OUT...
ONE PAPER, PLEASE.
!?
NEWS PAPER
2012.
GREECE
ITALY
EGYPT
AFRICA
The posters are appearing all around the world.
Could this be performance art? Or a message of some kind?
NEWS
WHOA ...
......
I'M THINKING ALIENS...
NO WAY.
HEH-HEH... WE NAILED THE ZEITGEIST! TOTALLY TRENDING!

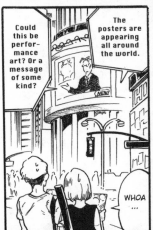

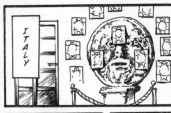

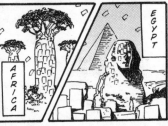

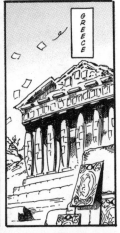

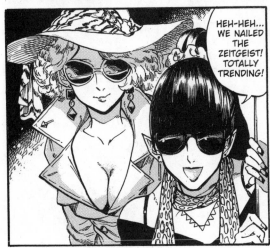

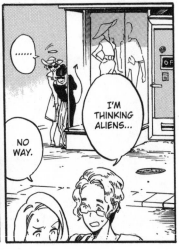

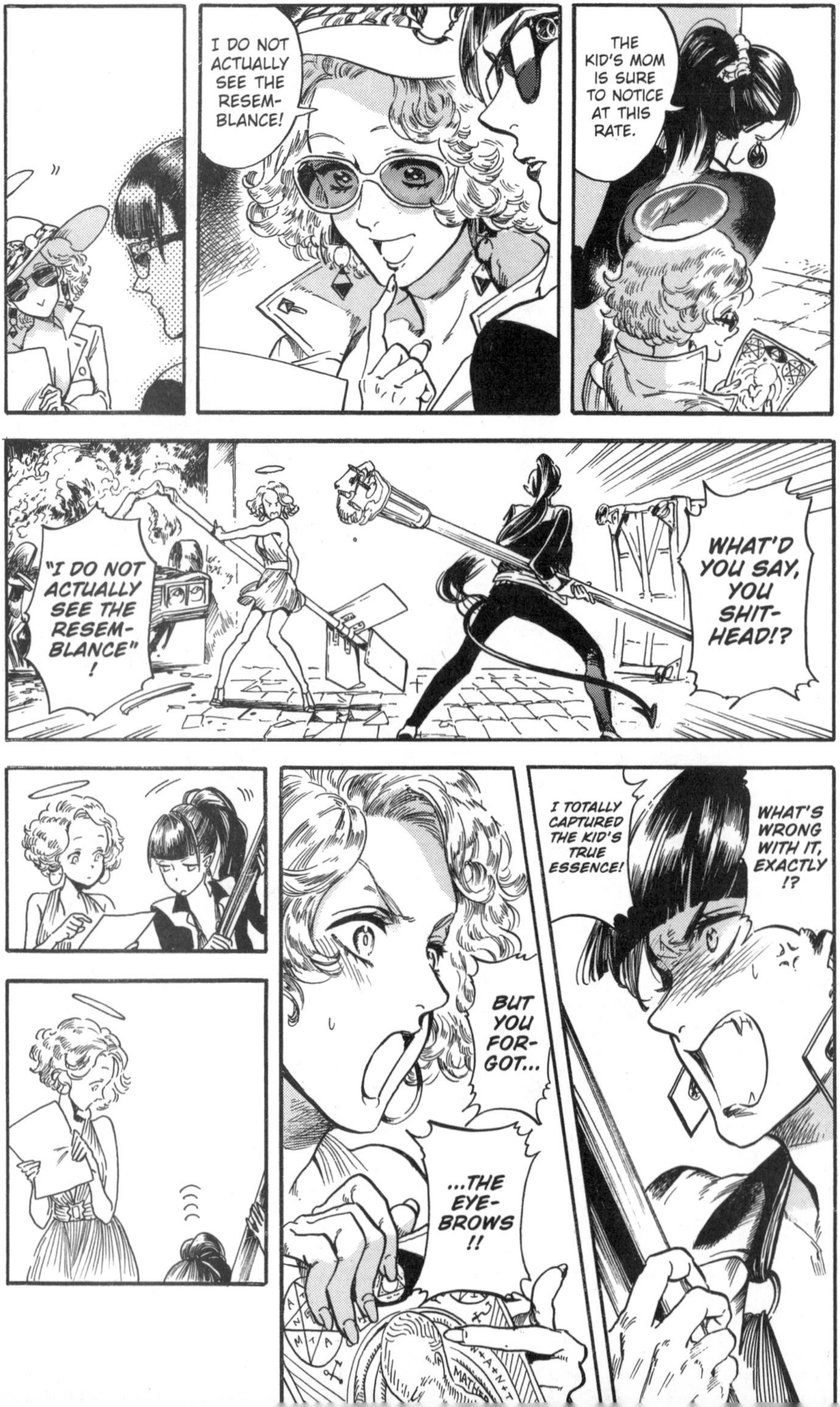
THE KID'S MOM IS SURE TO NOTICE AT THIS RATE.
I DO NOT ACTUALLY SEE THE RESEMBLANCE!
WHAT'D YOU SAY, YOU SHITHEAD!?
"I DO NOT ACTUALLY SEE THE RESEMBLANCE"!
WHAT'S WRONG WITH IT, EXACTLY!?
I TOTALLY CAPTURED THE KID'S TRUE ESSENCE!
BUT YOU FORGOT...
...THE EYEBROWS!!

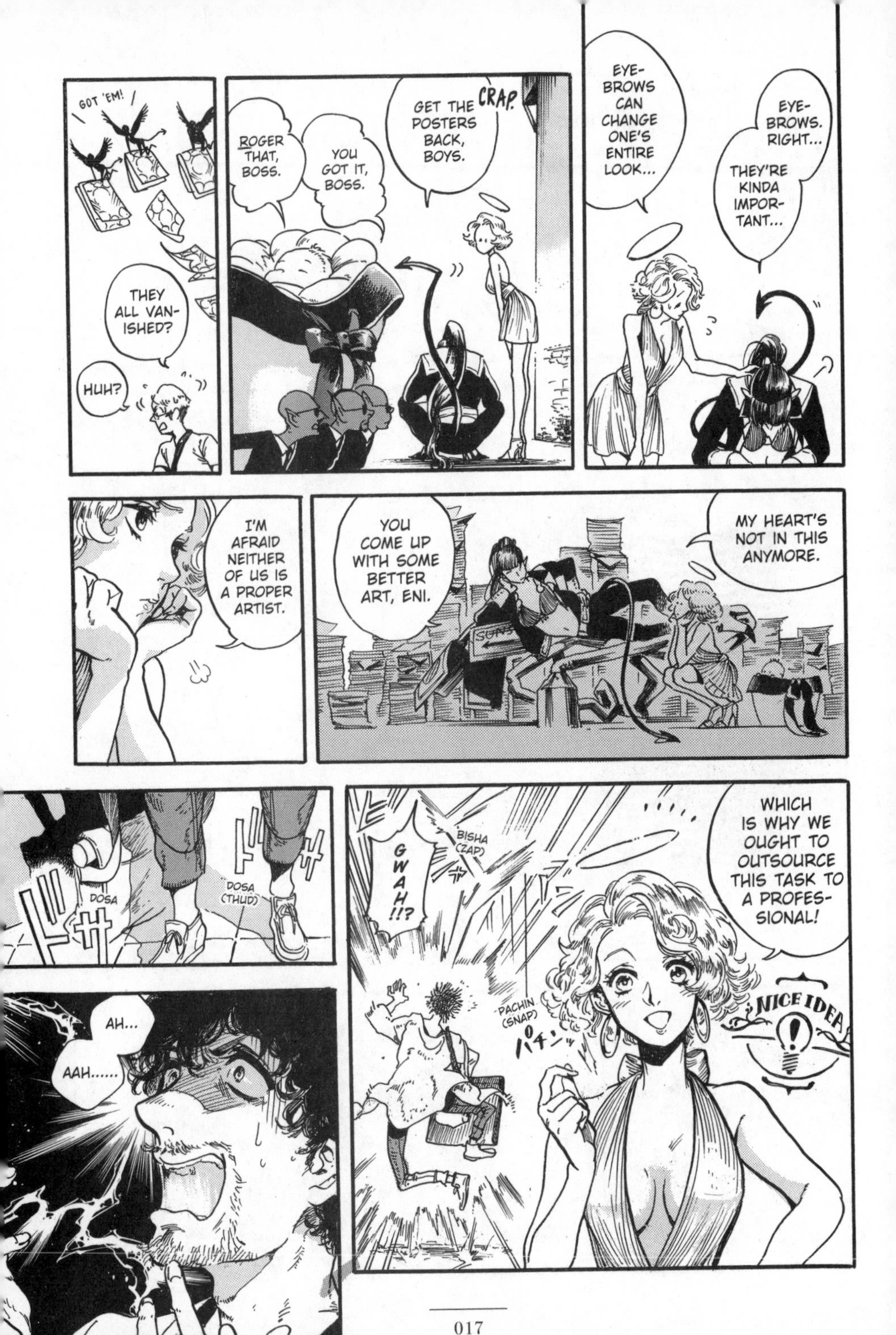
EYE-BROWS. RIGHT...
THEY'RE KINDA IMPORTANT...
EYE-BROWS CAN CHANGE ONE'S ENTIRE LOOK...
CRAP.
GET THE POSTERS BACK, BOYS.
YOU GOT IT, BOSS.
ROGER THAT, BOSS.
GOT 'EM!
THEY ALL VANISHED?
HUH?
MY HEART'S NOT IN THIS ANYMORE.
YOU COME UP WITH SOME BETTER ART, ENI.
I'M AFRAID NEITHER OF US IS A PROPER ARTIST.
WHICH IS WHY WE OUGHT TO OUTSOURCE THIS TASK TO A PROFESSIONAL!
NICE IDEA
PACHIN (SNAP)
BISHA (ZAP)
GWAH!!?
DOSA (THUD)
DOSA
AH...
AAH......

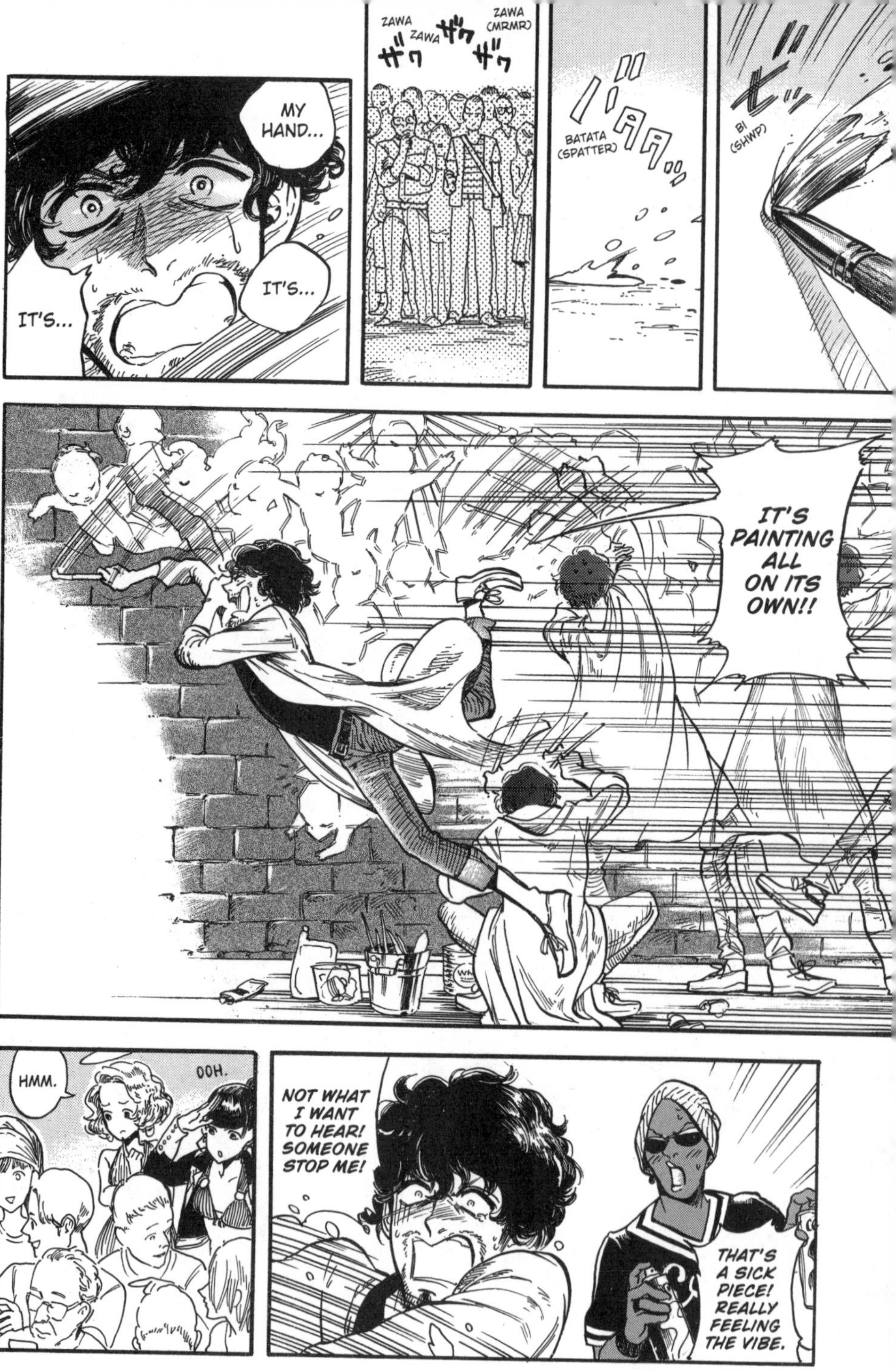
BI (SHWP)
BATATA (SPATTER)
ZAWA (MRMR)
ZAWA
ZAWA
MY HAND...
IT'S...
IT'S...
IT'S PAINTING ALL ON ITS OWN!!
THAT'S A SICK PIECE! REALLY FEELING THE VIBE.
NOT WHAT I WANT TO HEAR! SOMEONE STOP ME!
OOH.
HMM.

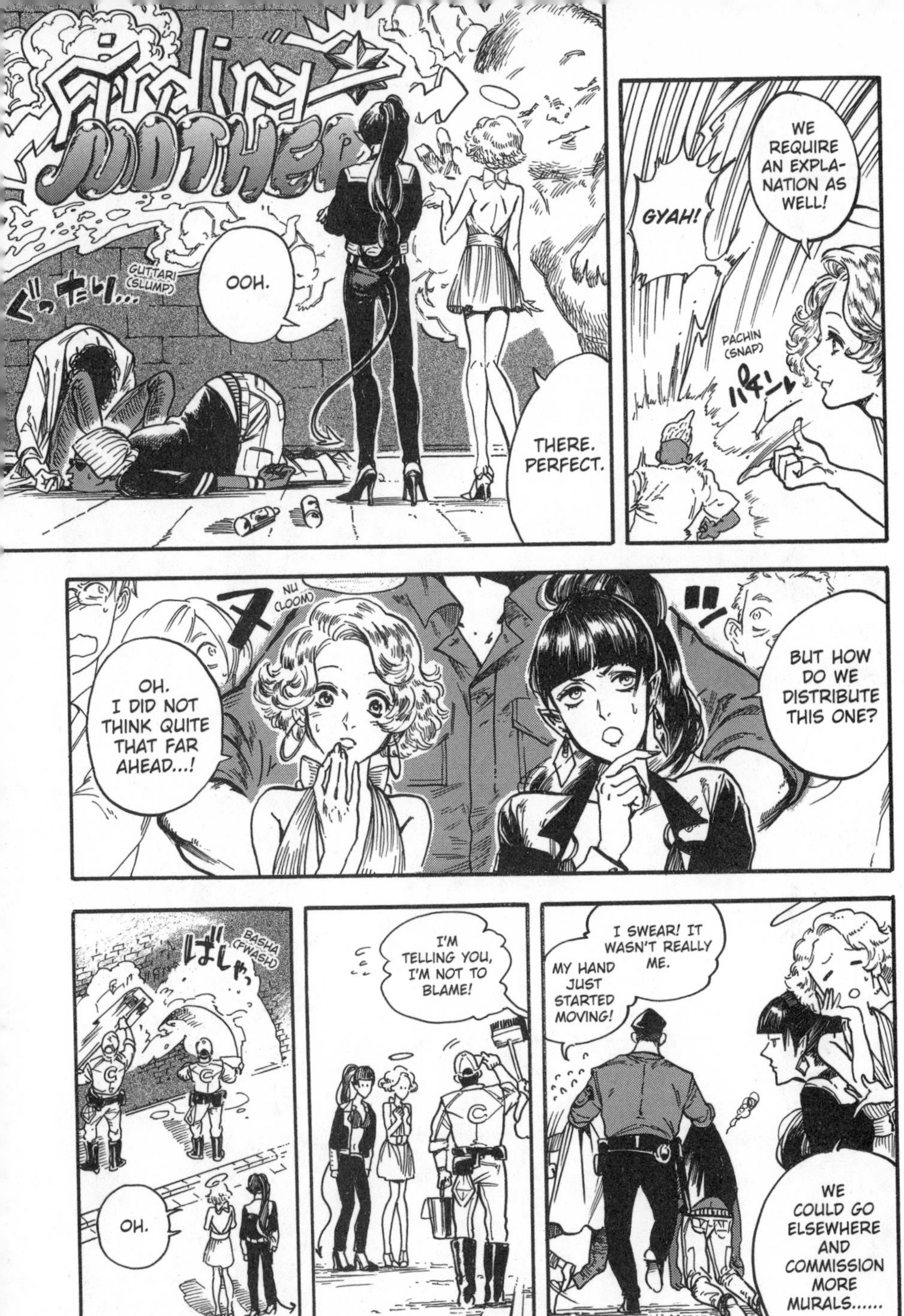
WE REQUIRE AN EXPLANATION AS WELL!
GYAH!
PACHIN (SNAP)
Finding MOTHER
THERE. PERFECT.
OOH.
GUTTARI (SLUMP)
BUT HOW DO WE DISTRIBUTE THIS ONE?
NU (LOOM)
OH. I DID NOT THINK QUITE THAT FAR AHEAD...!
I SWEAR! IT WASN'T REALLY ME.
MY HAND JUST STARTED MOVING!
WE COULD GO ELSEWHERE AND COMMISSION MORE MURALS......
I'M TELLING YOU, I'M NOT TO BLAME!
BASHA (FWASH)
OH.

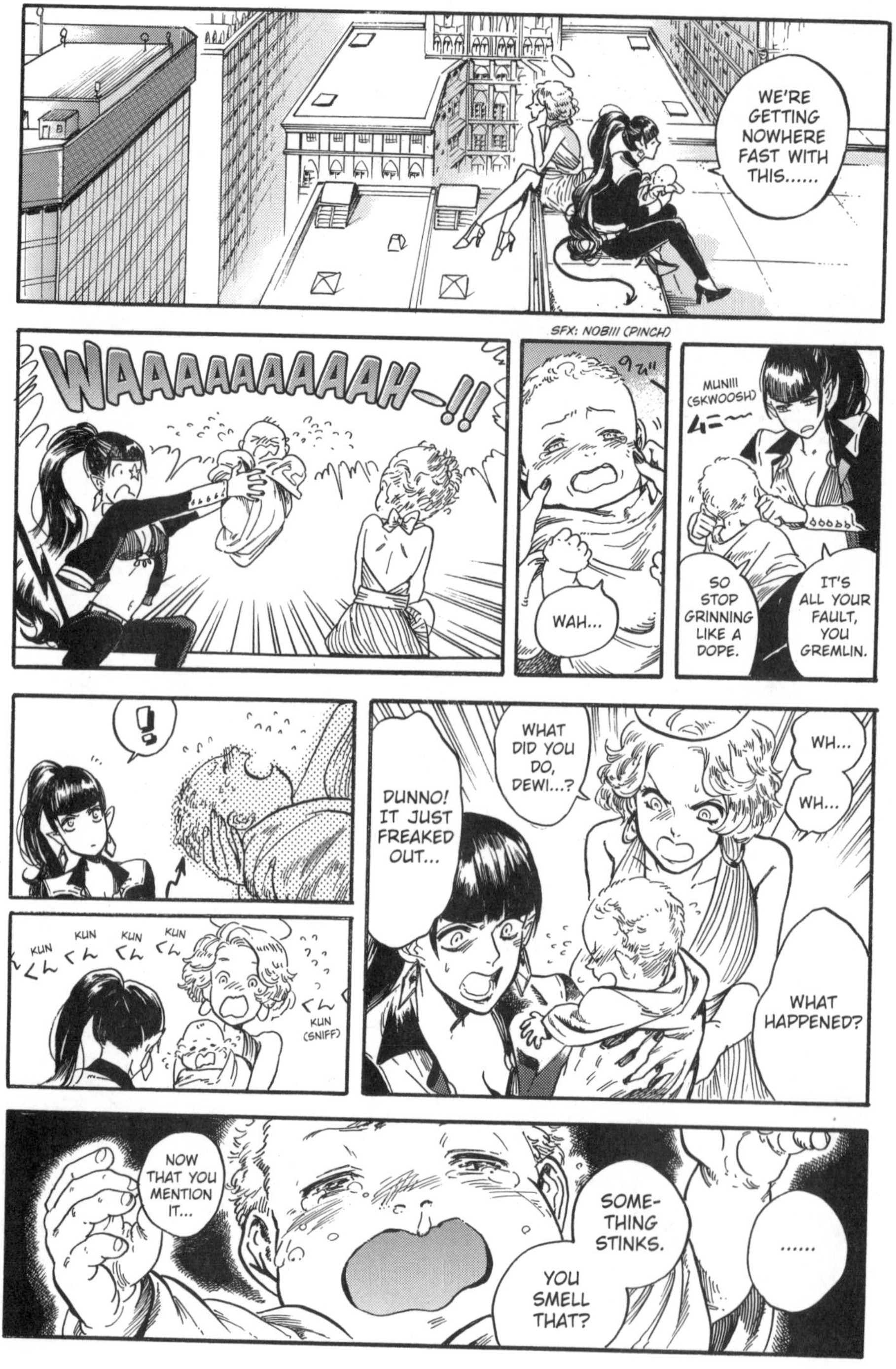
WE'RE GETTING NOWHERE FAST WITH THIS......
SFX: NOBIII (PINCH)
MUNIII (SKWOOSH)
IT'S ALL YOUR FAULT, YOU GREMLIN.
SO STOP GRINNING LIKE A DOPE.
WAH...
WAAAAAAAAAH-!!
WH...
WH...
WHAT DID YOU DO, DEWI...?
DUNNO! IT JUST FREAKED OUT...
WHAT HAPPENED?
!
KUN KUN KUN KUN
KUN (SNIFF)
......
SOME-THING STINKS.
YOU SMELL THAT?
NOW THAT YOU MENTION IT...

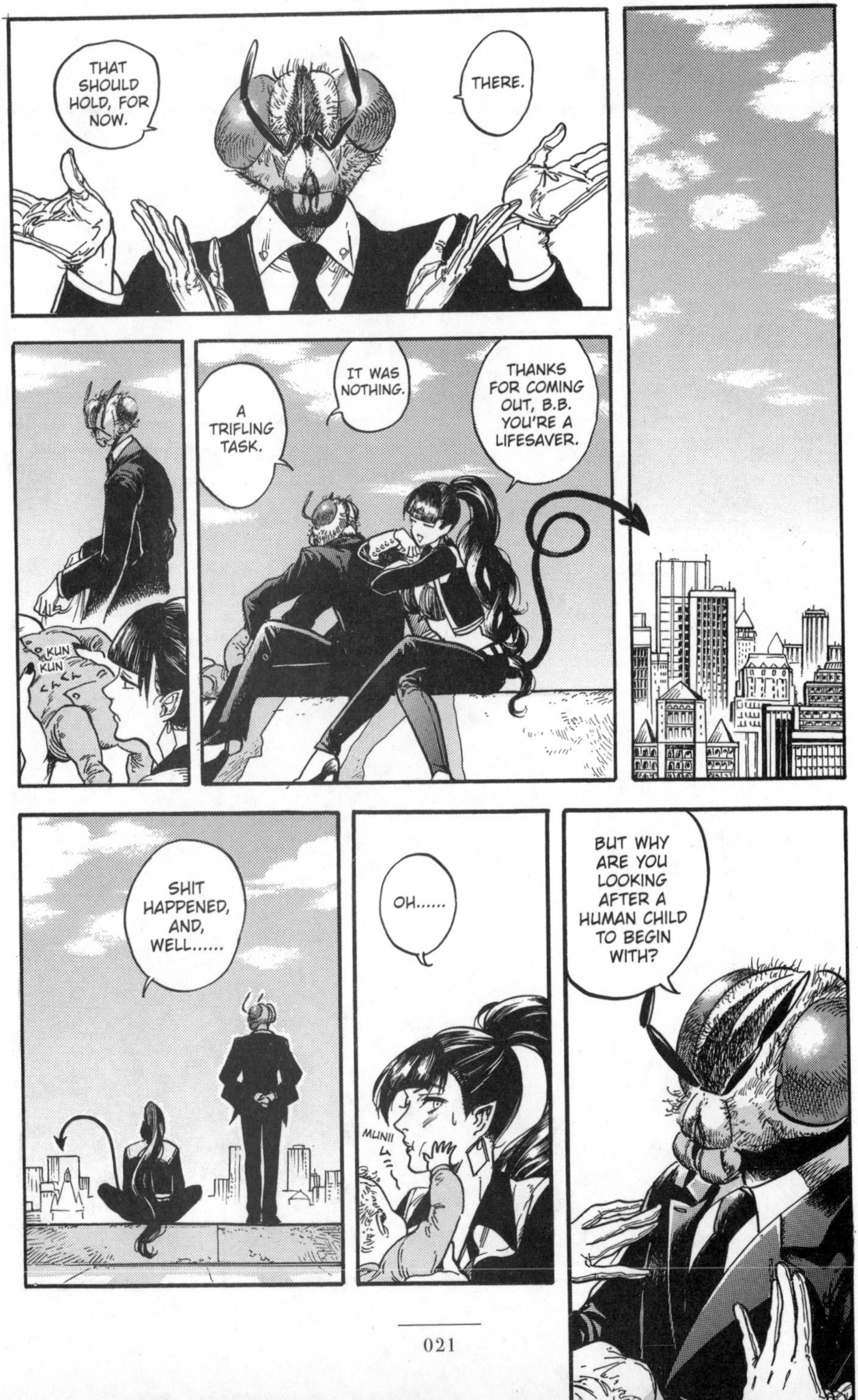
THERE.
THAT SHOULD HOLD, FOR NOW.
THANKS FOR COMING OUT, B.B. YOU'RE A LIFESAVER.
IT WAS NOTHING.
A TRIFLING TASK.
KUN KUN
BUT WHY ARE YOU LOOKING AFTER A HUMAN CHILD TO BEGIN WITH?
OH......
MUNI!
SHIT HAPPENED, AND, WELL......

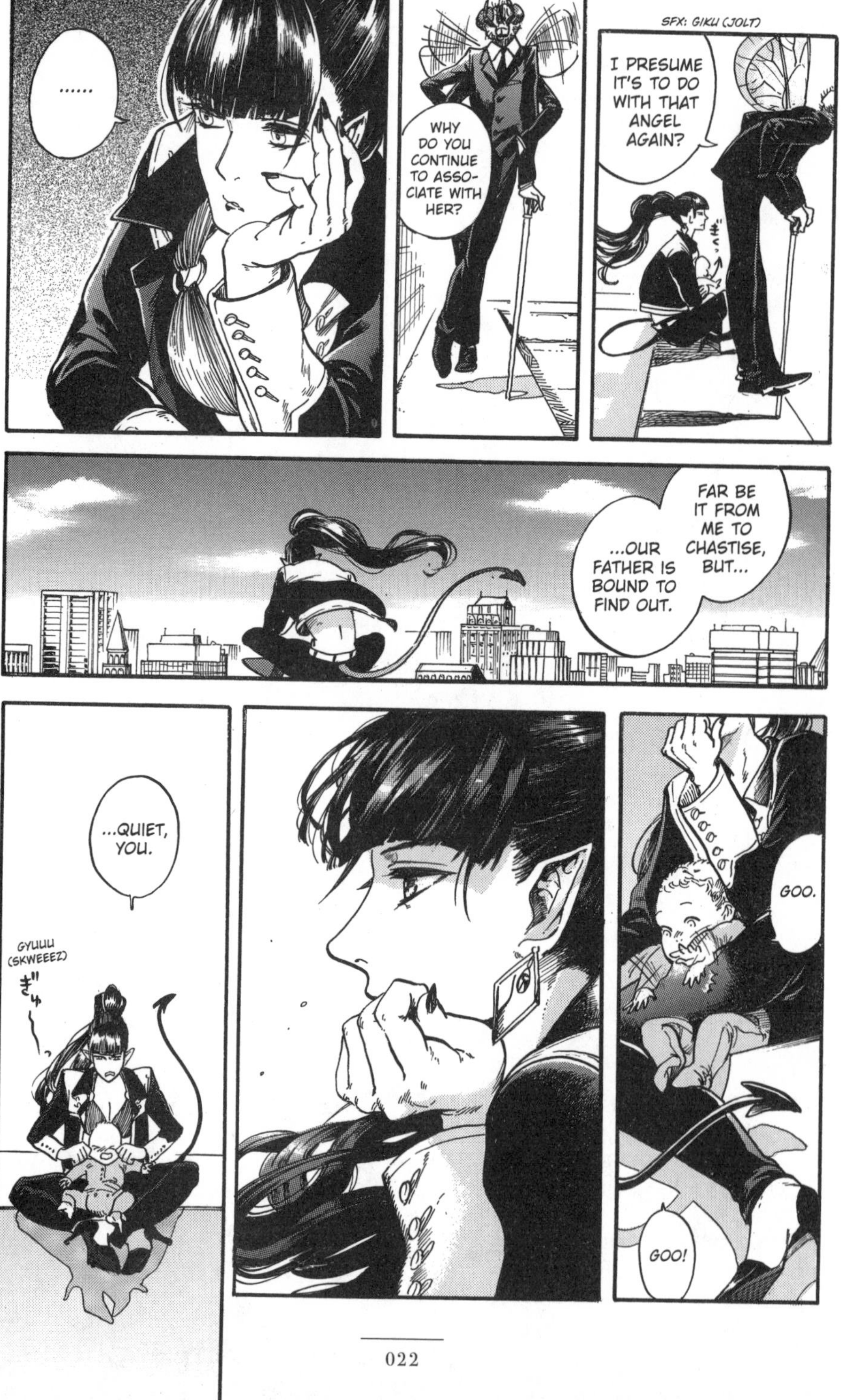
SFX: GIKU (JOLT)
I PRESUME IT'S TO DO WITH THAT ANGEL AGAIN?
WHY DO YOU CONTINUE TO ASSOCIATE WITH HER?
......
FAR BE IT FROM ME TO CHASTISE, BUT...
...OUR FATHER IS BOUND TO FIND OUT.
GOO.
GOO!
...QUIET, YOU.
GYUUU (SKWEEEZ)

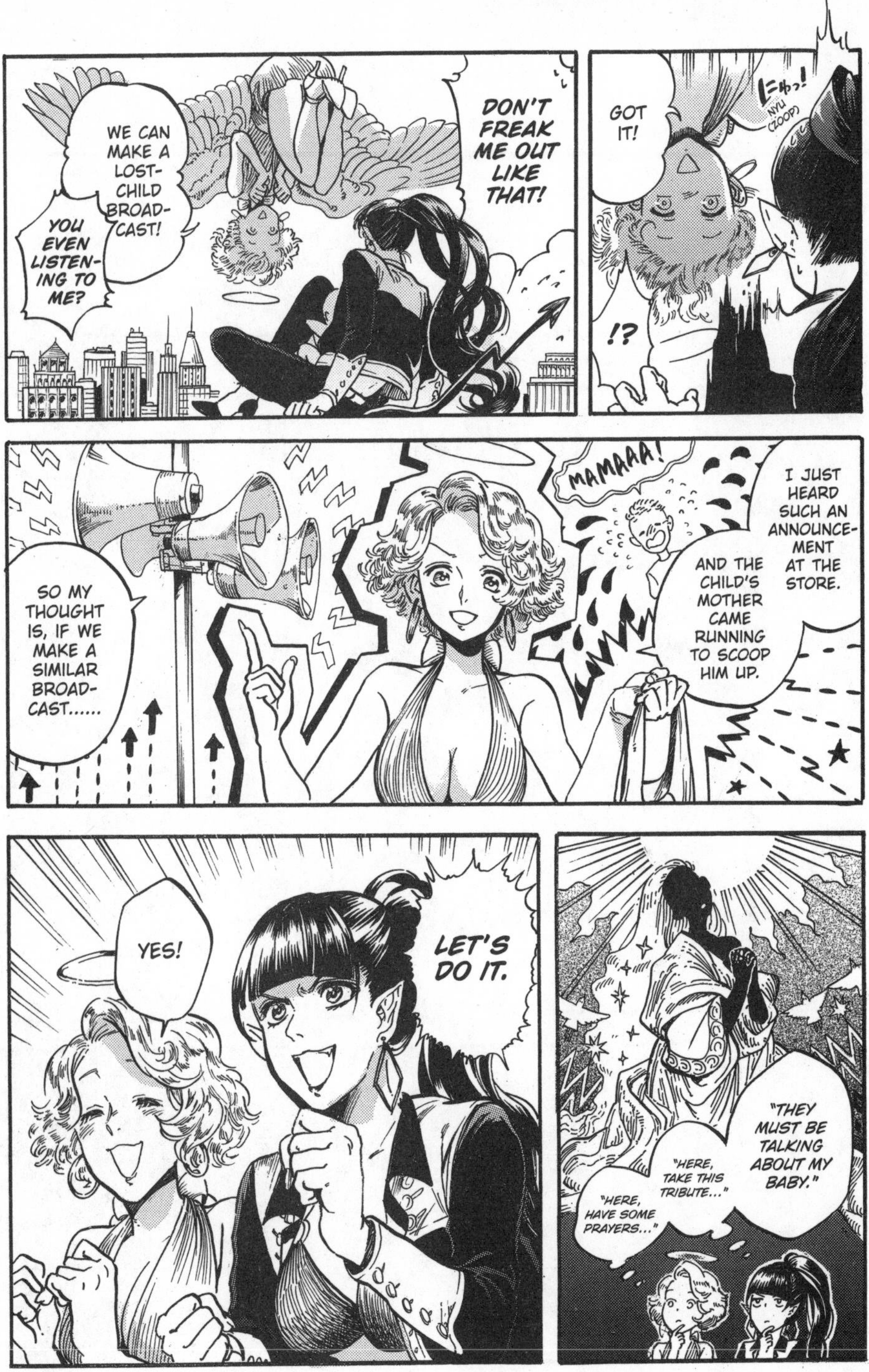
GOT IT!
にゅっ!
NYU (ZOOP)
!?
DON'T FREAK ME OUT LIKE THAT!
WE CAN MAKE A LOST-CHILD BROAD-CAST!
YOU EVEN LISTEN-ING TO ME?
MAMAAA!
I JUST HEARD SUCH AN ANNOUNCE-MENT AT THE STORE.
AND THE CHILD'S MOTHER CAME RUNNING TO SCOOP HIM UP.
SO MY THOUGHT IS, IF WE MAKE A SIMILAR BROAD-CAST......
"THEY MUST BE TALKING ABOUT MY BABY."
"HERE, TAKE THIS TRIBUTE..."
"HERE, HAVE SOME PRAYERS..."
LET'S DO IT.
YES!

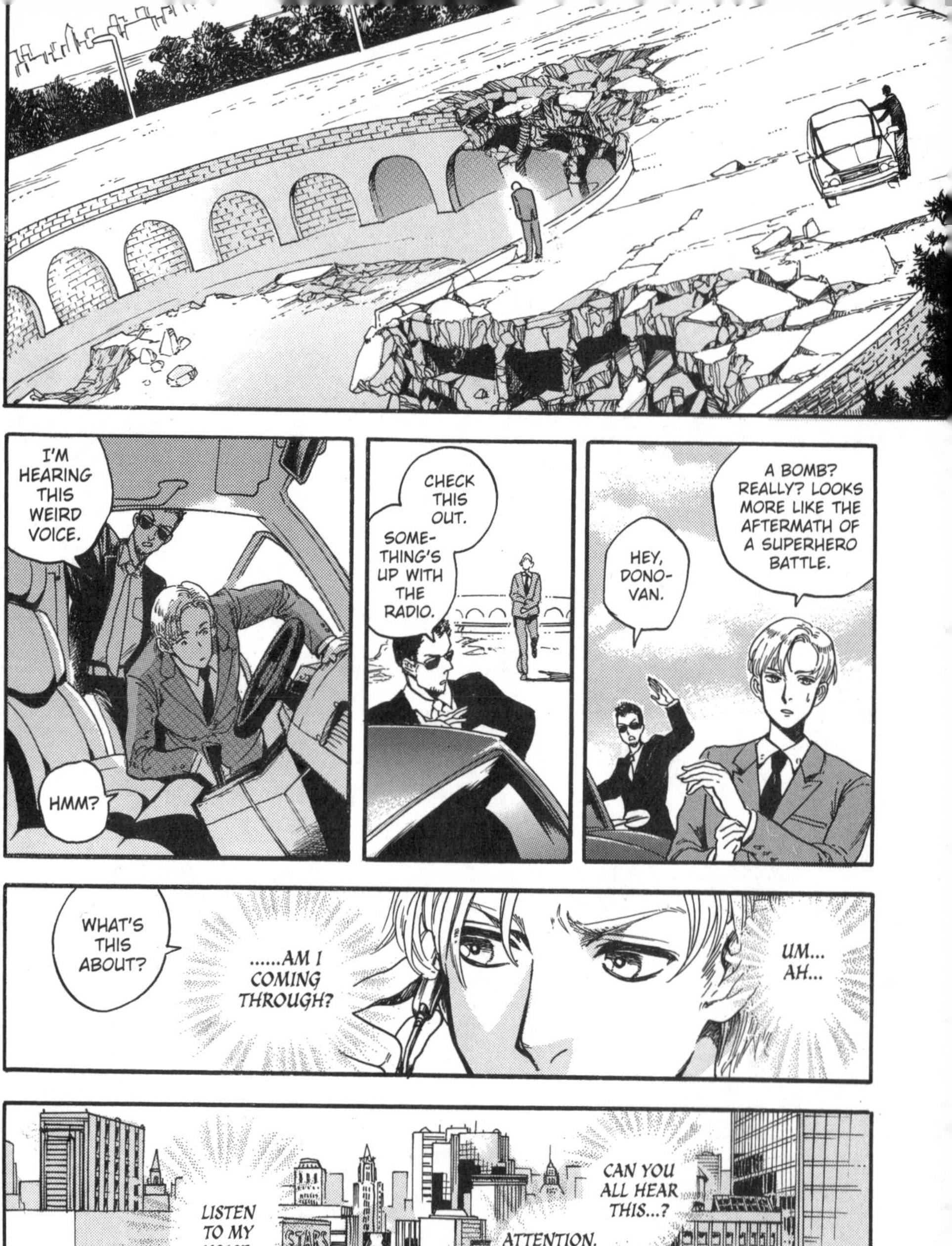
A BOMB? REALLY? LOOKS MORE LIKE THE AFTERMATH OF A SUPERHERO BATTLE.
HEY, DONO-VAN.
CHECK THIS OUT.
SOME-THING'S UP WITH THE RADIO.
I'M HEARING THIS WEIRD VOICE.
HMM?
UM... AH...
......AM I COMING THROUGH?
WHAT'S THIS ABOUT?
CAN YOU ALL HEAR THIS...?
ATTENTION, HUMANS, O BLESSED CHILDREN OF GOD...
LISTEN TO MY VOICE.

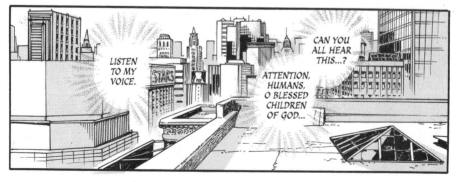

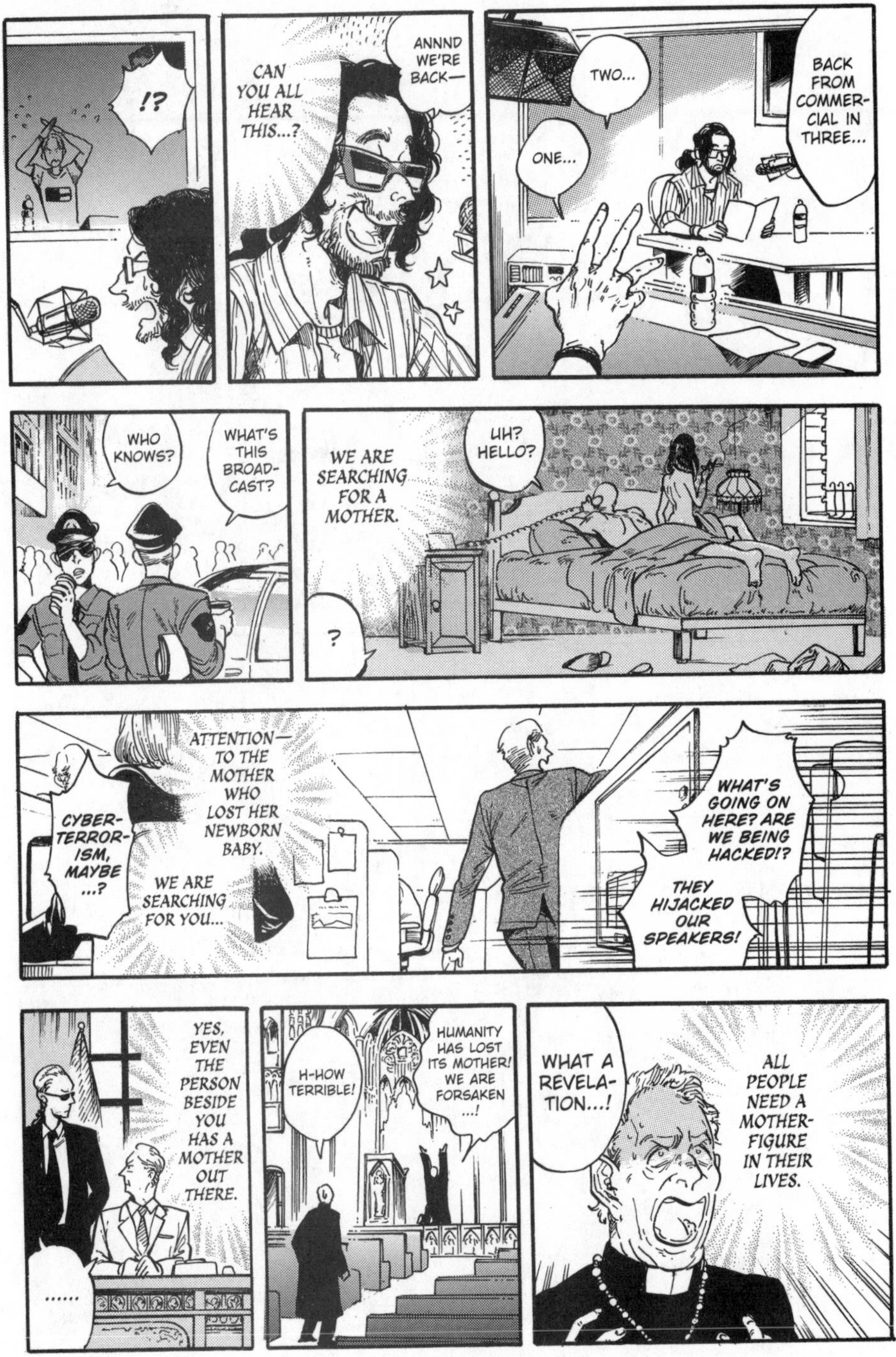
BACK FROM COMMERCIAL IN THREE...
TWO...
ONE...
ANNND WE'RE BACK—
CAN YOU ALL HEAR THIS...?
!?
UH? HELLO?
WE ARE SEARCHING FOR A MOTHER.
?
WHAT'S THIS BROADCAST?
WHO KNOWS?
WHAT'S GOING ON HERE? ARE WE BEING HACKED!?
THEY HIJACKED OUR SPEAKERS!
ATTENTION— TO THE MOTHER WHO LOST HER NEWBORN BABY.
CYBER-TERRORISM, MAYBE ...?
WE ARE SEARCHING FOR YOU...
ALL PEOPLE NEED A MOTHER-FIGURE IN THEIR LIVES.
WHAT A REVELATION...!
HUMANITY HAS LOST ITS MOTHER! WE ARE FORSAKEN ...!
H-HOW TERRIBLE!
YES, EVEN THE PERSON BESIDE YOU HAS A MOTHER OUT THERE.
......

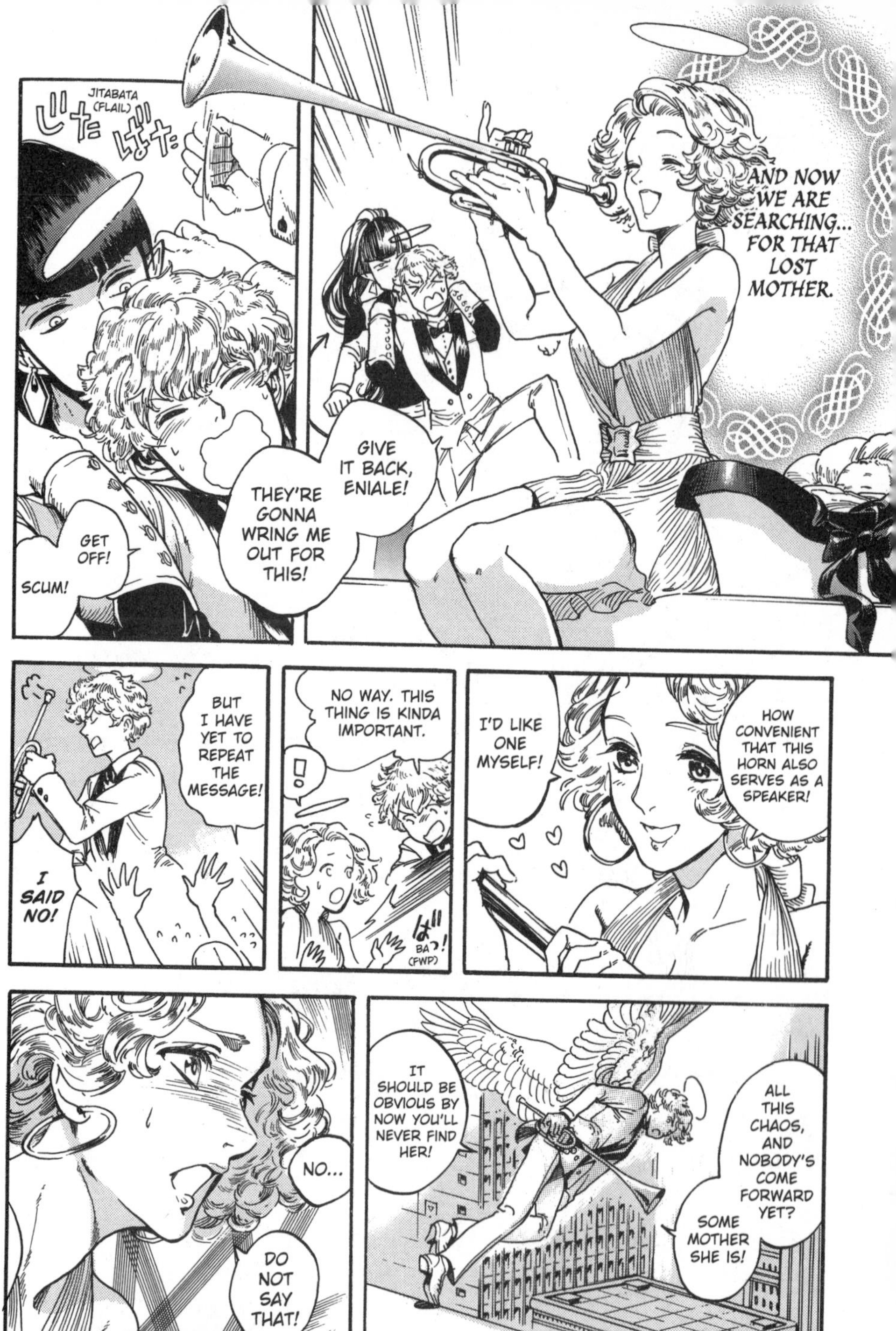
AND NOW WE ARE SEARCHING... FOR THAT LOST MOTHER.
GIVE IT BACK, ENIALE!
THEY'RE GONNA WRING ME OUT FOR THIS!
JITABATA (FLAIL)
GET OFF!
SCUM!
HOW CONVENIENT THAT THIS HORN ALSO SERVES AS A SPEAKER!
I'D LIKE ONE MYSELF!
NO WAY. THIS THING IS KINDA IMPORTANT.
!
BAっ! (FWP)
BUT I HAVE YET TO REPEAT THE MESSAGE!
I SAID NO!
ALL THIS CHAOS, AND NOBODY'S COME FORWARD YET?
SOME MOTHER SHE IS!
IT SHOULD BE OBVIOUS BY NOW YOU'LL NEVER FIND HER!
NO...
DO NOT SAY THAT!

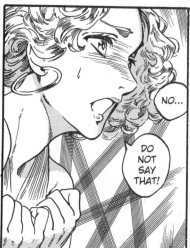

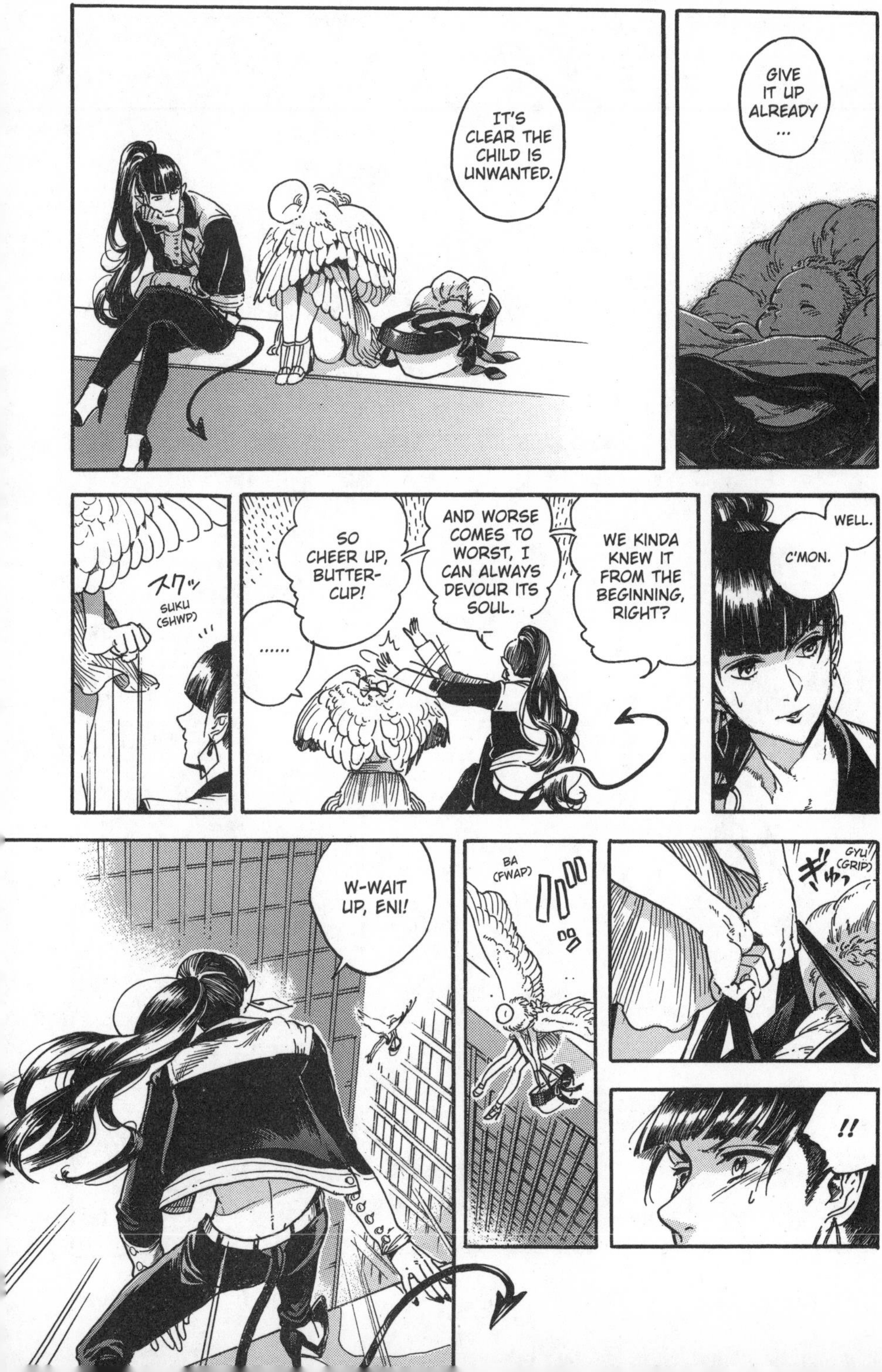
GIVE IT UP ALREADY ...
IT'S CLEAR THE CHILD IS UNWANTED.
WELL.
C'MON.
WE KINDA KNEW IT FROM THE BEGINNING, RIGHT?
AND WORSE COMES TO WORST, I CAN ALWAYS DEVOUR ITS SOUL.
SO CHEER UP, BUTTER-CUP!
......
スクッ
SUKU (SHWP)
ぎゅっ
GYU (GRIP)
!!
BA (FWAP)
W-WAIT UP, ENI!

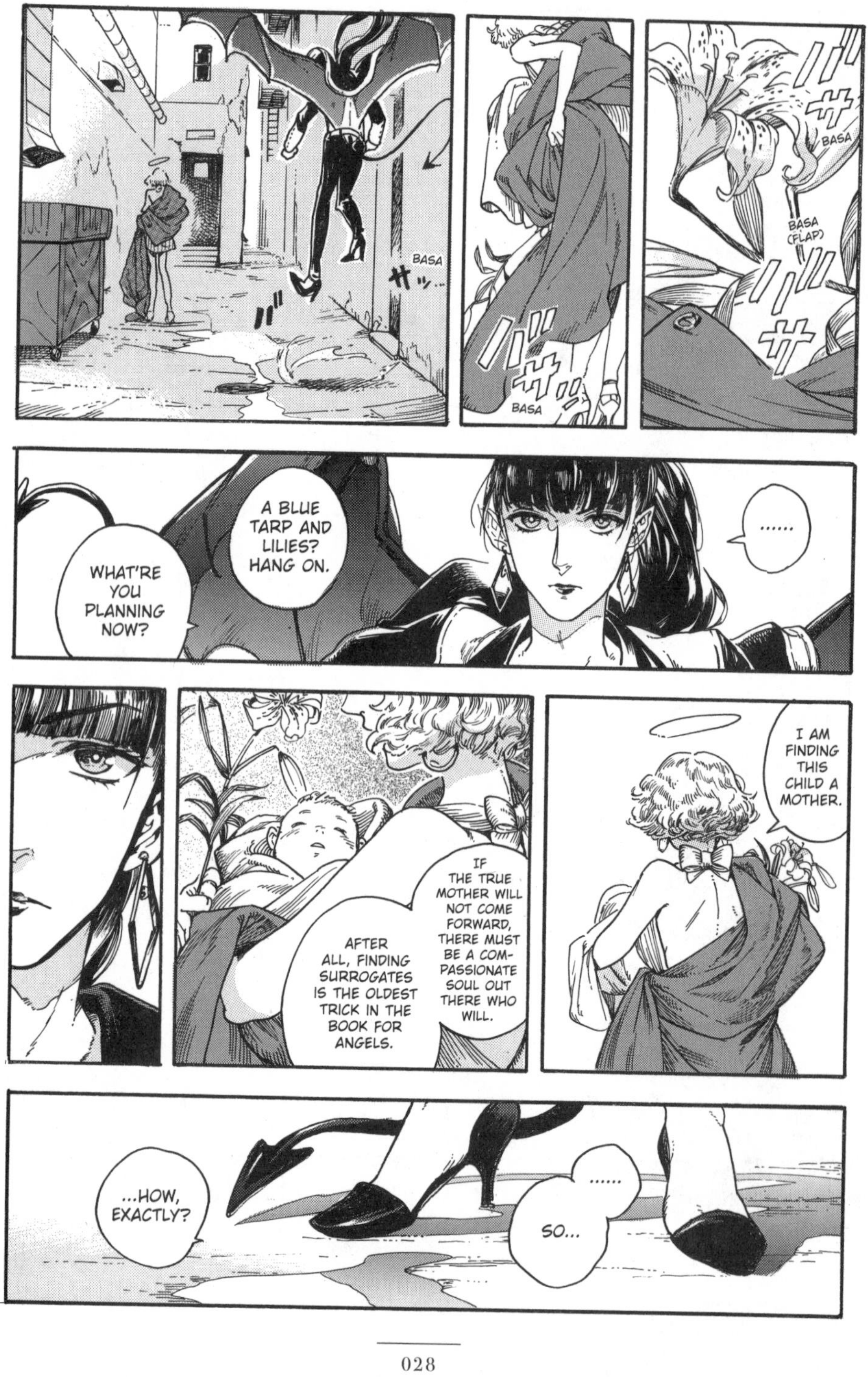

BASA
BASA (FLAP)
BASA
BASA
......
A BLUE TARP AND LILIES? HANG ON.
WHAT'RE YOU PLANNING NOW?
I AM FINDING THIS CHILD A MOTHER.
IF THE TRUE MOTHER WILL NOT COME FORWARD, THERE MUST BE A COM-PASSIONATE SOUL OUT THERE WHO WILL.
AFTER ALL, FINDING SURROGATES IS THE OLDEST TRICK IN THE BOOK FOR ANGELS.
......
SO...
...HOW, EXACTLY?

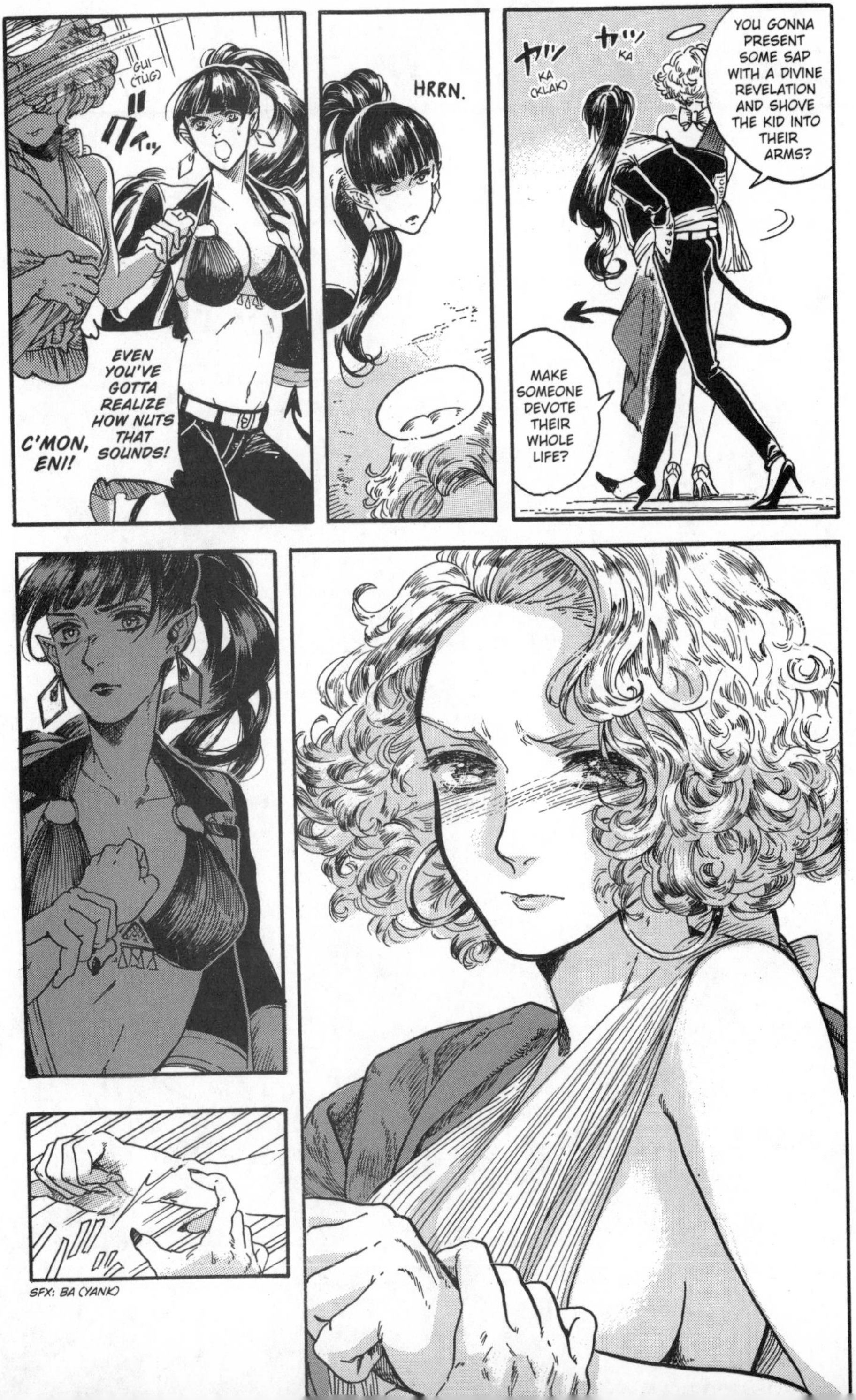
KA
KA (KLAK)
YOU GONNA PRESENT SOME SAP WITH A DIVINE REVELATION AND SHOVE THE KID INTO THEIR ARMS?
MAKE SOMEONE DEVOTE THEIR WHOLE LIFE?
HRRN.
GUI (TUG)
EVEN YOU'VE GOTTA REALIZE HOW NUTS THAT SOUNDS!
C'MON, ENI!
SFX: BA (YANK)

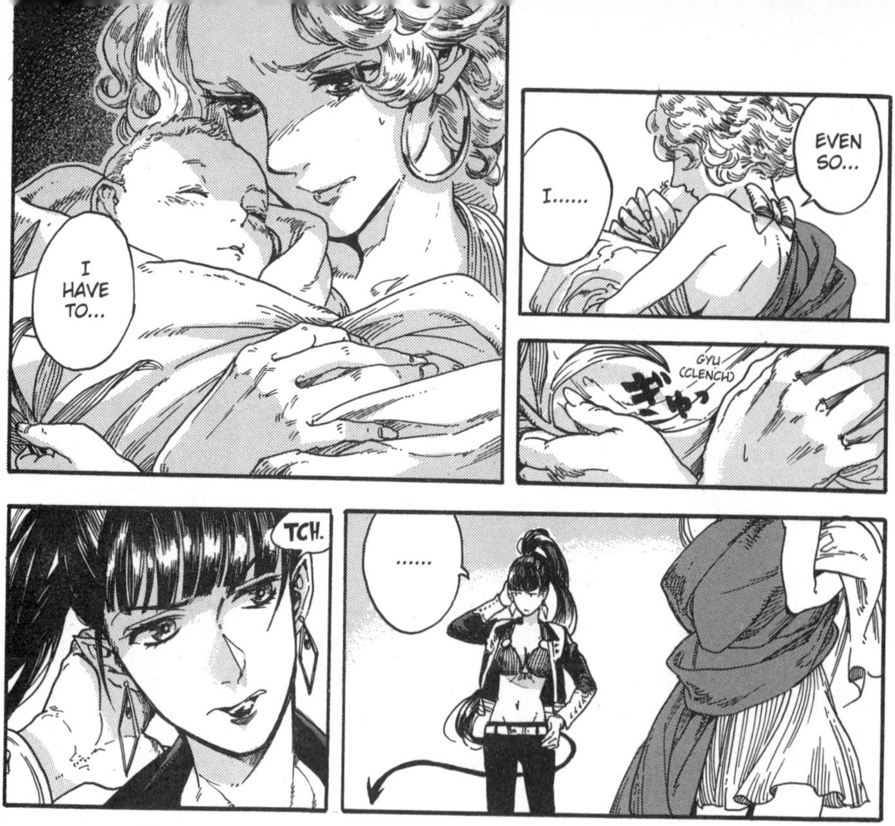
EVEN SO...
I......
GYU (CLENCH)
I HAVE TO...
......
TCH.

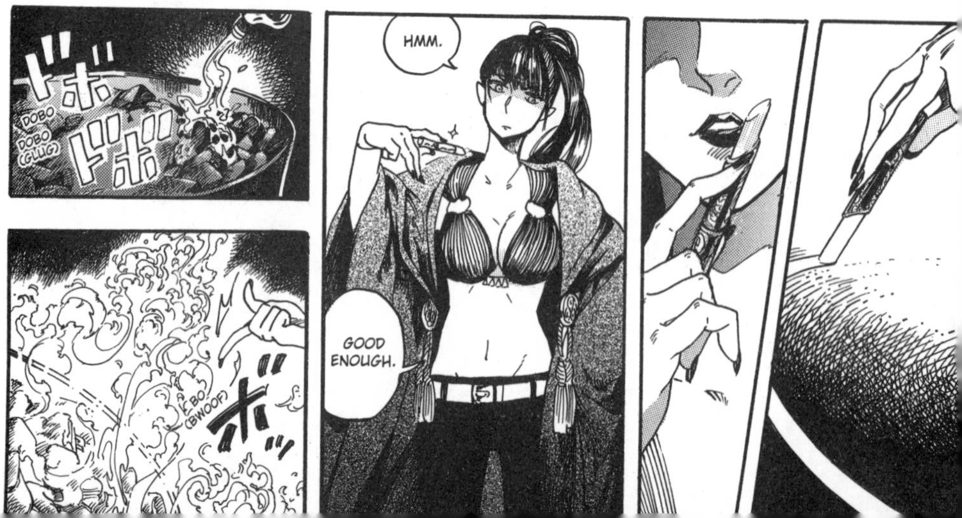
HMM.
GOOD ENOUGH.
DOBO DOBO (GLUG)
BO (BWOOF)

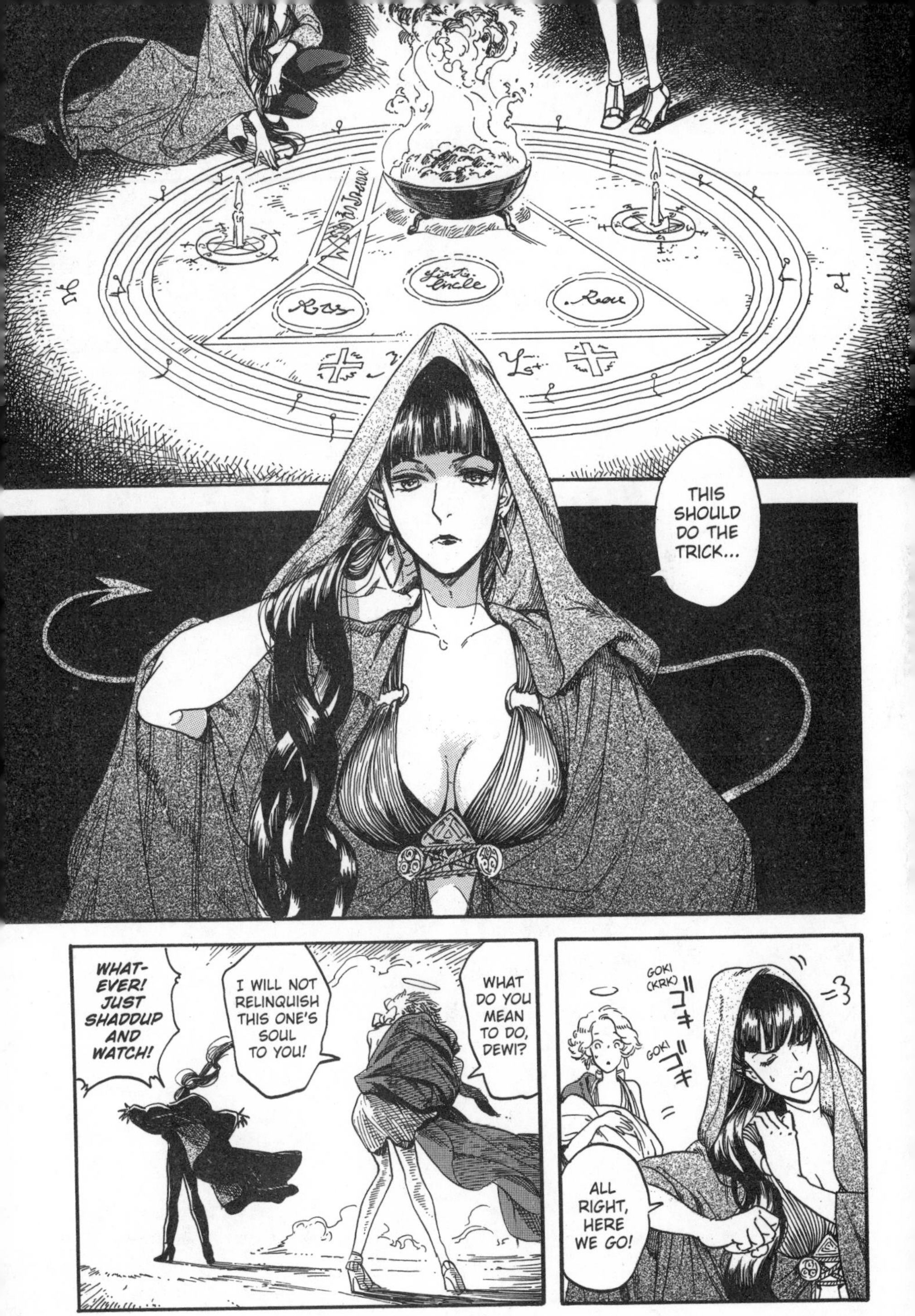
THIS SHOULD DO THE TRICK...
GOKI (KRK)
GOKI
ALL RIGHT, HERE WE GO!
WHAT DO YOU MEAN TO DO, DEWI?
I WILL NOT RELINQUISH THIS ONE'S SOUL TO YOU!
WHAT-EVER! JUST SHADDUP AND WATCH!

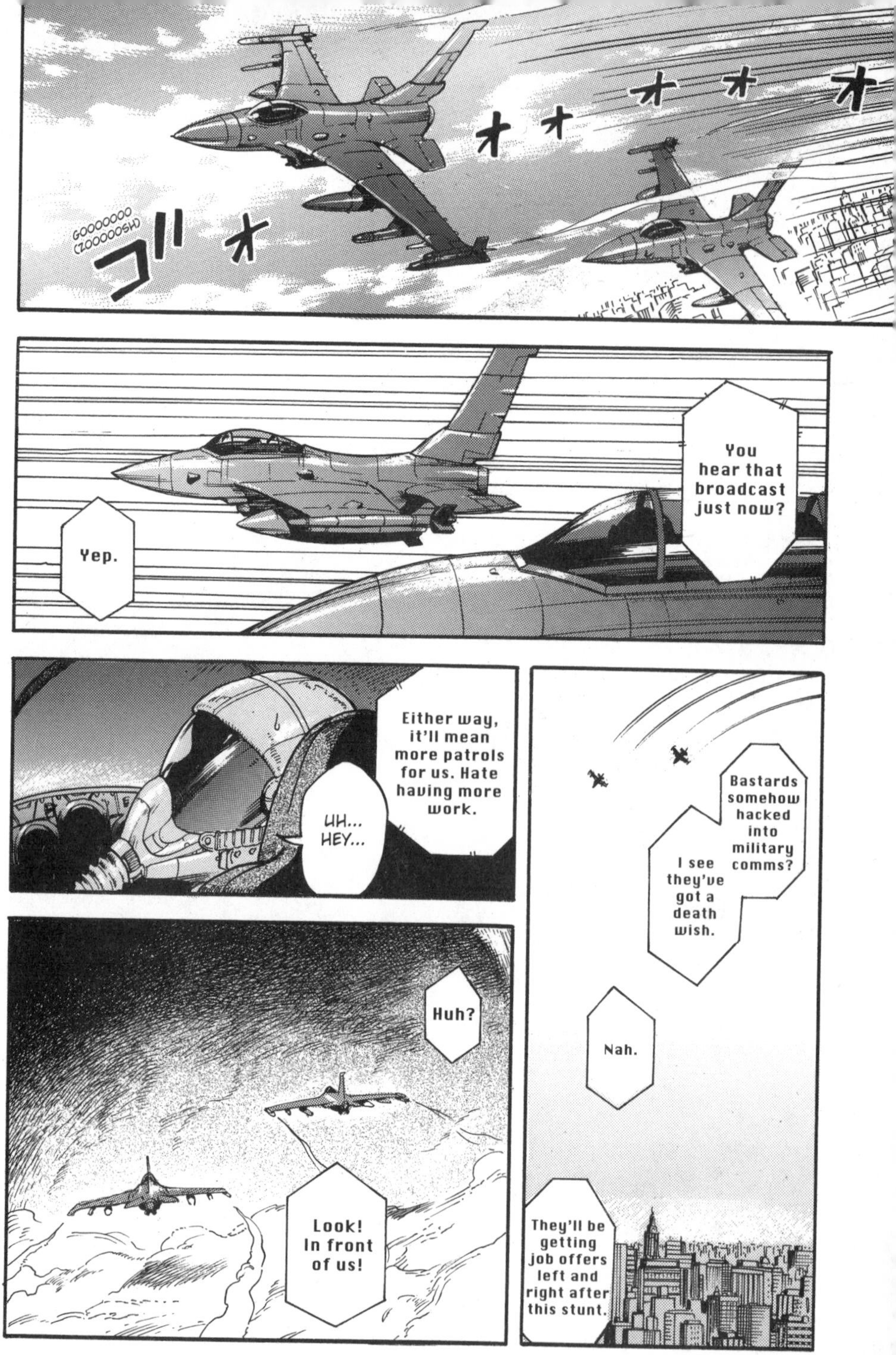
GOOOOOOO
(ZOOOOOSH)
You hear that broadcast just now?
Yep.
Bastards somehow hacked into military comms?
I see they've got a death wish.
Nah.
They'll be getting job offers left and right after this stunt.
Either way, it'll mean more patrols for us. Hate having more work.
UH... HEY...
Huh?
Look! In front of us!

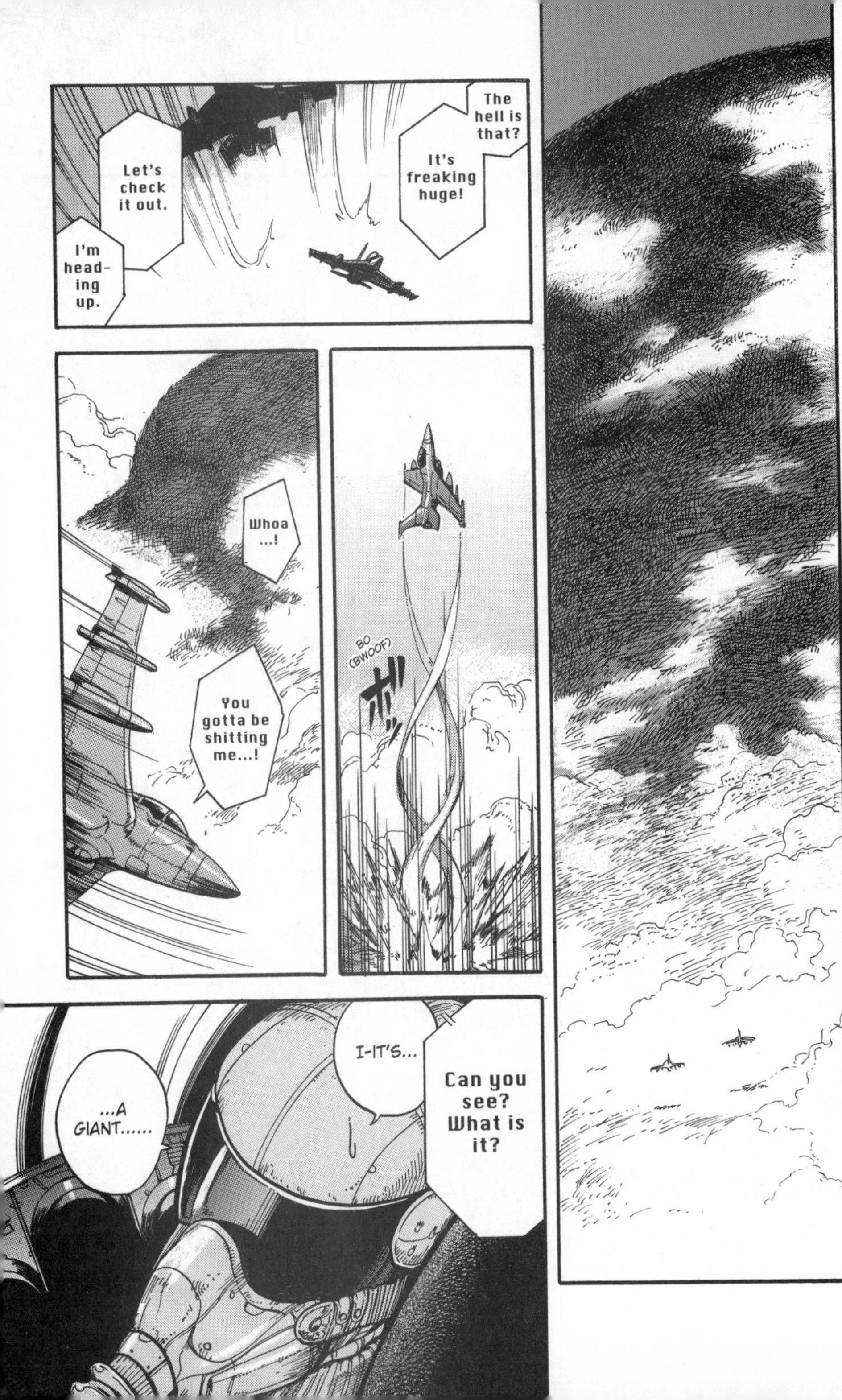
The hell is that?
It's freaking huge!
Let's check it out.
I'm heading up.
BO (BWOOF)
ボッ
Whoa ...!
You gotta be shitting me...!
Can you see? What is it?
I-IT'S...
...A GIANT......

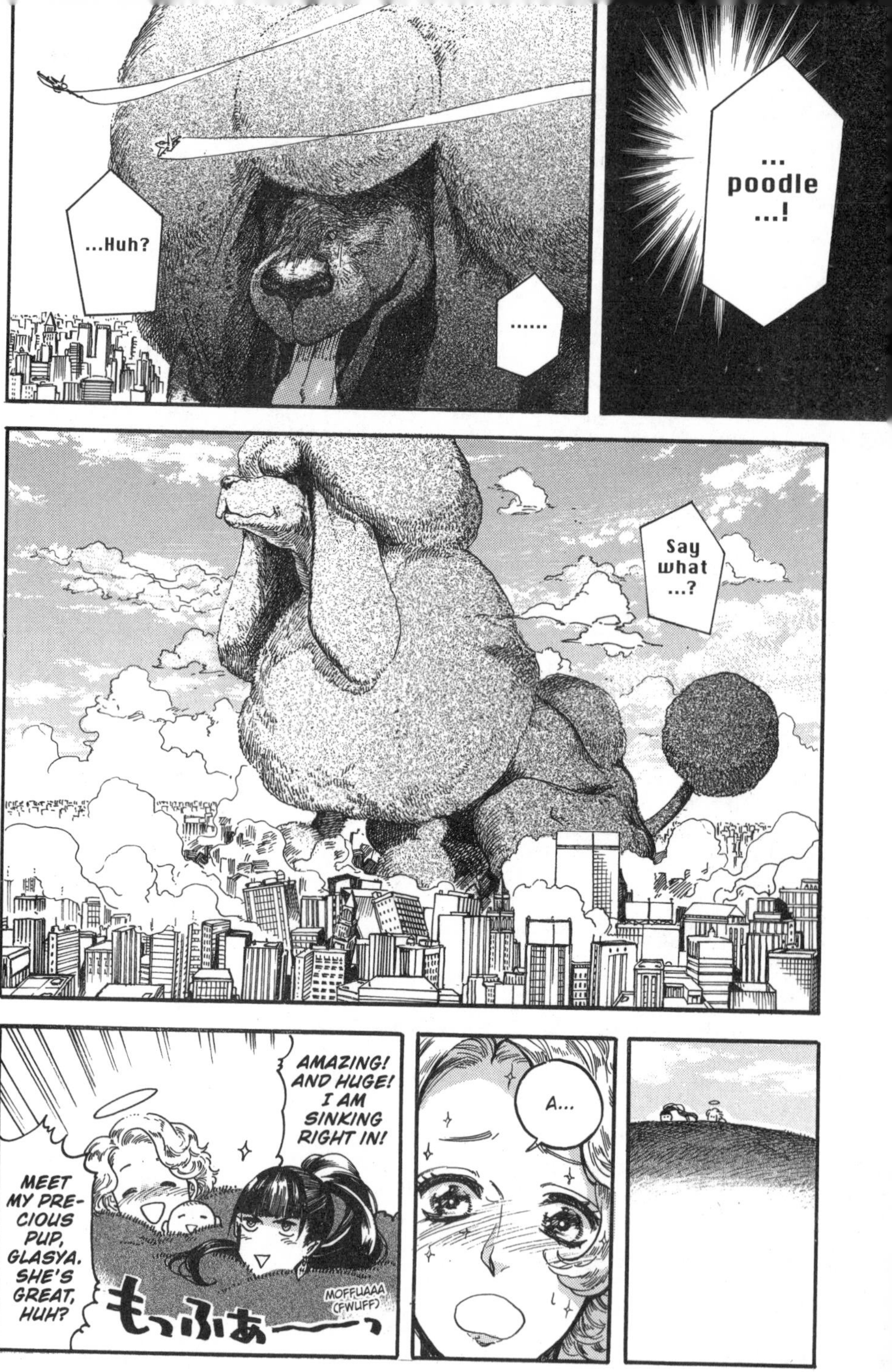

... poodle ...!
......
...Huh?
Say what ...?
A...
AMAZING! AND HUGE! I AM SINKING RIGHT IN!
MOFFUAAA (FWUFF)
もっふぁ〜〜っ
MEET MY PRECIOUS PUP, GLASYA. SHE'S GREAT, HUH?

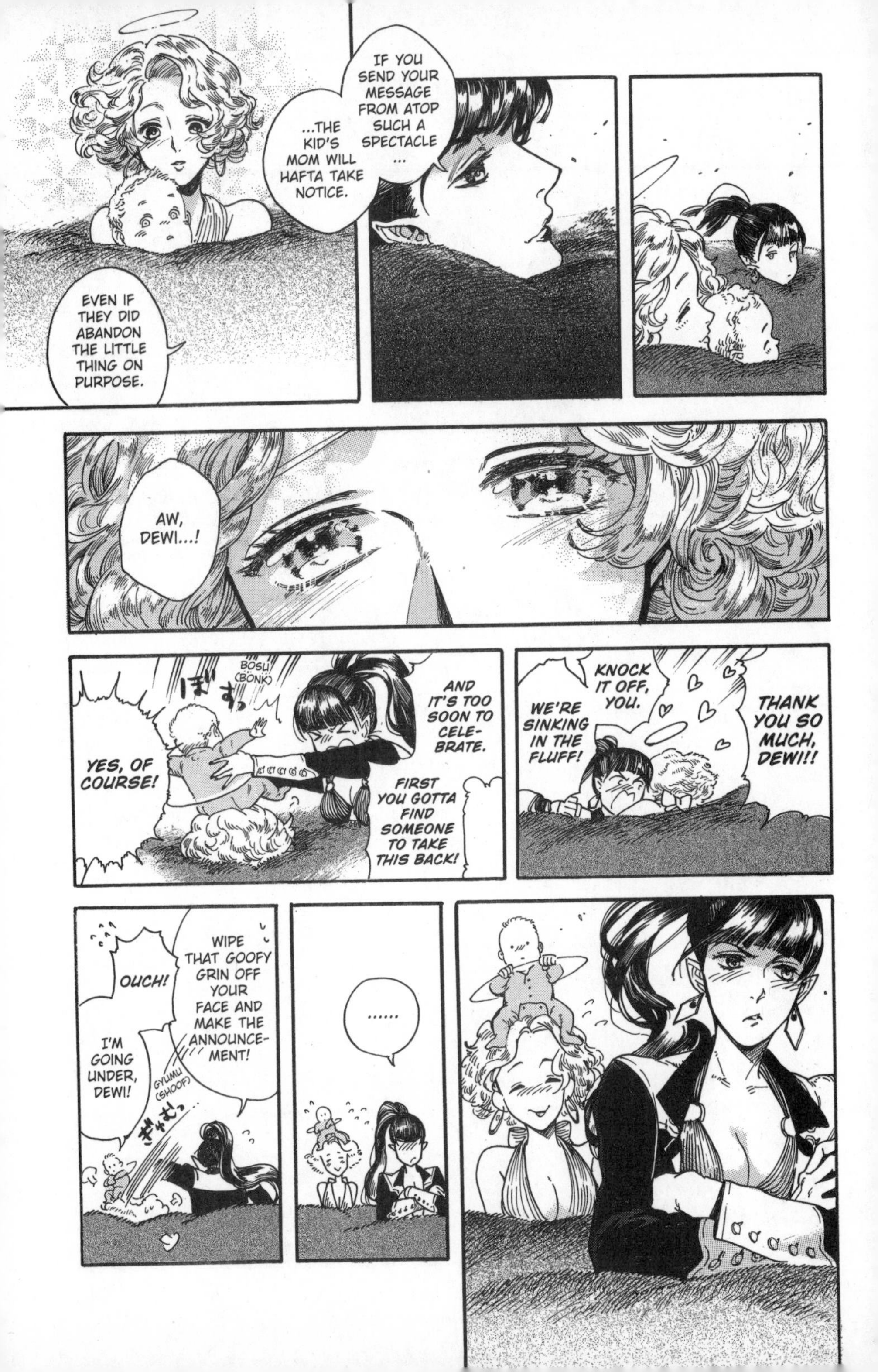

IF YOU SEND YOUR MESSAGE FROM ATOP SUCH A SPECTACLE...
...THE KID'S MOM WILL HAFTA TAKE NOTICE.
EVEN IF THEY DID ABANDON THE LITTLE THING ON PURPOSE.
AW, DEWI...!
THANK YOU SO MUCH, DEWI!!
KNOCK IT OFF, YOU.
WE'RE SINKING IN THE FLUFF!
AND IT'S TOO SOON TO CELE-BRATE.
FIRST YOU GOTTA FIND SOMEONE TO TAKE THIS BACK!
BOSU (BONK)
ぼすっ
YES, OF COURSE!
......
WIPE THAT GOOFY GRIN OFF YOUR FACE AND MAKE THE ANNOUNCE-MENT!
OUCH!
GYUMU (SHOOF)
ぎゅむっ
I'M GOING UNDER, DEWI!

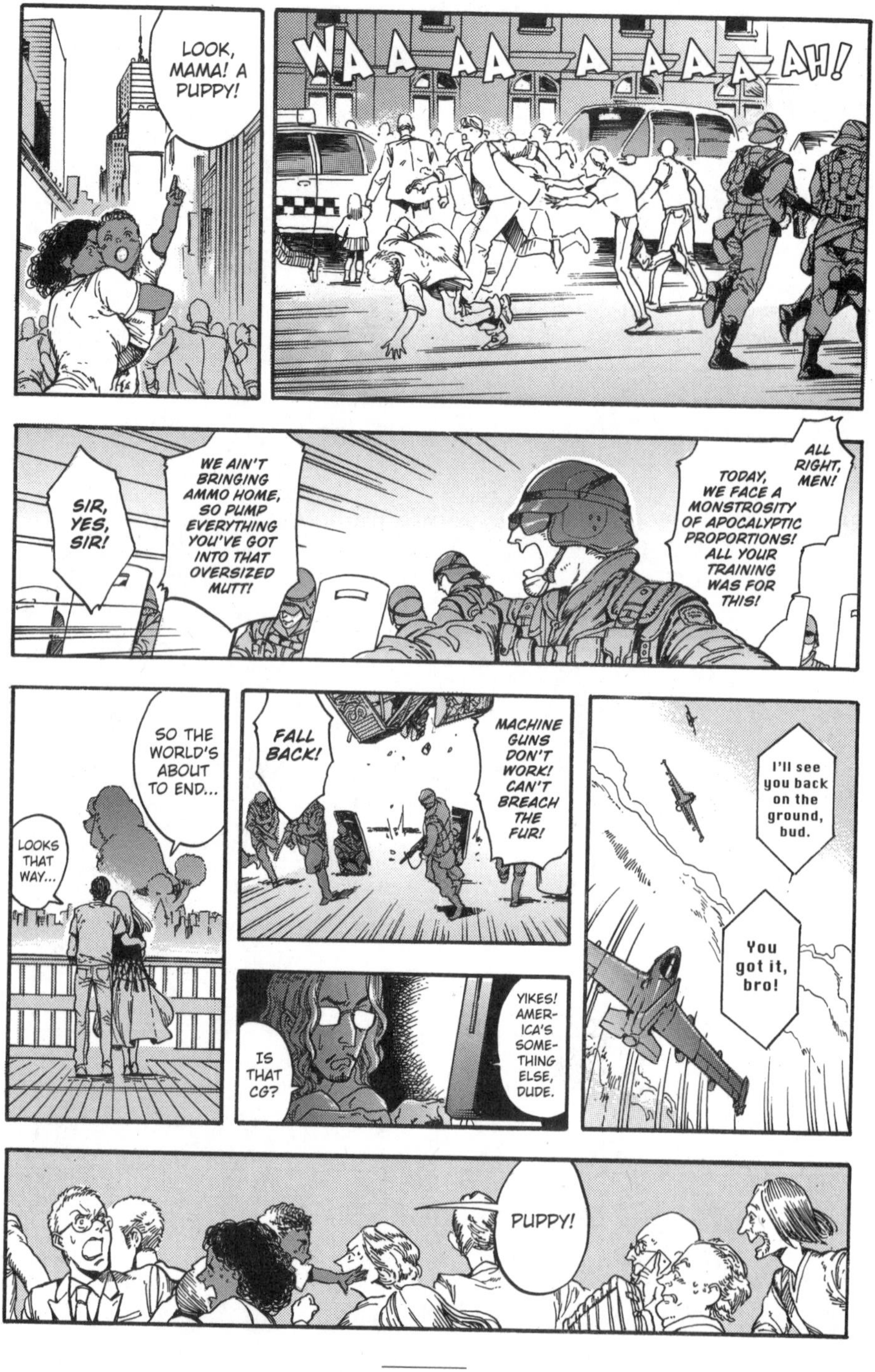
WAAAAAAAAAH!
LOOK, MAMA! A PUPPY!
ALL RIGHT, MEN!
TODAY, WE FACE A MONSTROSITY OF APOCALYPTIC PROPORTIONS! ALL YOUR TRAINING WAS FOR THIS!
WE AIN'T BRINGING AMMO HOME, SO PUMP EVERYTHING YOU'VE GOT INTO THAT OVERSIZED MUTT!
SIR, YES, SIR!
I'll see you back on the ground, bud.
You got it, bro!
MACHINE GUNS DON'T WORK! CAN'T BREACH THE FUR!
FALL BACK!
YIKES! AMERICA'S SOMETHING ELSE, DUDE.
IS THAT CG?
SO THE WORLD'S ABOUT TO END...
LOOKS THAT WAY...
PUPPY!

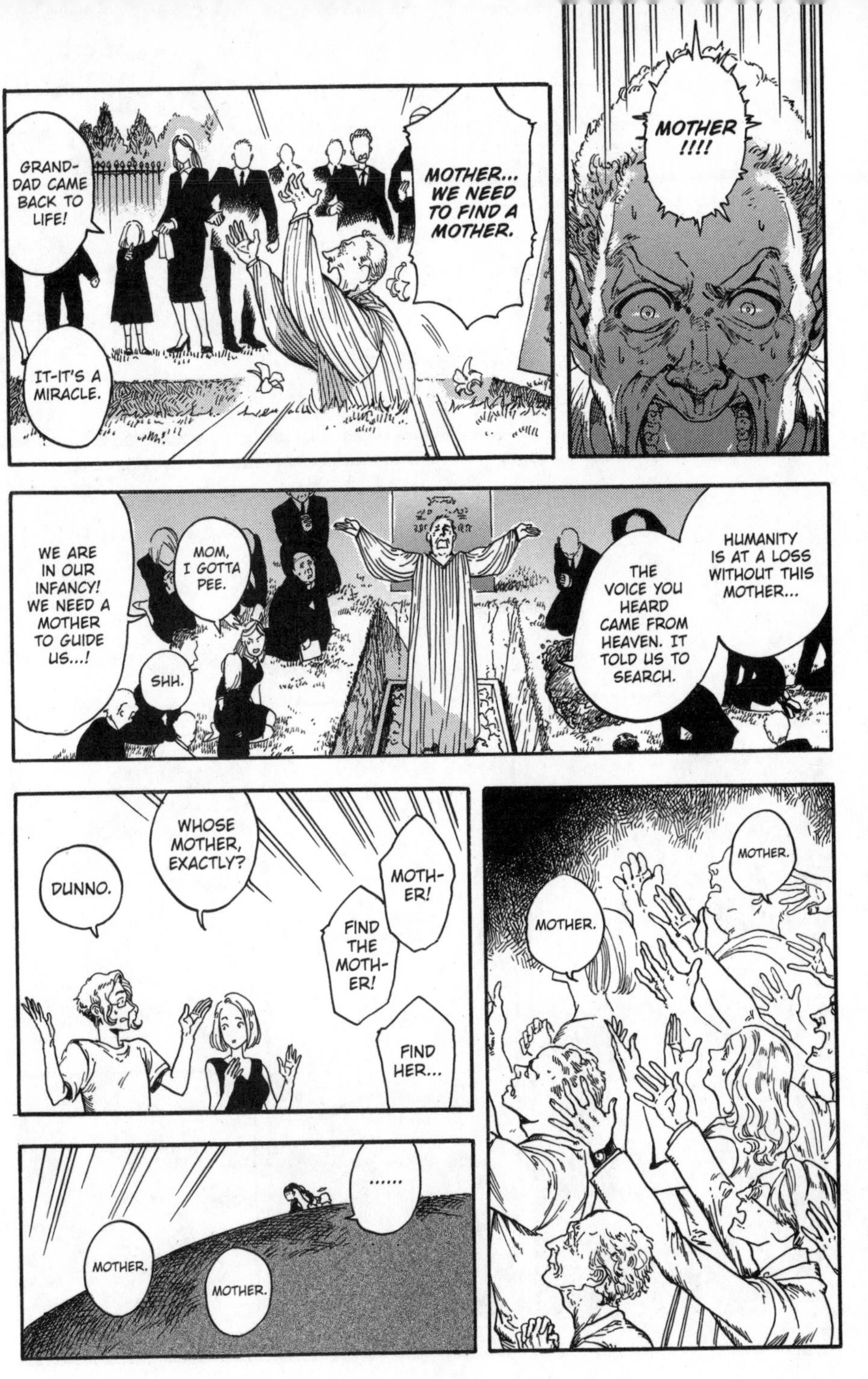
MOTHER !!!!
MOTHER... WE NEED TO FIND A MOTHER.
GRAND-DAD CAME BACK TO LIFE!
IT-IT'S A MIRACLE.
HUMANITY IS AT A LOSS WITHOUT THIS MOTHER...
THE VOICE YOU HEARD CAME FROM HEAVEN. IT TOLD US TO SEARCH.
MOM, I GOTTA PEE.
WE ARE IN OUR INFANCY! WE NEED A MOTHER TO GUIDE US...!
SHH.
MOTHER.
MOTHER.
MOTH-ER!
FIND THE MOTH-ER!
FIND HER...
WHOSE MOTHER, EXACTLY?
DUNNO.
......
MOTHER.
MOTHER.

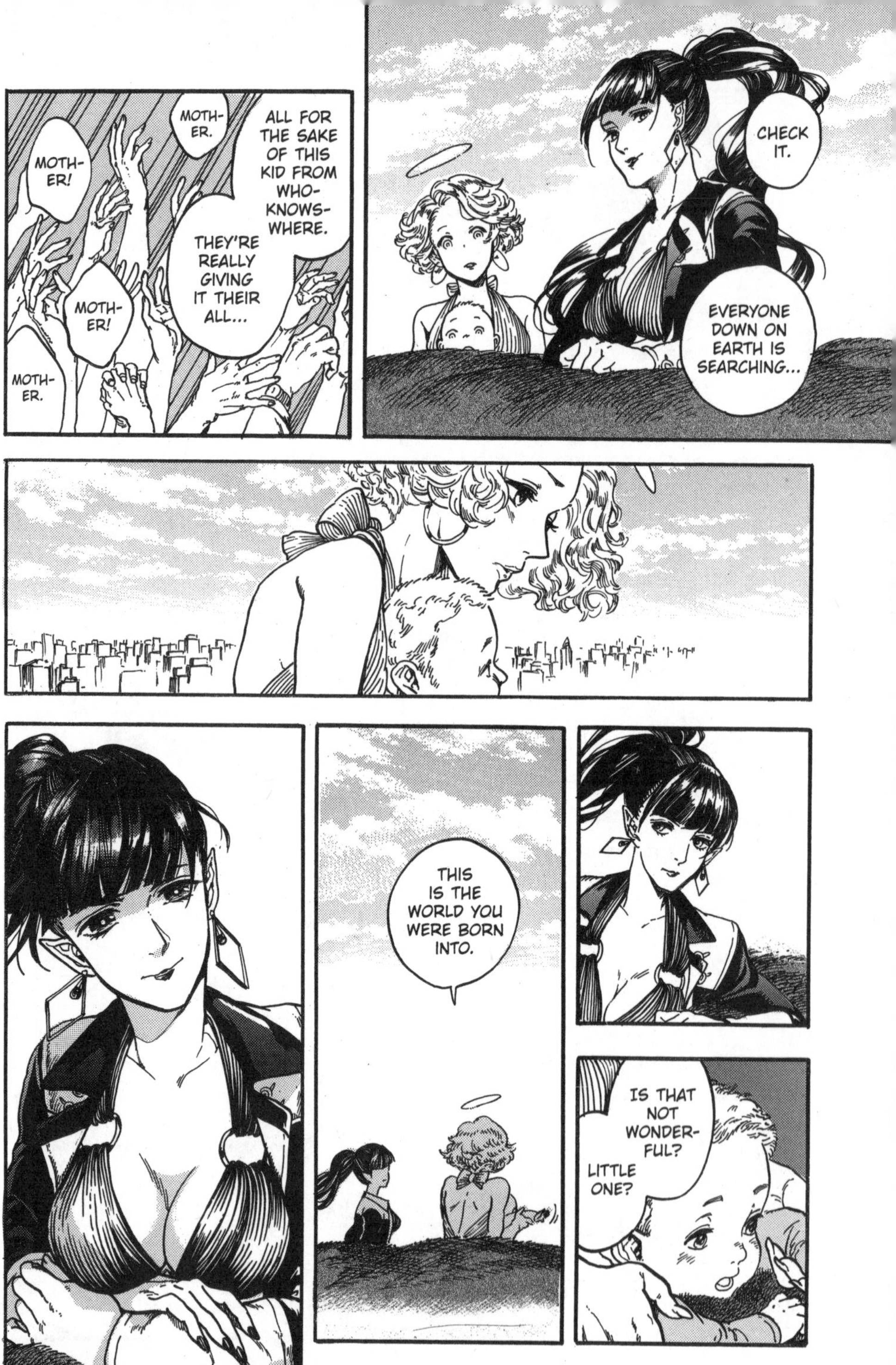
CHECK IT.
EVERYONE DOWN ON EARTH IS SEARCHING...
ALL FOR THE SAKE OF THIS KID FROM WHO-KNOWS-WHERE.
MOTH-ER.
MOTH-ER!
THEY'RE REALLY GIVING IT THEIR ALL...
MOTH-ER!
MOTH-ER.
IS THAT NOT WONDER-FUL?
LITTLE ONE?
THIS IS THE WORLD YOU WERE BORN INTO.

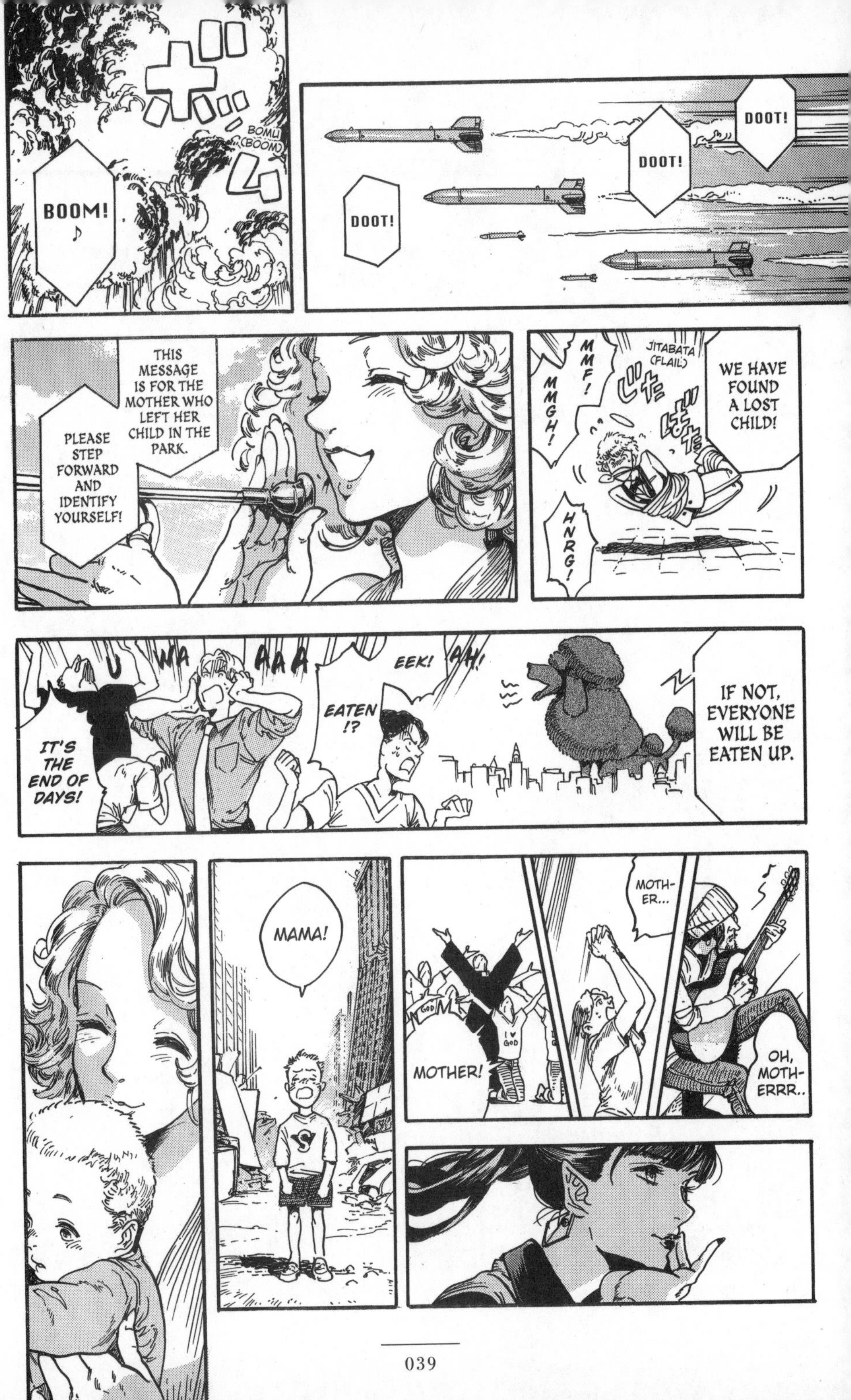
DOOT!
DOOT!
DOOT!
BOMU (BOOM)
BOOM! ♪
WE HAVE FOUND A LOST CHILD!
JITABATA (FLAIL)
MMF!
MMGH!
HNRG!
THIS MESSAGE IS FOR THE MOTHER WHO LEFT HER CHILD IN THE PARK.
PLEASE STEP FORWARD AND IDENTIFY YOURSELF!
IF NOT, EVERYONE WILL BE EATEN UP.
AH!
EEK!
EATEN!?
U WA AAA
IT'S THE END OF DAYS!
MOTH-ER...
OH, MOTH-ERRR..
MOTHER!
MAMA!

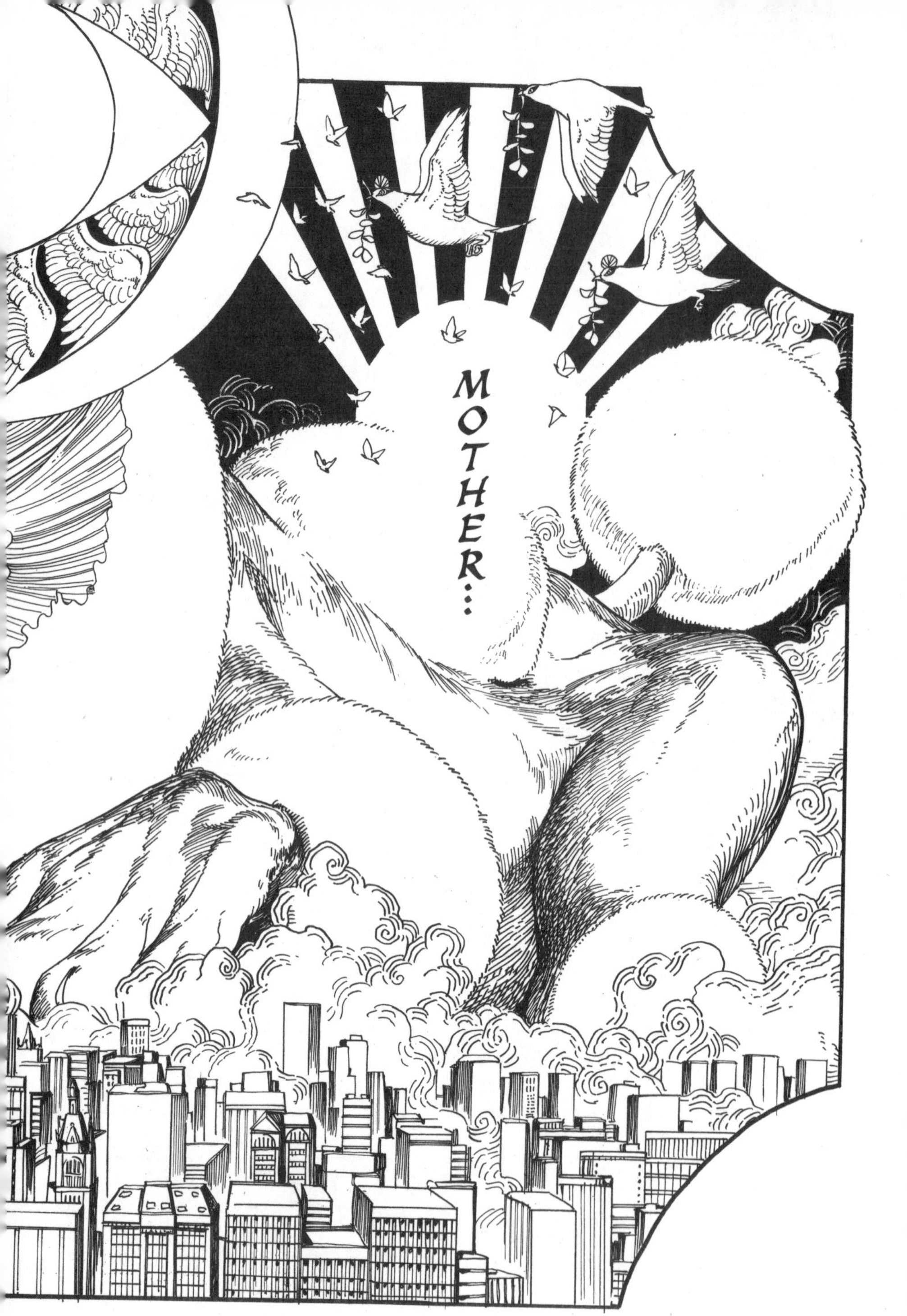
MOTHER...

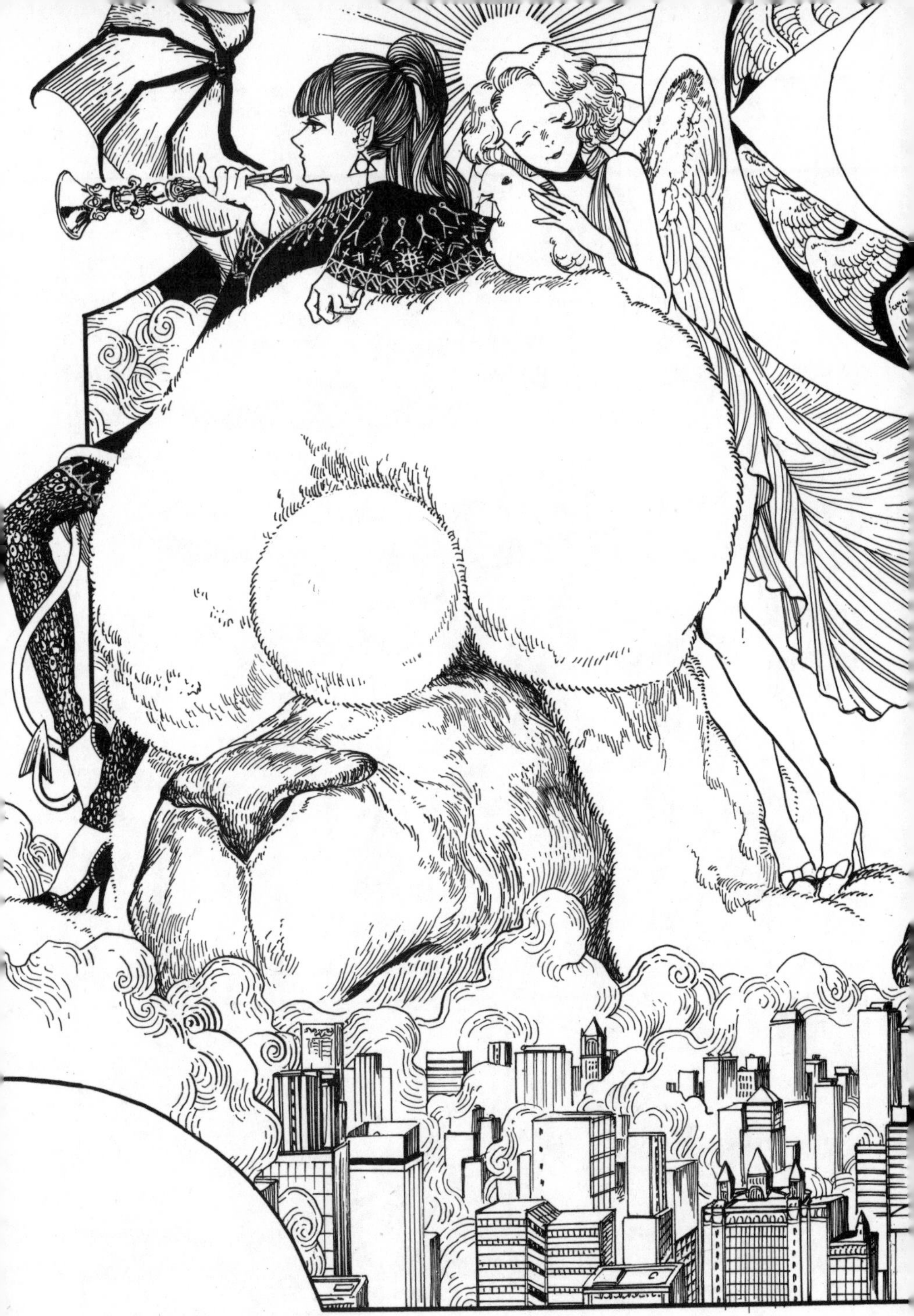

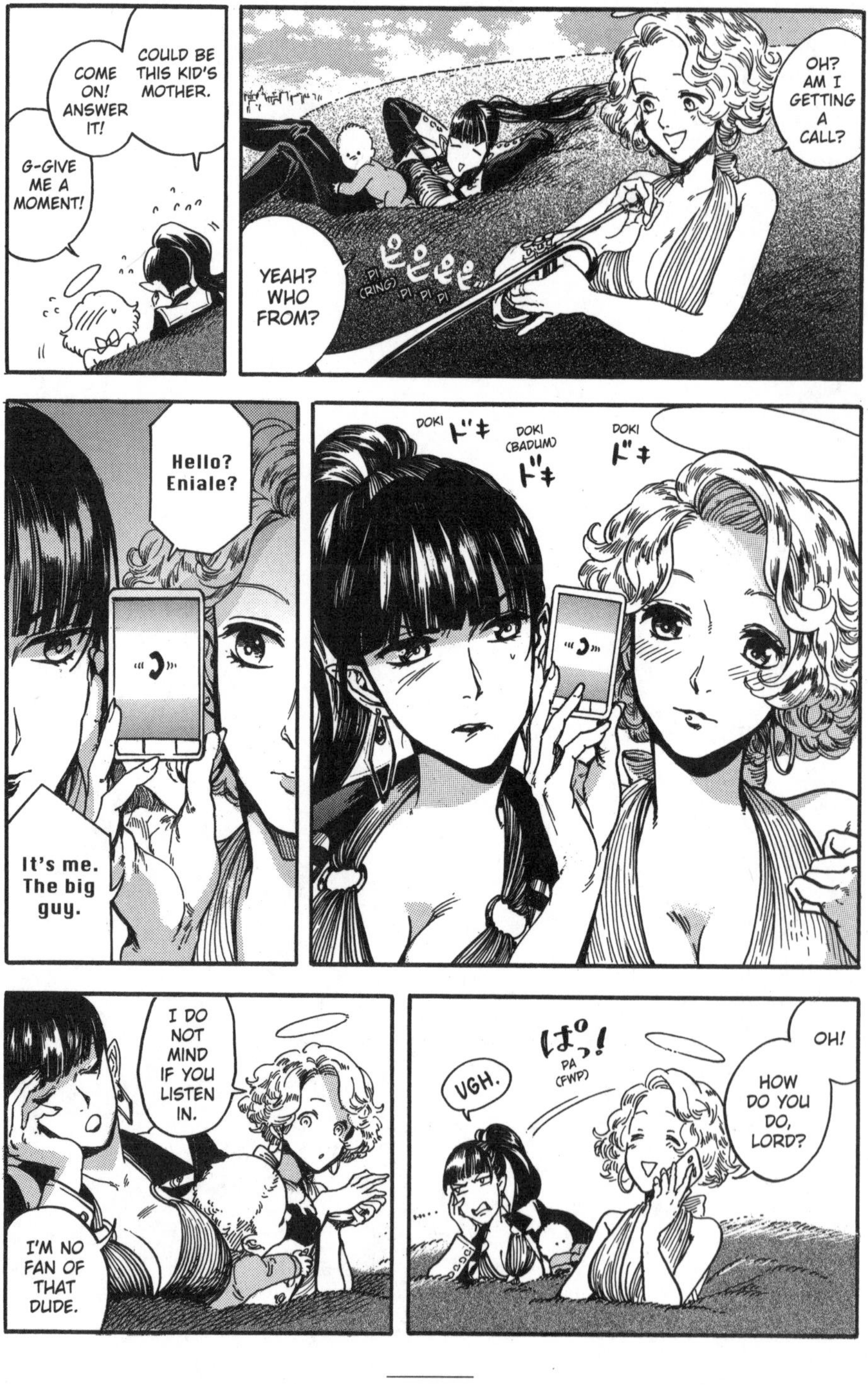
OH? AM I GETTING A CALL?
ピピピピ
PI (RING) PI PI PI
YEAH? WHO FROM?
COULD BE THIS KID'S MOTHER.
COME ON! ANSWER IT!
G-GIVE ME A MOMENT!
DOKI ドキ
DOKI (BADUM) ドキ
DOKI ドキ
Hello? Eniale?
It's me. The big guy.
OH!
HOW DO YOU DO, LORD?
ぱっ!
PA (FWP)
UGH.
I DO NOT MIND IF YOU LISTEN IN.
I'M NO FAN OF THAT DUDE.

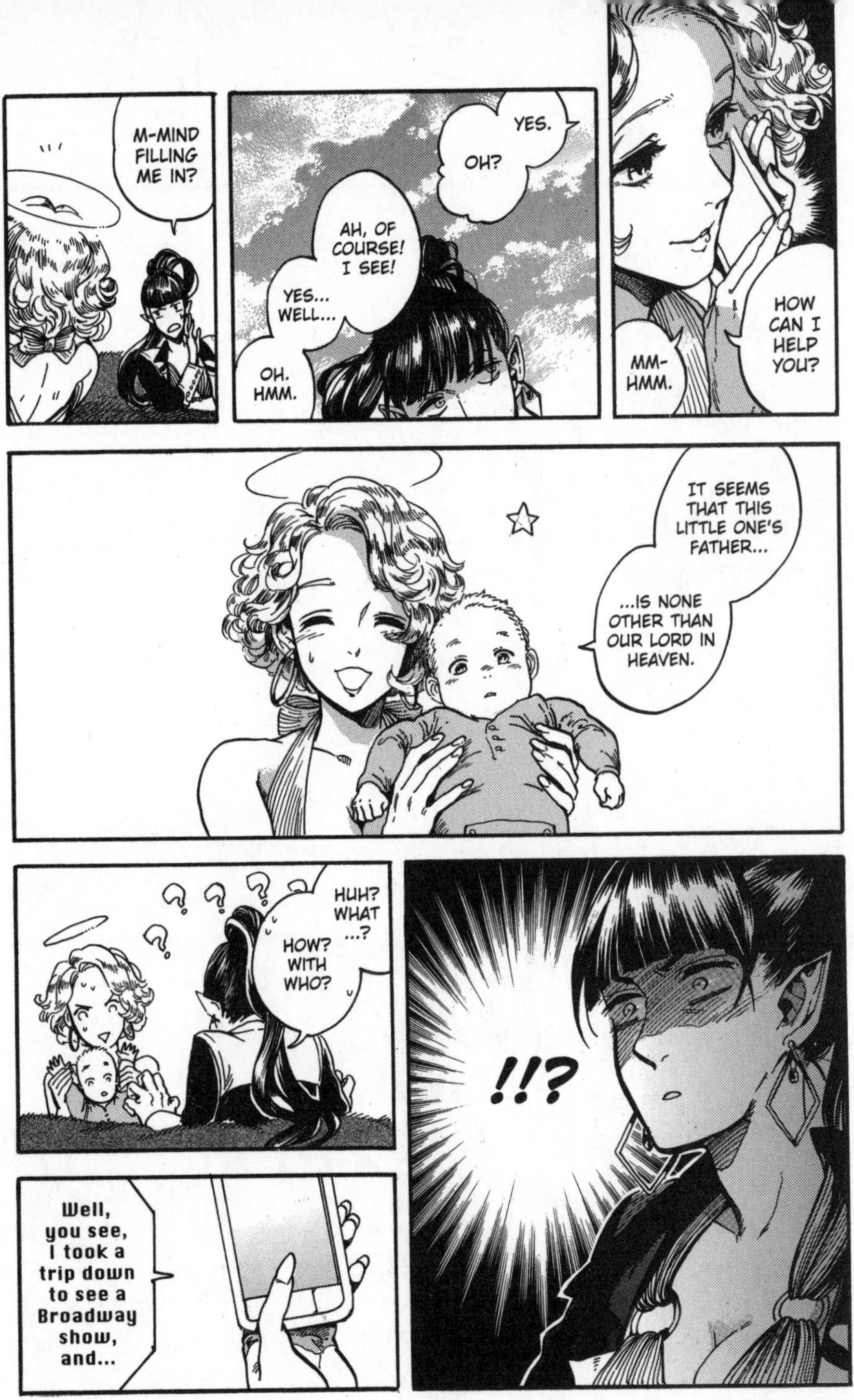
HOW CAN I HELP YOU?
MM-HMM.
YES.
OH?
AH, OF COURSE! I SEE!
YES... WELL...
OH. HMM.
M-MIND FILLING ME IN?
IT SEEMS THAT THIS LITTLE ONE'S FATHER...
...IS NONE OTHER THAN OUR LORD IN HEAVEN.
!!?
HUH? WHAT ...?
HOW? WITH WHO?
Well, you see, I took a trip down to see a Broadway show, and...

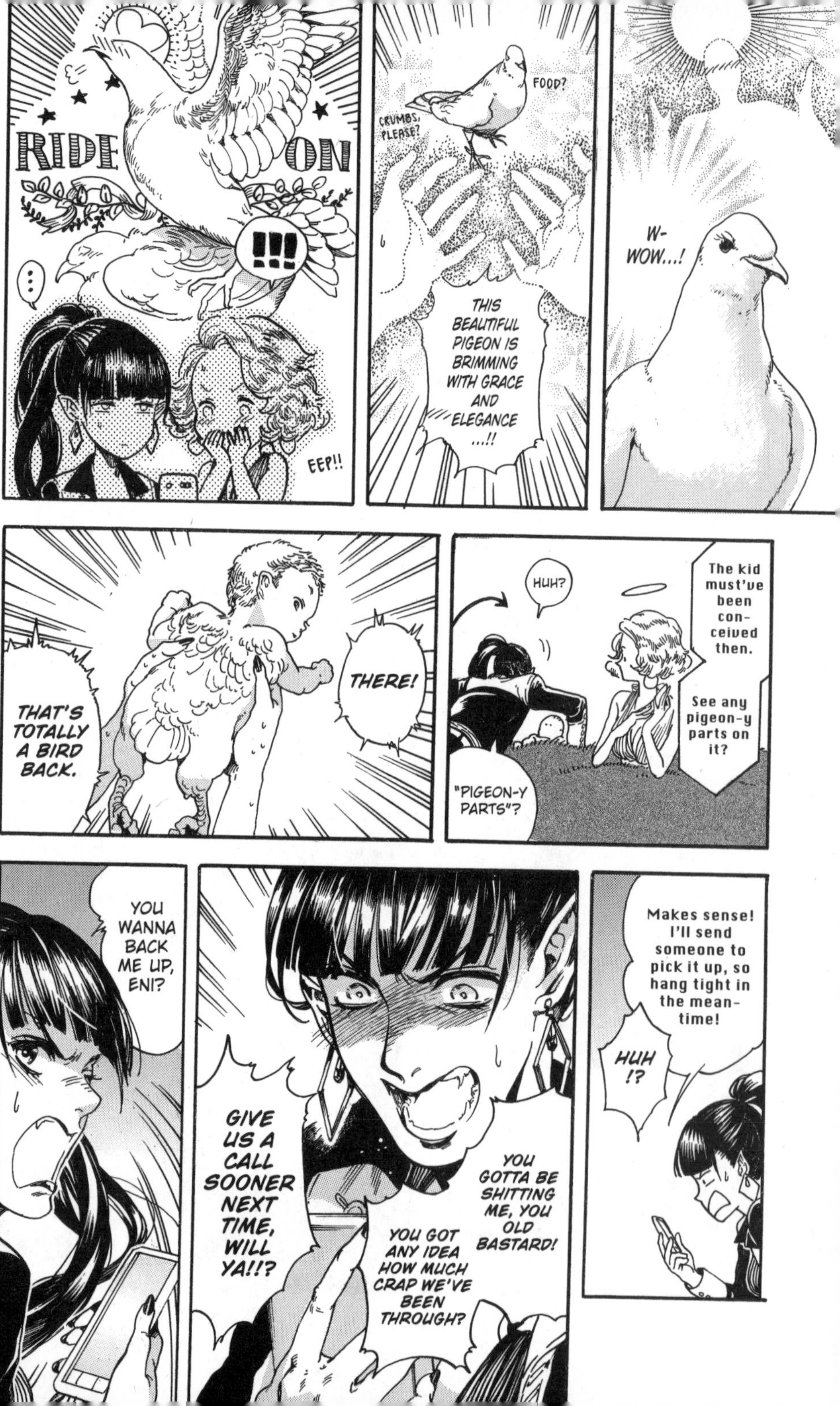
W-
WOW...!
FOOD?
CRUMBS, PLEASE?
THIS BEAUTIFUL PIGEON IS BRIMMING WITH GRACE AND ELEGANCE ...!!
RIDE ON
!!!
...
EEP!!
The kid must've been con-ceived then.
HUH?
See any pigeon-y parts on it?
"PIGEON-Y PARTS"?
THERE!
THAT'S TOTALLY A BIRD BACK.
Makes sense! I'll send someone to pick it up, so hang tight in the mean-time!
HUH !?
YOU GOTTA BE SHITTING ME, YOU OLD BASTARD!
YOU GOT ANY IDEA HOW MUCH CRAP WE'VE BEEN THROUGH?
GIVE US A CALL SOONER NEXT TIME, WILL YA!!?
YOU WANNA BACK ME UP, ENI?

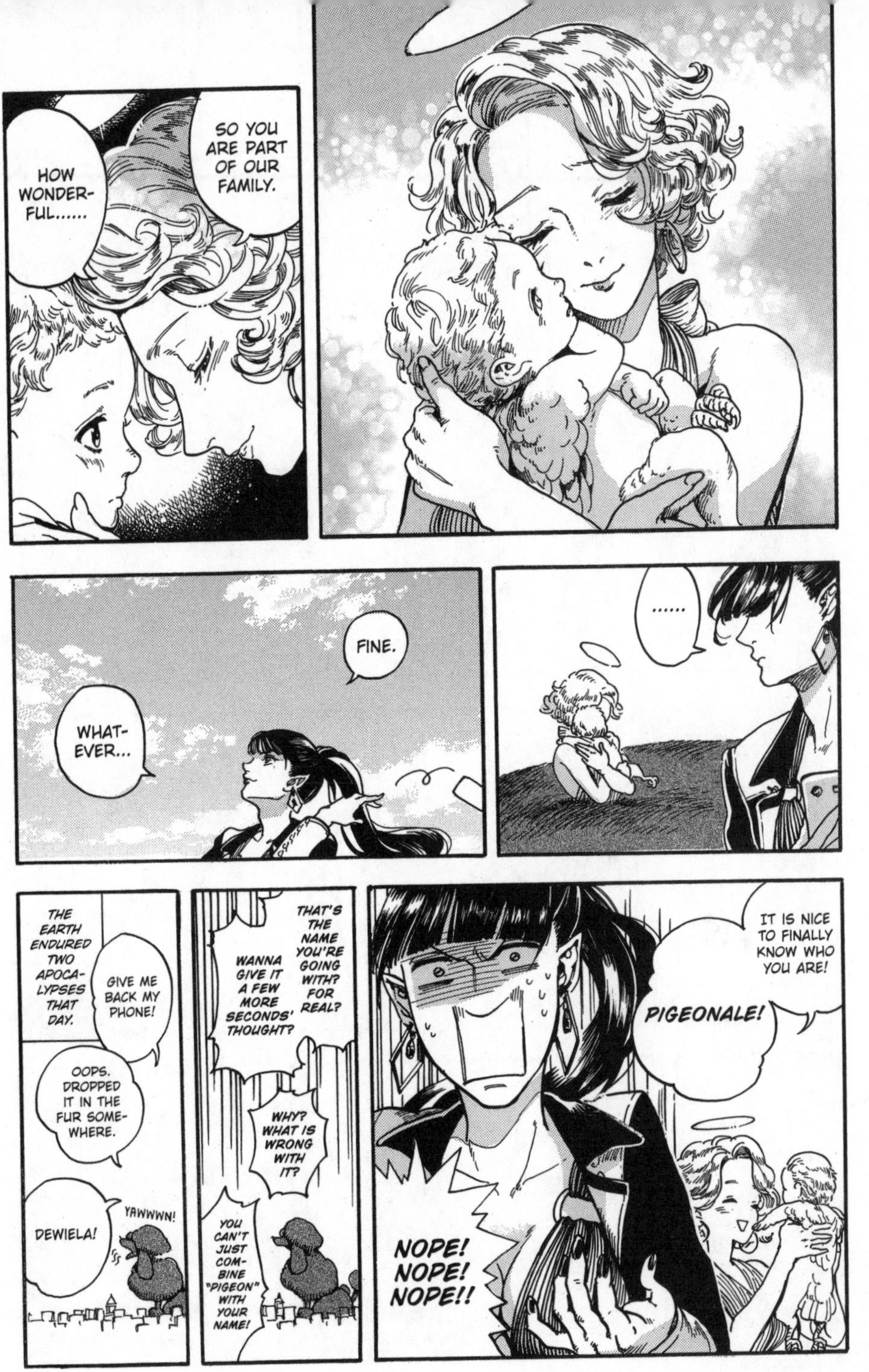
SO YOU ARE PART OF OUR FAMILY.
HOW WONDER-FUL......
......
FINE.
WHAT-EVER...
IT IS NICE TO FINALLY KNOW WHO YOU ARE!
PIGEONALE!
NOPE! NOPE! NOPE!!
THAT'S THE NAME YOU'RE GOING WITH? FOR REAL?
WANNA GIVE IT A FEW MORE SECONDS' THOUGHT?
WHY? WHAT IS WRONG WITH IT?
YOU CAN'T JUST COM-BINE "PIGEON" WITH YOUR NAME!
THE EARTH ENDURED TWO APOCA-LYPSES THAT DAY.
GIVE ME BACK MY PHONE!
OOPS. DROPPED IT IN THE FUR SOME-WHERE.
YAWWWN!
DEWIELA!

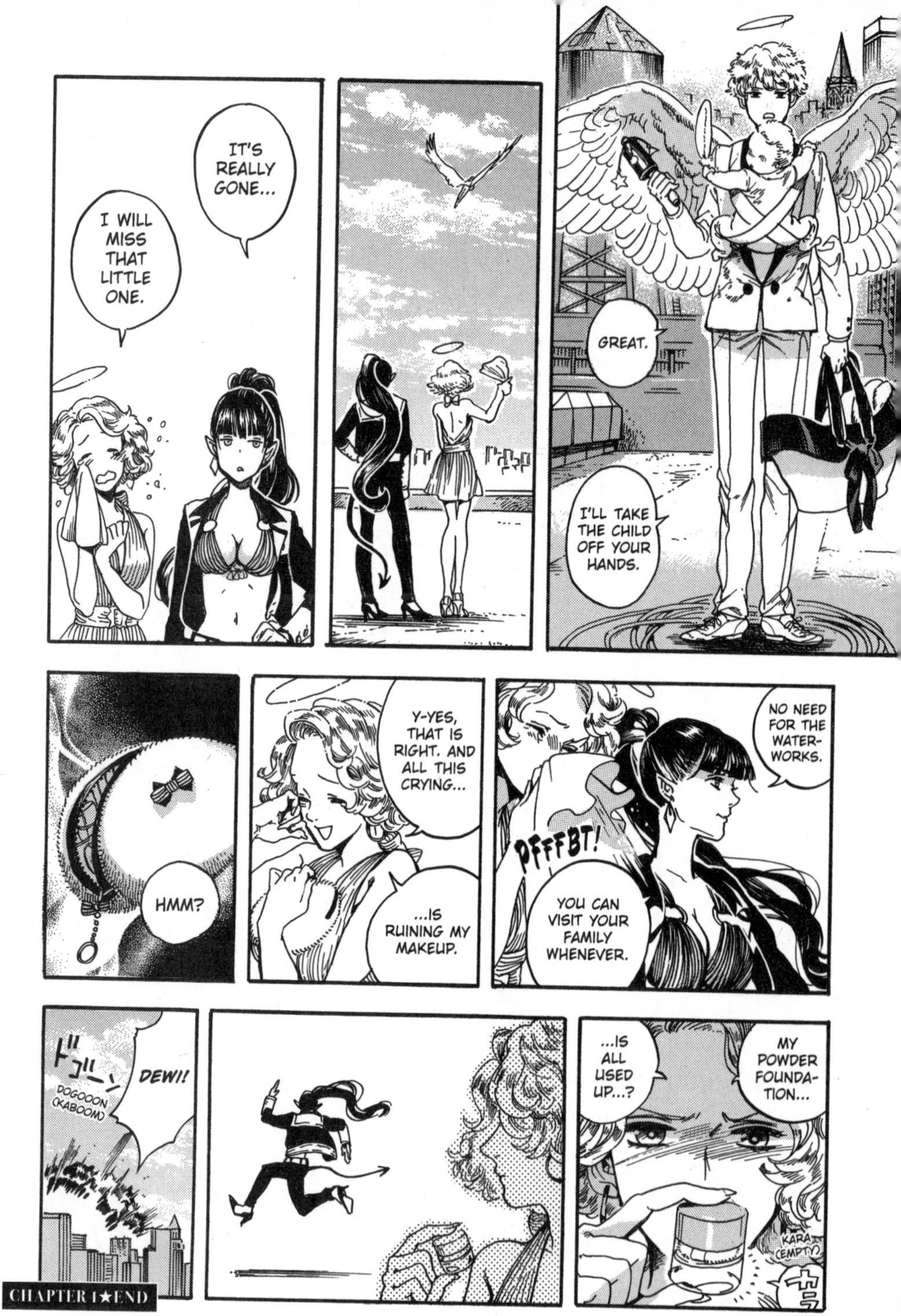
GREAT.
I'LL TAKE THE CHILD OFF YOUR HANDS.
IT'S REALLY GONE...
I WILL MISS THAT LITTLE ONE.
NO NEED FOR THE WATER-WORKS.
PFFFBT!
YOU CAN VISIT YOUR FAMILY WHENEVER.
Y-YES, THAT IS RIGHT. AND ALL THIS CRYING...
...IS RUINING MY MAKEUP.
HMM?
MY POWDER FOUNDATION...
...IS ALL USED UP...?
KARA (EMPTY)
DEWI!
DOGOOON (KABOOM)
CHAPTER 1★END

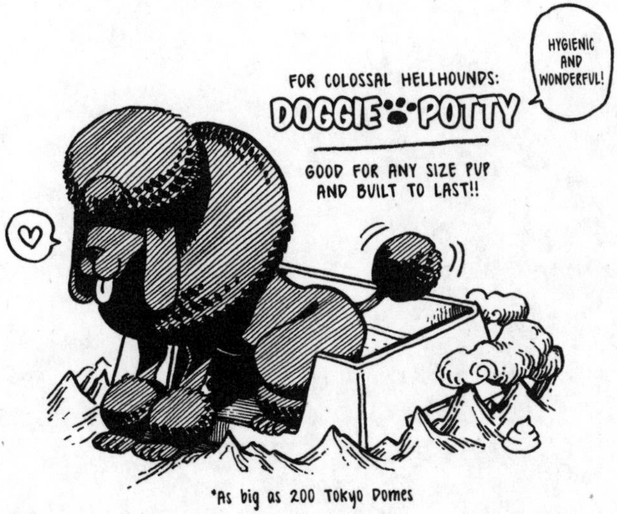
FOR COLOSSAL HELLHOUNDS:
DOGGIE POTTY
HYGIENIC AND WONDERFUL!
GOOD FOR ANY SIZE PUP AND BUILT TO LAST!!
*As big as 200 Tokyo Domes

ENIALE & DEWIELA

1

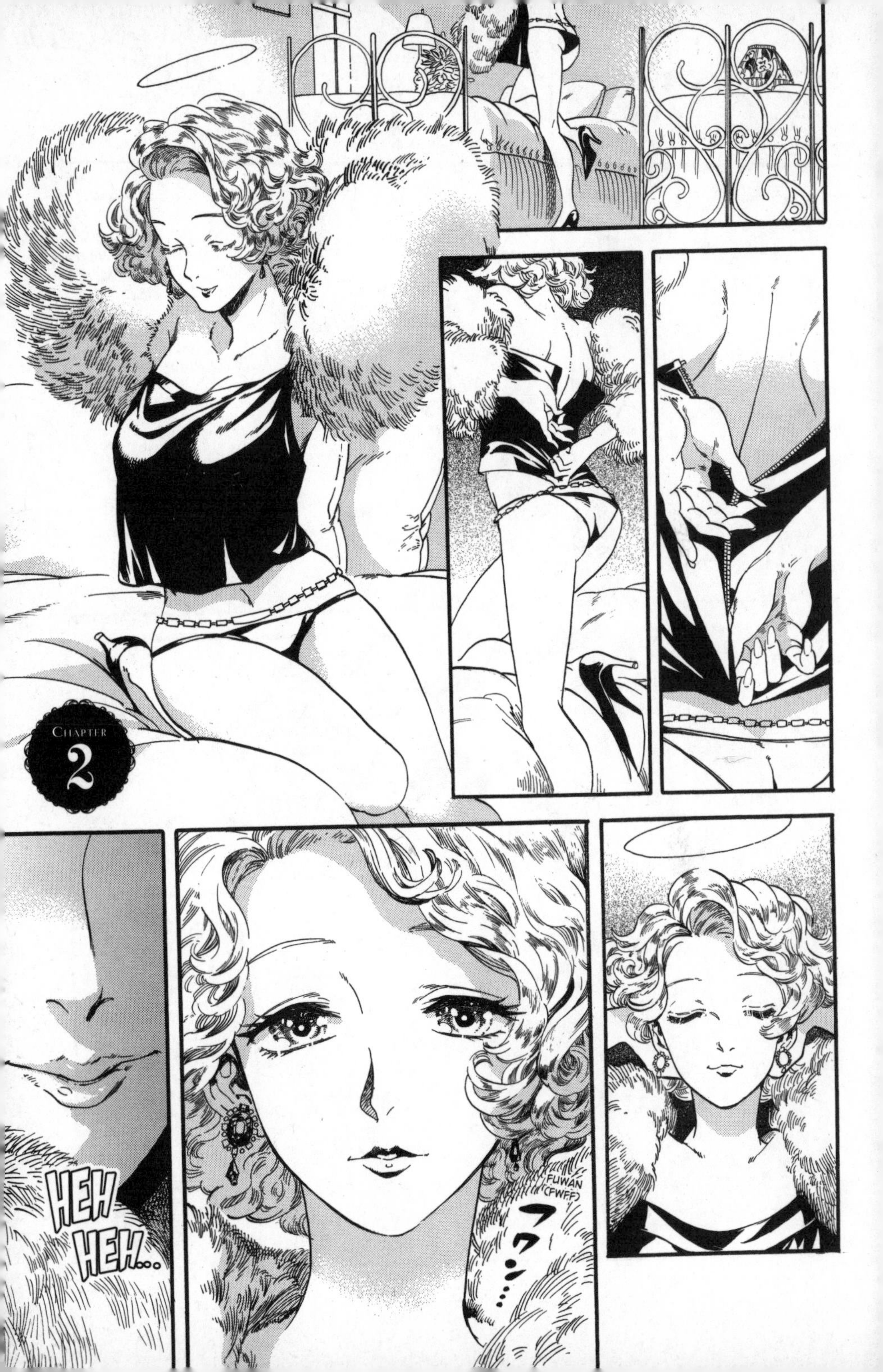
CHAPTER
2
FUWAN (FWFF)
HEH HEH...

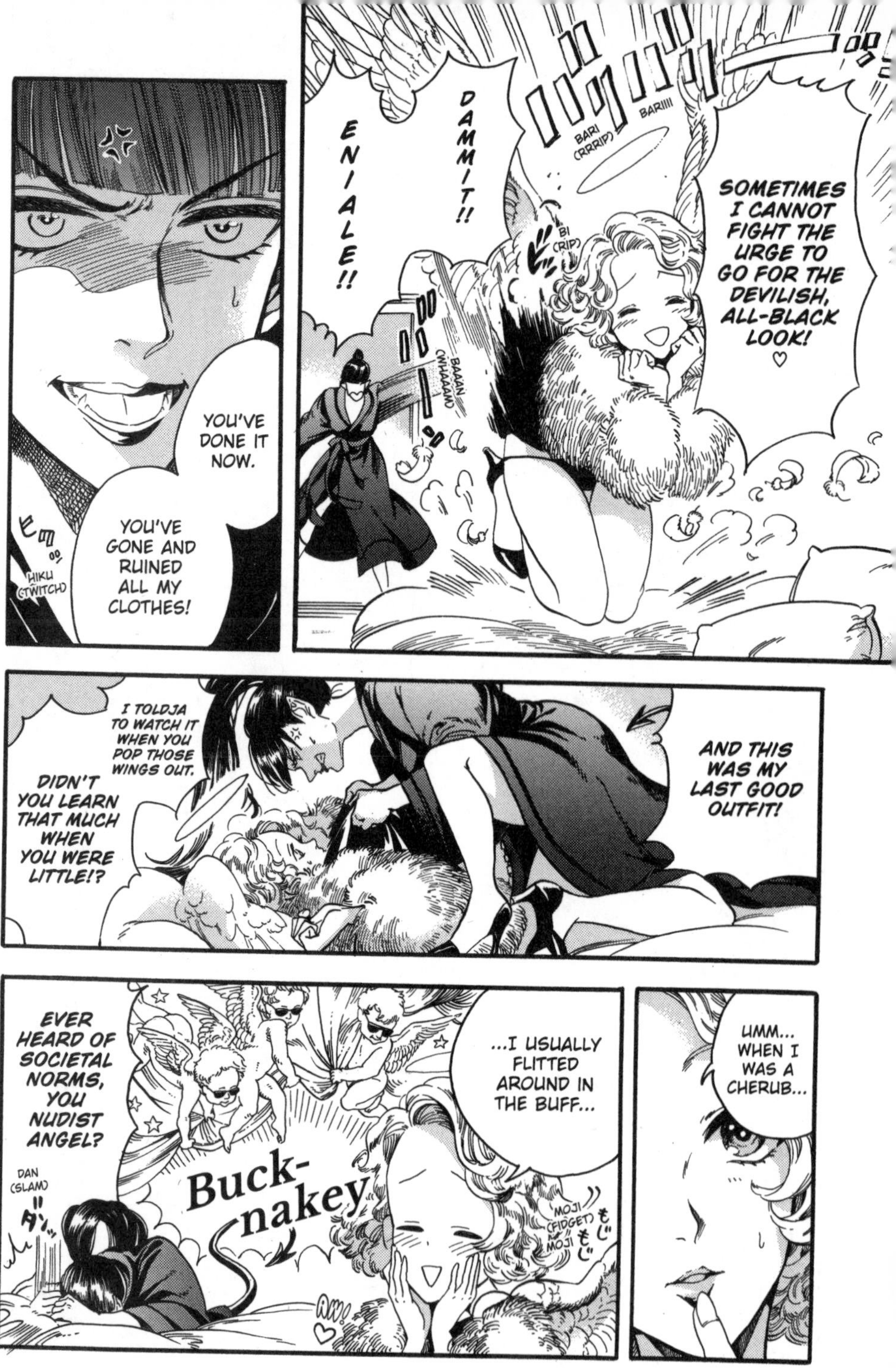
SOMETIMES I CANNOT FIGHT THE URGE TO GO FOR THE DEVILISH, ALL-BLACK LOOK! ♡
BARIIII
BARI (RRRIP)
DAMMIT!!
ENIALE!!
BI (RIP)
BAAAN (WHAAAM)
YOU'VE DONE IT NOW.
YOU'VE GONE AND RUINED ALL MY CLOTHES!
HIKU (TWITCH)
AND THIS WAS MY LAST GOOD OUTFIT!
I TOLDJA TO WATCH IT WHEN YOU POP THOSE WINGS OUT.
DIDN'T YOU LEARN THAT MUCH WHEN YOU WERE LITTLE!?
UMM... WHEN I WAS A CHERUB...
...I USUALLY FLITTED AROUND IN THE BUFF...
MOJI (FIDGET) MOJI
AW! ♡
Buck-nakey
EVER HEARD OF SOCIETAL NORMS, YOU NUDIST ANGEL?
DAN (SLAM)

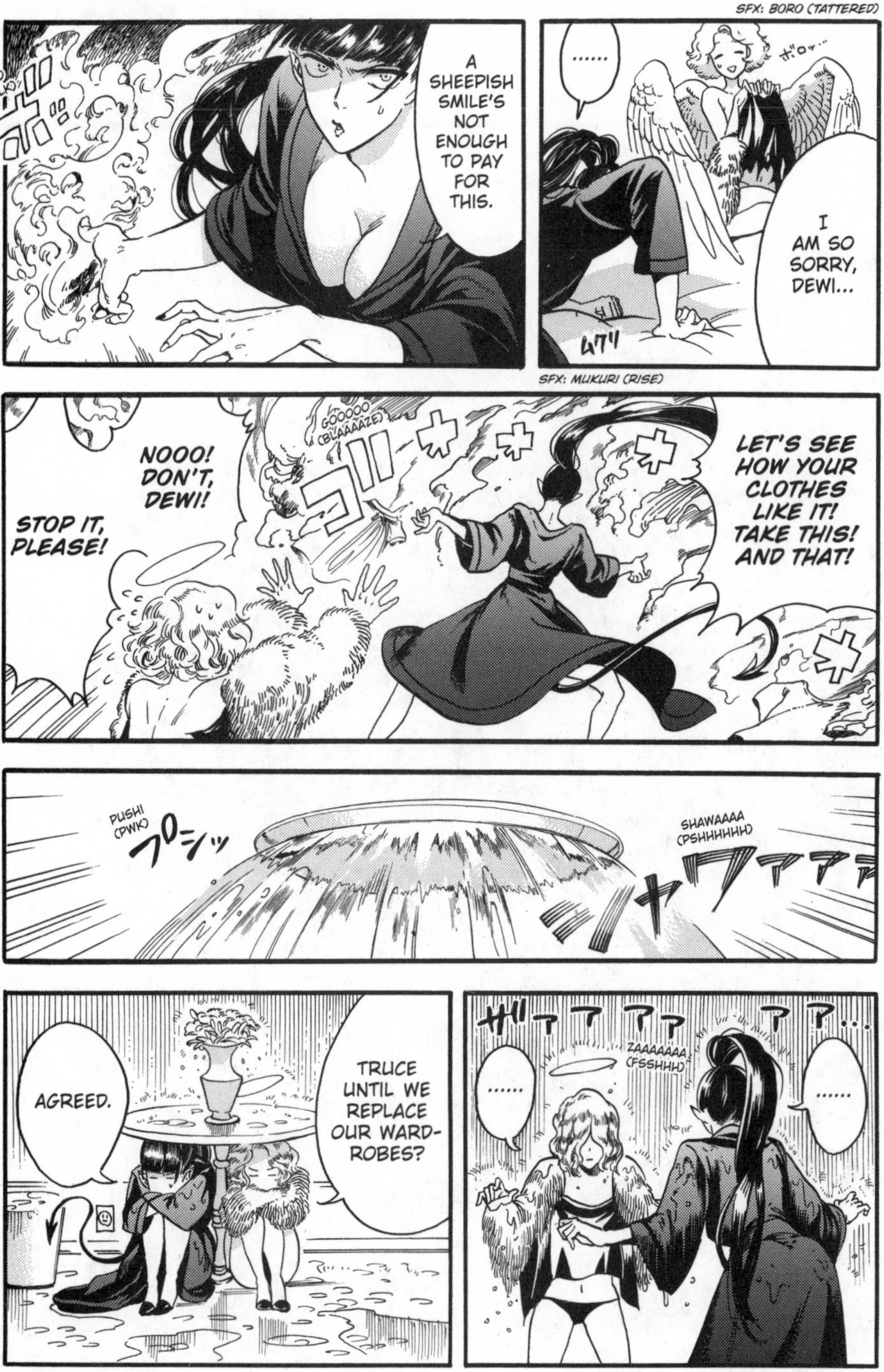
SFX: BORO (TATTERED)
......
I AM SO SORRY, DEWI...
SFX: MUKURI (RISE)
BO (FLK)
A SHEEPISH SMILE'S NOT ENOUGH TO PAY FOR THIS.
LET'S SEE HOW YOUR CLOTHES LIKE IT! TAKE THIS! AND THAT!
GOOOOO (BLAAAAZE)
NOOO! DON'T, DEWI!
STOP IT, PLEASE!
SHAWAAAA (PSHHHHHH)
PUSHI (PWK)
......
ZAAAAAAA (FSSHHH)
......
TRUCE UNTIL WE REPLACE OUR WARD-ROBES?
AGREED.

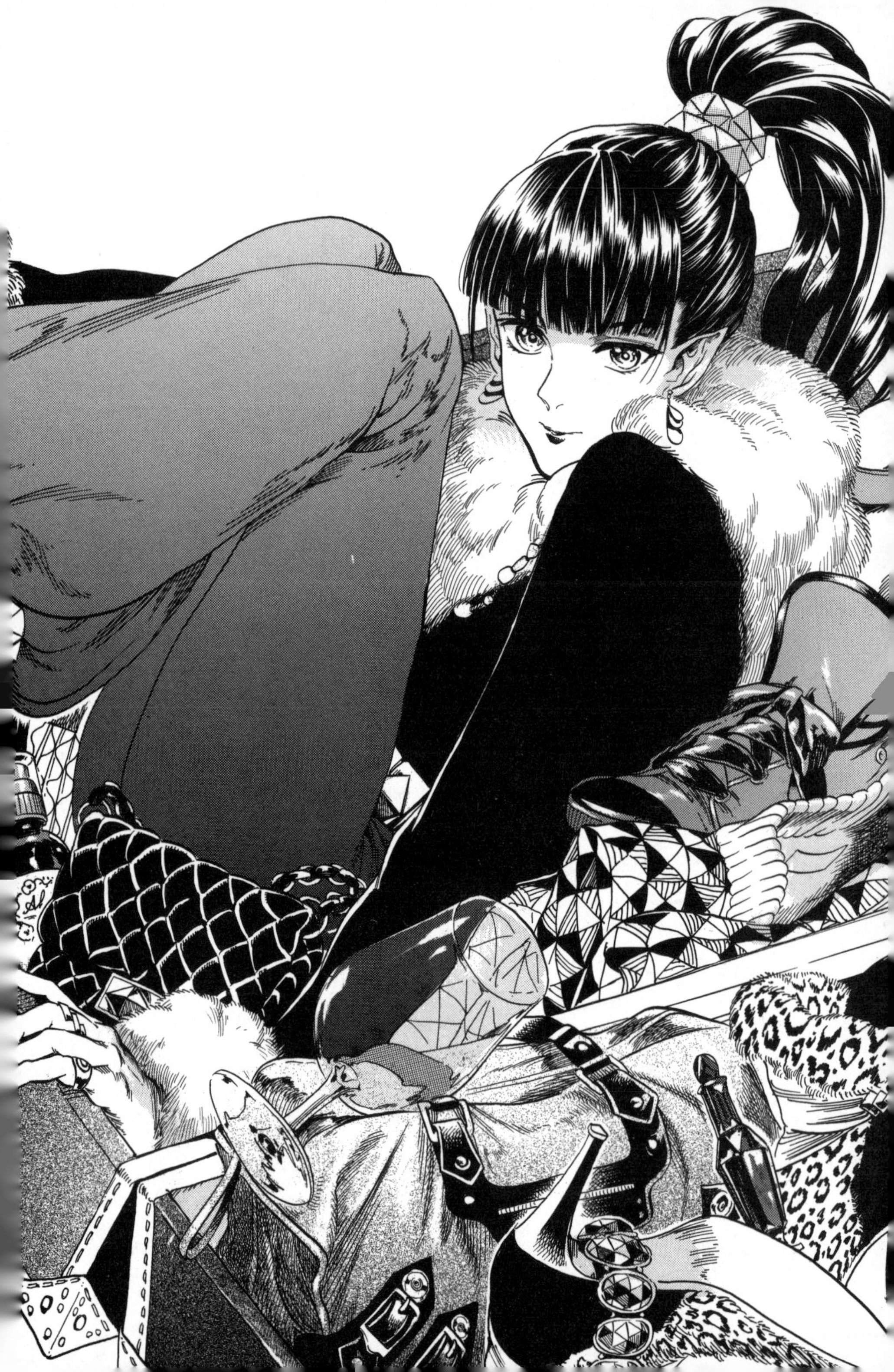

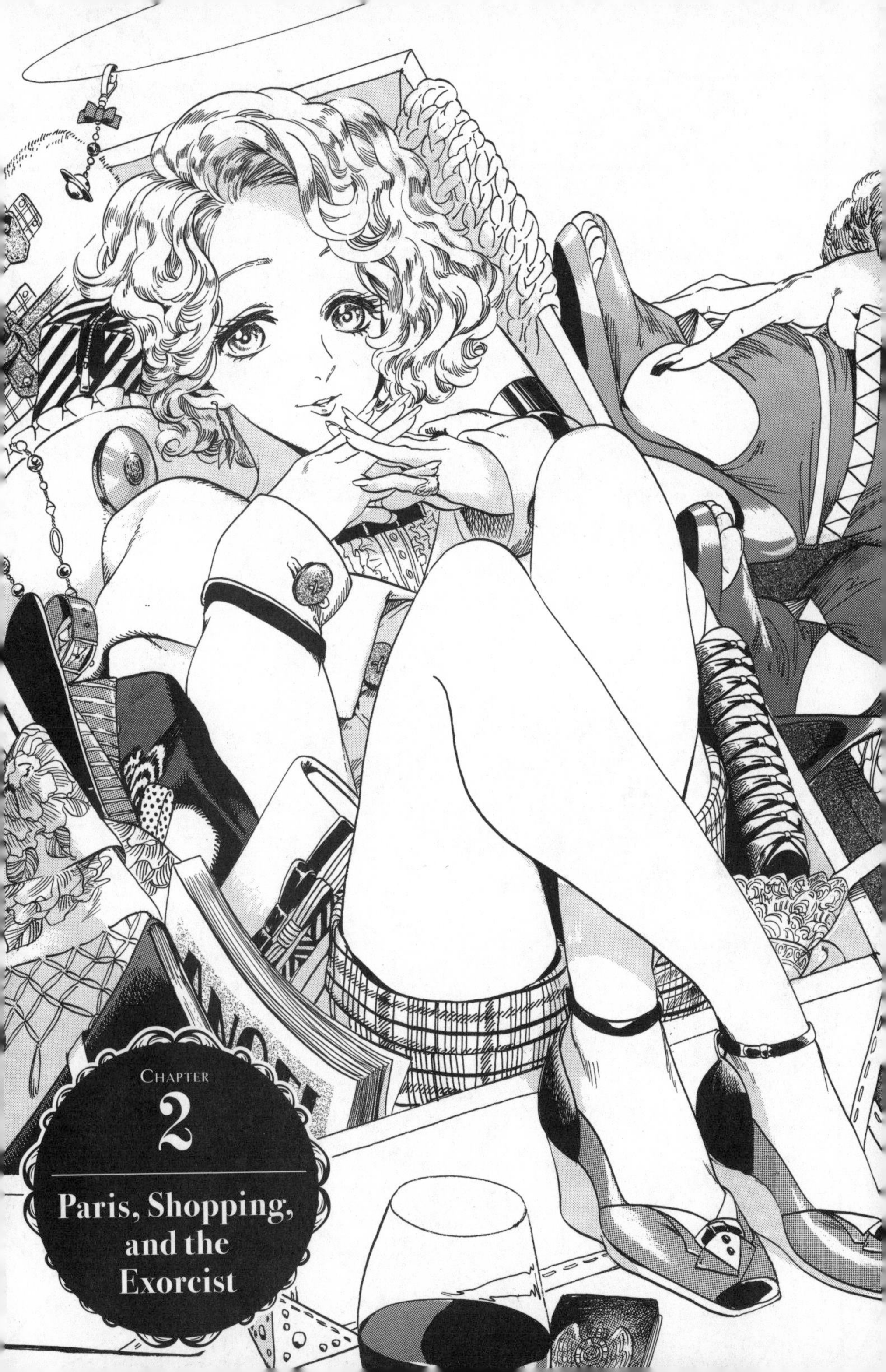
CHAPTER
2
Paris, Shopping, and the Exorcist

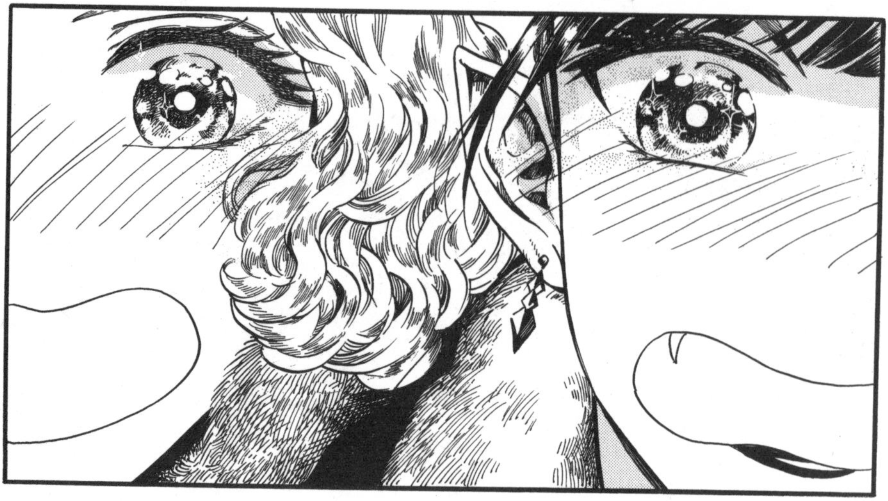

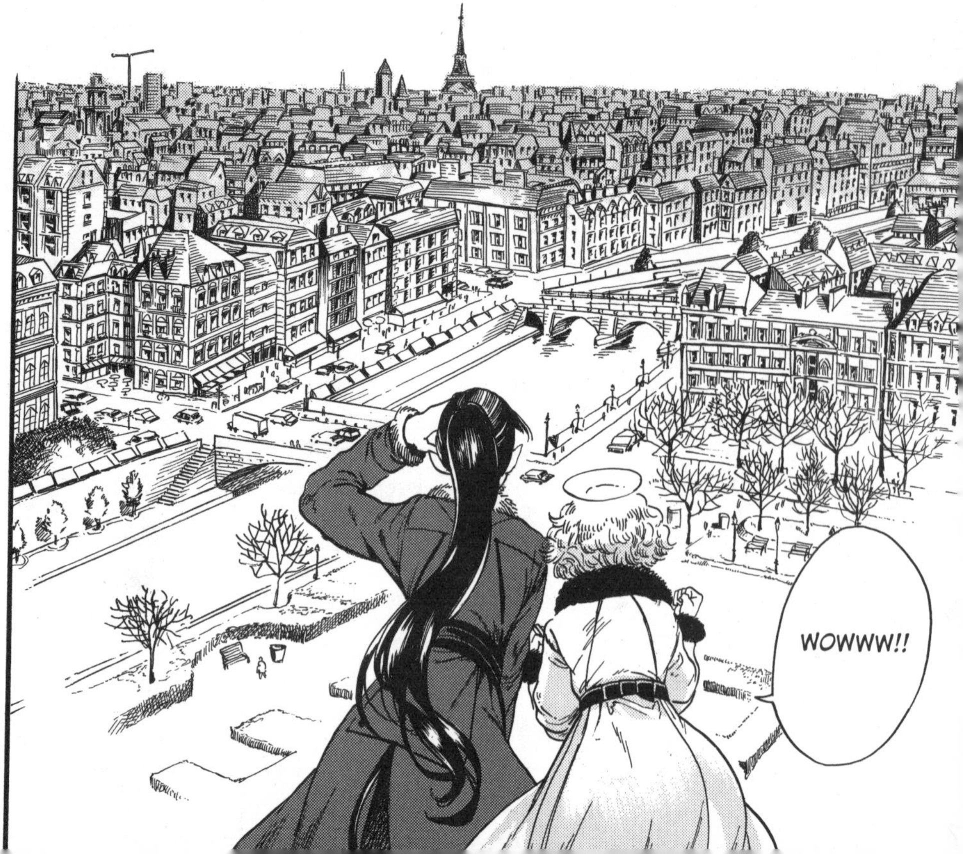
WOWWW!!

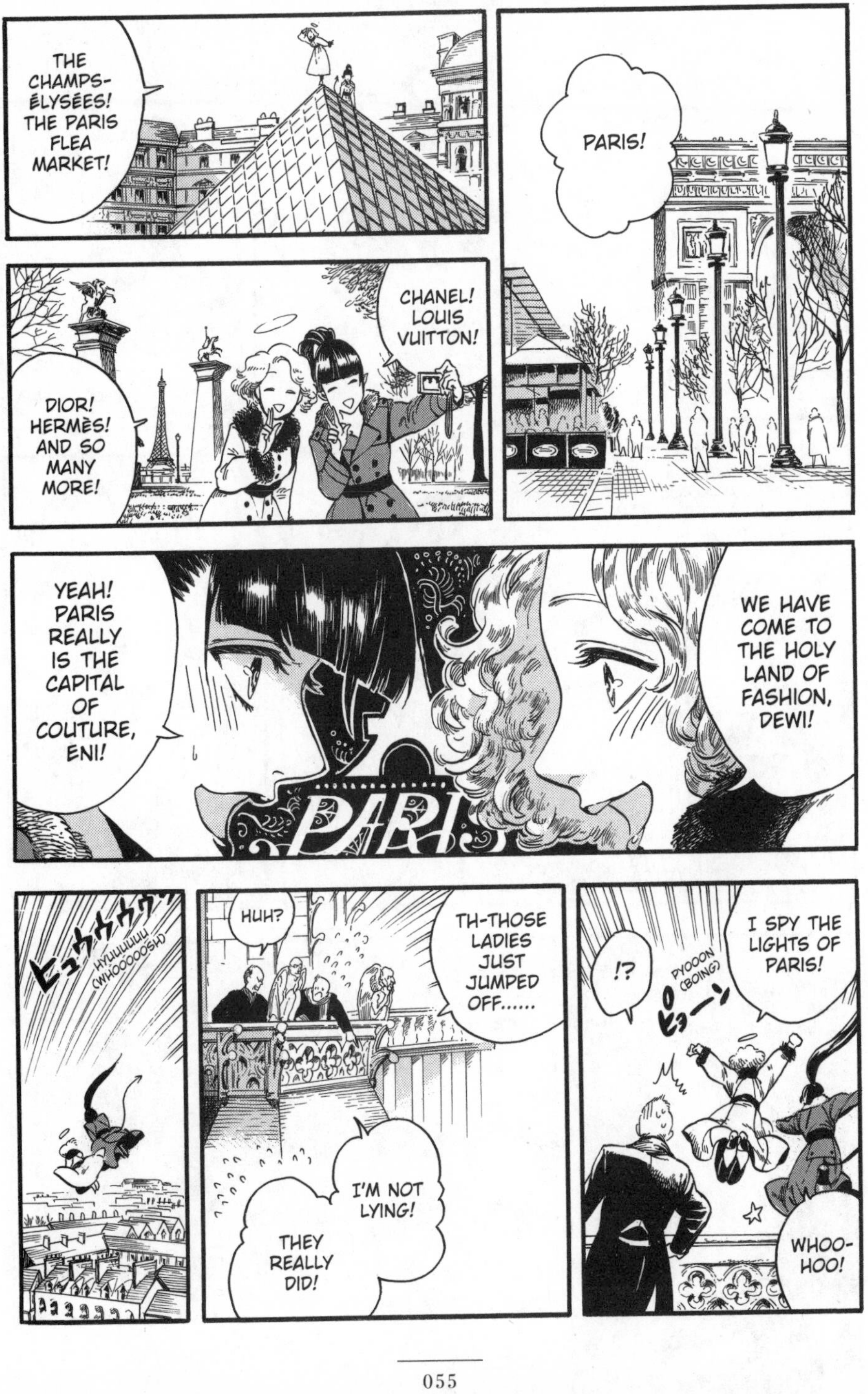
PARIS!
THE CHAMPS-ÉLYSÉES! THE PARIS FLEA MARKET!
CHANEL! LOUIS VUITTON!
DIOR! HERMÈS! AND SO MANY MORE!
WE HAVE COME TO THE HOLY LAND OF FASHION, DEWI!
YEAH! PARIS REALLY IS THE CAPITAL OF COUTURE, ENI!
I SPY THE LIGHTS OF PARIS!
!?
ピョーン
PYOOON (BOING)
WHOO-HOO!
TH-THOSE LADIES JUST JUMPED OFF......
HUH?
I'M NOT LYING!
THEY REALLY DID!
ヒュウウウウ
HYUuuuuuu (WHOOOOOOSH)

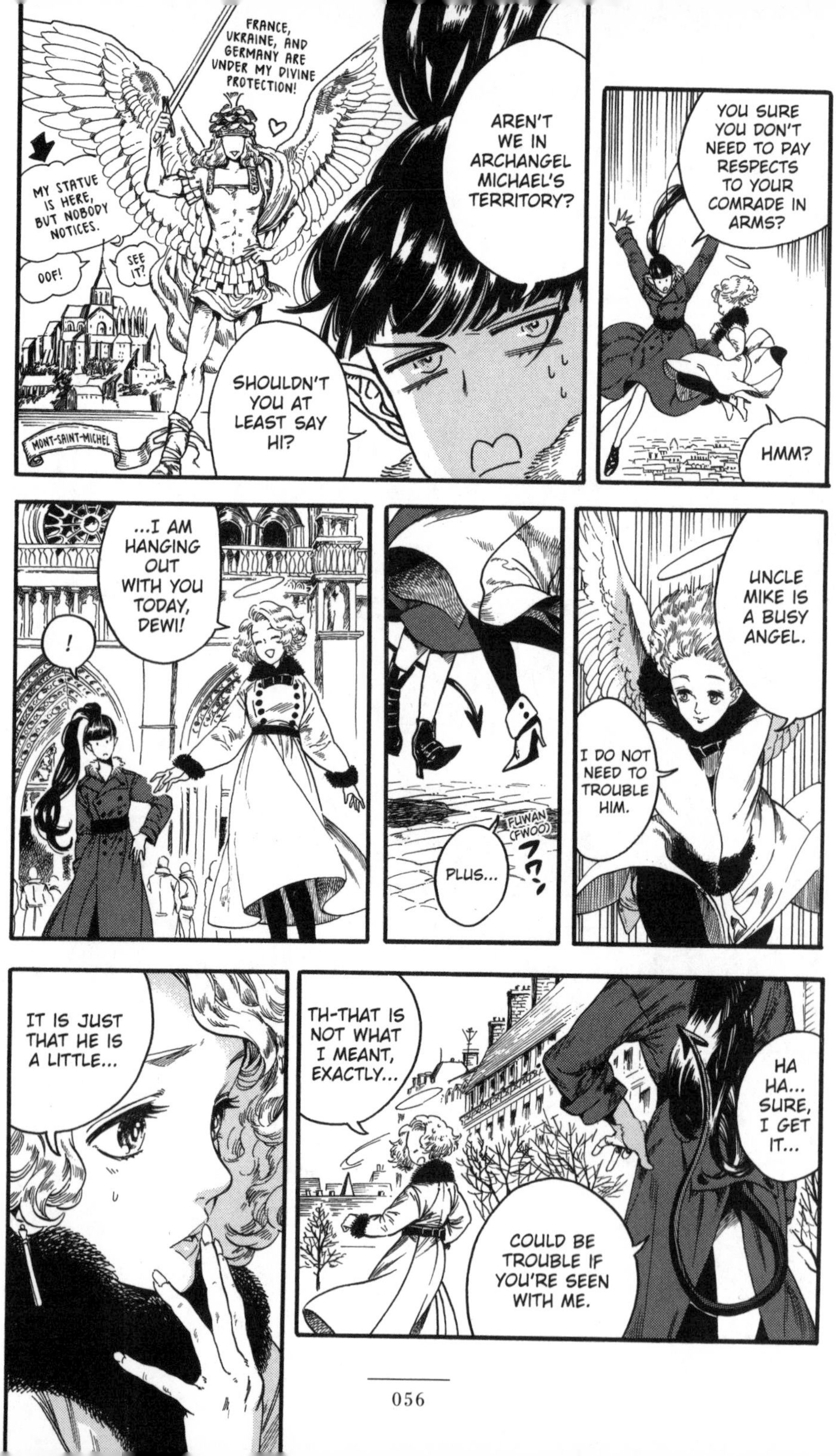
YOU SURE YOU DON'T NEED TO PAY RESPECTS TO YOUR COMRADE IN ARMS?
HMM?
AREN'T WE IN ARCHANGEL MICHAEL'S TERRITORY?
SHOULDN'T YOU AT LEAST SAY HI?
FRANCE, UKRAINE, AND GERMANY ARE UNDER MY DIVINE PROTECTION!
MY STATUE IS HERE, BUT NOBODY NOTICES.
SEE IT?
OOF!
MONT-SAINT-MICHEL
UNCLE MIKE IS A BUSY ANGEL.
I DO NOT NEED TO TROUBLE HIM.
FUWAN (FWOO)
PLUS...
...I AM HANGING OUT WITH YOU TODAY, DEWI!
!
HA HA... SURE, I GET IT...
COULD BE TROUBLE IF YOU'RE SEEN WITH ME.
TH-THAT IS NOT WHAT I MEANT, EXACTLY...
IT IS JUST THAT HE IS A LITTLE...

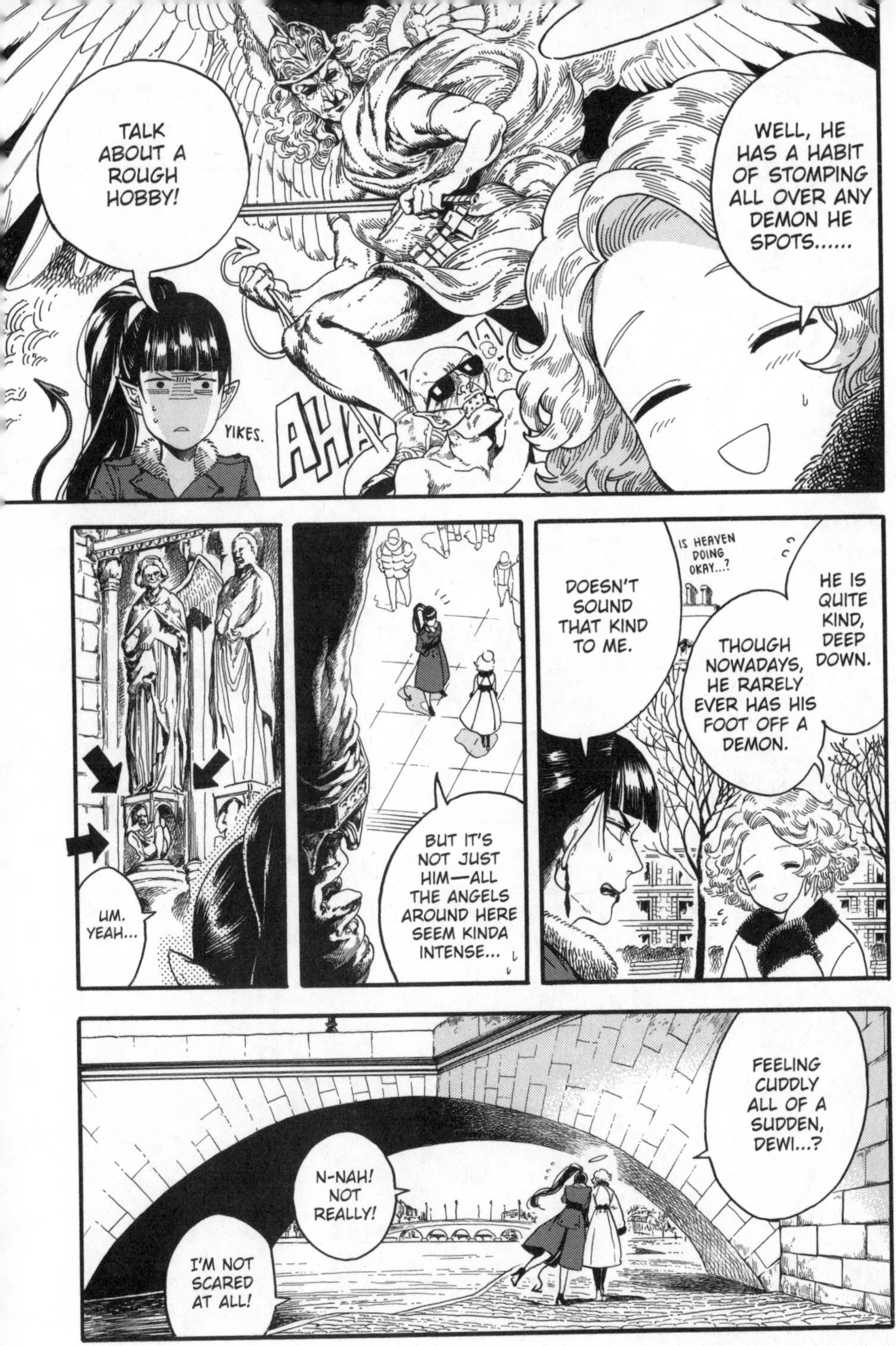
WELL, HE HAS A HABIT OF STOMPING ALL OVER ANY DEMON HE SPOTS......
TALK ABOUT A ROUGH HOBBY!
AHA
YIKES.
HE IS QUITE KIND, DEEP DOWN.
DOESN'T SOUND THAT KIND TO ME.
THOUGH NOWADAYS, HE RARELY EVER HAS HIS FOOT OFF A DEMON.
IS HEAVEN DOING OKAY...?
BUT IT'S NOT JUST HIM—ALL THE ANGELS AROUND HERE SEEM KINDA INTENSE...
UM. YEAH...
FEELING CUDDLY ALL OF A SUDDEN, DEWI...?
N-NAH! NOT REALLY!
I'M NOT SCARED AT ALL!

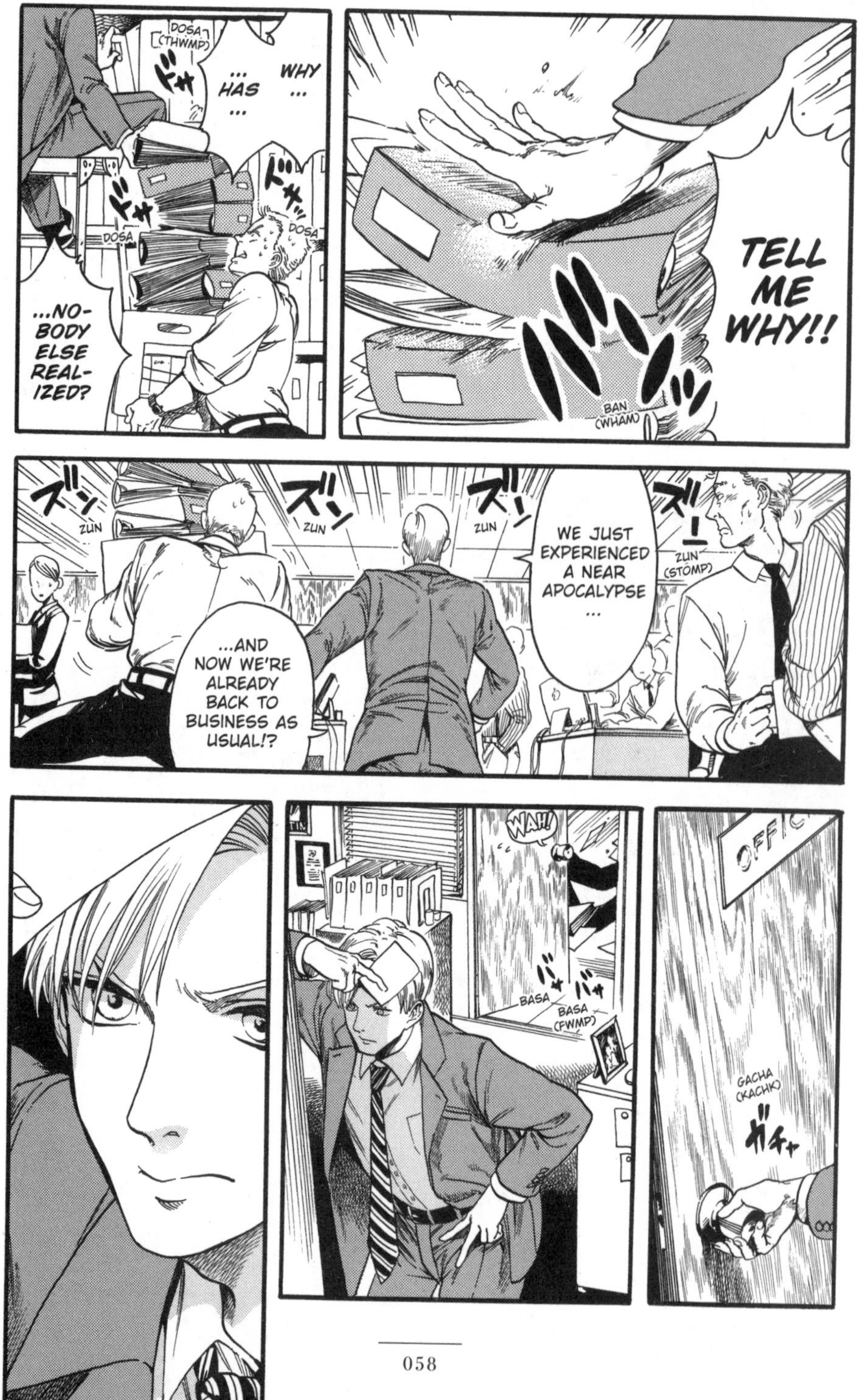
TELL ME WHY!!
BAN (WHAM)
DOSA (THWMP)
WHY ...
... HAS ...
DOSA
DOSA
...NOBODY ELSE REALIZED?
ZUN (STOMP)
WE JUST EXPERIENCED A NEAR APOCALYPSE ...
ZUN
ZUN
ZUN
...AND NOW WE'RE ALREADY BACK TO BUSINESS AS USUAL!?
OFFIC
GACHA (KACHK)
WAH!
BASA
BASA (FWMP)

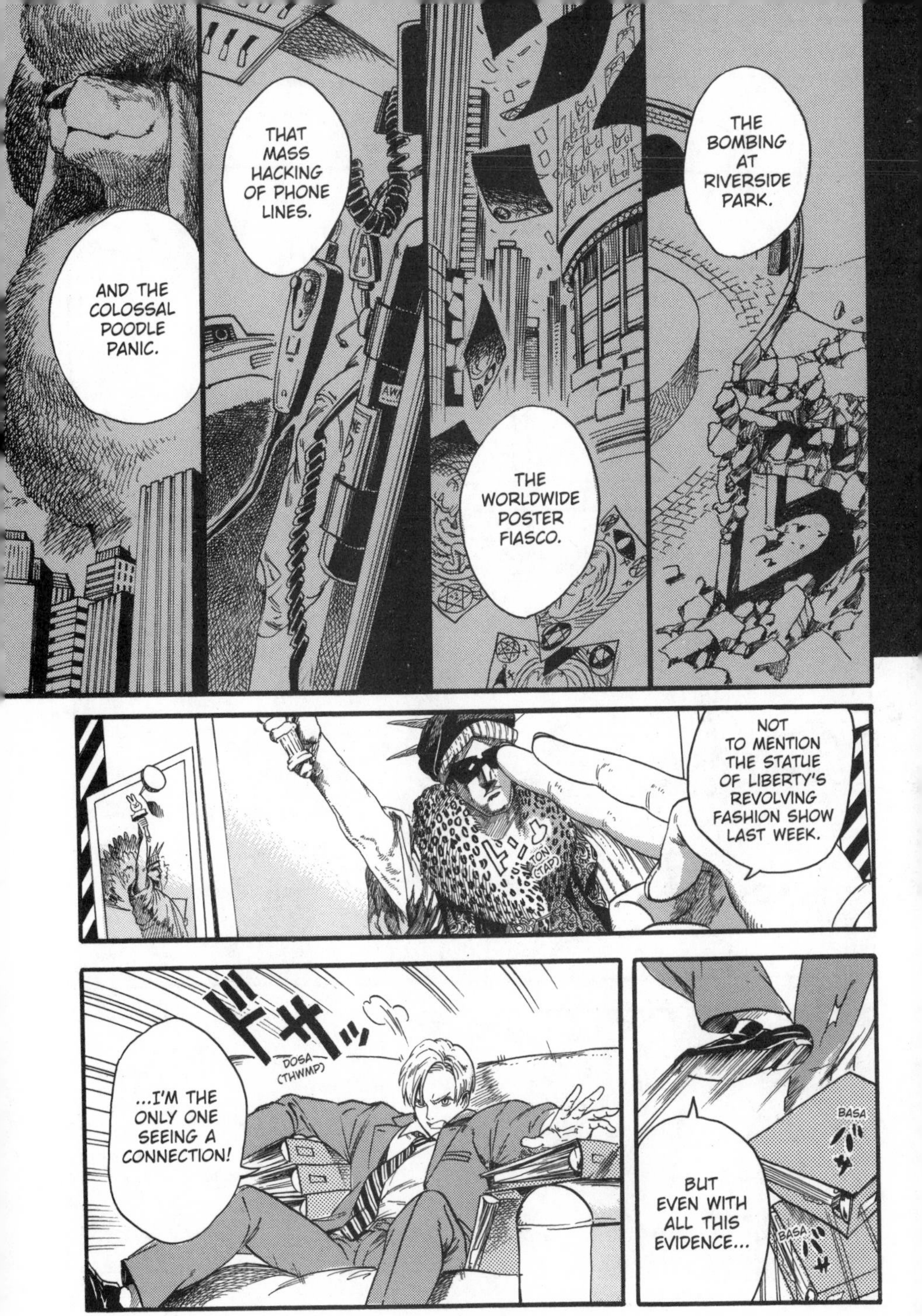
THE BOMBING AT RIVERSIDE PARK.
THE WORLDWIDE POSTER FIASCO.
THAT MASS HACKING OF PHONE LINES.
AND THE COLOSSAL POODLE PANIC.
NOT TO MENTION THE STATUE OF LIBERTY'S REVOLVING FASHION SHOW LAST WEEK.
TON (TAP)
BASA
BASA
BUT EVEN WITH ALL THIS EVIDENCE...
DOSA (THWMP)
...I'M THE ONLY ONE SEEING A CONNECTION!

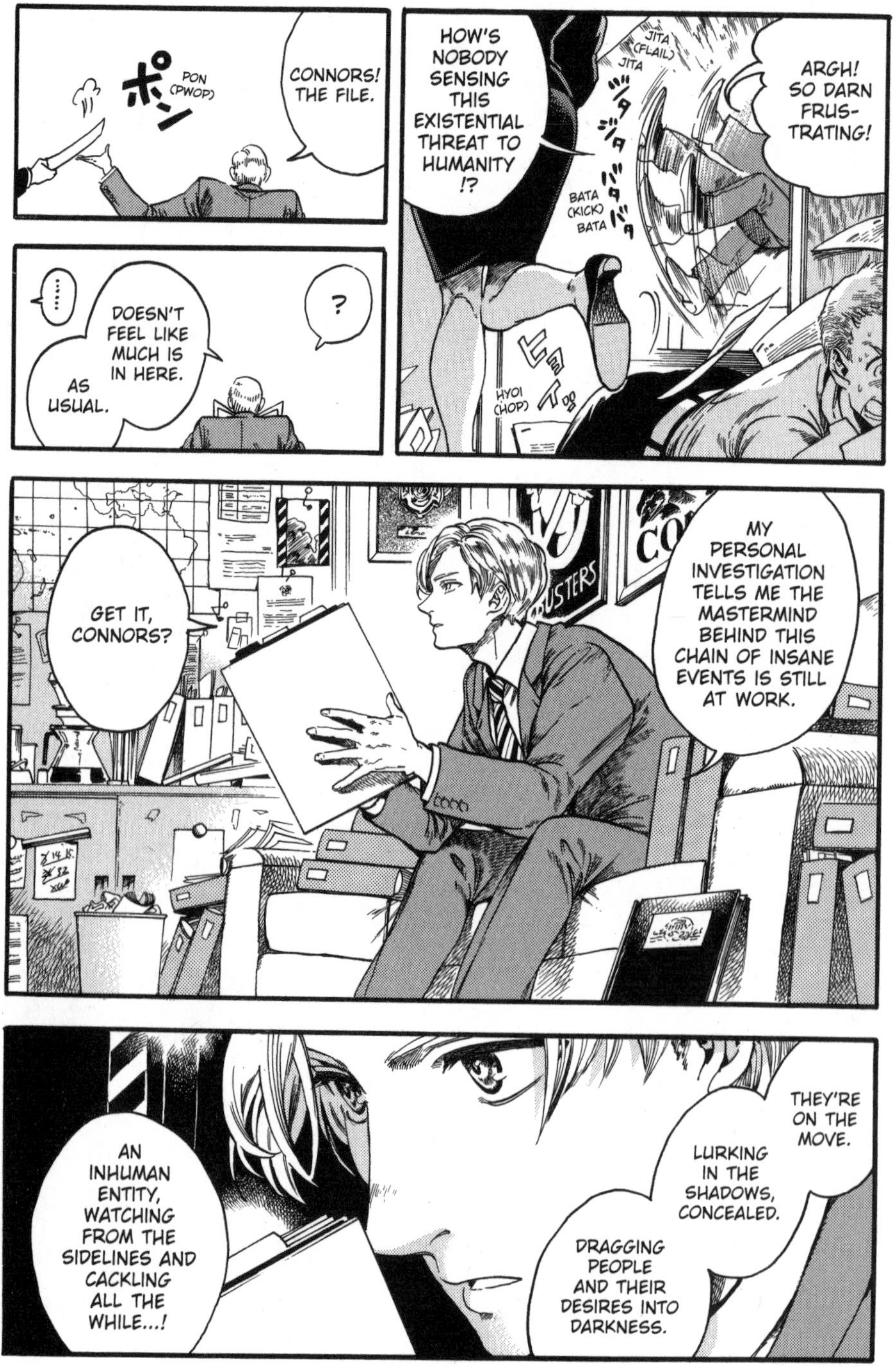
ARGH! SO DARN FRUS-TRATING!
JITA (FLAIL) JITA
HOW'S NOBODY SENSING THIS EXISTENTIAL THREAT TO HUMANITY !?
BATA (KICK) BATA
HYOI (HOP)
CONNORS! THE FILE.
PON (PWOP)
?
DOESN'T FEEL LIKE MUCH IS IN HERE.
AS USUAL.
......
MY PERSONAL INVESTIGATION TELLS ME THE MASTERMIND BEHIND THIS CHAIN OF INSANE EVENTS IS STILL AT WORK.
GET IT, CONNORS?
THEY'RE ON THE MOVE.
LURKING IN THE SHADOWS, CONCEALED.
DRAGGING PEOPLE AND THEIR DESIRES INTO DARKNESS.
AN INHUMAN ENTITY, WATCHING FROM THE SIDELINES AND CACKLING ALL THE WHILE...!

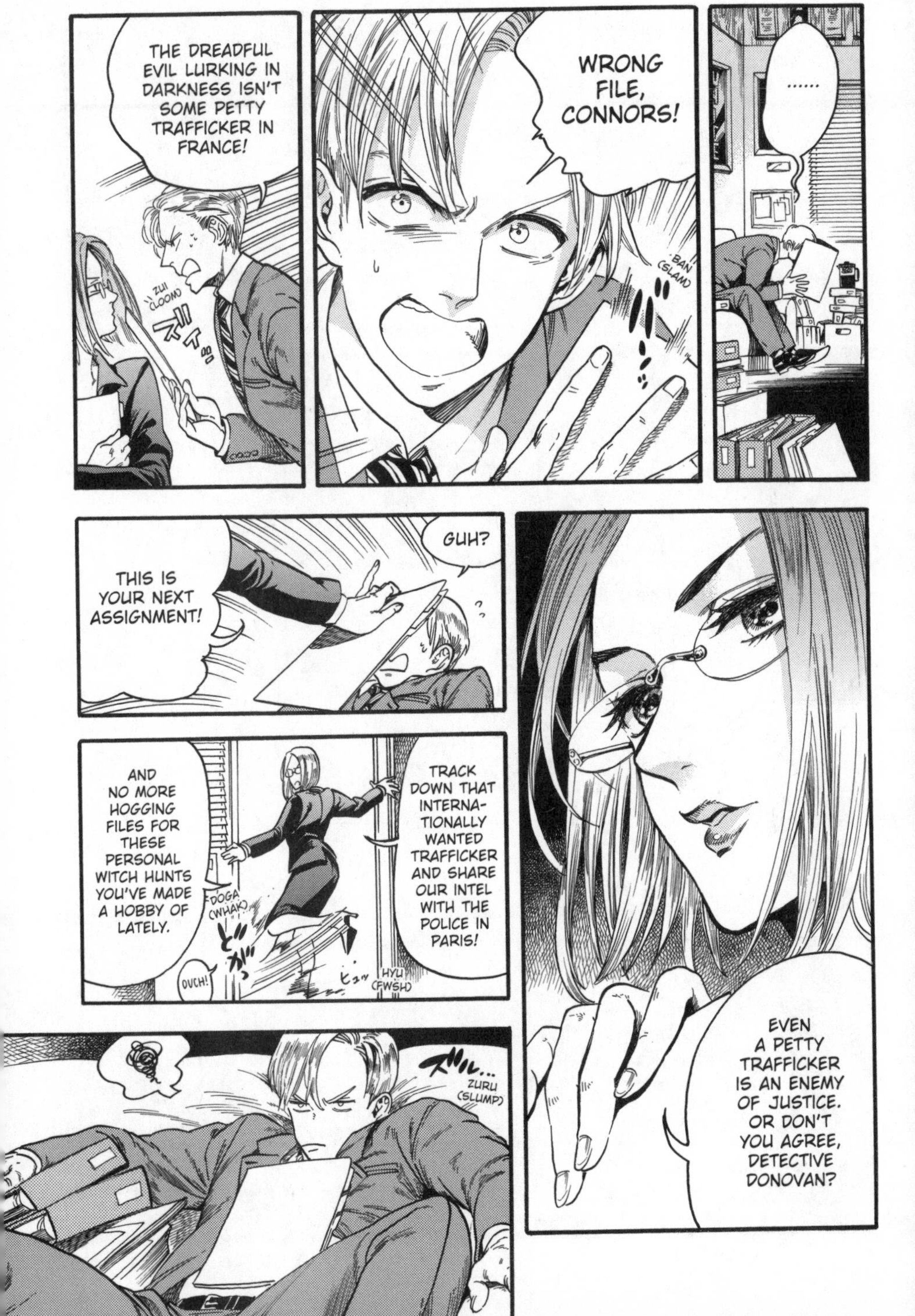
......
WRONG FILE, CONNORS!
BAN (SLAM)
THE DREADFUL EVIL LURKING IN DARKNESS ISN'T SOME PETTY TRAFFICKER IN FRANCE!
ZUI (LOOM)
EVEN A PETTY TRAFFICKER IS AN ENEMY OF JUSTICE. OR DON'T YOU AGREE, DETECTIVE DONOVAN?
GUH?
THIS IS YOUR NEXT ASSIGNMENT!
TRACK DOWN THAT INTERNATIONALLY WANTED TRAFFICKER AND SHARE OUR INTEL WITH THE POLICE IN PARIS!
AND NO MORE HOGGING FILES FOR THESE PERSONAL WITCH HUNTS YOU'VE MADE A HOBBY OF LATELY.
DOGA (WHAK)
HYU (FWSH)
OUCH!
ZURU (SLUMP)

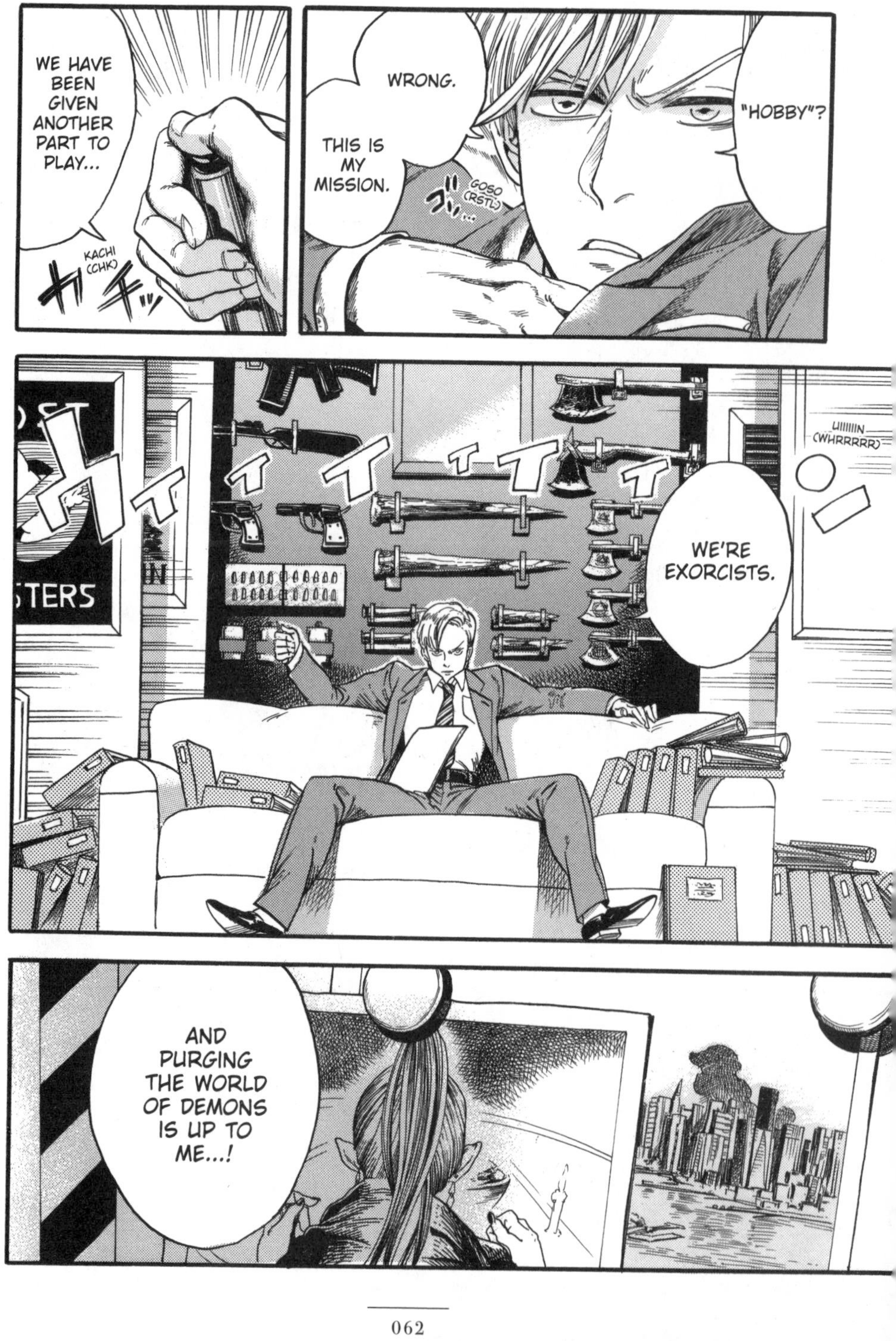
"HOBBY"?
WRONG.
THIS IS MY MISSION.
GOSO (RSTL)
WE HAVE BEEN GIVEN ANOTHER PART TO PLAY...
KACHI (CHK)
UIIIIIN (WHRRRRR)
WE'RE EXORCISTS.
AND PURGING THE WORLD OF DEMONS IS UP TO ME...!

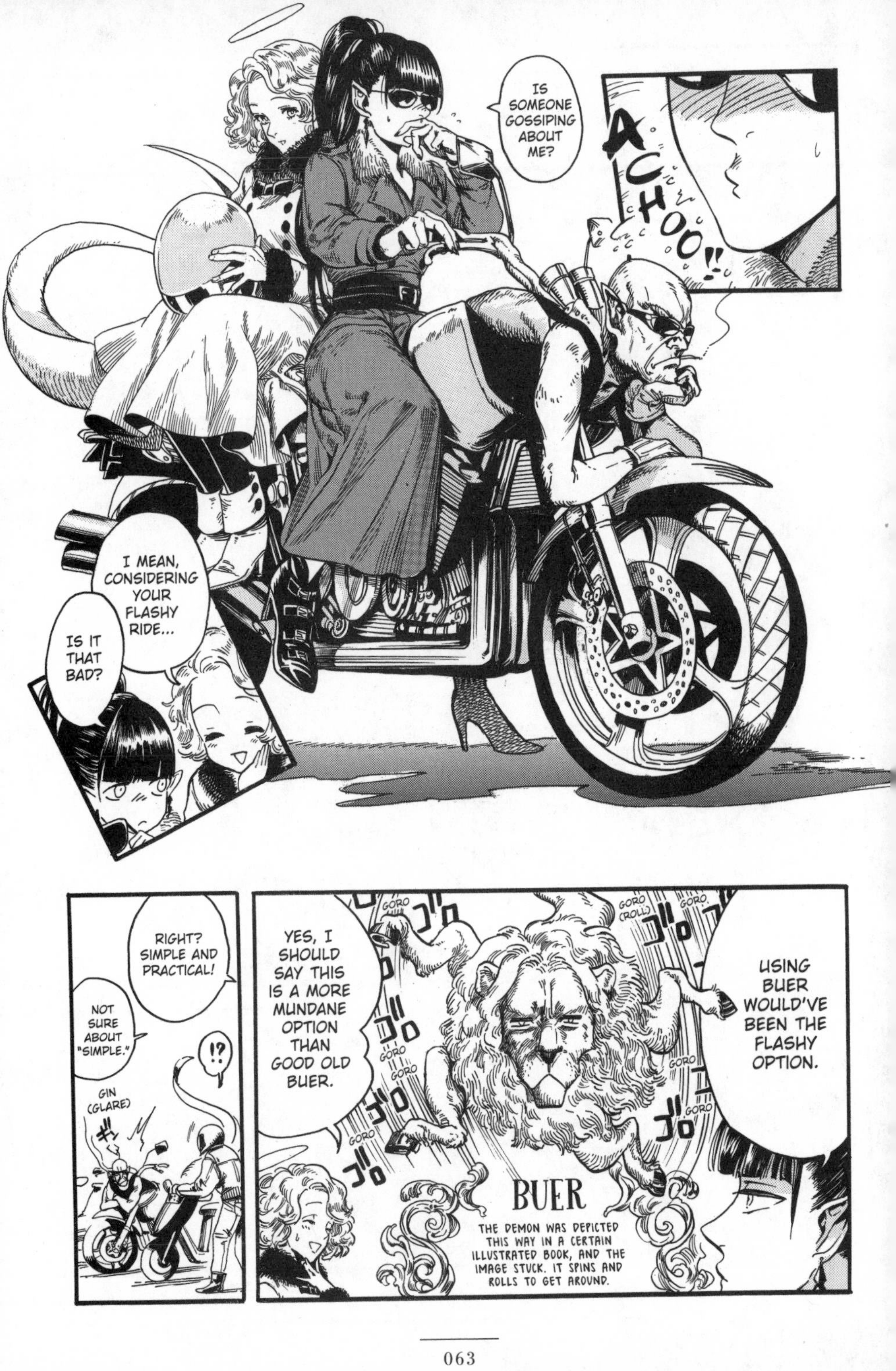
ACHOO!!
IS SOMEONE GOSSIPING ABOUT ME?
I MEAN, CONSIDERING YOUR FLASHY RIDE...
IS IT THAT BAD?
USING BUER WOULD'VE BEEN THE FLASHY OPTION.
GORO (ROLL)
GORO
GORO
GORO
GORO
GORO
GORO
GORO
YES, I SHOULD SAY THIS IS A MORE MUNDANE OPTION THAN GOOD OLD BUER.
BUER
THE DEMON WAS DEPICTED THIS WAY IN A CERTAIN ILLUSTRATED BOOK, AND THE IMAGE STUCK. IT SPINS AND ROLLS TO GET AROUND.
RIGHT? SIMPLE AND PRACTICAL!
NOT SURE ABOUT "SIMPLE."
!?
GIN (GLARE)

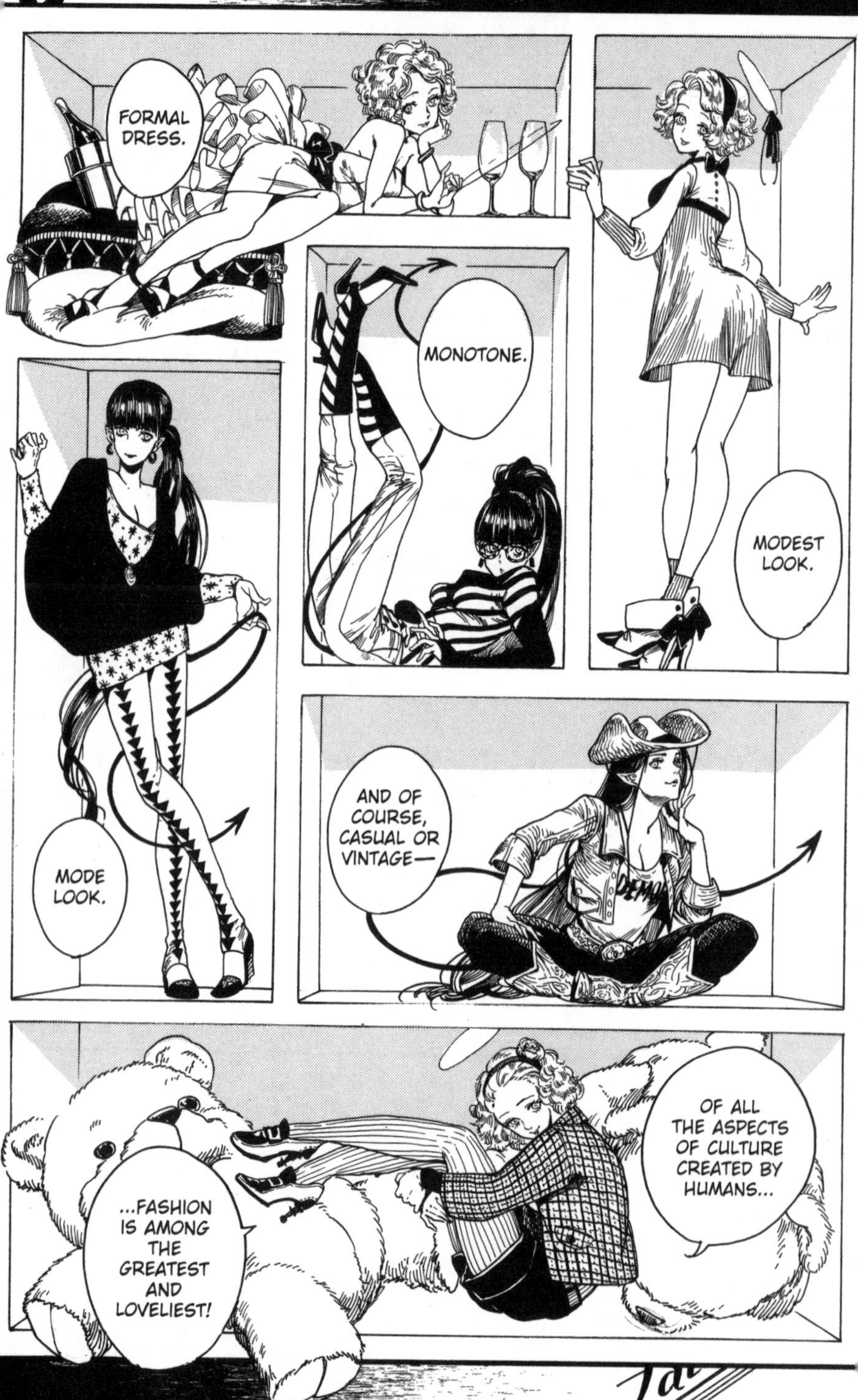
MODEST LOOK.
FORMAL DRESS.
MONOTONE.
MODE LOOK.
AND OF COURSE, CASUAL OR VINTAGE—
OF ALL THE ASPECTS OF CULTURE CREATED BY HUMANS...
...FASHION IS AMONG THE GREATEST AND LOVELIEST!

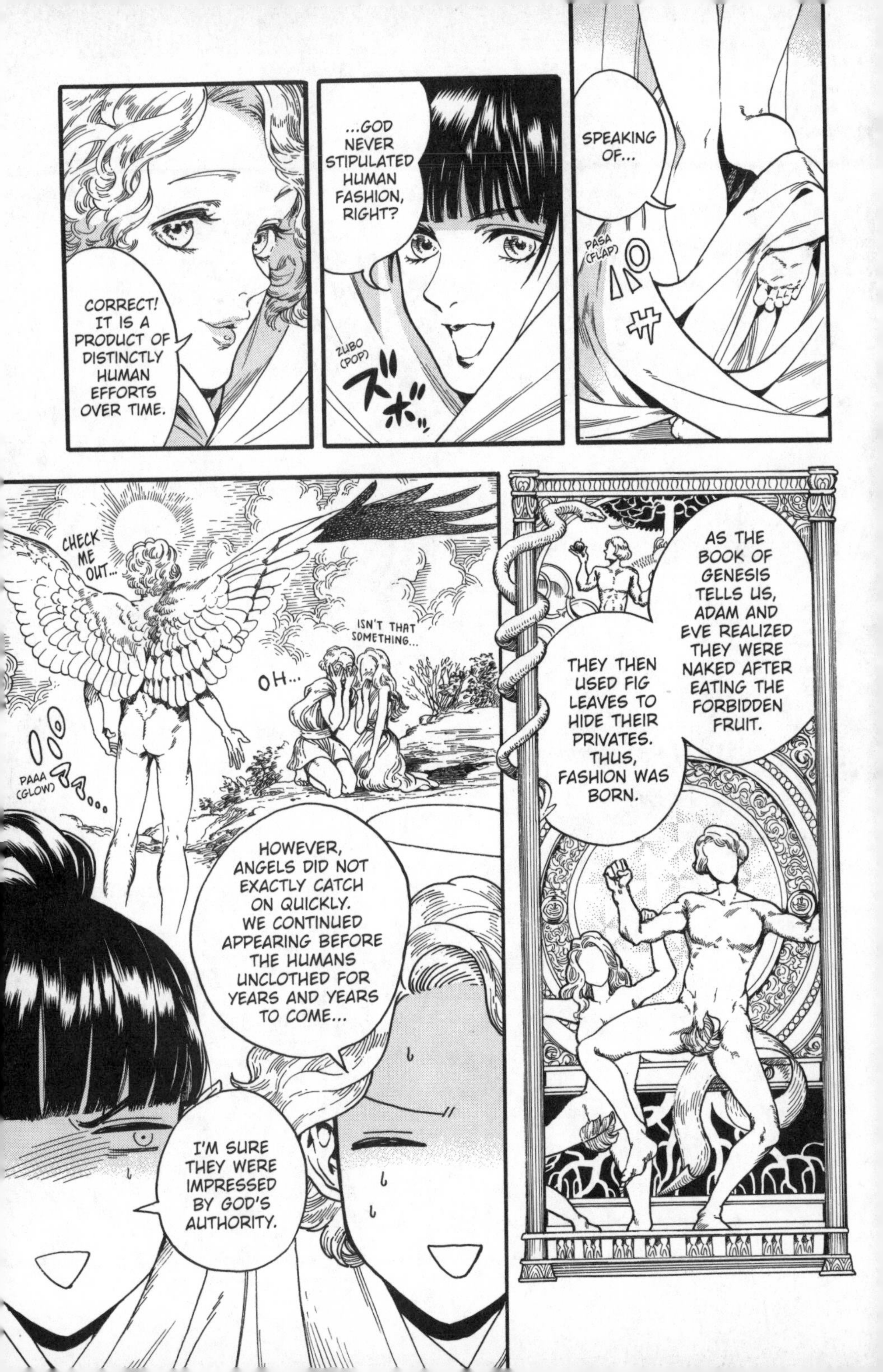
SPEAKING OF...
PASA (FLAP)
...GOD NEVER STIPULATED HUMAN FASHION, RIGHT?
ZUBO (POP)
CORRECT! IT IS A PRODUCT OF DISTINCTLY HUMAN EFFORTS OVER TIME.
AS THE BOOK OF GENESIS TELLS US, ADAM AND EVE REALIZED THEY WERE NAKED AFTER EATING THE FORBIDDEN FRUIT.
THEY THEN USED FIG LEAVES TO HIDE THEIR PRIVATES. THUS, FASHION WAS BORN.
CHECK ME OUT...
ISN'T THAT SOMETHING...
OH...
PAAA (GLOW)
HOWEVER, ANGELS DID NOT EXACTLY CATCH ON QUICKLY. WE CONTINUED APPEARING BEFORE THE HUMANS UNCLOTHED FOR YEARS AND YEARS TO COME...
I'M SURE THEY WERE IMPRESSED BY GOD'S AUTHORITY.

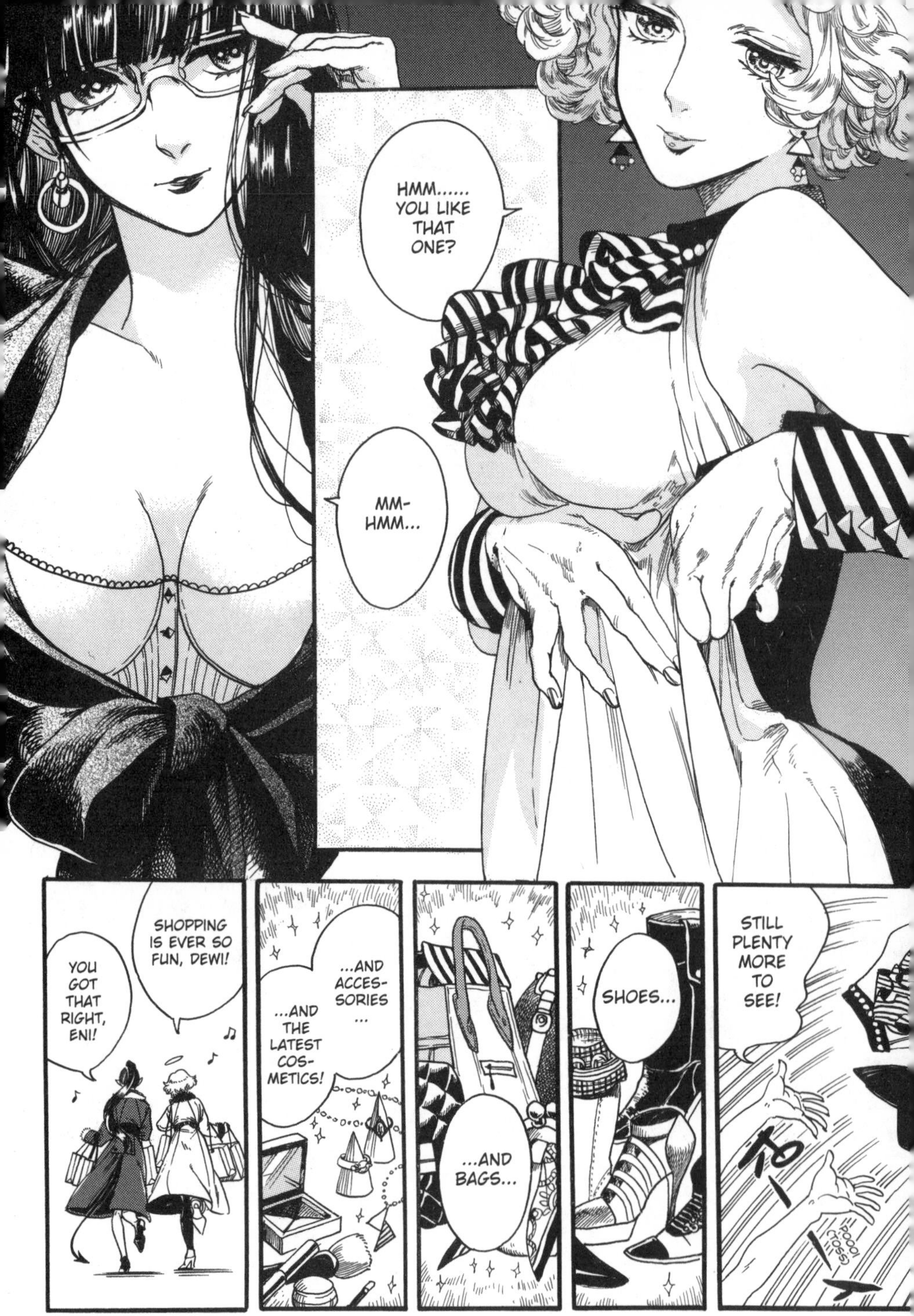
HMM...... YOU LIKE THAT ONE?
MM-HMM...
STILL PLENTY MORE TO SEE!
POOON (TOSS)
SHOES...
...AND BAGS...
...AND ACCES-SORIES ...
...AND THE LATEST COS-METICS!
SHOPPING IS EVER SO FUN, DEWI!
YOU GOT THAT RIGHT, ENI!

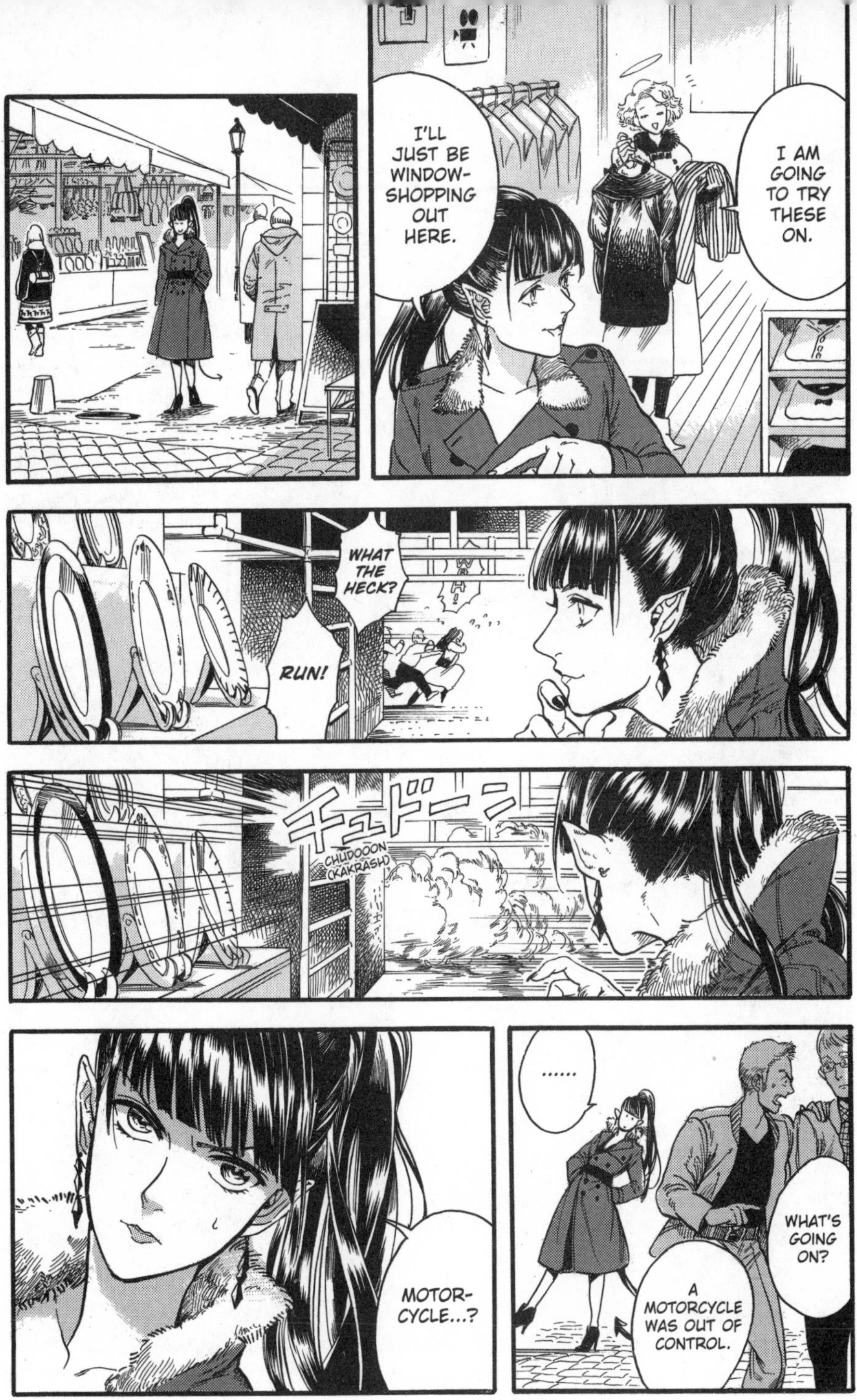
I AM GOING TO TRY THESE ON.
I'LL JUST BE WINDOW-SHOPPING OUT HERE.
WAH!
WHAT THE HECK?
RUN!
チュドーン
CHUDOOON (KAKRASH)
......
WHAT'S GOING ON?
A MOTORCYCLE WAS OUT OF CONTROL.
MOTOR-CYCLE...?

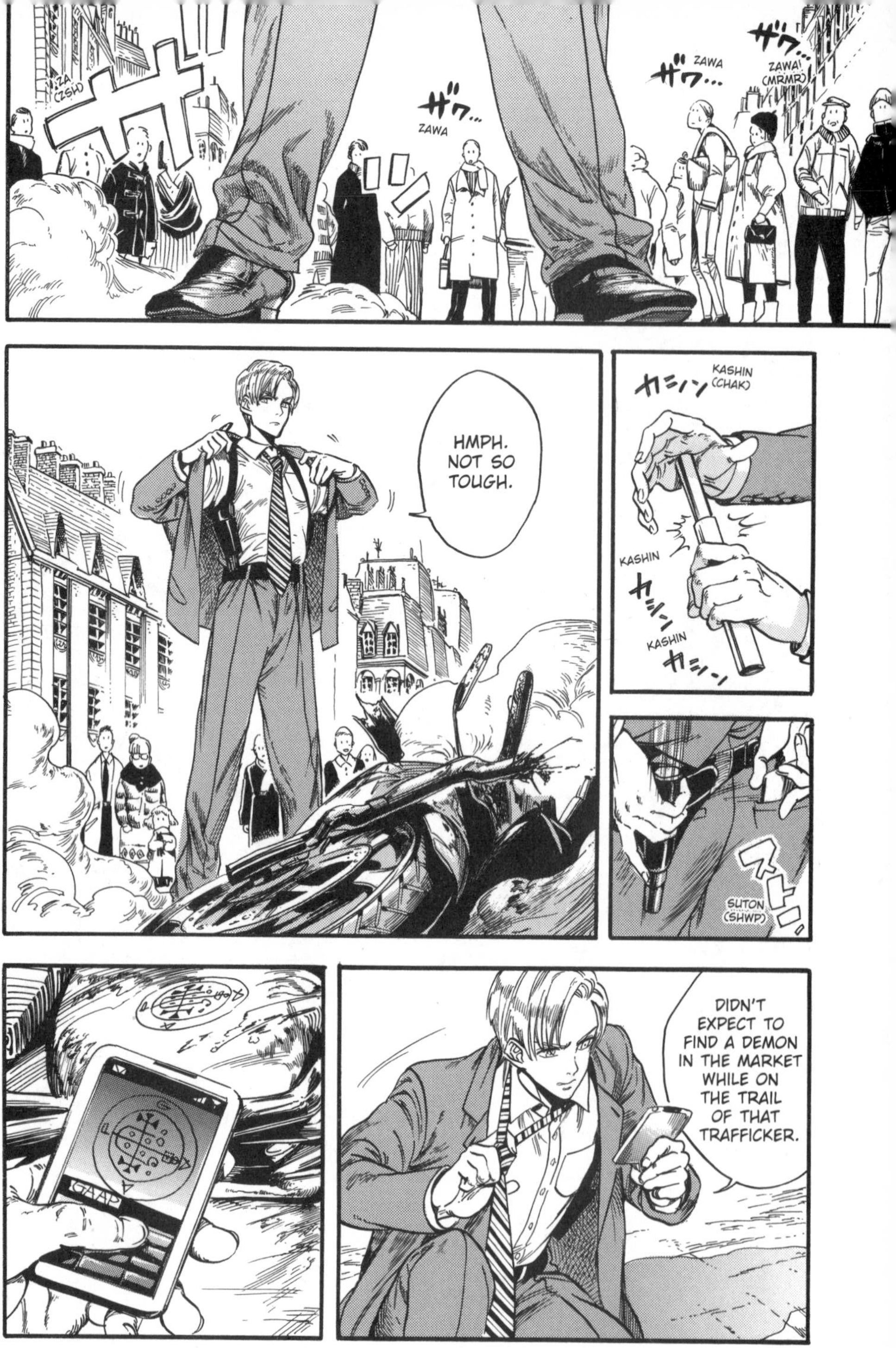
ZAWA (MRMR)
ZAWA
ZAWA
ZA (ZSH)
KASHIN (CHAK)
KASHIN
KASHIN
SUTON (SHWP)
HMPH. NOT SO TOUGH.
DIDN'T EXPECT TO FIND A DEMON IN THE MARKET WHILE ON THE TRAIL OF THAT TRAFFICKER.
GAAP

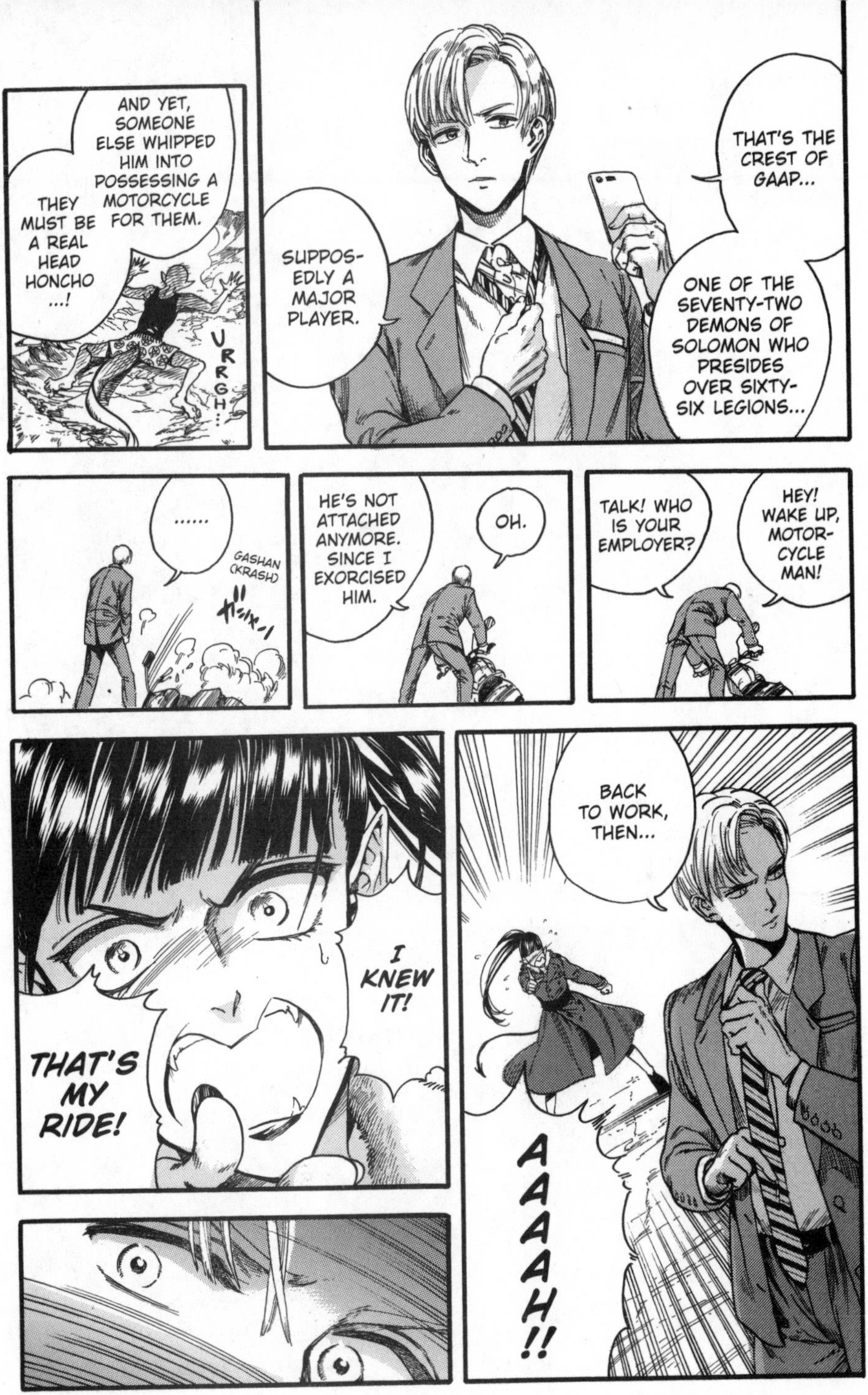
THAT'S THE CREST OF GAAP...
ONE OF THE SEVENTY-TWO DEMONS OF SOLOMON WHO PRESIDES OVER SIXTY-SIX LEGIONS...
SUPPOSEDLY A MAJOR PLAYER.
AND YET, SOMEONE ELSE WHIPPED HIM INTO POSSESSING A MOTORCYCLE FOR THEM.
THEY MUST BE A REAL HEAD HONCHO ...!
URRGH...
HEY! WAKE UP, MOTORCYCLE MAN!
TALK! WHO IS YOUR EMPLOYER?
OH.
HE'S NOT ATTACHED ANYMORE. SINCE I EXORCISED HIM.
......
GASHAN (KRASH)
BACK TO WORK, THEN...
AAAAAH!!
I KNEW IT!
THAT'S MY RIDE!

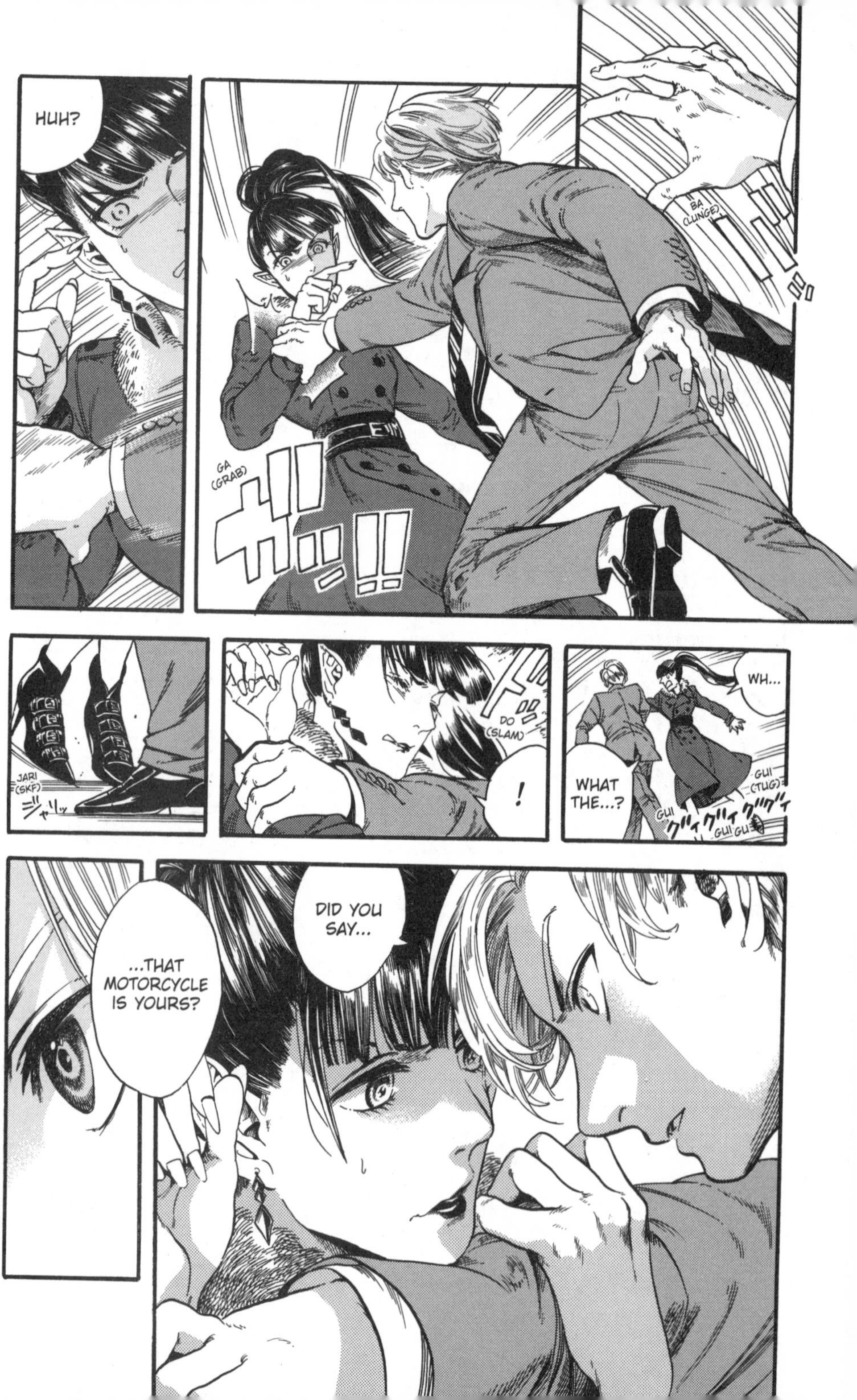
BA (LUNGE)
GA (GRAB)
HUH?
WH...
WHAT THE...?
GUI (TUG)
GUI
GUI
GUI
DO (SLAM)
!
JARI (SKF)
DID YOU SAY...
...THAT MOTORCYCLE IS YOURS?

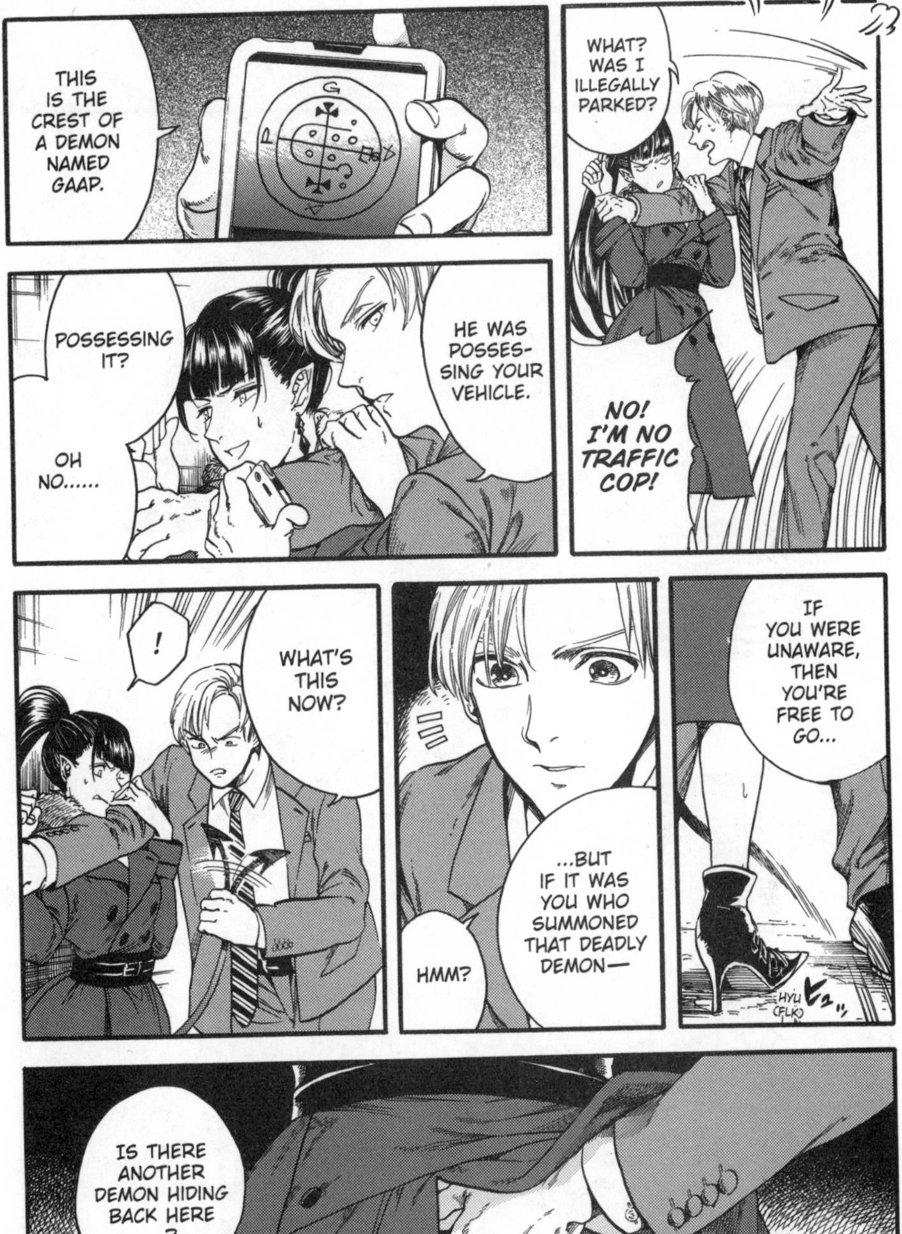
WHAT? WAS I ILLEGALLY PARKED?
NO! I'M NO TRAFFIC COP!
THIS IS THE CREST OF A DEMON NAMED GAAP.
HE WAS POSSES-SING YOUR VEHICLE.
POSSESSING IT?
OH NO......
IF YOU WERE UNAWARE, THEN YOU'RE FREE TO GO...
HYU (FLK)
...BUT IF IT WAS YOU WHO SUMMONED THAT DEADLY DEMON—
HMM?
WHAT'S THIS NOW?
!
IS THERE ANOTHER DEMON HIDING BACK HERE ...?
SURU (SLIP)

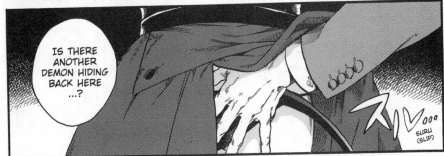

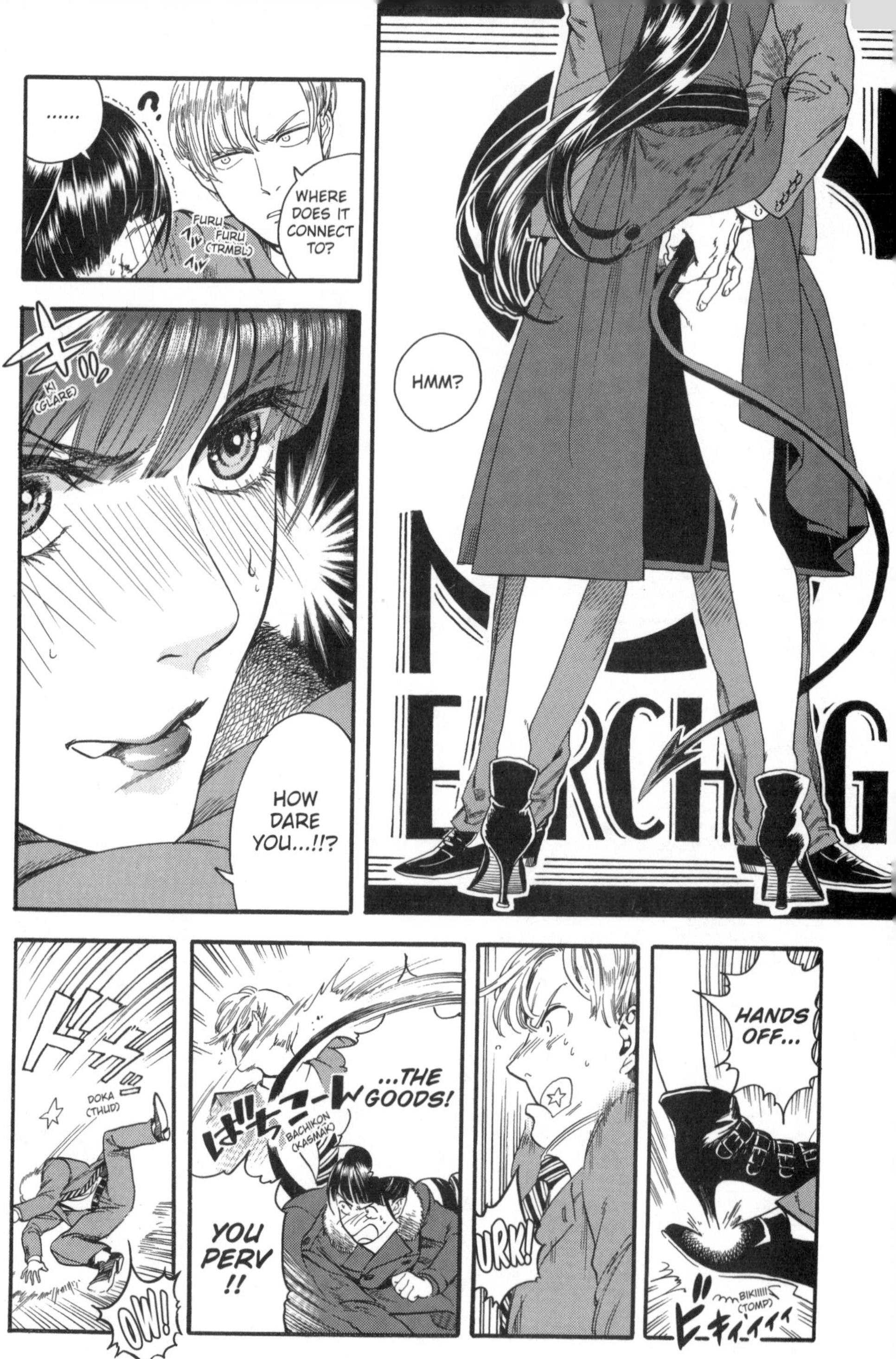
HMM?
......
?
WHERE DOES IT CONNECT TO?
FURU FURU (TRMBL)
KI (GLARE)
HOW DARE YOU...!!?
HANDS OFF...
BIKIIIII (TOMP)
URK!
...THE GOODS!
BACHIKON (KASMAK)
YOU PERV !!
DOKA (THUD)
OW!

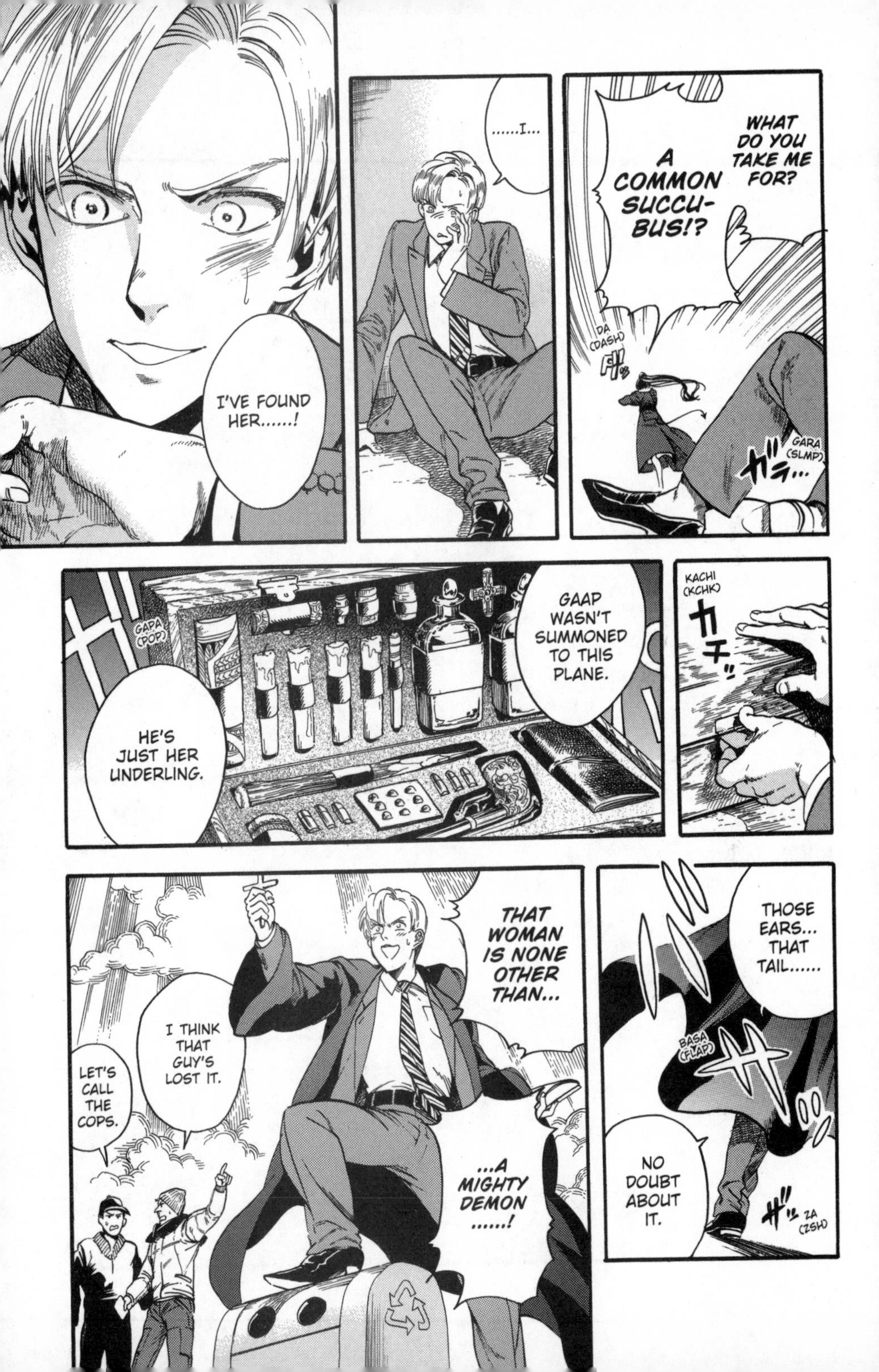
WHAT DO YOU TAKE ME FOR?
A COMMON SUCCU-BUS!?
DA (DASH)
GARA (SLMP)
......I...
I'VE FOUND HER......!
KACHI (KCHK)
GAAP WASN'T SUMMONED TO THIS PLANE.
GAPA (POP)
HE'S JUST HER UNDERLING.
THOSE EARS... THAT TAIL......
BASA (FLAP)
NO DOUBT ABOUT IT.
ZA (ZSH)
THAT WOMAN IS NONE OTHER THAN...
...A MIGHTY DEMON ......!
I THINK THAT GUY'S LOST IT.
LET'S CALL THE COPS.

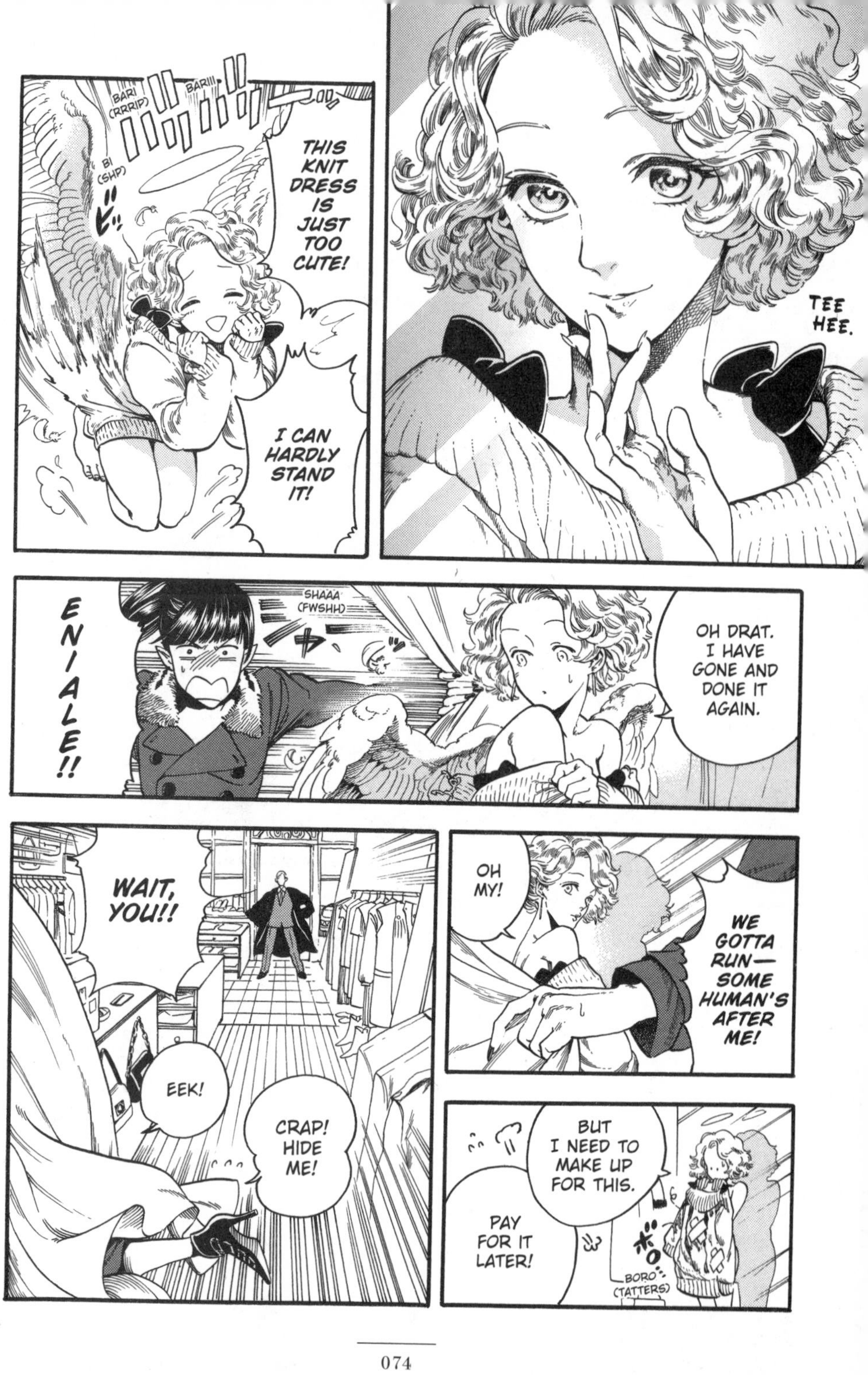
TEE HEE.
BARI (RRRIP)
BARIII
BI (SHP)
THIS KNIT DRESS IS JUST TOO CUTE!
I CAN HARDLY STAND IT!
OH DRAT. I HAVE GONE AND DONE IT AGAIN.
SHAAA (FWSHH)
ENIALE!!
WE GOTTA RUN—SOME HUMAN'S AFTER ME!
OH MY!
BUT I NEED TO MAKE UP FOR THIS.
PAY FOR IT LATER!
BORO (TATTERS)
WAIT, YOU!!
EEK!
CRAP! HIDE ME!

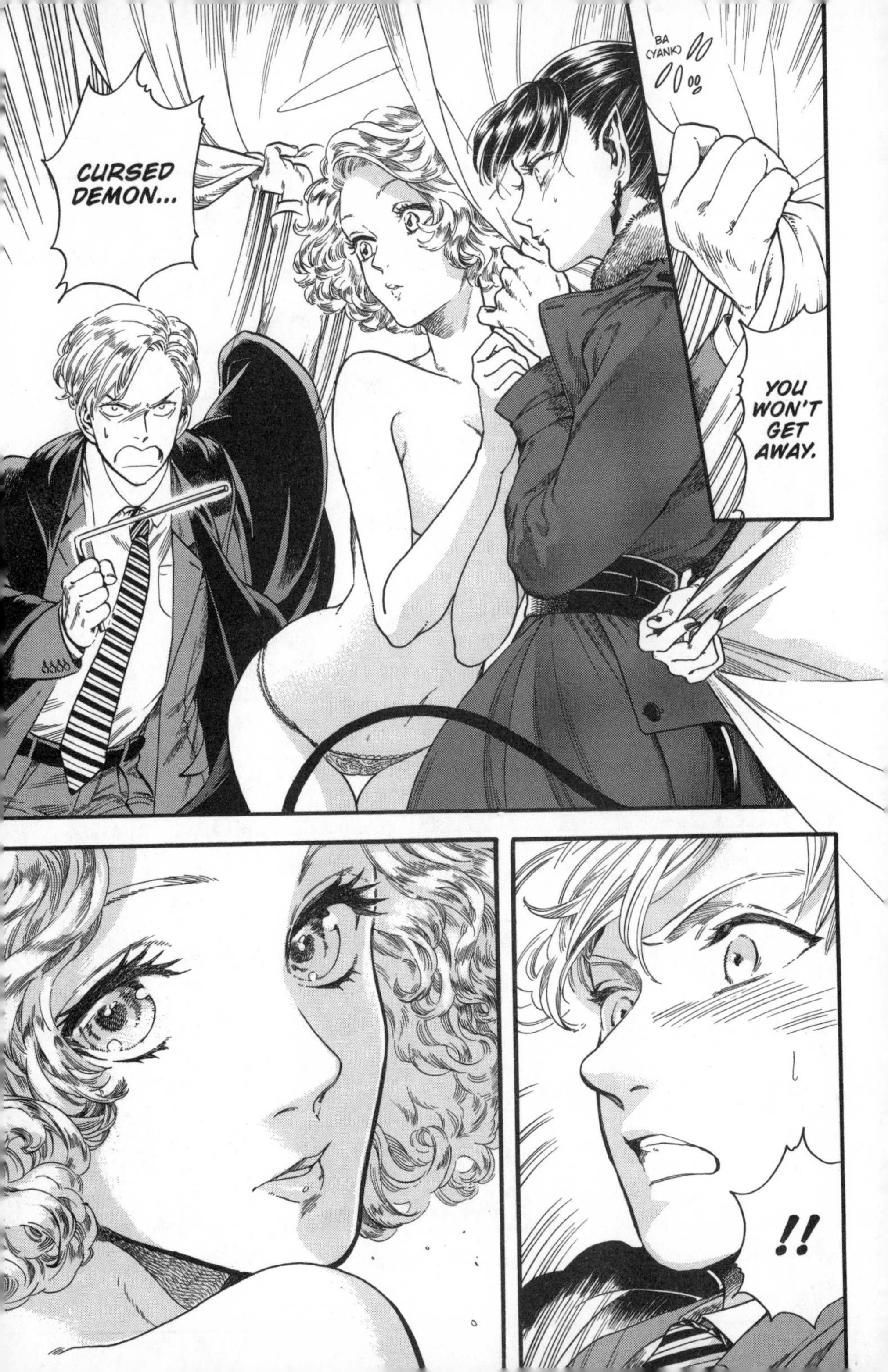
BA (YANK)
YOU WON'T GET AWAY.
CURSED DEMON...
!!

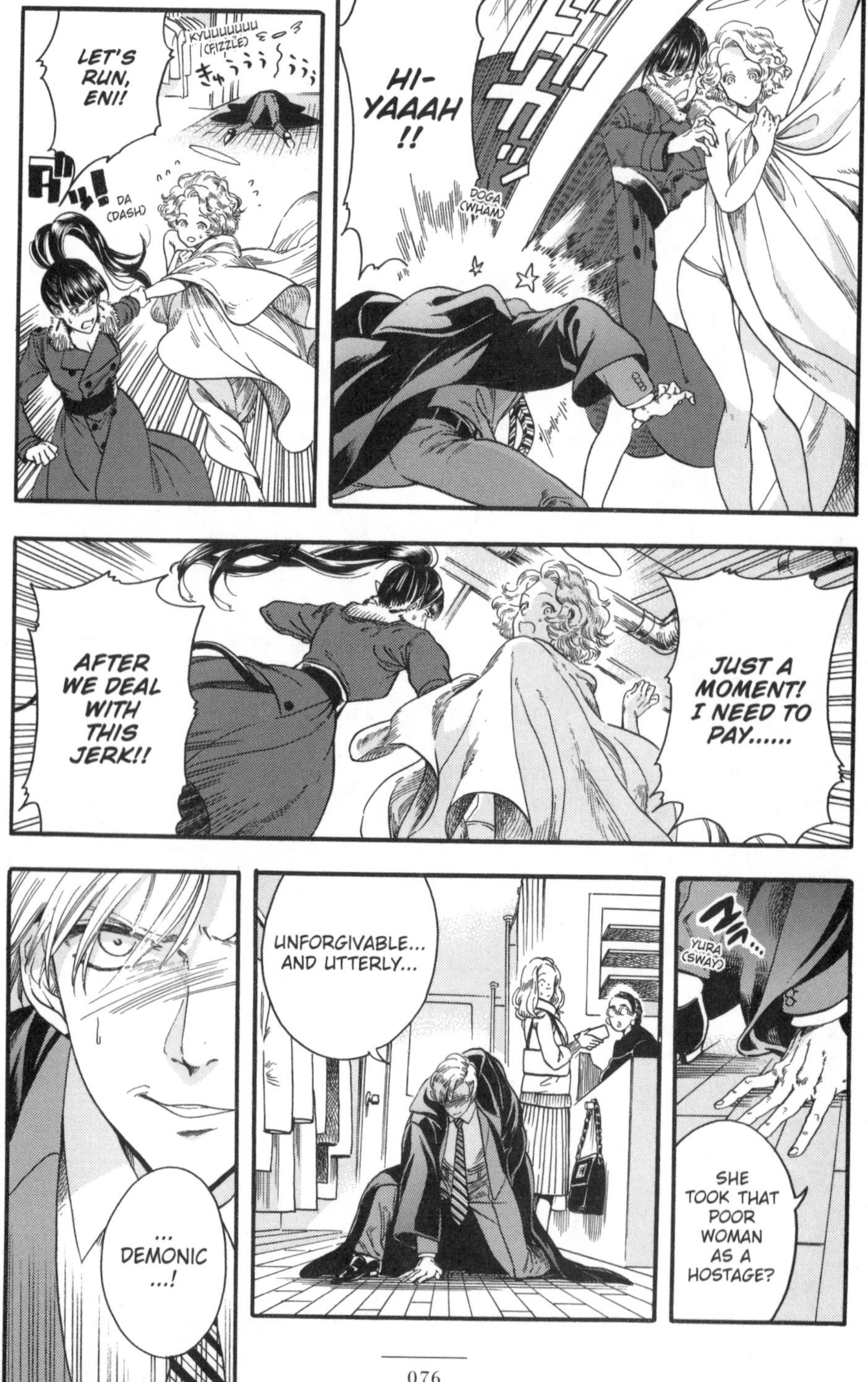
HI-YAAAH!!
DOGA (WHAM)
LET'S RUN, ENI!
KYUUUUUUU (FIZZLE)
DA (DASH)
JUST A MOMENT! I NEED TO PAY......
AFTER WE DEAL WITH THIS JERK!!
YURA (SWAY)
SHE TOOK THAT POOR WOMAN AS A HOSTAGE?
UNFORGIVABLE... AND UTTERLY...
...DEMONIC...!

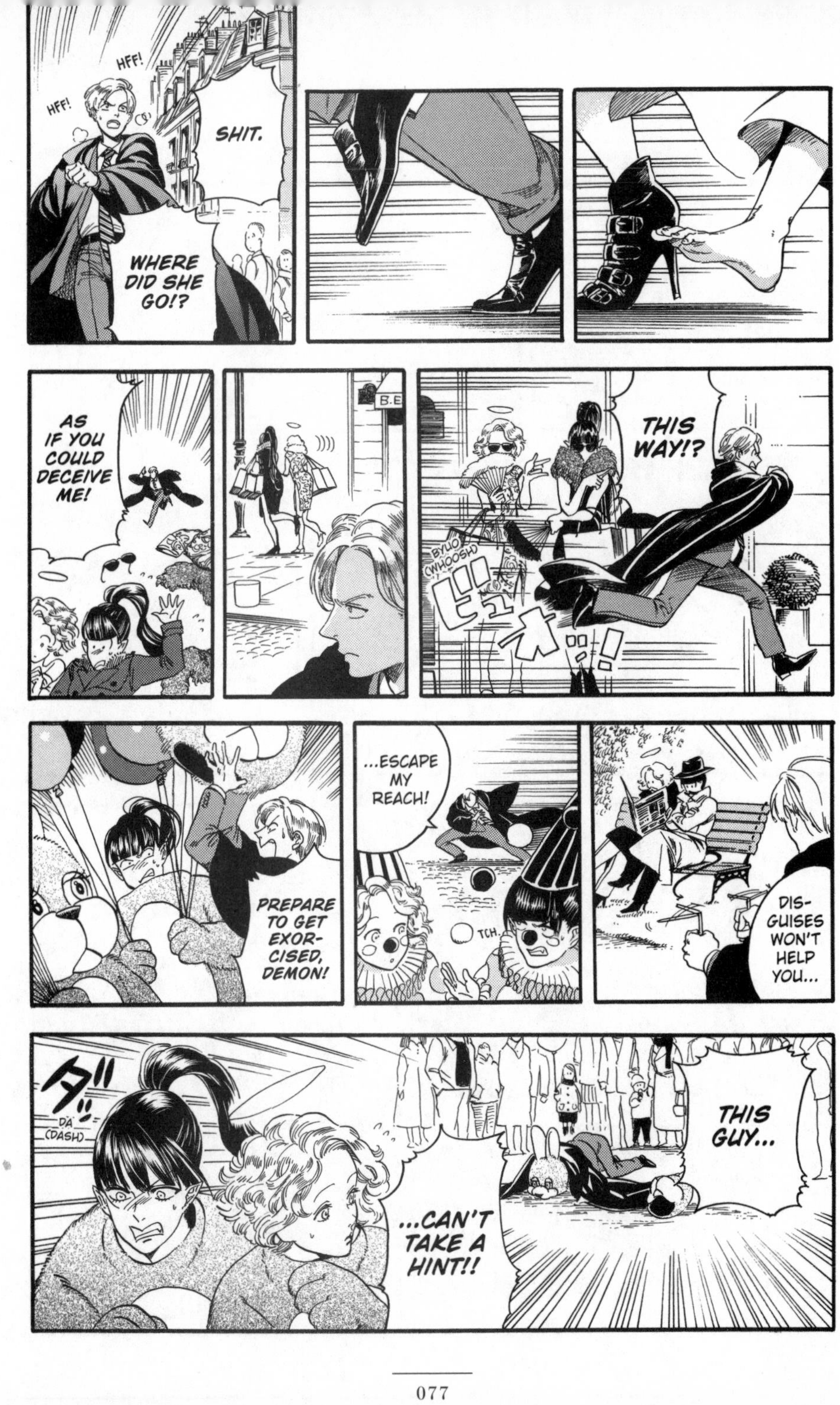
HFF!
HFF!
SHIT.
WHERE DID SHE GO!?
THIS WAY!?
BYUO (WHOOSH)
AS IF YOU COULD DECEIVE ME!
DIS-GUISES WON'T HELP YOU...
...ESCAPE MY REACH!
TCH.
PREPARE TO GET EXOR-CISED, DEMON!
THIS GUY...
...CAN'T TAKE A HINT!!
DA (DASH)

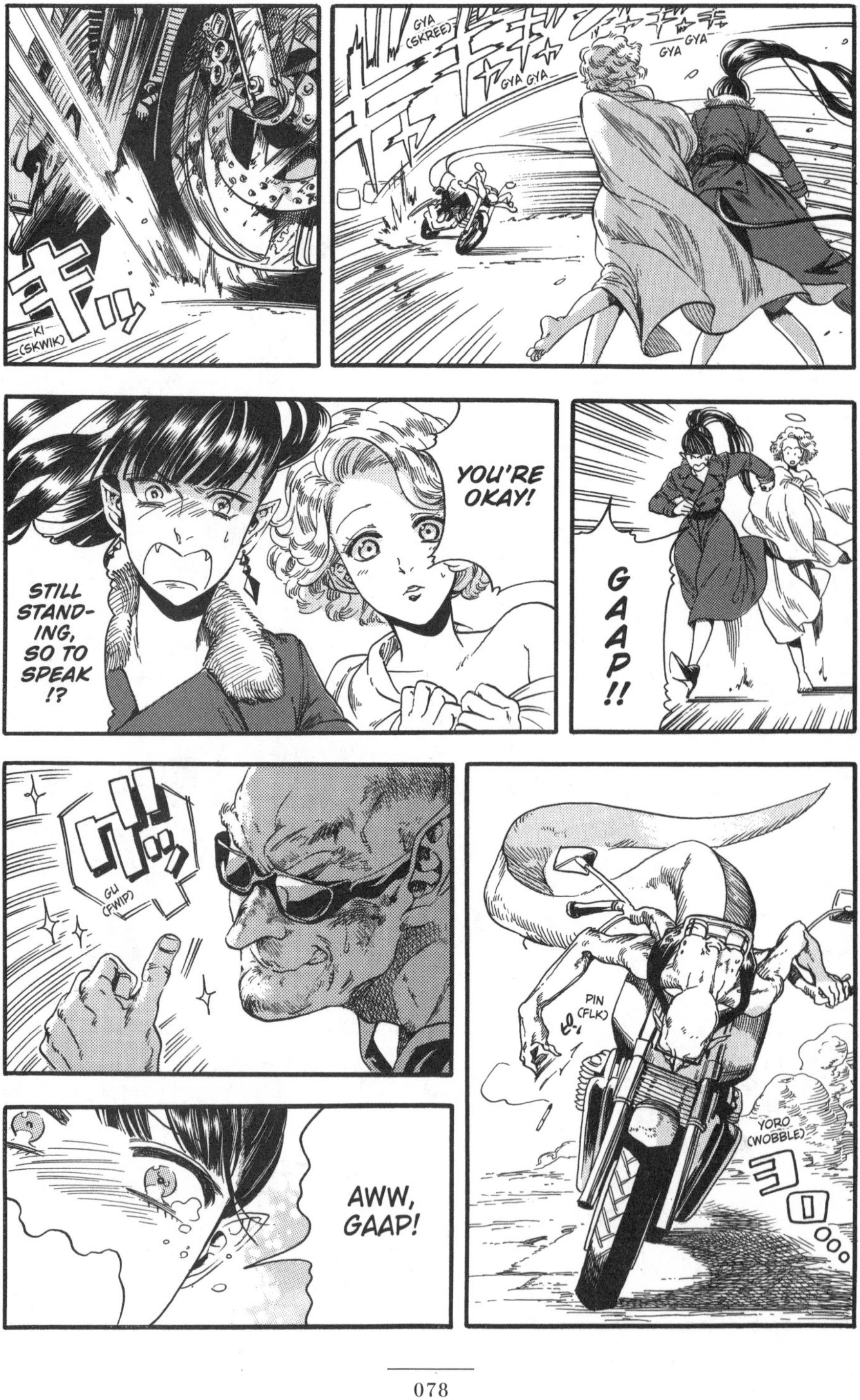
GYA (SKREE)
GYA GYA
GYA GYA
KI (SKWIK)
GAAP!!
YOU'RE OKAY!
STILL STANDING, SO TO SPEAK!?
PIN (FLK)
YORO (WOBBLE)
GU (FWIP)
AWW, GAAP!

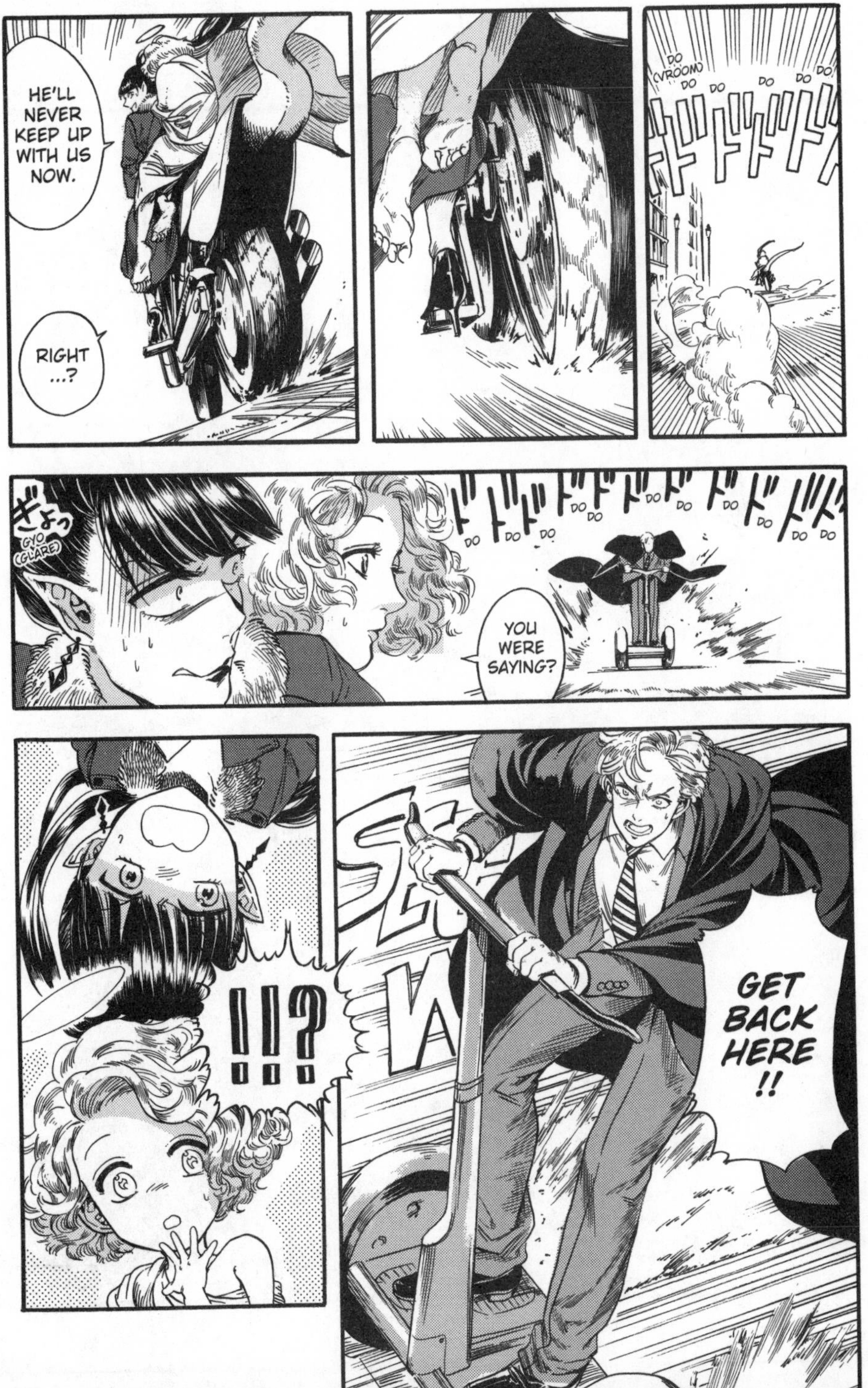
DO (VROOM) DO DO DO DO DO
HE'LL NEVER KEEP UP WITH US NOW.
RIGHT ...?
DO DO DO DO DO DO DO DO DO DO DO
YOU WERE SAYING?
ぎょっ GYO (GLARE)
GET BACK HERE !!
!!?

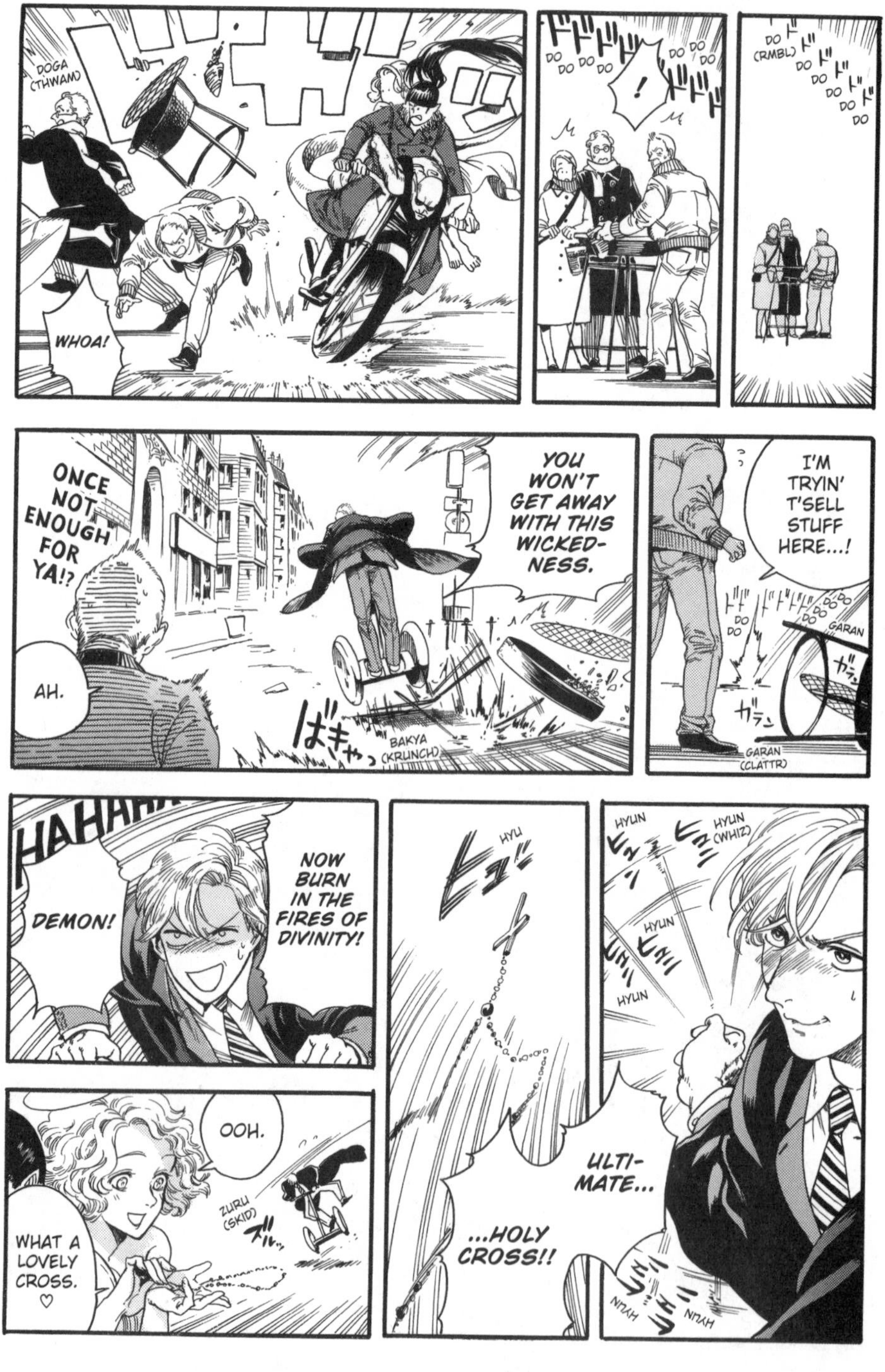
DO (RMBL) DO DO DO DO DO DO
DO DO DO DO
!
DO DO DO
DOGA (THWAM)
WHOA!
I'M TRYIN' T'SELL STUFF HERE...!
DO DO DO DO
GARAN
GARAN (CLATTR)
YOU WON'T GET AWAY WITH THIS WICKED-NESS.
ONCE NOT ENOUGH FOR YA!?
AH.
BAKYA (KRUNCH)
HYUN HYUN (WHIZ)
HYUN
HYUN
ULTI-MATE...
...HOLY CROSS!!
HYUN HYUN
HYU
NOW BURN IN THE FIRES OF DIVINITY!
DEMON!
OOH.
ZURU (SKID)
WHAT A LOVELY CROSS. ♡

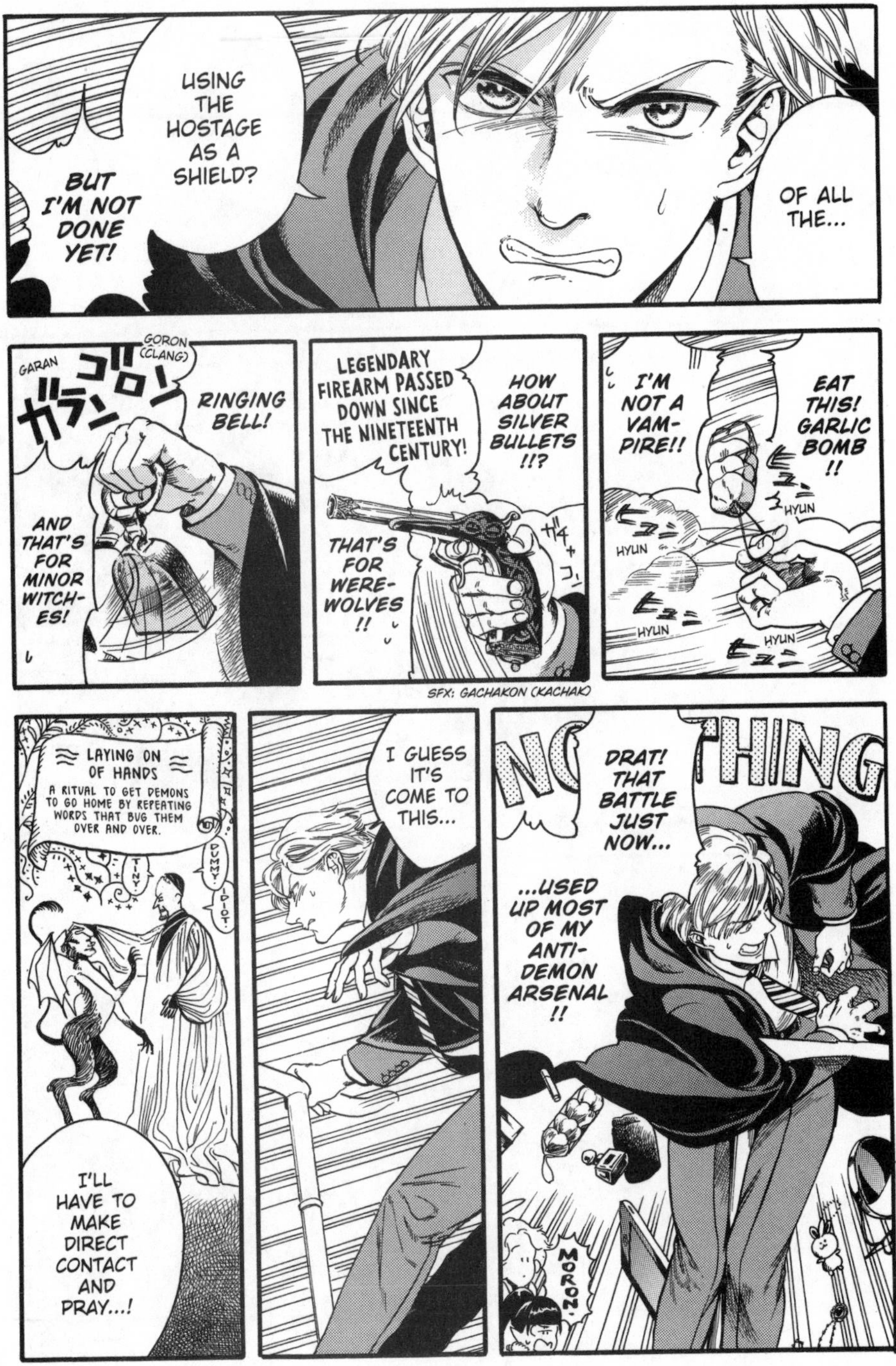
OF ALL THE...
USING THE HOSTAGE AS A SHIELD?
BUT I'M NOT DONE YET!
EAT THIS! GARLIC BOMB!!
I'M NOT A VAMPIRE!!
HYUN
HYUN
HYUN
HYUN
HOW ABOUT SILVER BULLETS!!?
LEGENDARY FIREARM PASSED DOWN SINCE THE NINETEENTH CENTURY!
THAT'S FOR WEREWOLVES!!
SFX: GACHAKON (KACHAK)
RINGING BELL!
ゴロン
GORON (CLANG)
ガラン
GARAN
AND THAT'S FOR MINOR WITCHES!
NOTHING
DRAT! THAT BATTLE JUST NOW...
...USED UP MOST OF MY ANTI-DEMON ARSENAL!!
MORON.
I GUESS IT'S COME TO THIS...
LAYING ON OF HANDS
A RITUAL TO GET DEMONS TO GO HOME BY REPEATING WORDS THAT BUG THEM OVER AND OVER.
DUMMY. IDIOT.
TINY.
I'LL HAVE TO MAKE DIRECT CONTACT AND PRAY...!

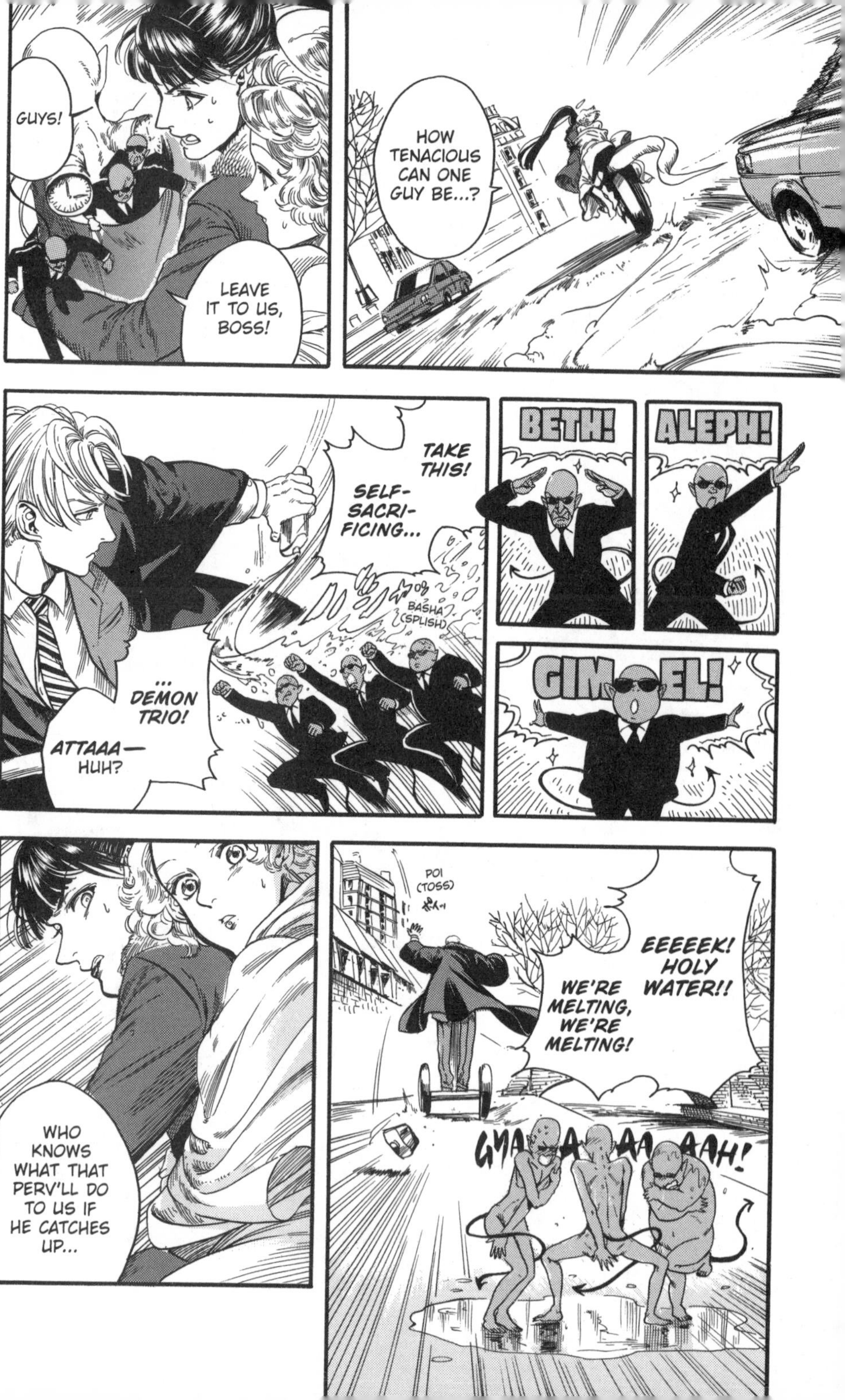
HOW TENACIOUS CAN ONE GUY BE...?
GUYS!
LEAVE IT TO US, BOSS!
ALEPH!
BETH!
GIMEL!
TAKE THIS!
SELF-SACRIFICING...
BASHA (SPLISH)
...DEMON TRIO!
ATTAAA—HUH?
POI (TOSS)
EEEEEK! HOLY WATER!!
WE'RE MELTING, WE'RE MELTING!
GYAAAAAAAH!
WHO KNOWS WHAT THAT PERV'LL DO TO US IF HE CATCHES UP...

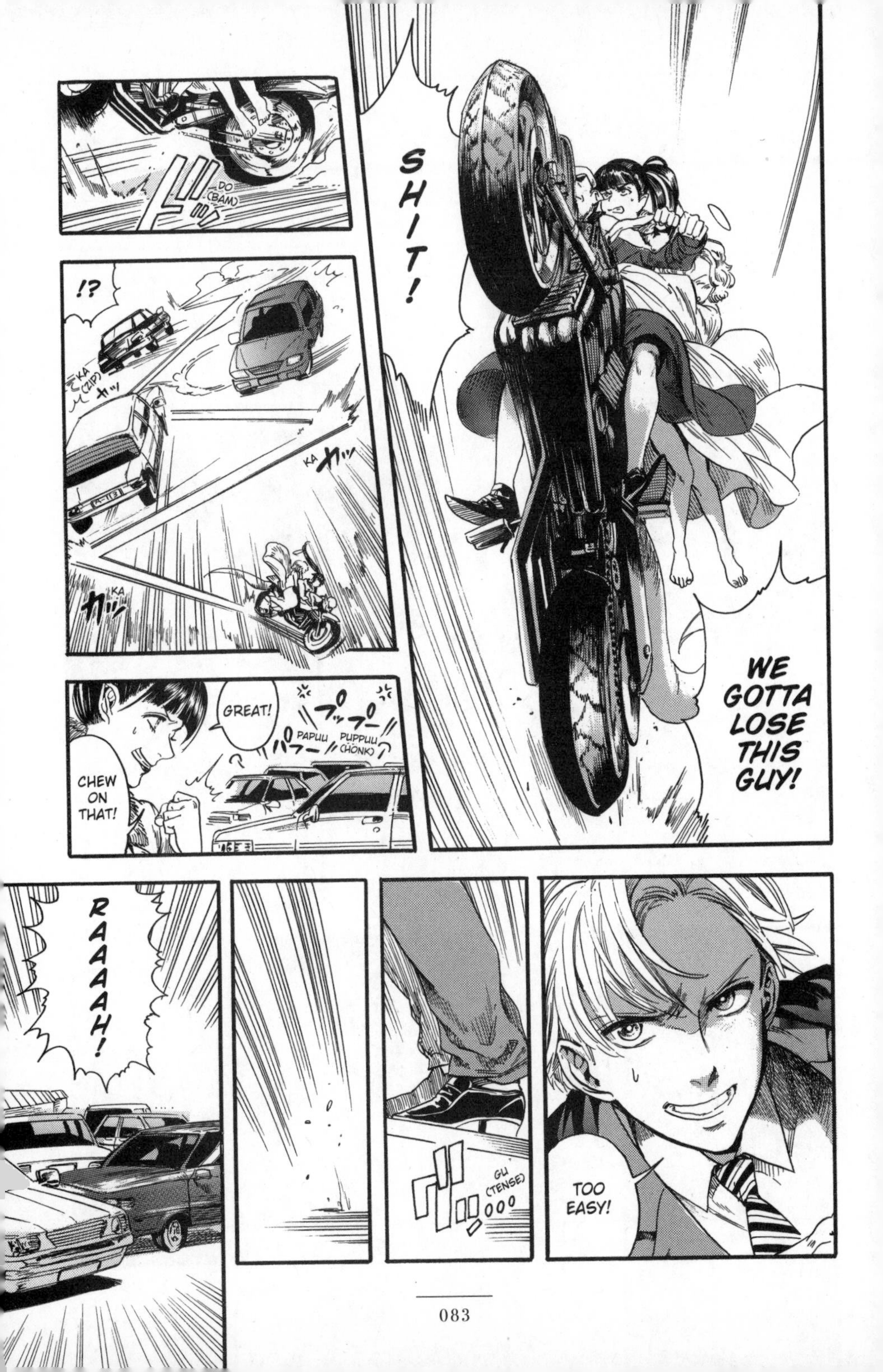
SHIT!
WE GOTTA LOSE THIS GUY!
DO (BAM)
!?
KA (ZIP)
KA
KA
GREAT!
PAPUU
PUPPUU (HONK)
CHEW ON THAT!
TOO EASY!
GU (TENSE)
RAAAAAH!

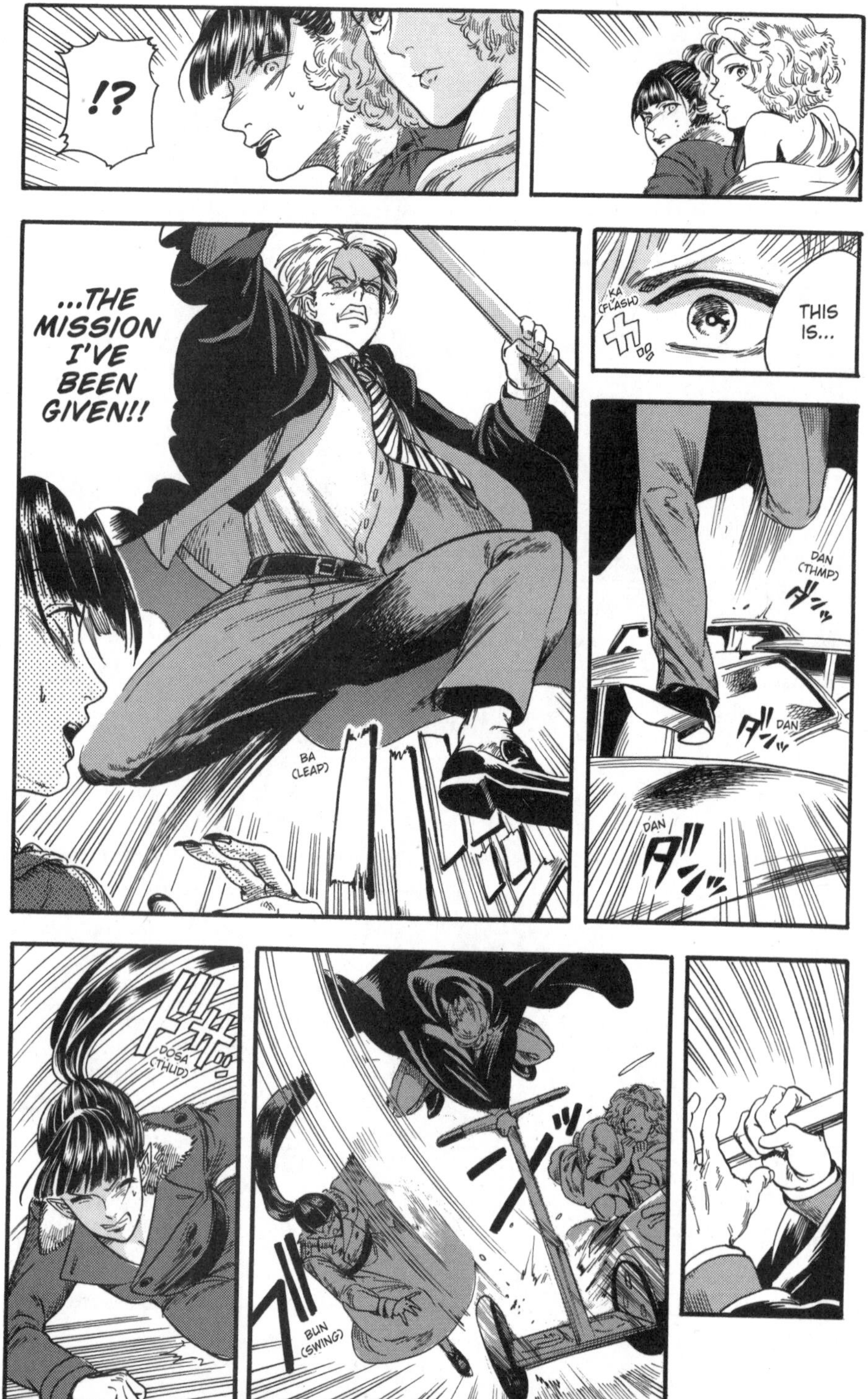
!?
THIS IS...
KA (FLASH)
カッ
DAN (THMP)
ダンッ
DAN
ダンッ
DAN
ダンッ
...THE MISSION I'VE BEEN GIVEN!!
BA (LEAP)
BUN (SWING)
DOSA (THUD)

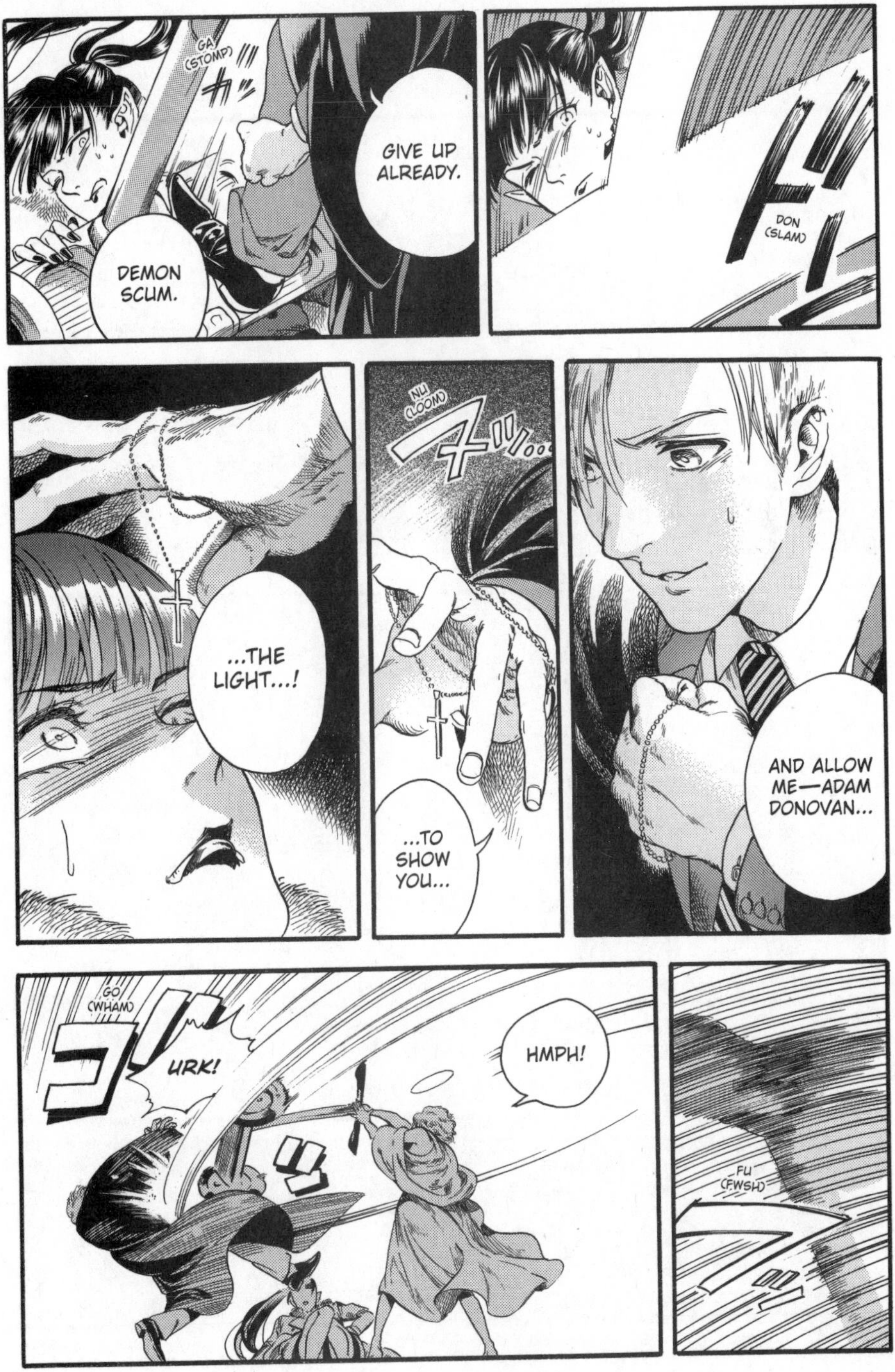
DON
(SLAM)
GA
(STOMP)
GIVE UP ALREADY.
DEMON SCUM.
AND ALLOW ME—ADAM DONOVAN...
NU
(LOOM)
...TO SHOW YOU...
...THE LIGHT...!
FU
(FWSH)
HMPH!
GO
(WHAM)
URK!

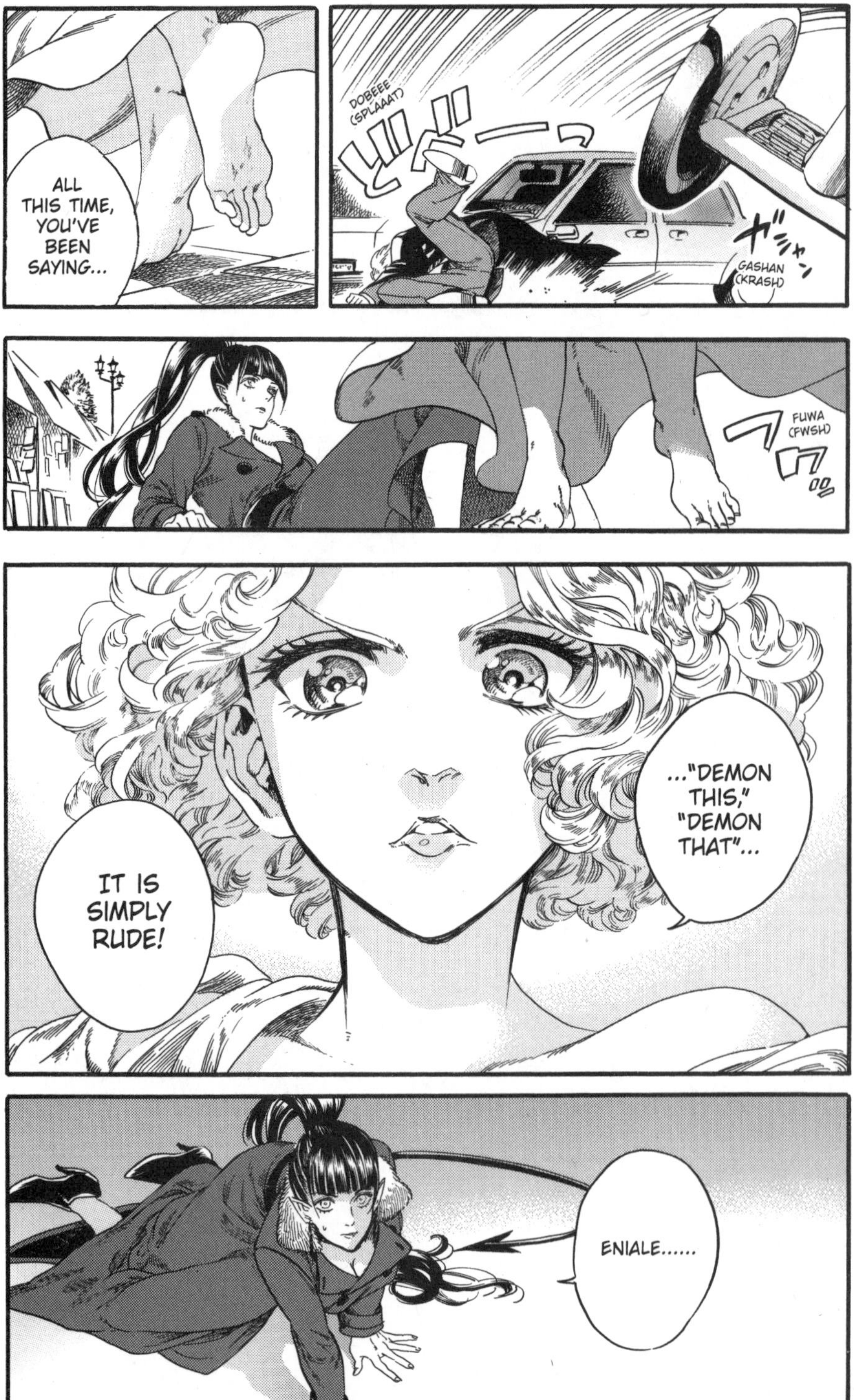
DOBEEE (SPLAAAT)
GASHAN (KRASH)
ALL THIS TIME, YOU'VE BEEN SAYING...
FUWA (FWSH)
..."DEMON THIS," "DEMON THAT"...
IT IS SIMPLY RUDE!
ENIALE......

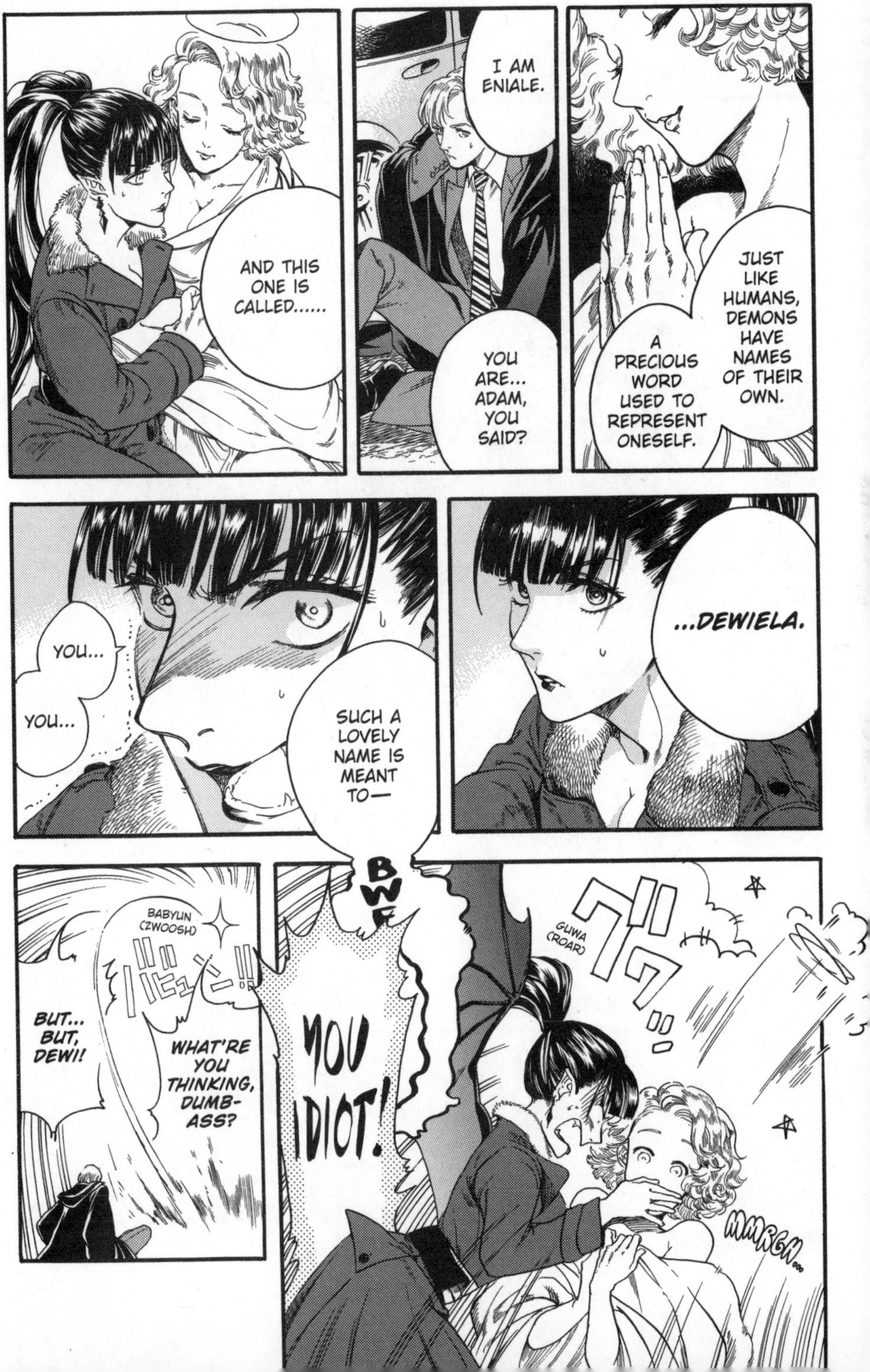
JUST LIKE HUMANS, DEMONS HAVE NAMES OF THEIR OWN.
A PRECIOUS WORD USED TO REPRESENT ONESELF.
I AM ENIALE.
YOU ARE... ADAM, YOU SAID?
AND THIS ONE IS CALLED......
...DEWIELA.
YOU...
YOU...
SUCH A LOVELY NAME IS MEANT TO—
BWF
GUWA (ROAR)
YOU IDIOT!
MMRGH...
BABYUN (ZWOOSH)
WHAT'RE YOU THINKING, DUMB-ASS?
BUT... BUT, DEWI!

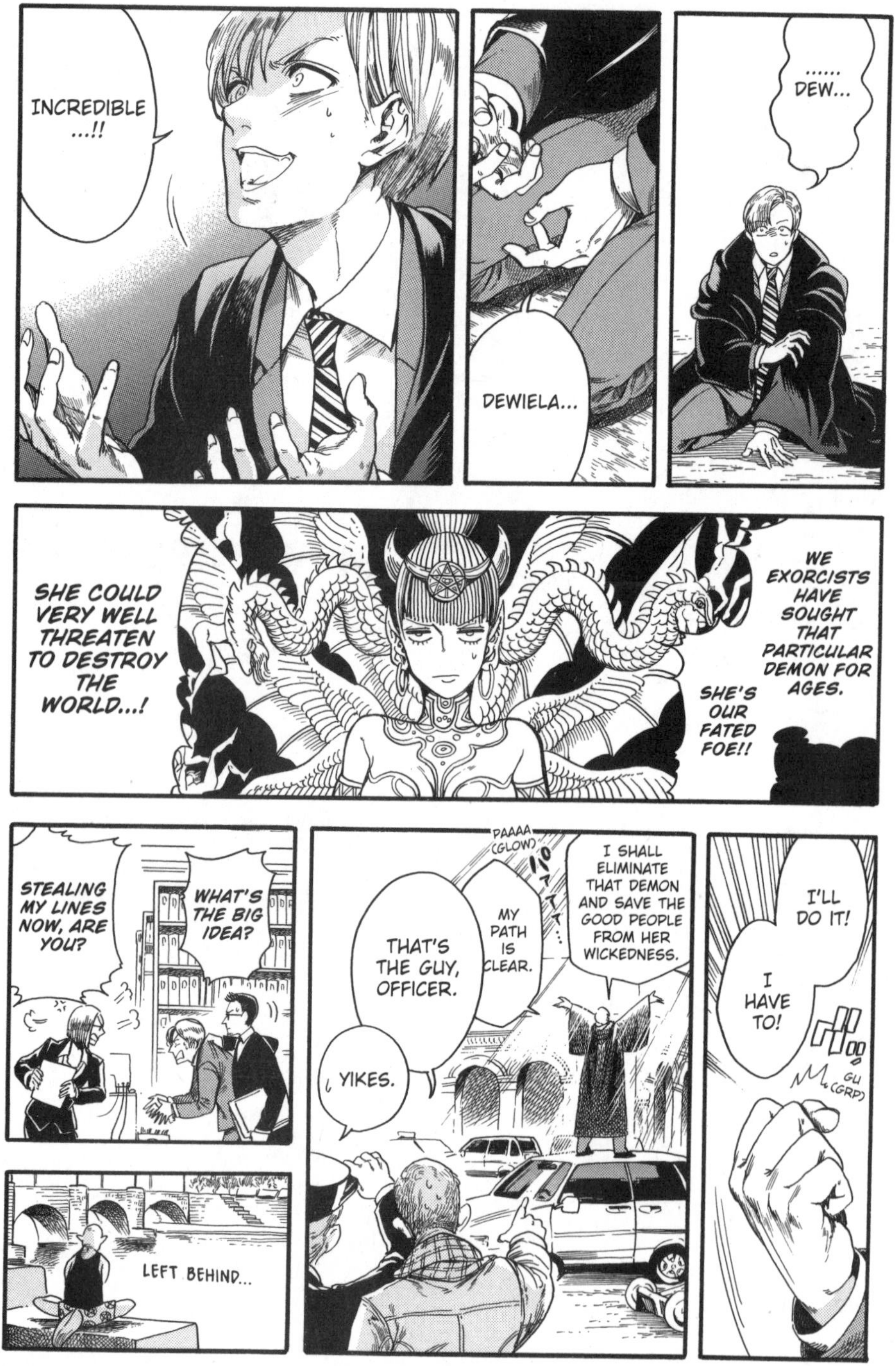
......
DEW...
DEWIELA...
INCREDIBLE ...!!
WE EXORCISTS HAVE SOUGHT THAT PARTICULAR DEMON FOR AGES.
SHE'S OUR FATED FOE!!
SHE COULD VERY WELL THREATEN TO DESTROY THE WORLD...!
I'LL DO IT!
I HAVE TO!
GU (GRP)
PAAAA (GLOW)
I SHALL ELIMINATE THAT DEMON AND SAVE THE GOOD PEOPLE FROM HER WICKEDNESS.
MY PATH IS CLEAR.
THAT'S THE GUY, OFFICER.
YIKES.
WHAT'S THE BIG IDEA?
STEALING MY LINES NOW, ARE YOU?
LEFT BEHIND...

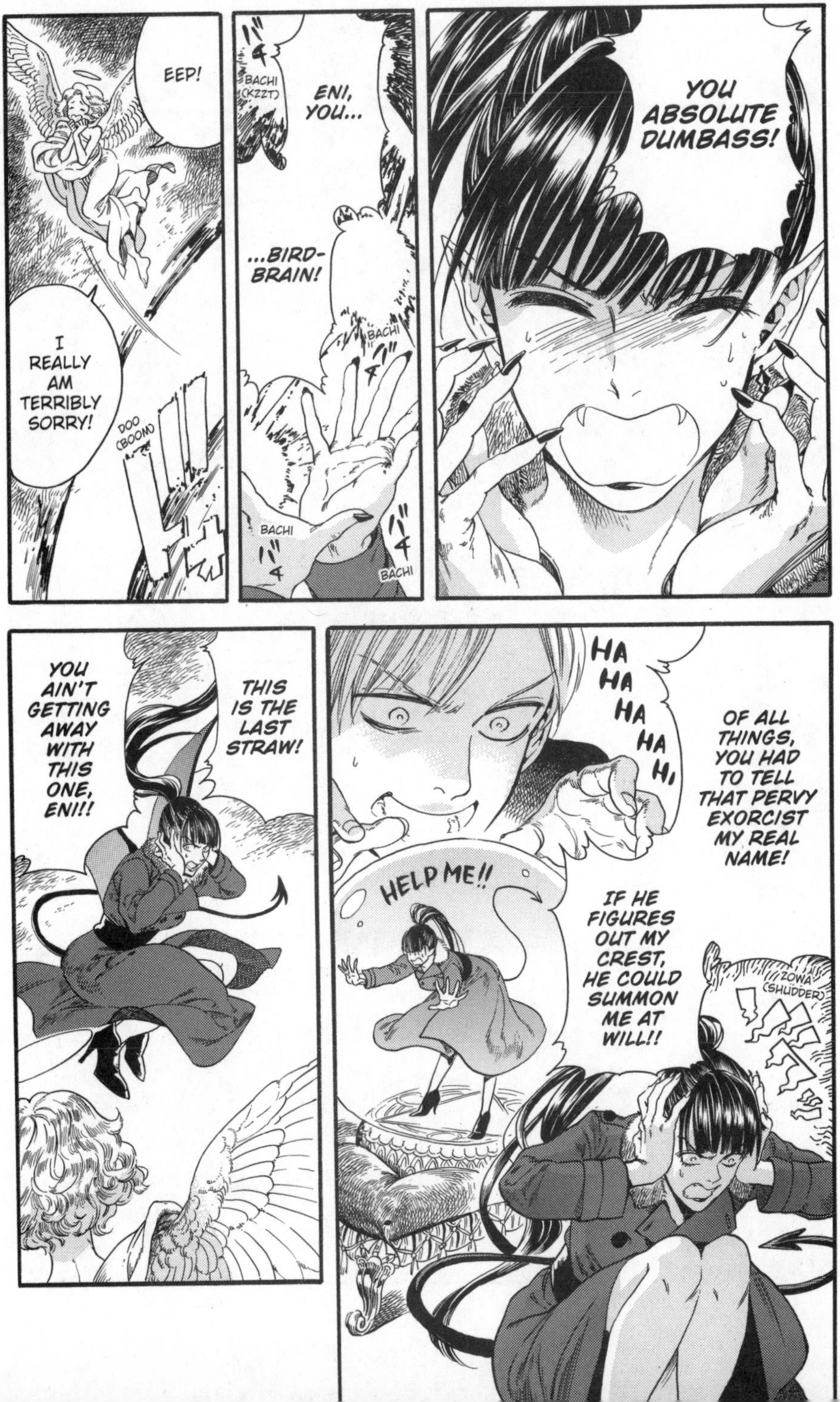
YOU ABSOLUTE DUMBASS!
BACHI (KZZT)
ENI, YOU...
...BIRD-BRAIN!
BACHI
BACHI
BACHI
EEP!
I REALLY AM TERRIBLY SORRY!
DOO (BOOM)
HA HA HA HA HI
OF ALL THINGS, YOU HAD TO TELL THAT PERVY EXORCIST MY REAL NAME!
HELP ME!!
IF HE FIGURES OUT MY CREST, HE COULD SUMMON ME AT WILL!!
ZOWA (SHUDDER)
THIS IS THE LAST STRAW!
YOU AIN'T GETTING AWAY WITH THIS ONE, ENI!!

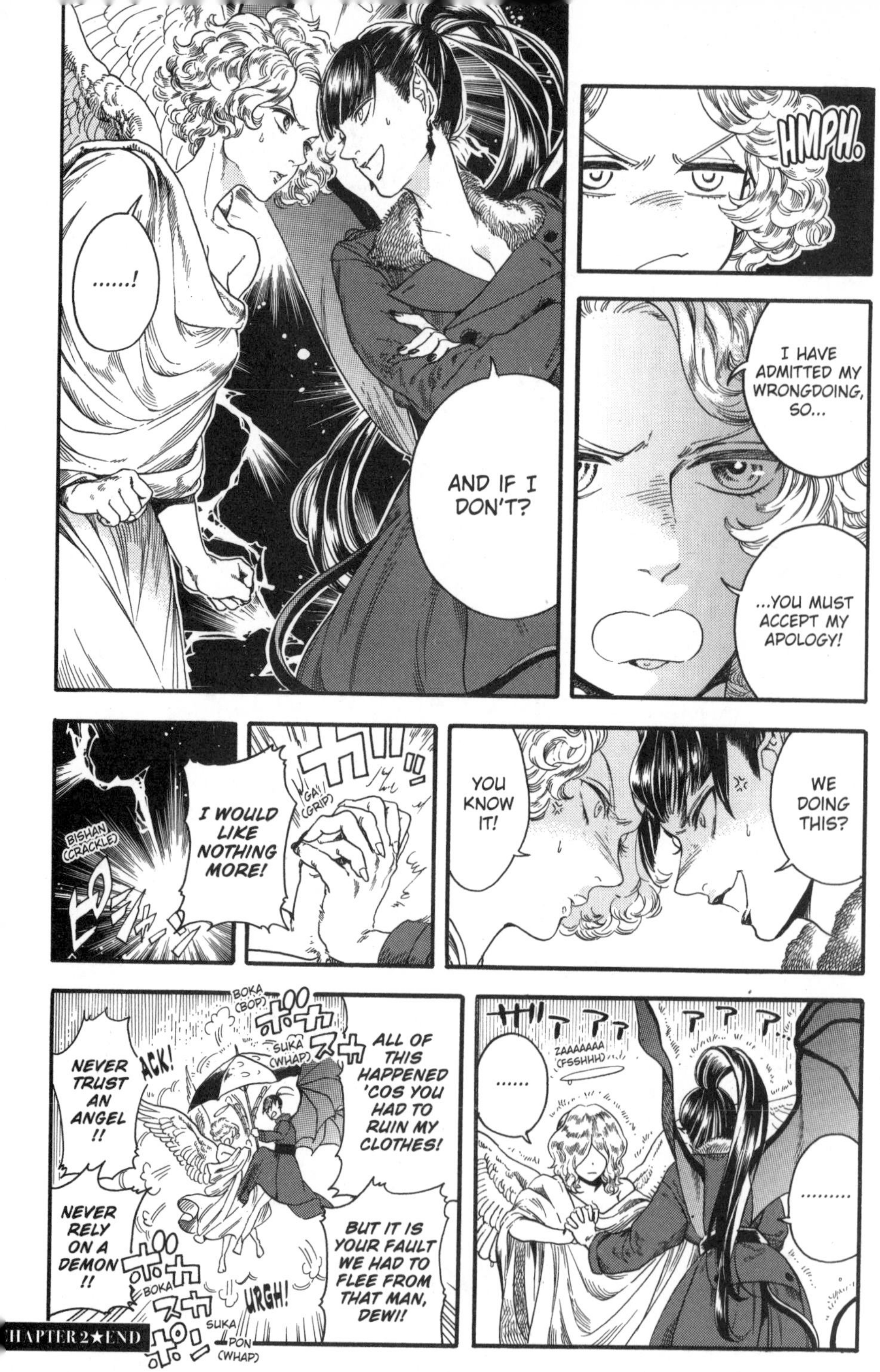
HMPH.
I HAVE ADMITTED MY WRONGDOING, SO...
...YOU MUST ACCEPT MY APOLOGY!
AND IF I DON'T?
......!
WE DOING THIS?
YOU KNOW IT!
GA (GRIP)
I WOULD LIKE NOTHING MORE!
BISHAN (CRACKLE)
ZAAAAAAA (FSSHHH)
....
......
ALL OF THIS HAPPENED 'COS YOU HAD TO RUIN MY CLOTHES!
BOKA (BOP)
SUKA (WHAP)
NEVER TRUST AN ANGEL!!
ACK!
BUT IT IS YOUR FAULT WE HAD TO FLEE FROM THAT MAN, DEWI!
NEVER RELY ON A DEMON!!
URGH!
BOKA
SUKA
PON (WHAP)
HAPTER 2★END

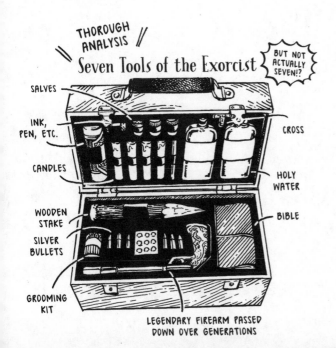

THOROUGH ANALYSIS

Seven Tools of the Exorcist

BUT NOT ACTUALLY SEVEN!?

SALVES

INK, PEN, ETC.

CANDLES

WOODEN STAKE

SILVER BULLETS

GROOMING KIT

CROSS

HOLY WATER

BIBLE

LEGENDARY FIREARM PASSED DOWN OVER GENERATIONS

ENIALE & DEWIELA

1

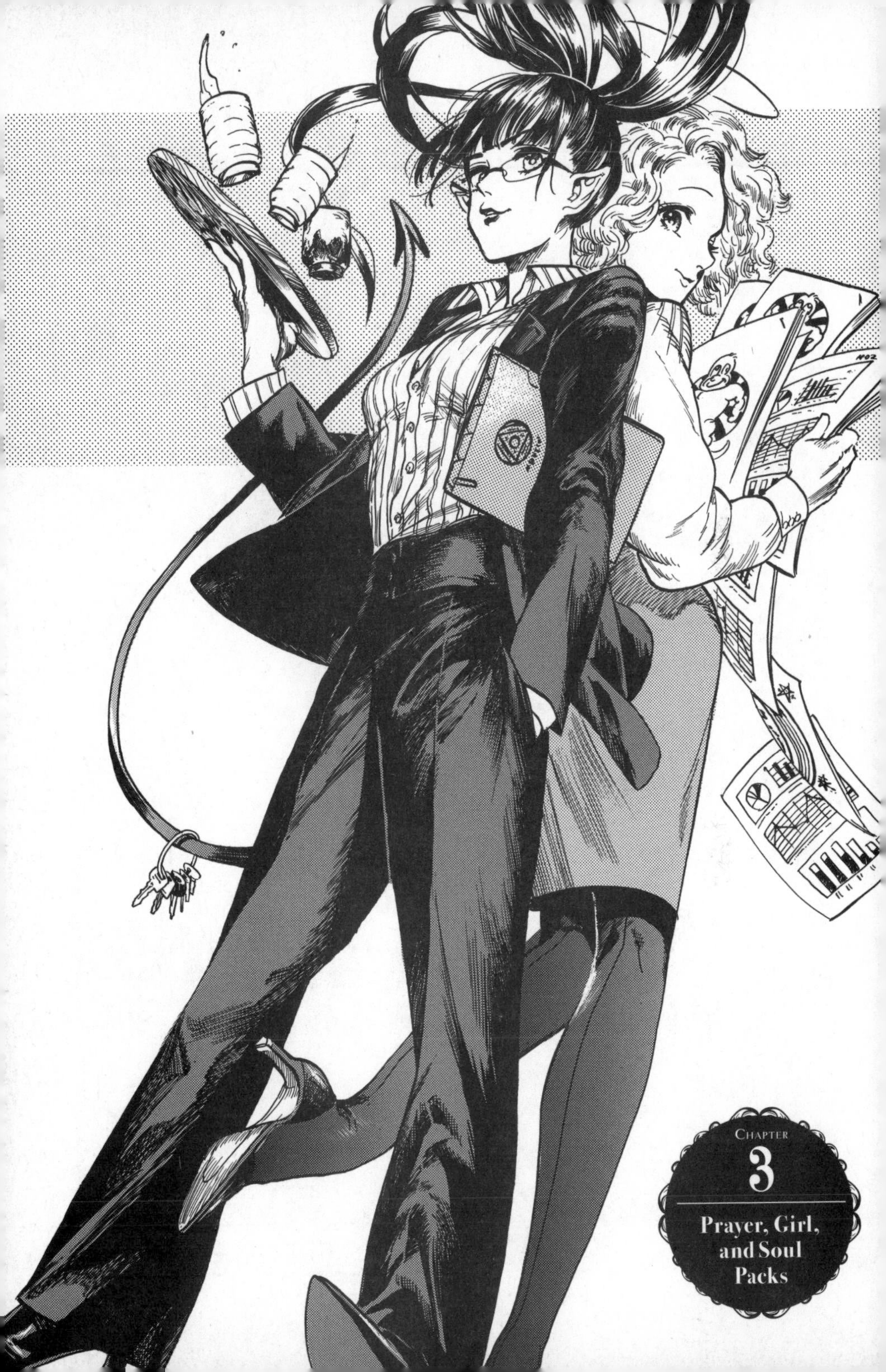
CHAPTER
3
Prayer, Girl, and Soul Packs

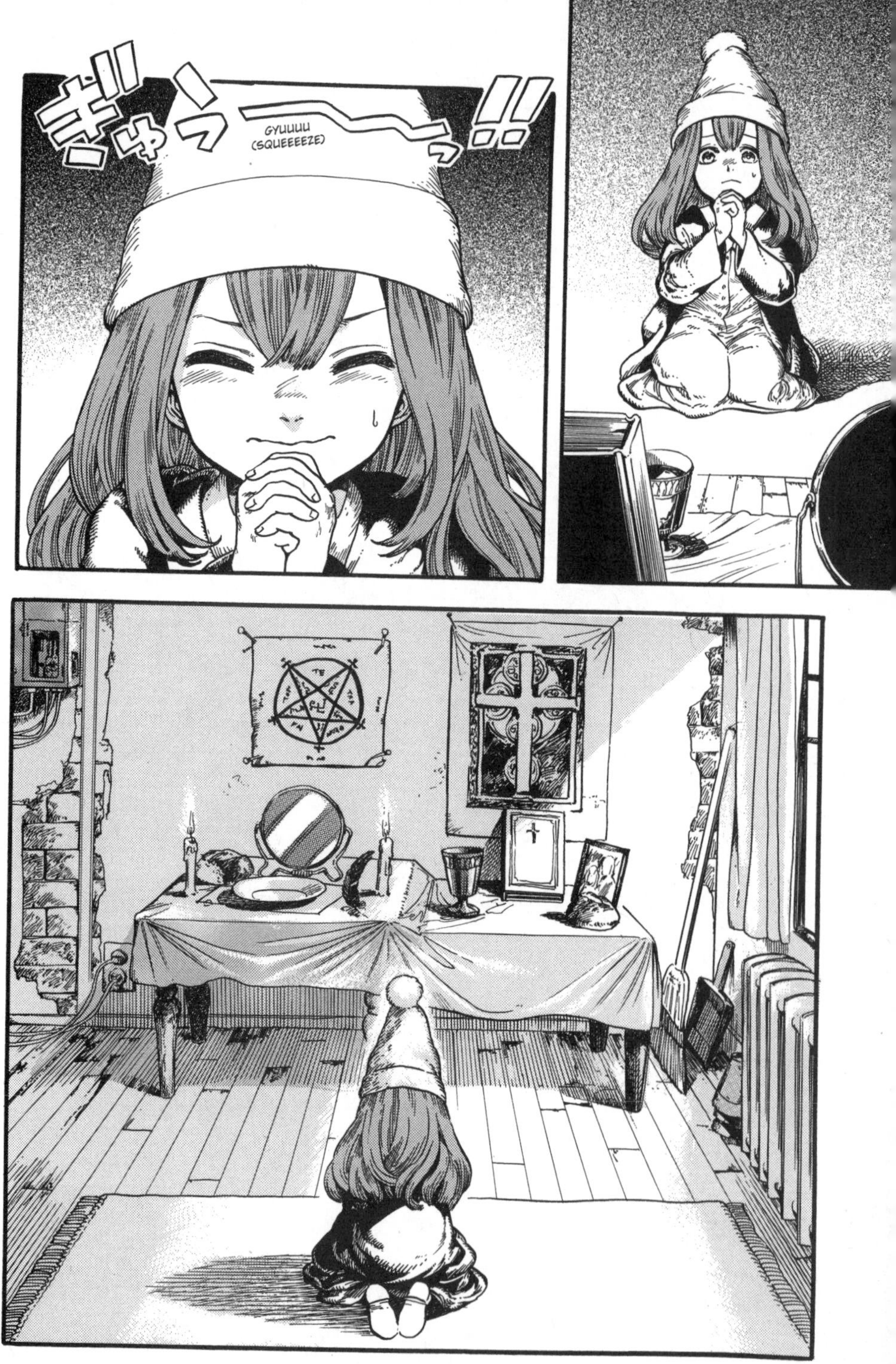
ぎゅう〜〜っ!!
GYUUUU (SQUEEEEZE)

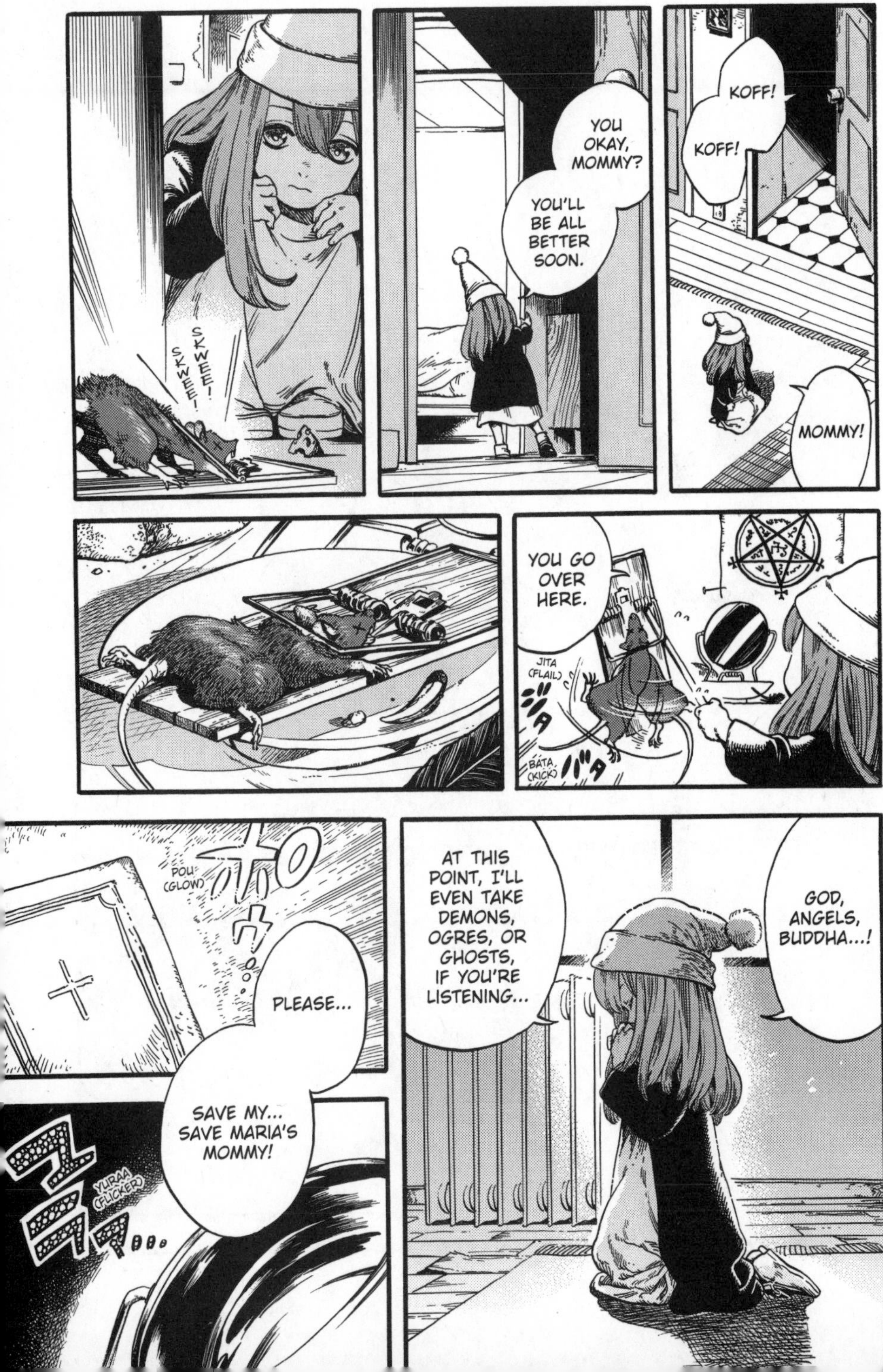
KOFF!
KOFF!
MOMMY!
YOU OKAY, MOMMY?
YOU'LL BE ALL BETTER SOON.
SKWEE! SKWEE!
YOU GO OVER HERE.
JITA (FLAIL)
BATA (KICK)
GOD, ANGELS, BUDDHA...!
AT THIS POINT, I'LL EVEN TAKE DEMONS, OGRES, OR GHOSTS, IF YOU'RE LISTENING...
POU (GLOW)
PLEASE...
SAVE MY... SAVE MARIA'S MOMMY!
YURAA (FLICKER)

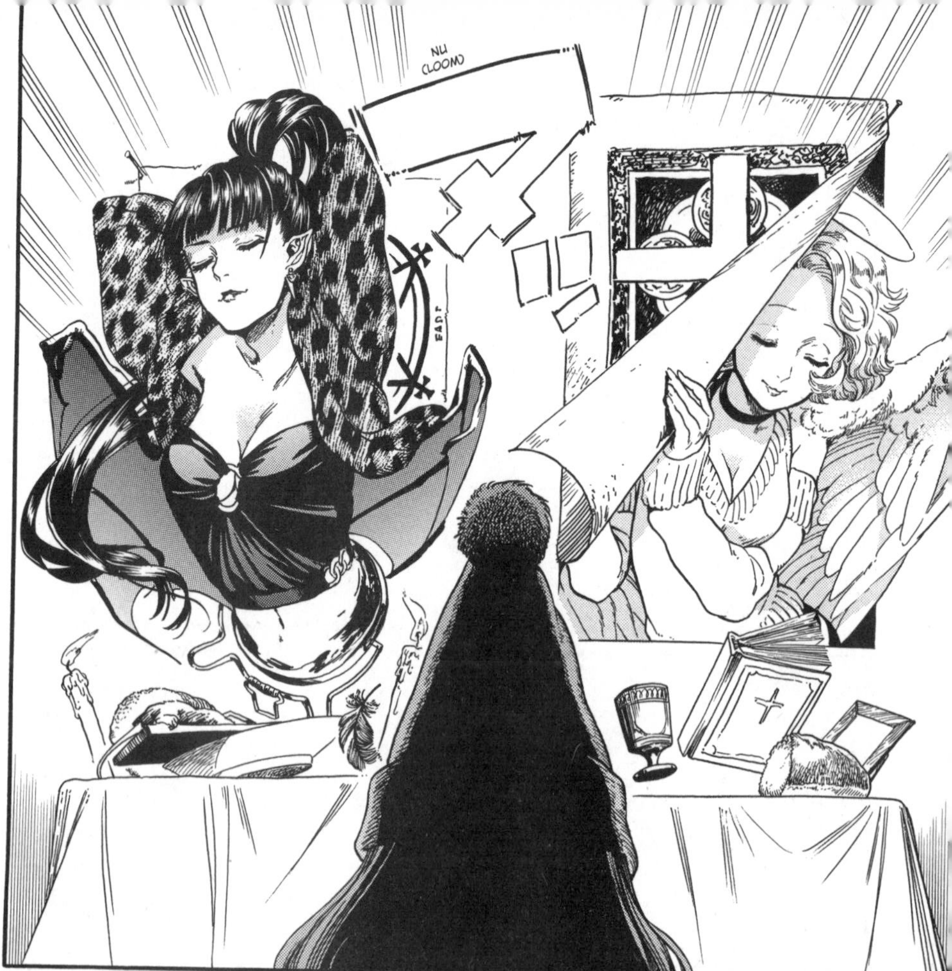
NU
(LOOM)
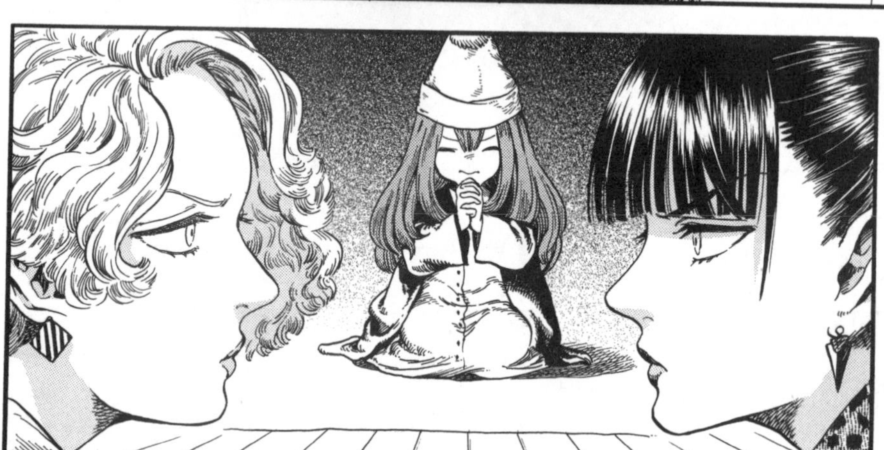

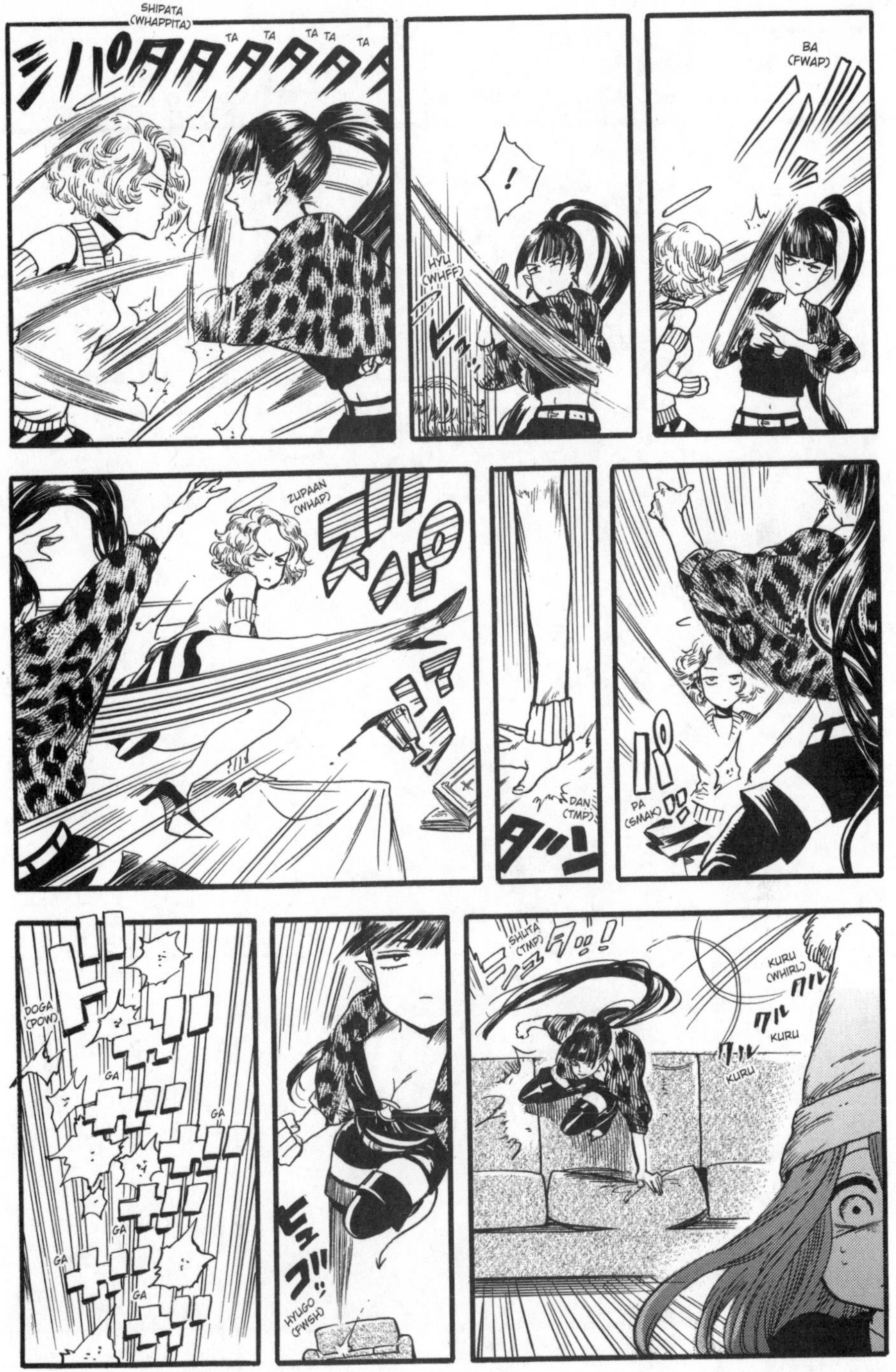
BA
(FWAP)
!
HYU
(WHFF)
SHIPATA
(WHAPPITA)
TA TA TA TA TA
PA
(SMAK)
DAN
(TMP)
ZUPAAN
(WHAP)
SHUTA
(TMP)
KURU
(WHIRL)
KURU
KURU
HYUGO
(FWSH)
DOGA
(POW)
GA
GA
GA
GA
GA

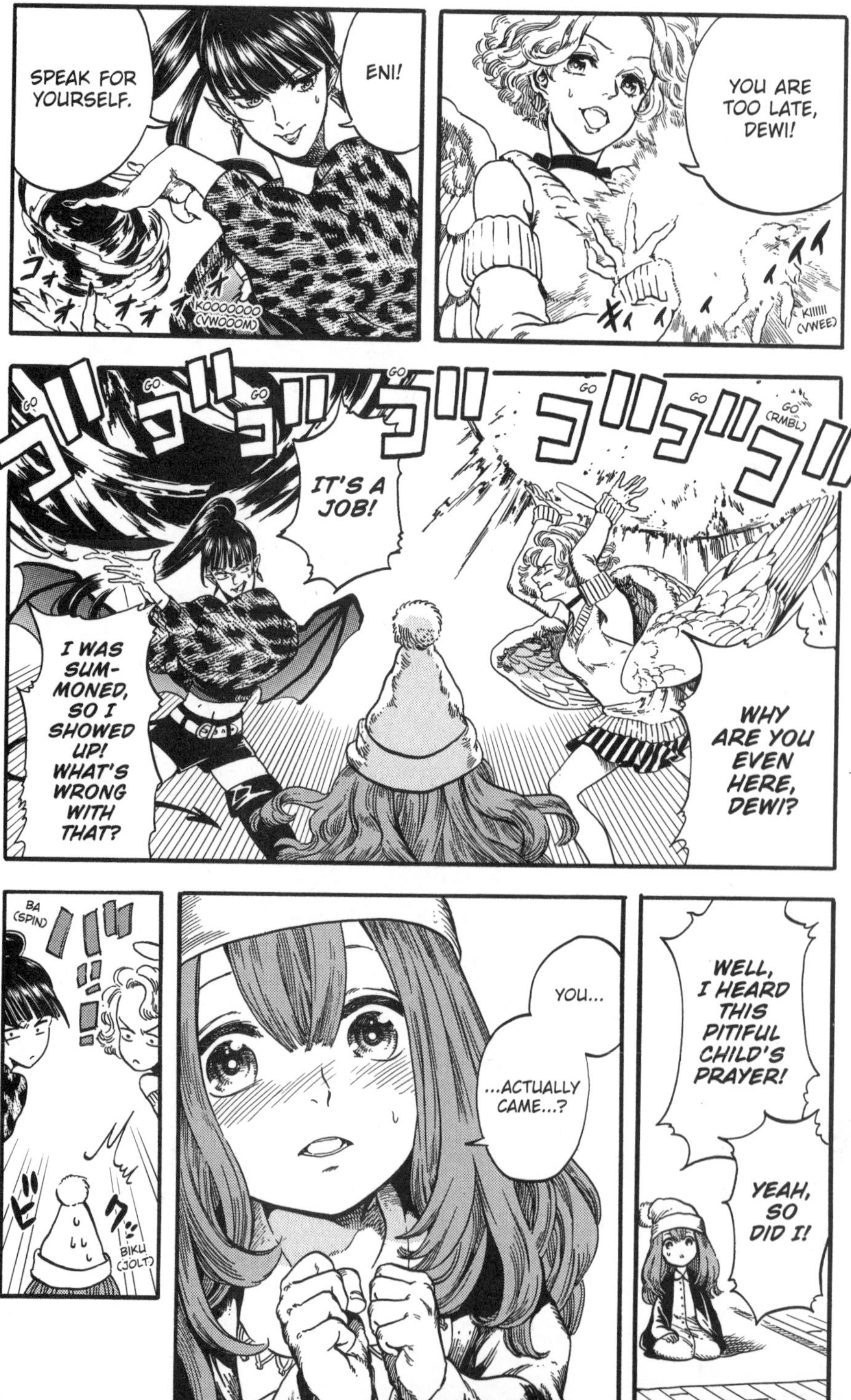
YOU ARE TOO LATE, DEWI!
KIIIII (VWEE)
ENI!
SPEAK FOR YOURSELF.
KOOOOOOO (VWOOOM)
GO GO GO (RMBL)
GO GO GO GO
WHY ARE YOU EVEN HERE, DEWI?
IT'S A JOB!
I WAS SUM-MONED, SO I SHOWED UP! WHAT'S WRONG WITH THAT?
WELL, I HEARD THIS PITIFUL CHILD'S PRAYER!
YEAH, SO DID I!
YOU...
...ACTUALLY CAME...?
BA (SPIN)
BIKU (JOLT)

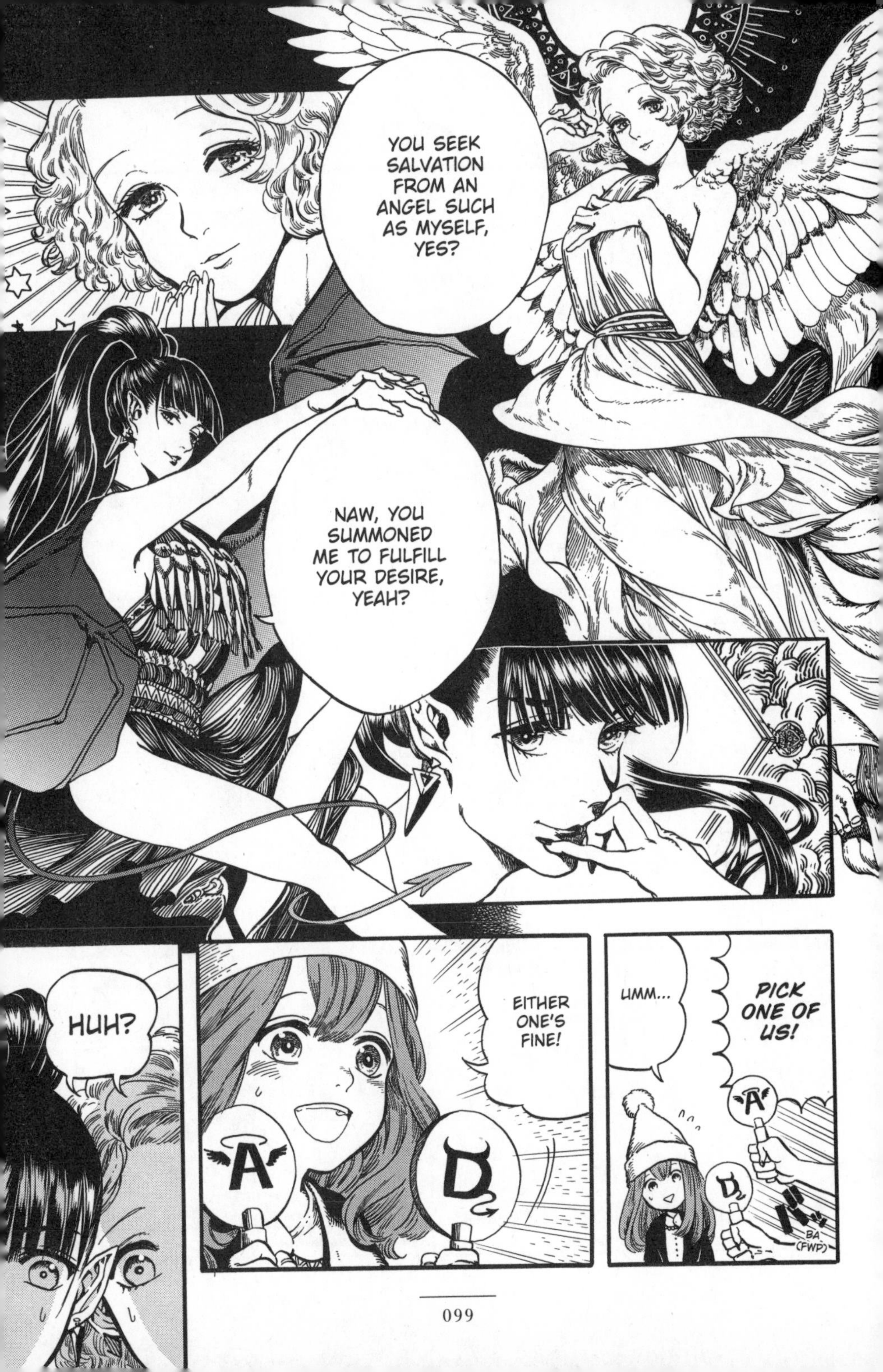
YOU SEEK SALVATION FROM AN ANGEL SUCH AS MYSELF, YES?
NAW, YOU SUMMONED ME TO FULFILL YOUR DESIRE, YEAH?
PICK ONE OF US!
UMM...
BA (FWP)
EITHER ONE'S FINE!
A
D
HUH?

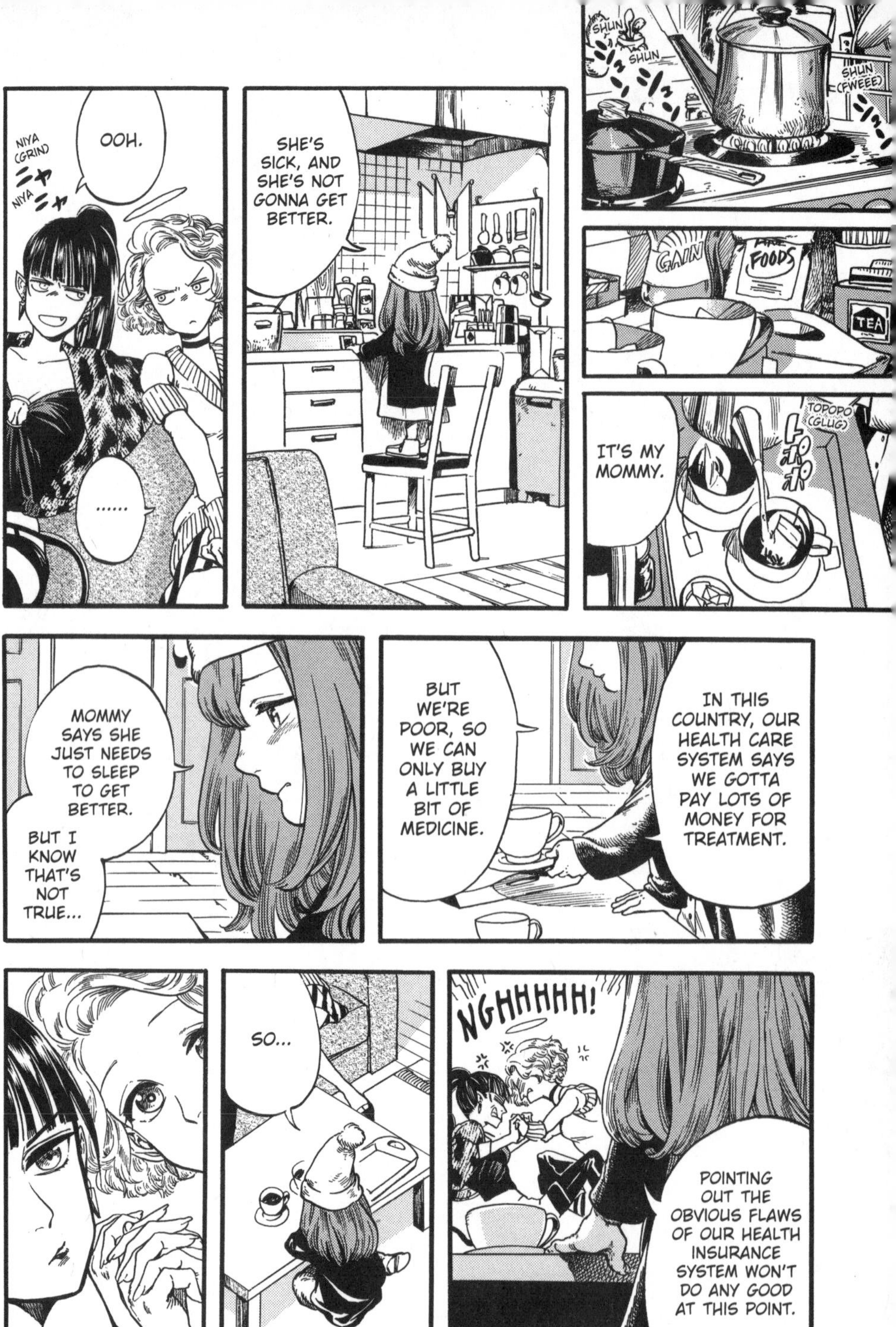
SHUN
SHUN
SHUN (FWEEEE)
IT'S MY MOMMY.
TOPOPO (GLUG)
SHE'S SICK, AND SHE'S NOT GONNA GET BETTER.
OOH.
NIYA (GRIND) NIYA
......
IN THIS COUNTRY, OUR HEALTH CARE SYSTEM SAYS WE GOTTA PAY LOTS OF MONEY FOR TREATMENT.
BUT WE'RE POOR, SO WE CAN ONLY BUY A LITTLE BIT OF MEDICINE.
MOMMY SAYS SHE JUST NEEDS TO SLEEP TO GET BETTER.
BUT I KNOW THAT'S NOT TRUE...
NGHHHHH!
POINTING OUT THE OBVIOUS FLAWS OF OUR HEALTH INSURANCE SYSTEM WON'T DO ANY GOOD AT THIS POINT.
SO...

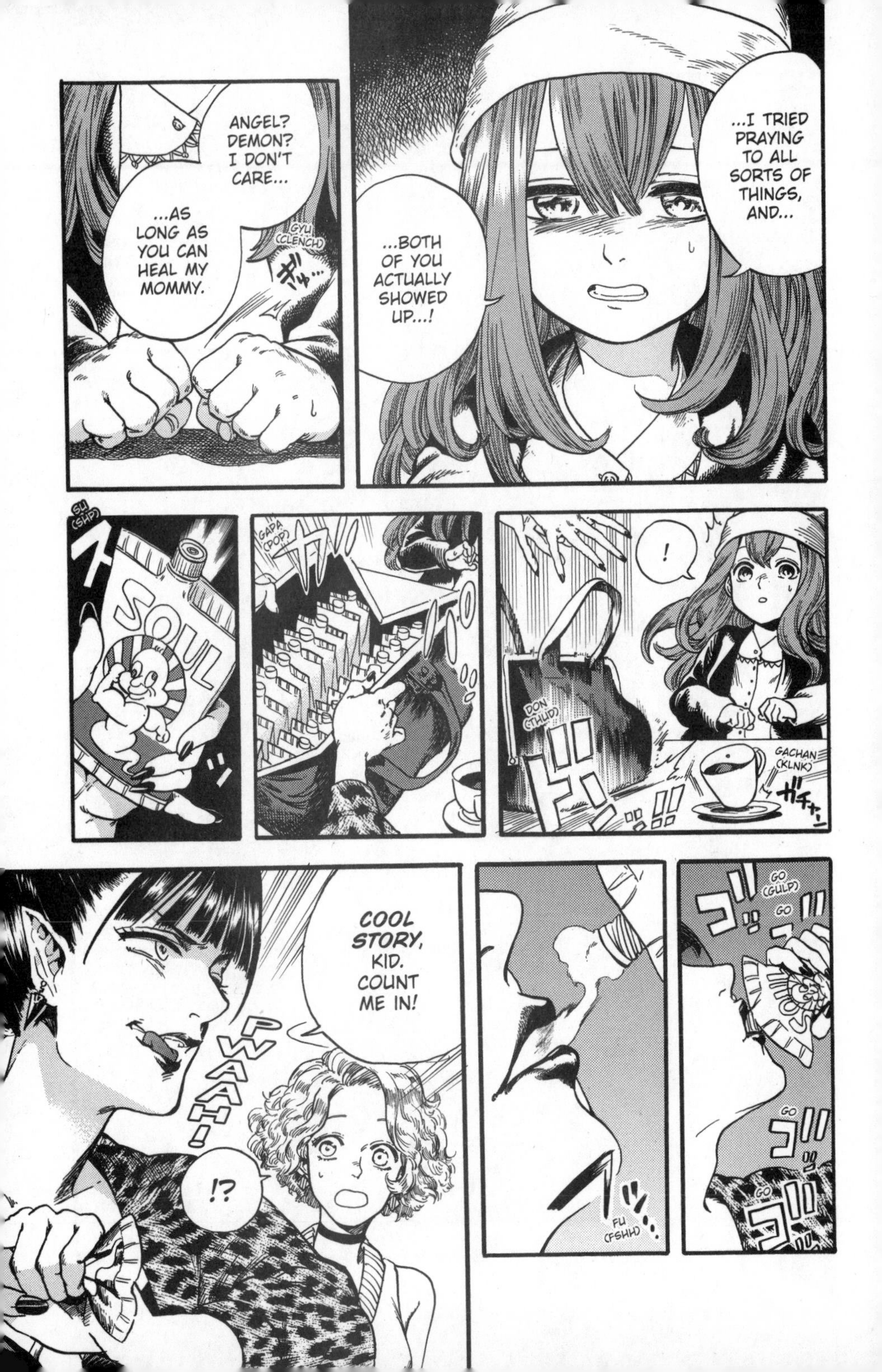
...I TRIED PRAYING TO ALL SORTS OF THINGS, AND...
...BOTH OF YOU ACTUALLY SHOWED UP...!
ANGEL? DEMON? I DON'T CARE...
...AS LONG AS YOU CAN HEAL MY MOMMY.
GYU (CLENCH)
!
DON (THUD)
GACHAN (KLNK)
GAPA (POP)
SU (SHP)
SOUL
GO (GULP)
GO
GO
GO
FU (FSHH)
COOL STORY, KID. COUNT ME IN!
PWAAAH!
!?

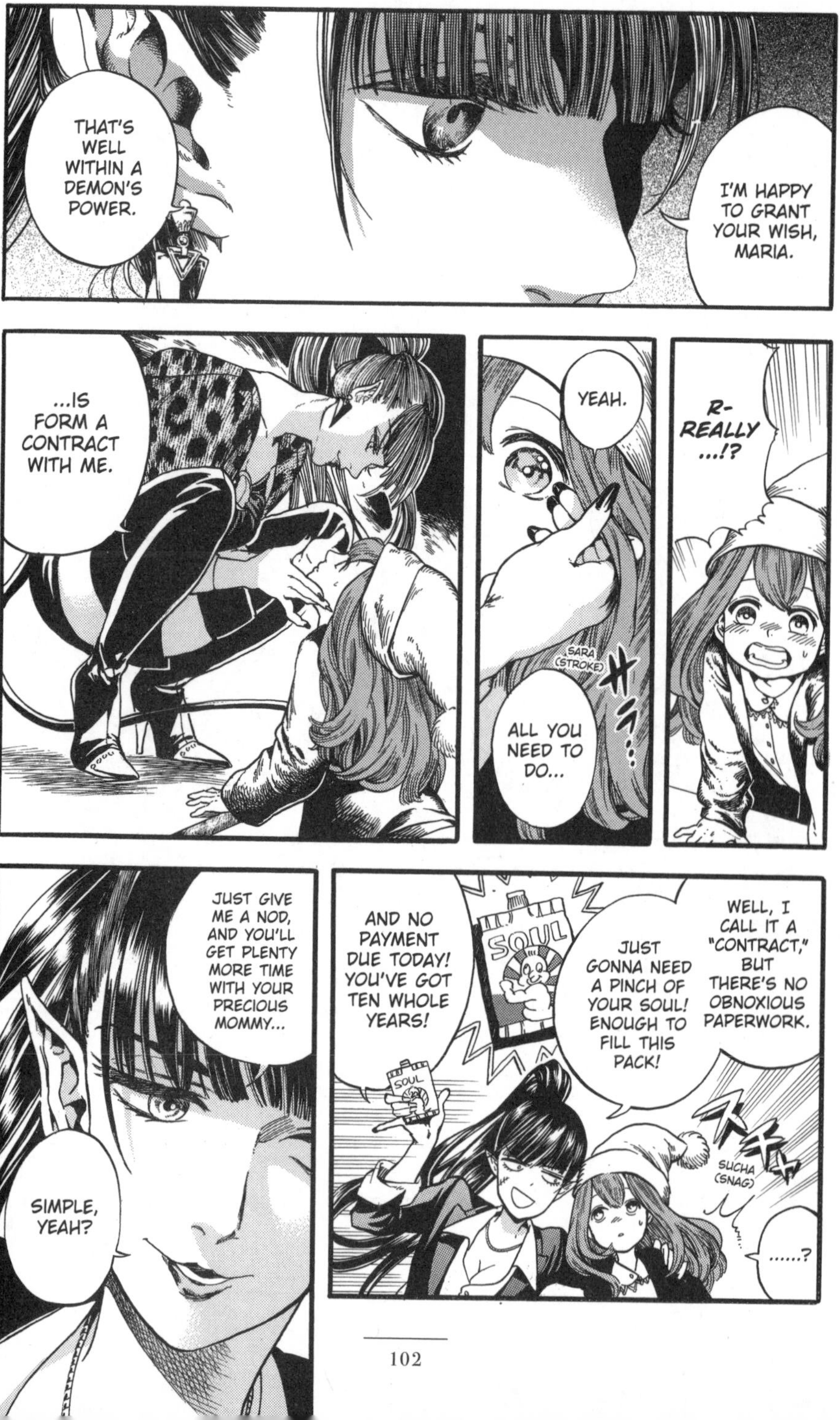
I'M HAPPY TO GRANT YOUR WISH, MARIA.
THAT'S WELL WITHIN A DEMON'S POWER.
R-REALLY ...!?
YEAH.
SARA (STROKE)
ALL YOU NEED TO DO...
...IS FORM A CONTRACT WITH ME.
WELL, I CALL IT A "CONTRACT," BUT THERE'S NO OBNOXIOUS PAPERWORK.
JUST GONNA NEED A PINCH OF YOUR SOUL! ENOUGH TO FILL THIS PACK!
SOUL
AND NO PAYMENT DUE TODAY! YOU'VE GOT TEN WHOLE YEARS!
SOUL
SUCHA (SNAG)
......?
JUST GIVE ME A NOD, AND YOU'LL GET PLENTY MORE TIME WITH YOUR PRECIOUS MOMMY...
SIMPLE, YEAH?

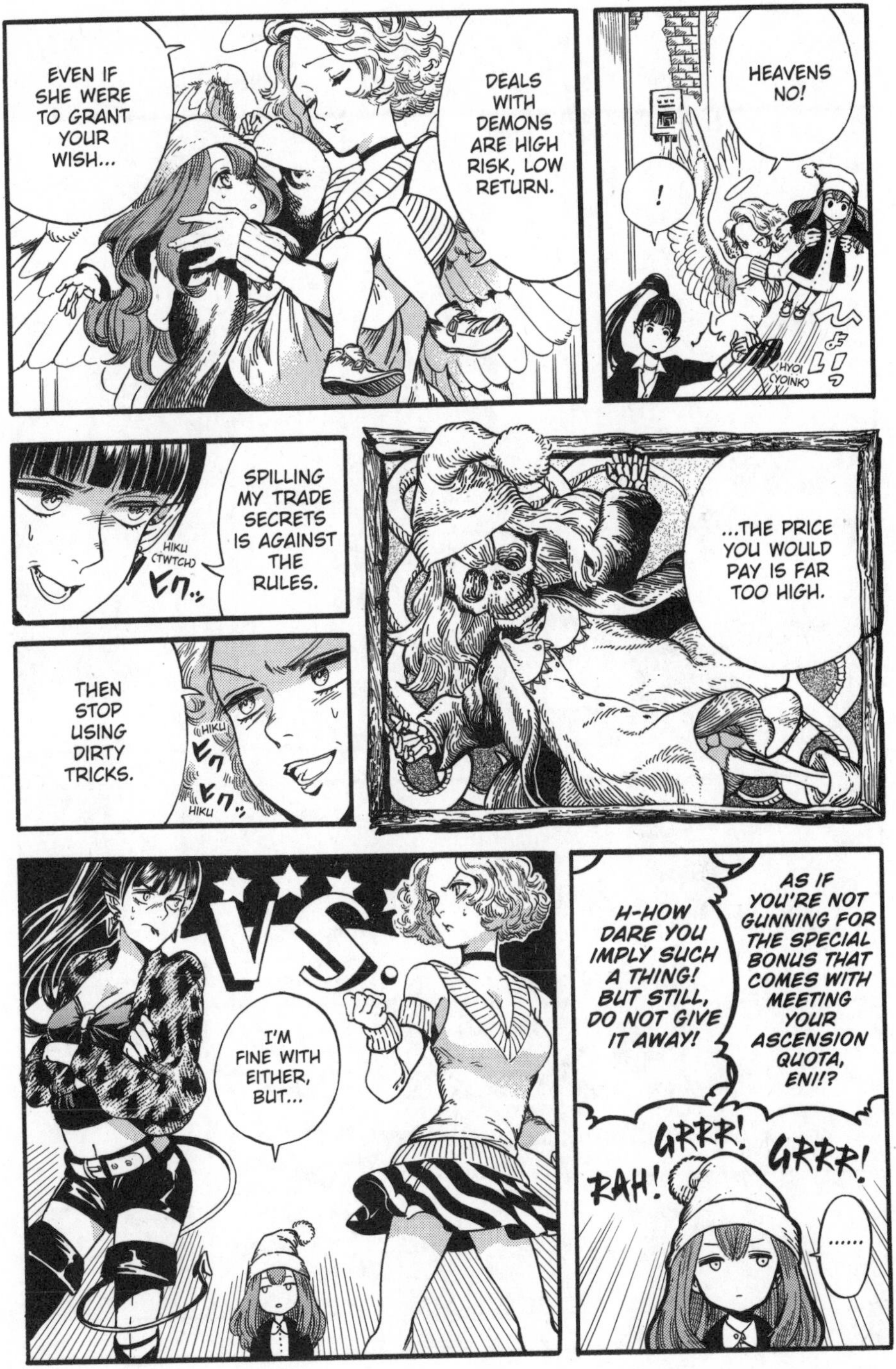
HEAVENS NO!
!
HYOI (YOINK)
DEALS WITH DEMONS ARE HIGH RISK, LOW RETURN.
EVEN IF SHE WERE TO GRANT YOUR WISH...
...THE PRICE YOU WOULD PAY IS FAR TOO HIGH.
SPILLING MY TRADE SECRETS IS AGAINST THE RULES.
HIKU (TWTCH)
ヒクッ
THEN STOP USING DIRTY TRICKS.
HIKU
ヒク
ヒクッ
HIKU
AS IF YOU'RE NOT GUNNING FOR THE SPECIAL BONUS THAT COMES WITH MEETING YOUR ASCENSION QUOTA, ENI!?
H-HOW DARE YOU IMPLY SUCH A THING! BUT STILL, DO NOT GIVE IT AWAY!
GRRR!
GRRR!
RAH!
......
VS.
I'M FINE WITH EITHER, BUT...

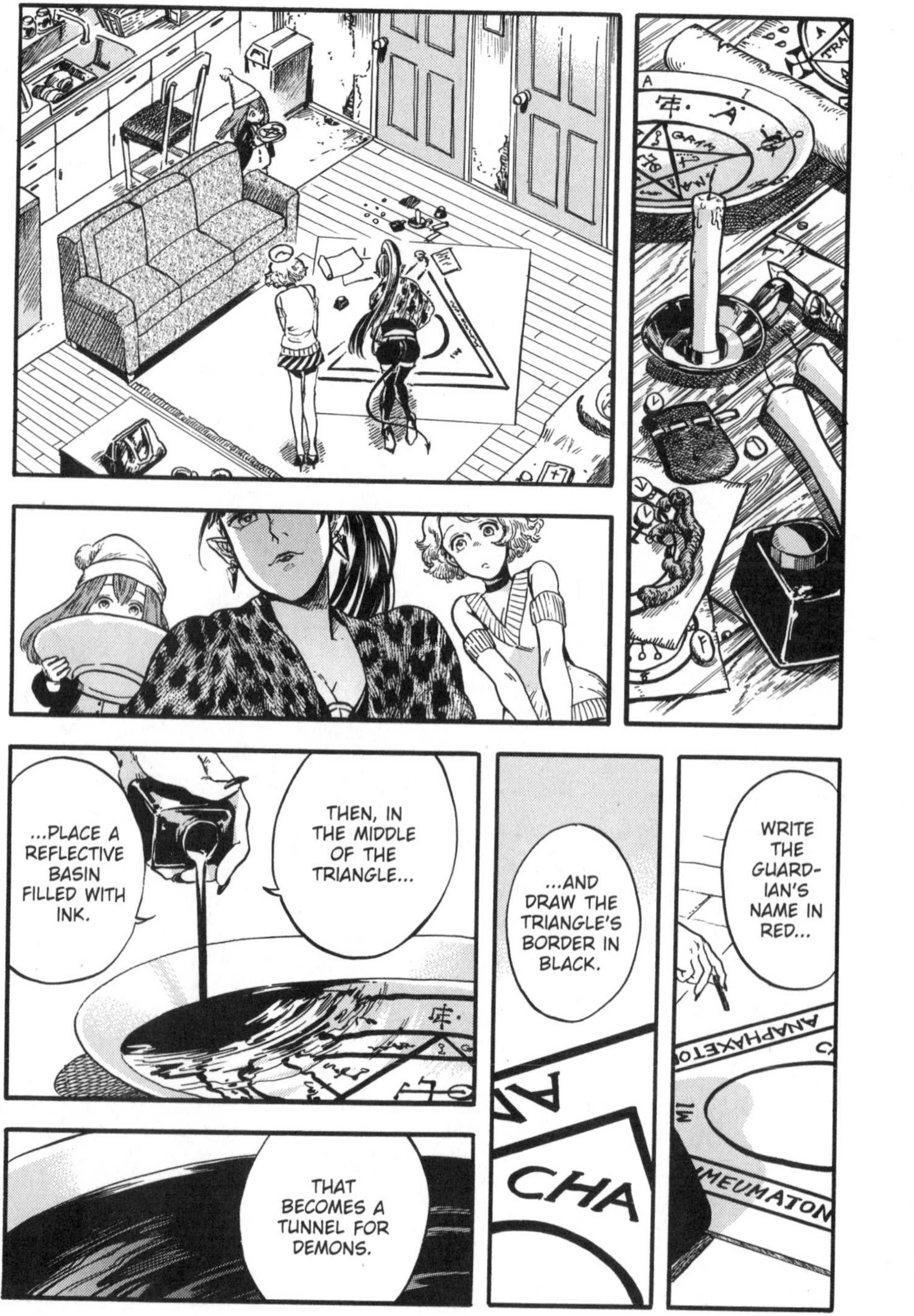
WRITE THE GUARDIAN'S NAME IN RED...
ANAPHAXETON
CHA
...AND DRAW THE TRIANGLE'S BORDER IN BLACK.
THEN, IN THE MIDDLE OF THE TRIANGLE...
...PLACE A REFLECTIVE BASIN FILLED WITH INK.
THAT BECOMES A TUNNEL FOR DEMONS.

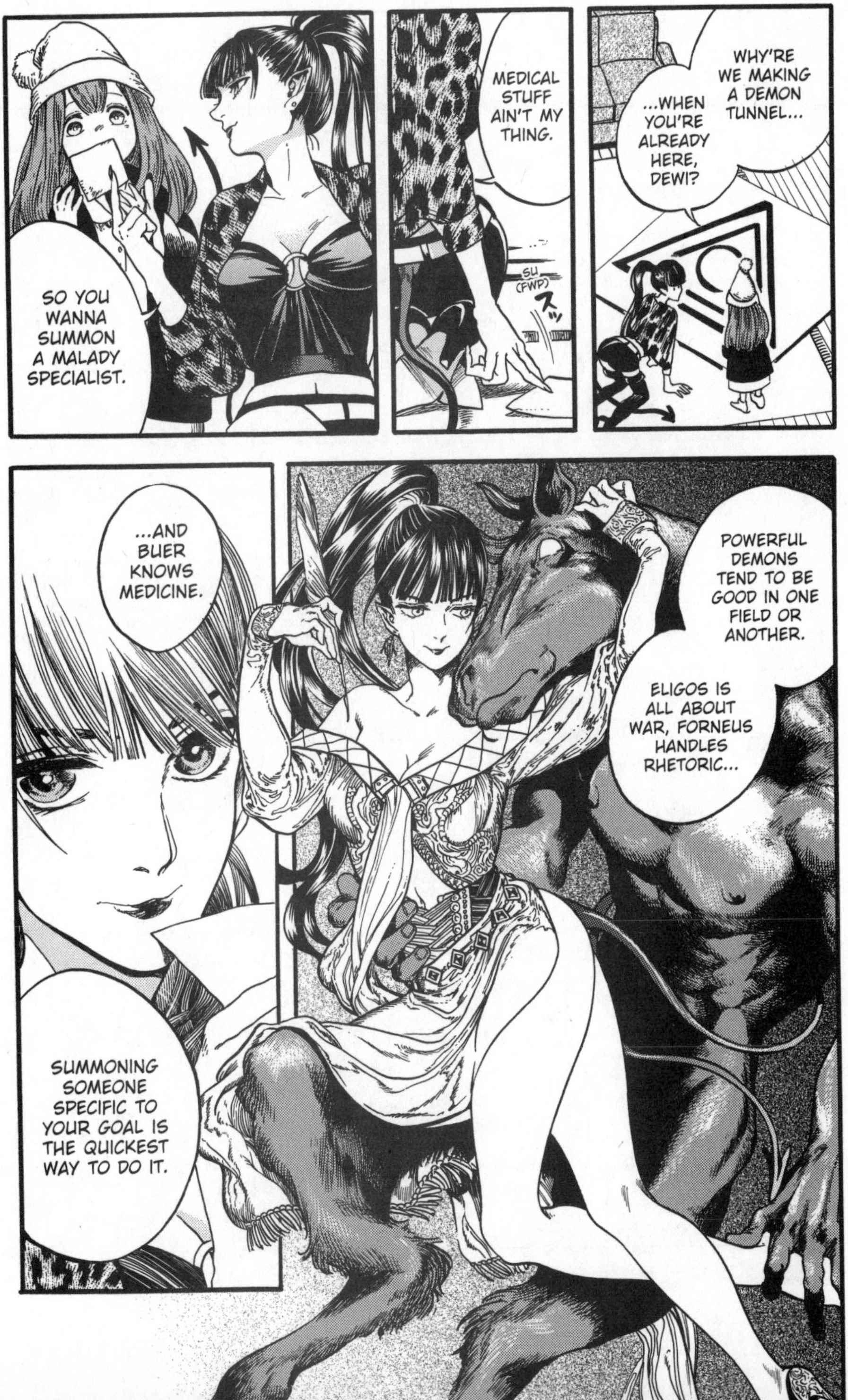
WHY'RE WE MAKING A DEMON TUNNEL...
...WHEN YOU'RE ALREADY HERE, DEWI?
MEDICAL STUFF AIN'T MY THING.
SU (FWP)
スッ
SO YOU WANNA SUMMON A MALADY SPECIALIST.
POWERFUL DEMONS TEND TO BE GOOD IN ONE FIELD OR ANOTHER.
ELIGOS IS ALL ABOUT WAR, FORNEUS HANDLES RHETORIC...
...AND BUER KNOWS MEDICINE.
SUMMONING SOMEONE SPECIFIC TO YOUR GOAL IS THE QUICKEST WAY TO DO IT.

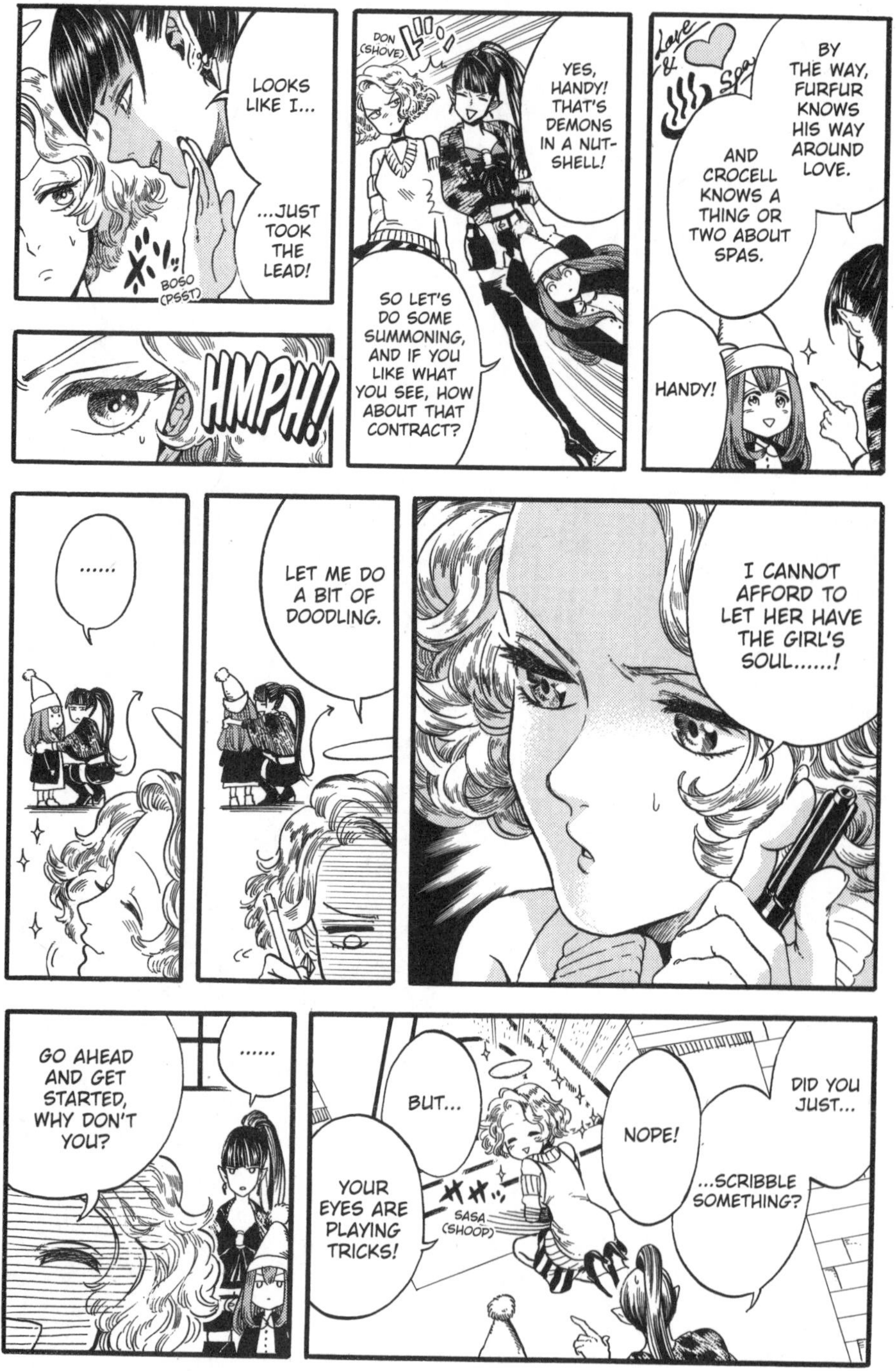

BY THE WAY, FURFUR KNOWS HIS WAY AROUND LOVE.
Love &
Spa
AND CROCELL KNOWS A THING OR TWO ABOUT SPAS.
HANDY!
DON (SHOVE)
YES, HANDY! THAT'S DEMONS IN A NUT-SHELL!
SO LET'S DO SOME SUMMONING, AND IF YOU LIKE WHAT YOU SEE, HOW ABOUT THAT CONTRACT?
LOOKS LIKE I...
...JUST TOOK THE LEAD!
BOSO (PSST)
HMPH!!
I CANNOT AFFORD TO LET HER HAVE THE GIRL'S SOUL......!
LET ME DO A BIT OF DOODLING.
......
DID YOU JUST...
...SCRIBBLE SOMETHING?
NOPE!
BUT...
YOUR EYES ARE PLAYING TRICKS!
SASA (SHOOP)
......
GO AHEAD AND GET STARTED, WHY DON'T YOU?

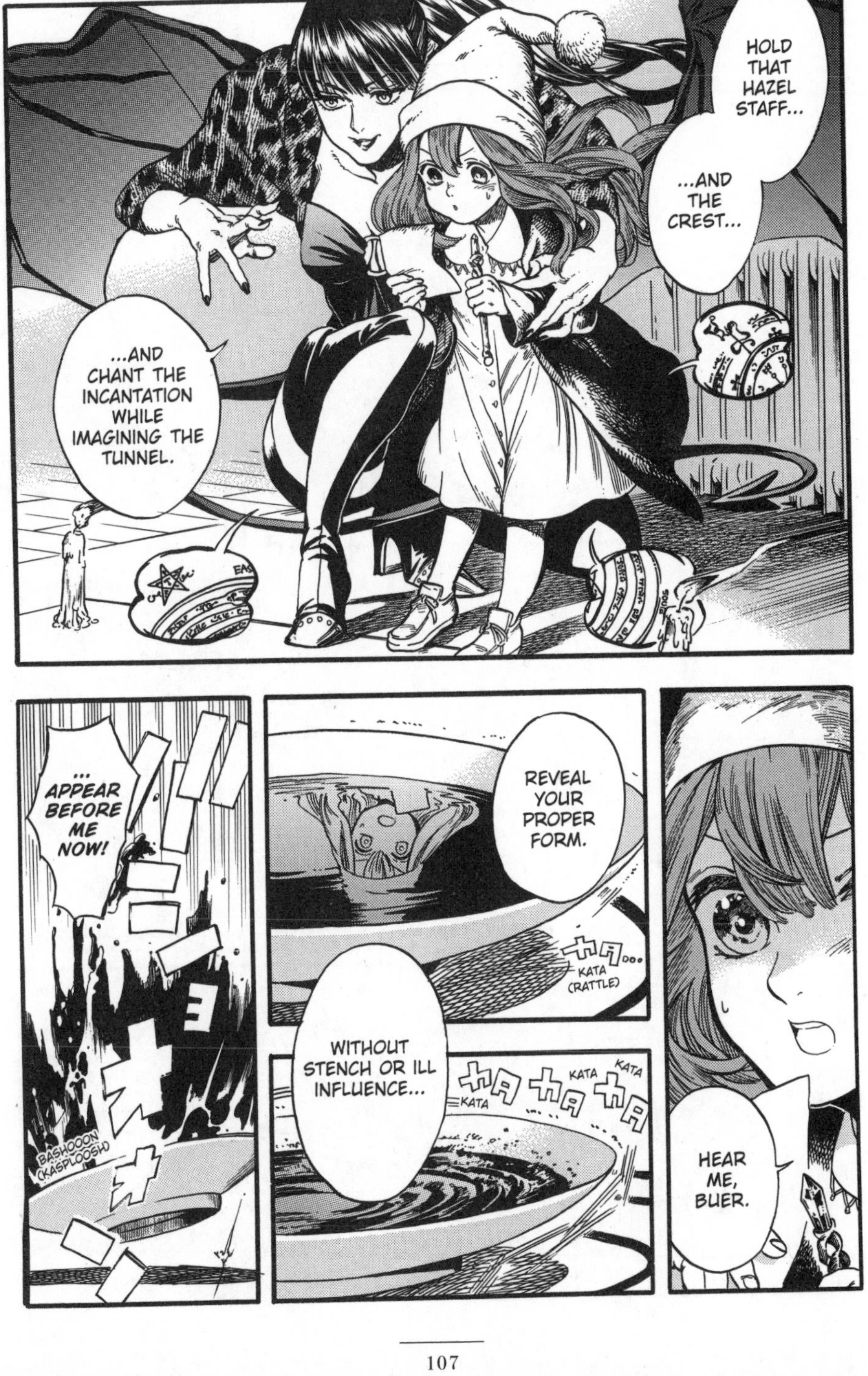
HOLD THAT HAZEL STAFF...
...AND THE CREST...
...AND CHANT THE INCANTATION WHILE IMAGINING THE TUNNEL.
HEAR ME, BUER.
REVEAL YOUR PROPER FORM.
KATA (RATTLE)
WITHOUT STENCH OR ILL INFLUENCE...
KATA
KATA
KATA
... APPEAR BEFORE ME NOW!
BASHOOON (KASPLOOSH)

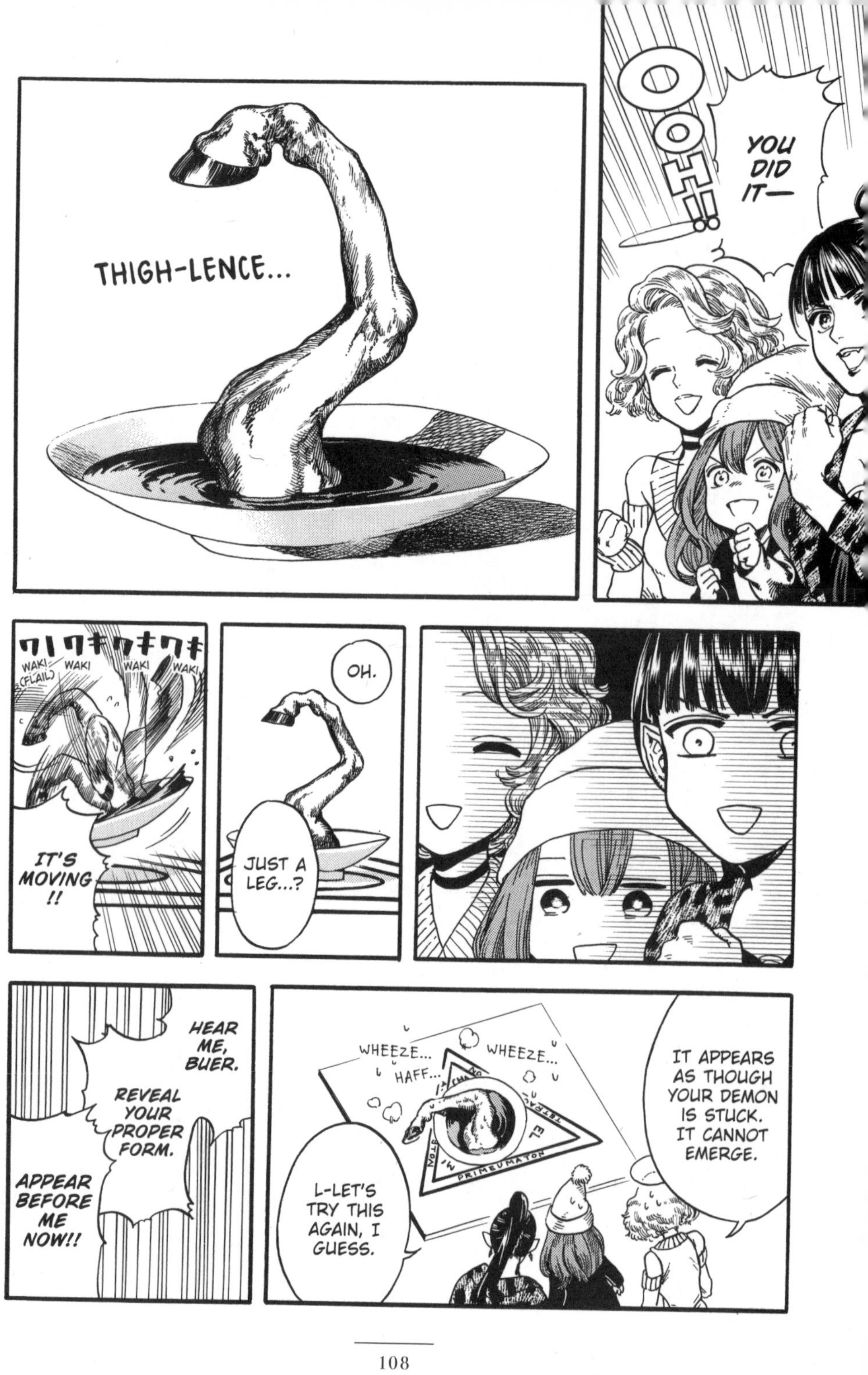
YOU DID IT—
OOOH!!
THIGH-LENCE...
OH.
JUST A LEG...?
ワキワキワキワキ
WAKI (FLAIL) WAKI WAKI WAKI
IT'S MOVING!!
IT APPEARS AS THOUGH YOUR DEMON IS STUCK. IT CANNOT EMERGE.
WHEEZE... WHEEZE...
HAFF...
PRIMEUMATON
L-LET'S TRY THIS AGAIN, I GUESS.
HEAR ME, BUER.
REVEAL YOUR PROPER FORM.
APPEAR BEFORE ME NOW!!

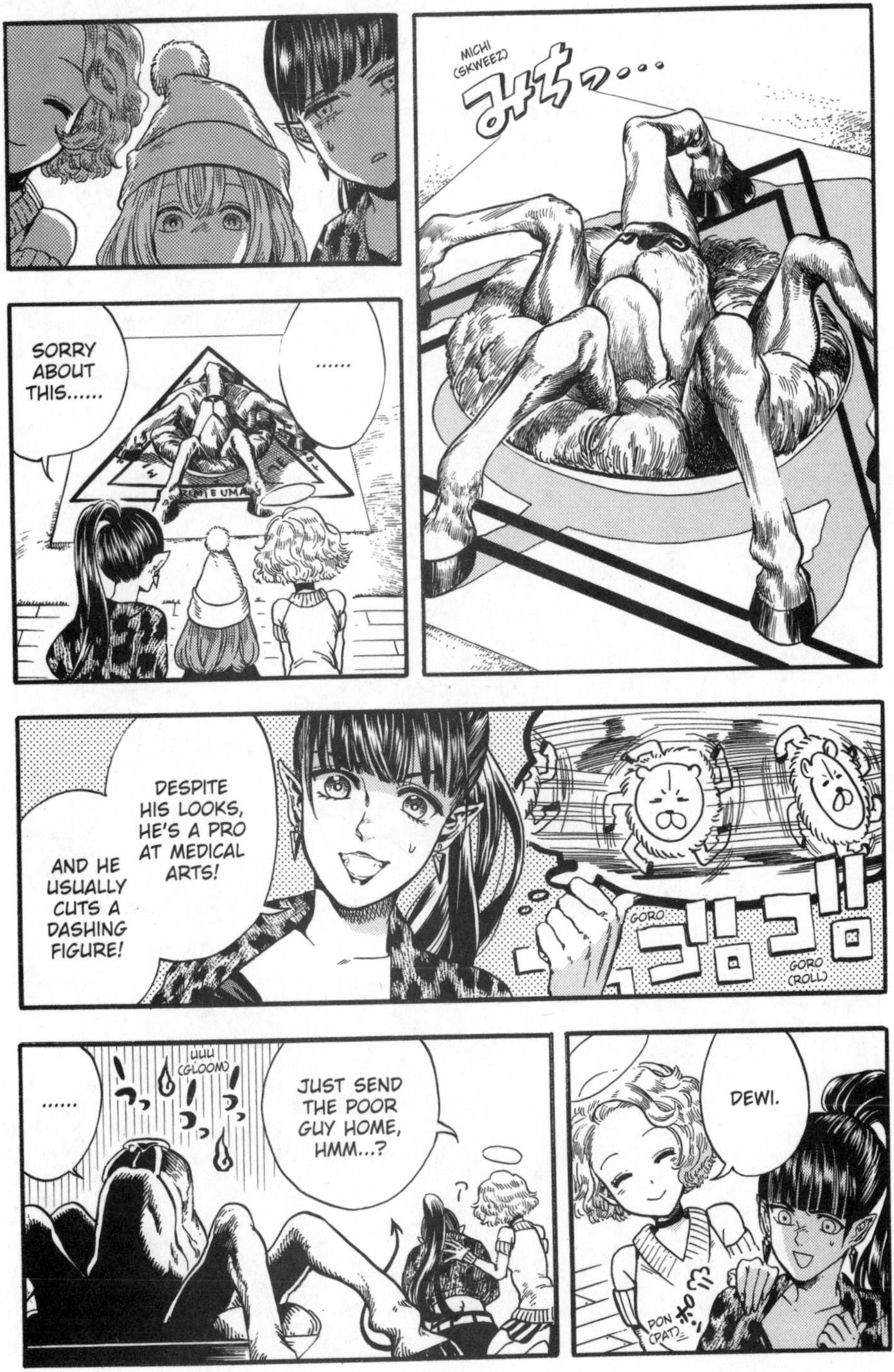
MICHI (SKWEEZ)
みちっ...
......
SORRY ABOUT THIS......
GORO GORO (ROLL)
DESPITE HIS LOOKS, HE'S A PRO AT MEDICAL ARTS!
AND HE USUALLY CUTS A DASHING FIGURE!
DEWI.
PON (PAT)
JUST SEND THE POOR GUY HOME, HMM...?
UUU (GLOOM)
......

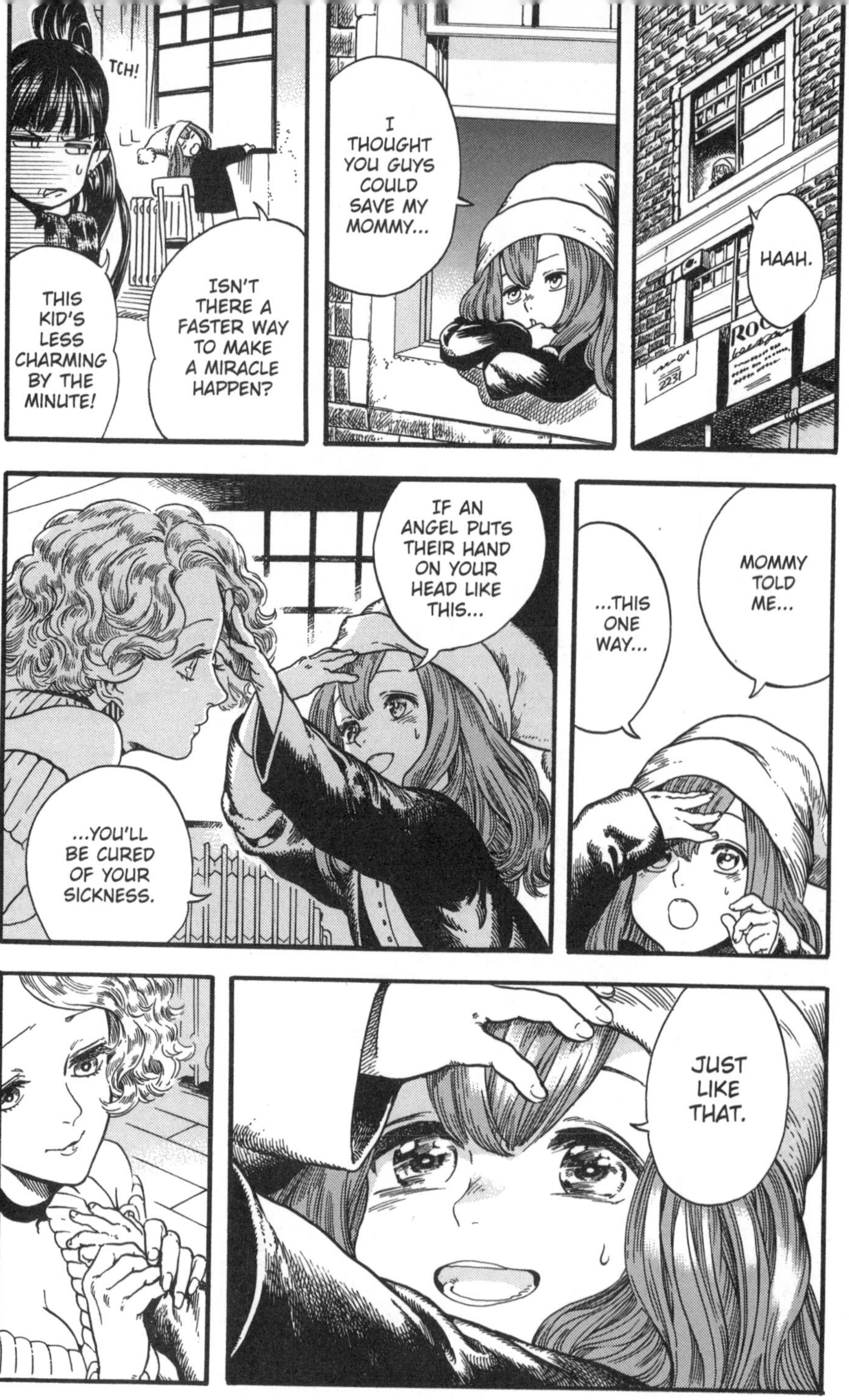
HAAH.
I THOUGHT YOU GUYS COULD SAVE MY MOMMY...
TCH!
ISN'T THERE A FASTER WAY TO MAKE A MIRACLE HAPPEN?
THIS KID'S LESS CHARMING BY THE MINUTE!
MOMMY TOLD ME...
...THIS ONE WAY...
IF AN ANGEL PUTS THEIR HAND ON YOUR HEAD LIKE THIS...
...YOU'LL BE CURED OF YOUR SICKNESS.
JUST LIKE THAT.

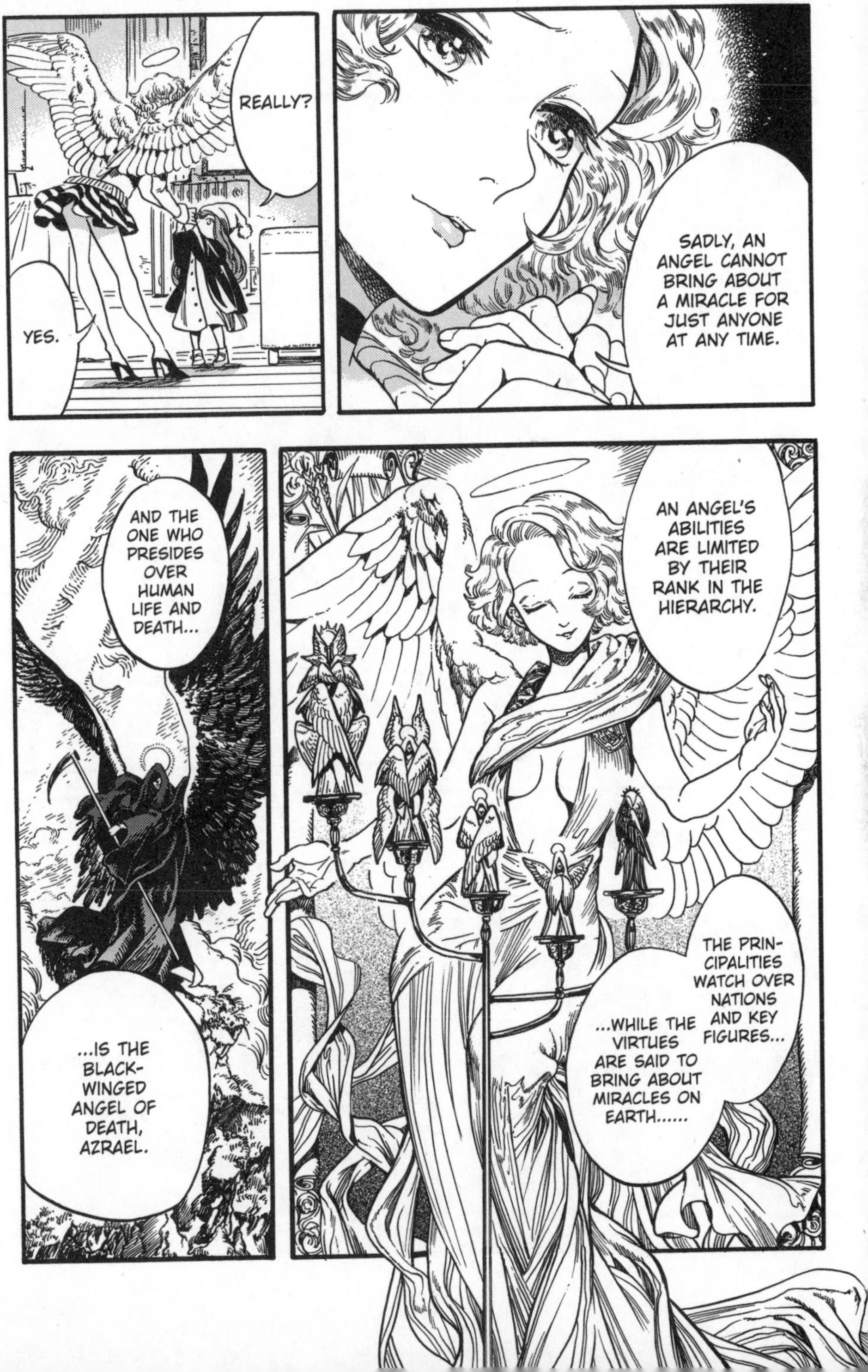
SADLY, AN ANGEL CANNOT BRING ABOUT A MIRACLE FOR JUST ANYONE AT ANY TIME.
REALLY?
YES.
AN ANGEL'S ABILITIES ARE LIMITED BY THEIR RANK IN THE HIERARCHY.
THE PRIN-CIPALITIES WATCH OVER NATIONS AND KEY FIGURES...
...WHILE THE VIRTUES ARE SAID TO BRING ABOUT MIRACLES ON EARTH......
AND THE ONE WHO PRESIDES OVER HUMAN LIFE AND DEATH...
...IS THE BLACK-WINGED ANGEL OF DEATH, AZRAEL.

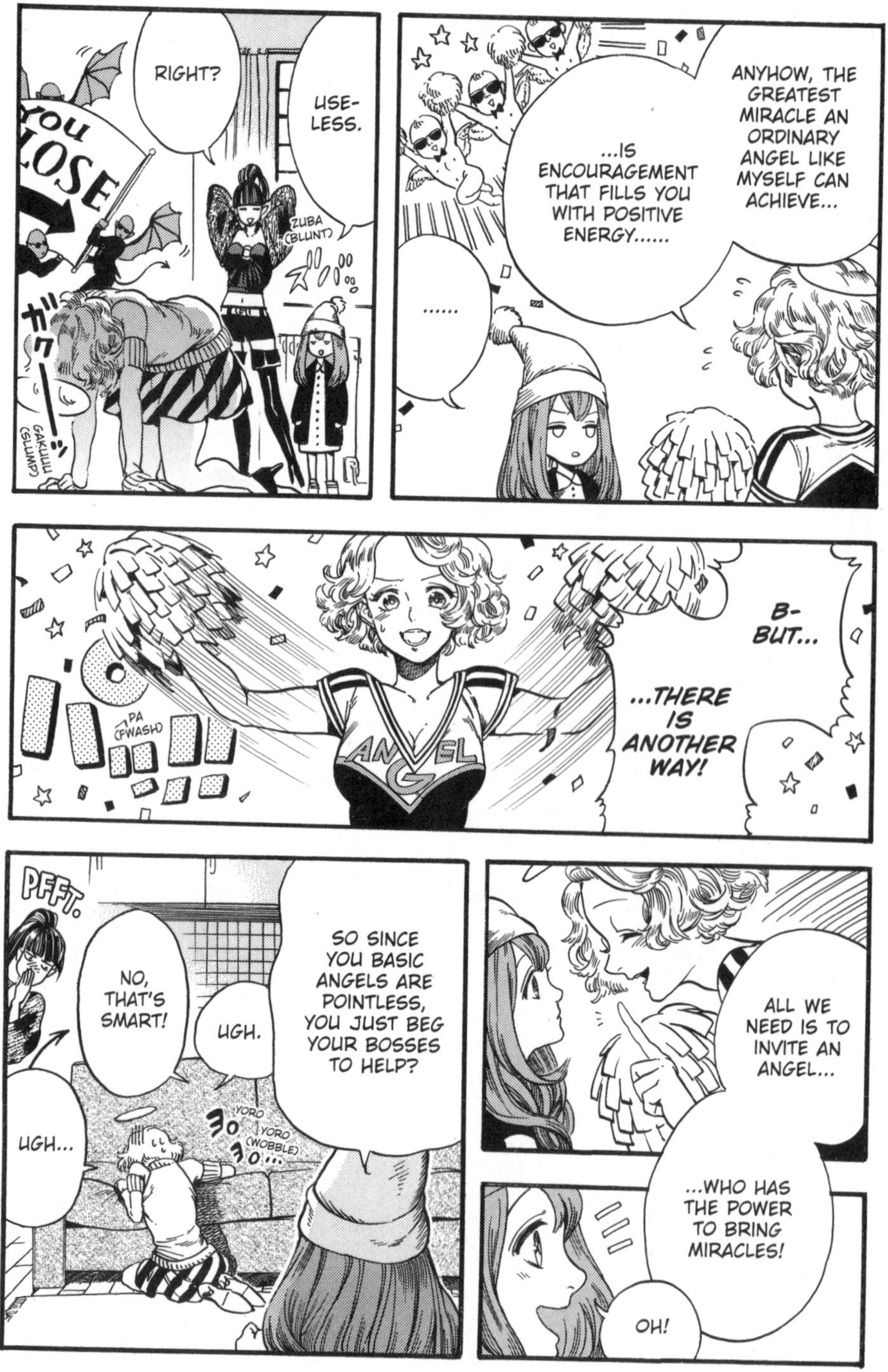
ANYHOW, THE GREATEST MIRACLE AN ORDINARY ANGEL LIKE MYSELF CAN ACHIEVE...
...IS ENCOURAGEMENT THAT FILLS YOU WITH POSITIVE ENERGY......
......
USE-LESS.
RIGHT?
ZUBA (BLUNT)
YOU LOSE
GAKUUUU (SLUMP)
B-BUT...
...THERE IS ANOTHER WAY!
PA (FWASH)
ANGEL
ALL WE NEED IS TO INVITE AN ANGEL...
...WHO HAS THE POWER TO BRING MIRACLES!
OH!
SO SINCE YOU BASIC ANGELS ARE POINTLESS, YOU JUST BEG YOUR BOSSES TO HELP?
UGH.
NO, THAT'S SMART!
PFFT.
UGH...
YORO YORO (WOBBLE)

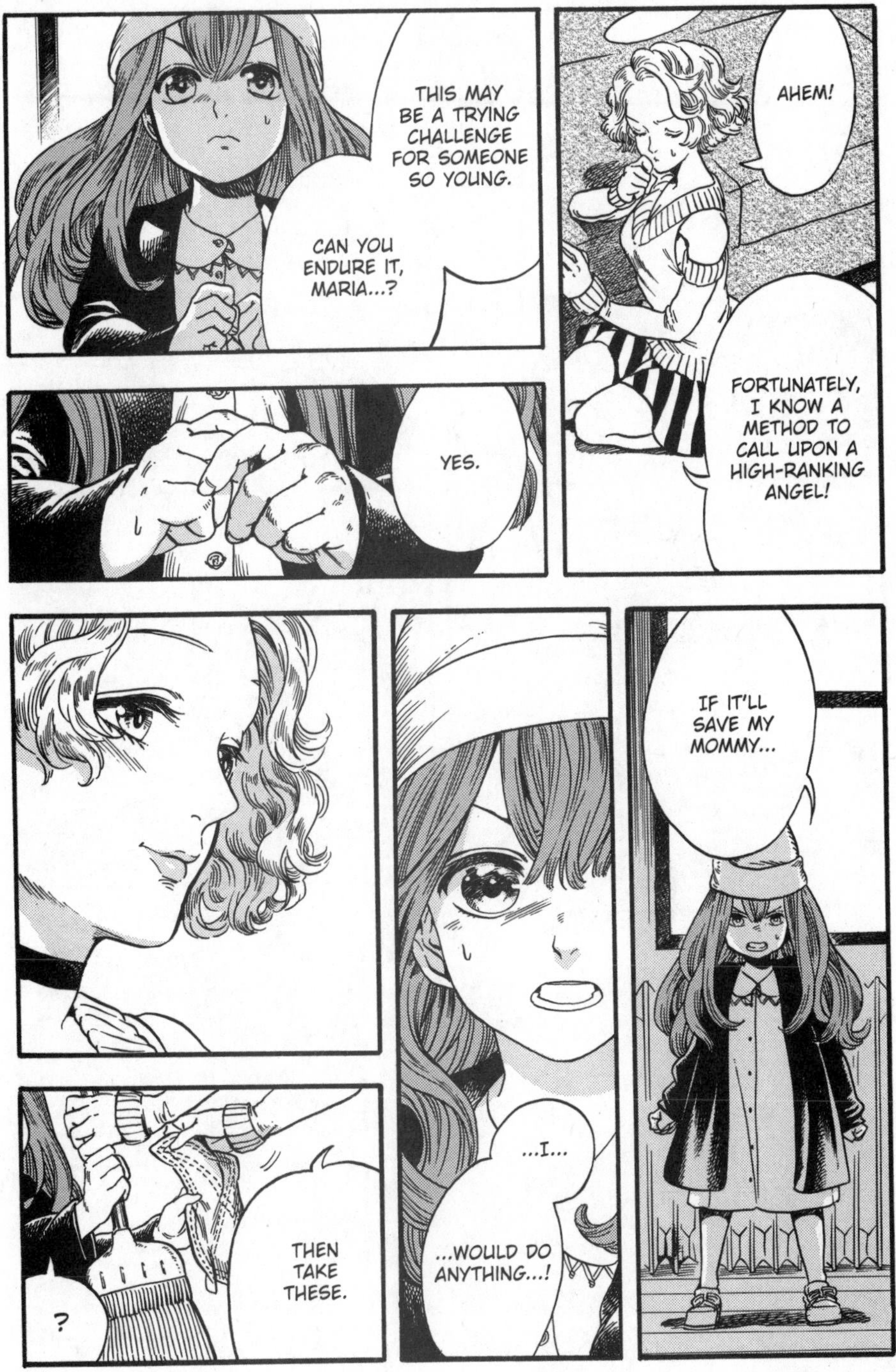
AHEM!
FORTUNATELY, I KNOW A METHOD TO CALL UPON A HIGH-RANKING ANGEL!
THIS MAY BE A TRYING CHALLENGE FOR SOMEONE SO YOUNG.
CAN YOU ENDURE IT, MARIA...?
YES.
IF IT'LL SAVE MY MOMMY...
...I...
...WOULD DO ANYTHING...!
THEN TAKE THESE.
?

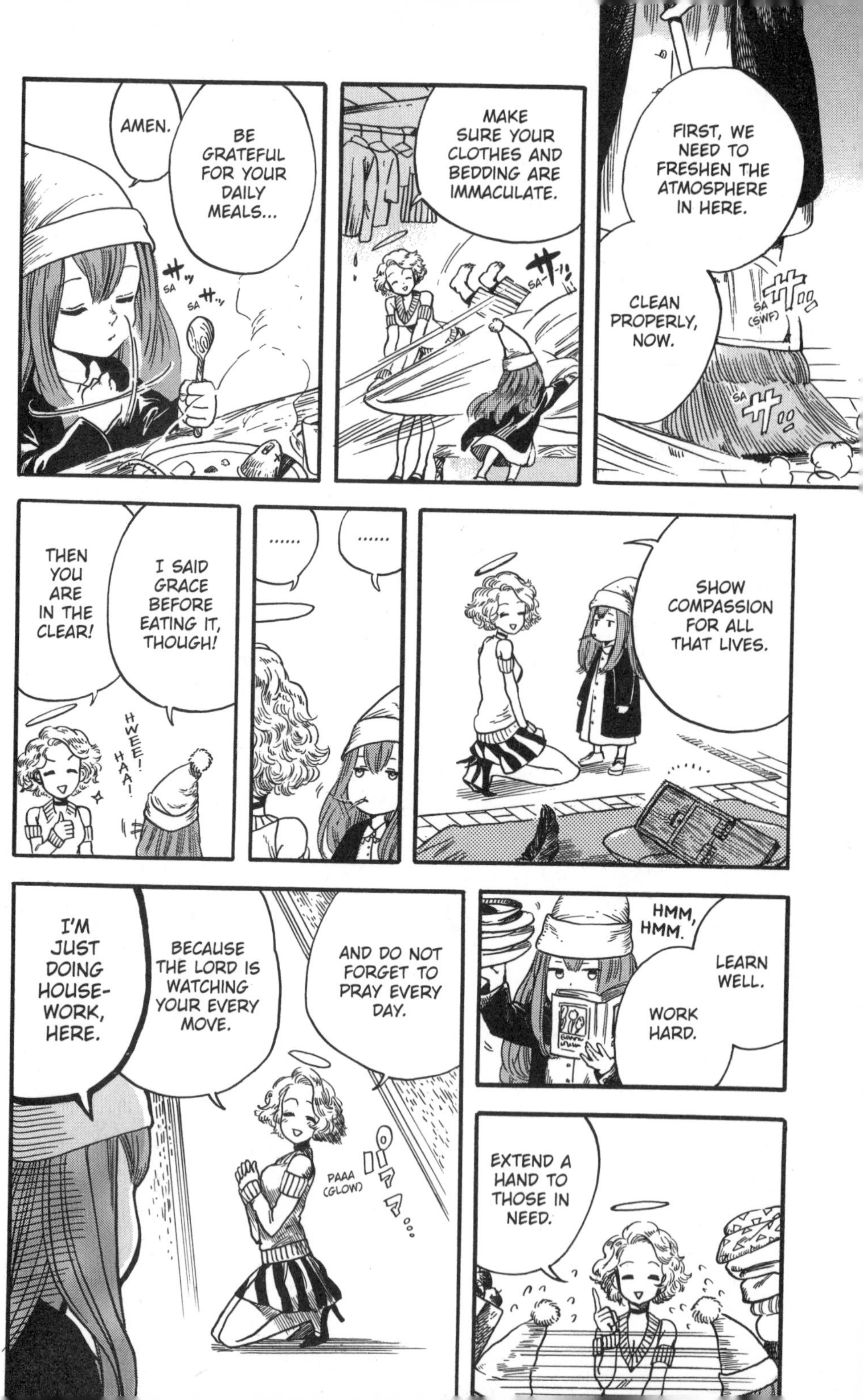
FIRST, WE NEED TO FRESHEN THE ATMOSPHERE IN HERE.
SA (SWF)
CLEAN PROPERLY, NOW.
SA
MAKE SURE YOUR CLOTHES AND BEDDING ARE IMMACULATE.
SA-
BE GRATEFUL FOR YOUR DAILY MEALS...
AMEN.
SA
SA
SHOW COMPASSION FOR ALL THAT LIVES.
......
......
I SAID GRACE BEFORE EATING IT, THOUGH!
THEN YOU ARE IN THE CLEAR!
HWEE! HAA!
HMM, HMM.
LEARN WELL.
WORK HARD.
EXTEND A HAND TO THOSE IN NEED.
AND DO NOT FORGET TO PRAY EVERY DAY.
BECAUSE THE LORD IS WATCHING YOUR EVERY MOVE.
PAAA (GLOW)
I'M JUST DOING HOUSE-WORK, HERE.

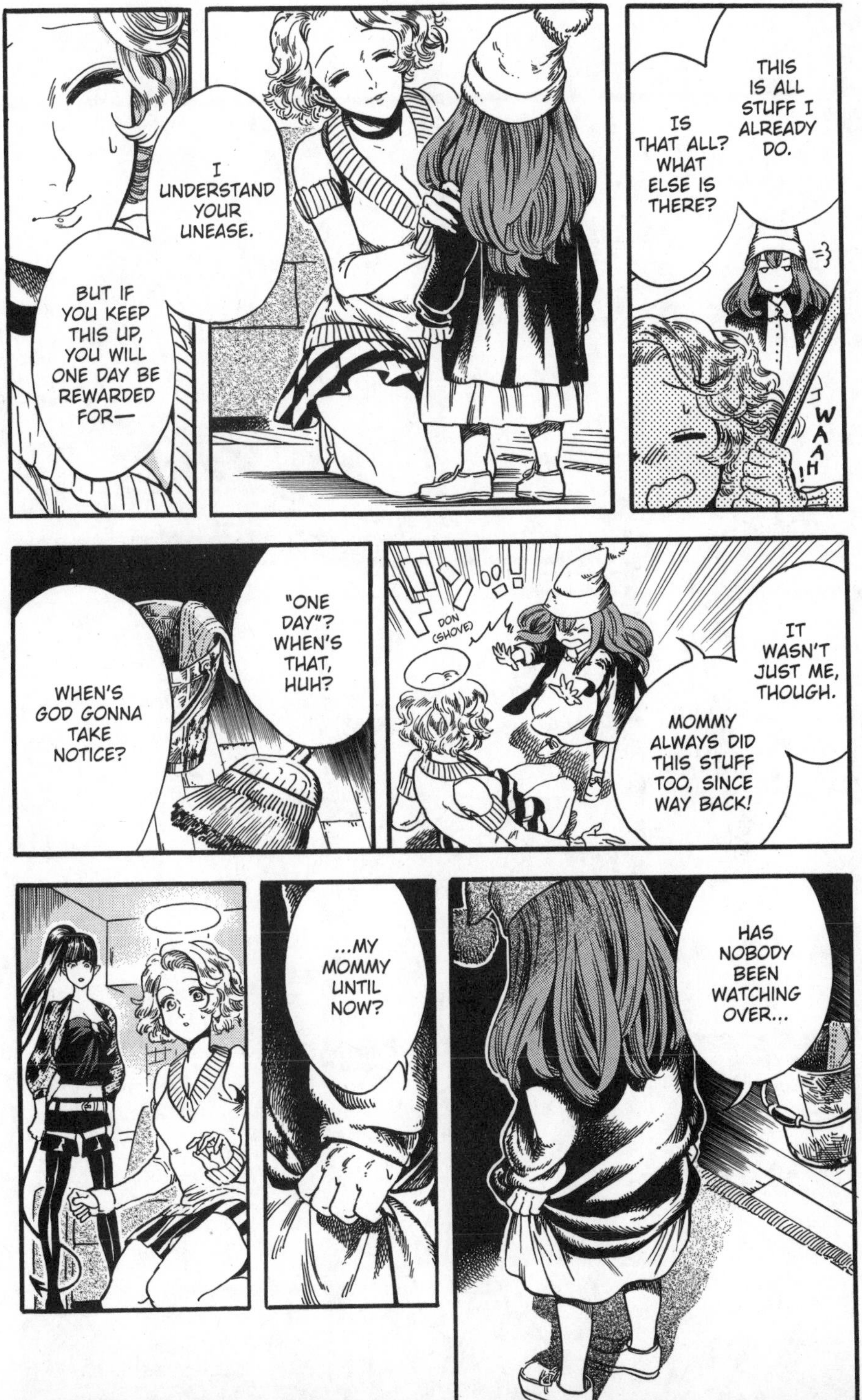
THIS IS ALL STUFF I ALREADY DO.
IS THAT ALL? WHAT ELSE IS THERE?
WAAAH!
I UNDERSTAND YOUR UNEASE.
BUT IF YOU KEEP THIS UP, YOU WILL ONE DAY BE REWARDED FOR—
IT WASN'T JUST ME, THOUGH.
MOMMY ALWAYS DID THIS STUFF TOO, SINCE WAY BACK!
DON (SHOVE)
"ONE DAY"? WHEN'S THAT, HUH?
WHEN'S GOD GONNA TAKE NOTICE?
HAS NOBODY BEEN WATCHING OVER...
...MY MOMMY UNTIL NOW?

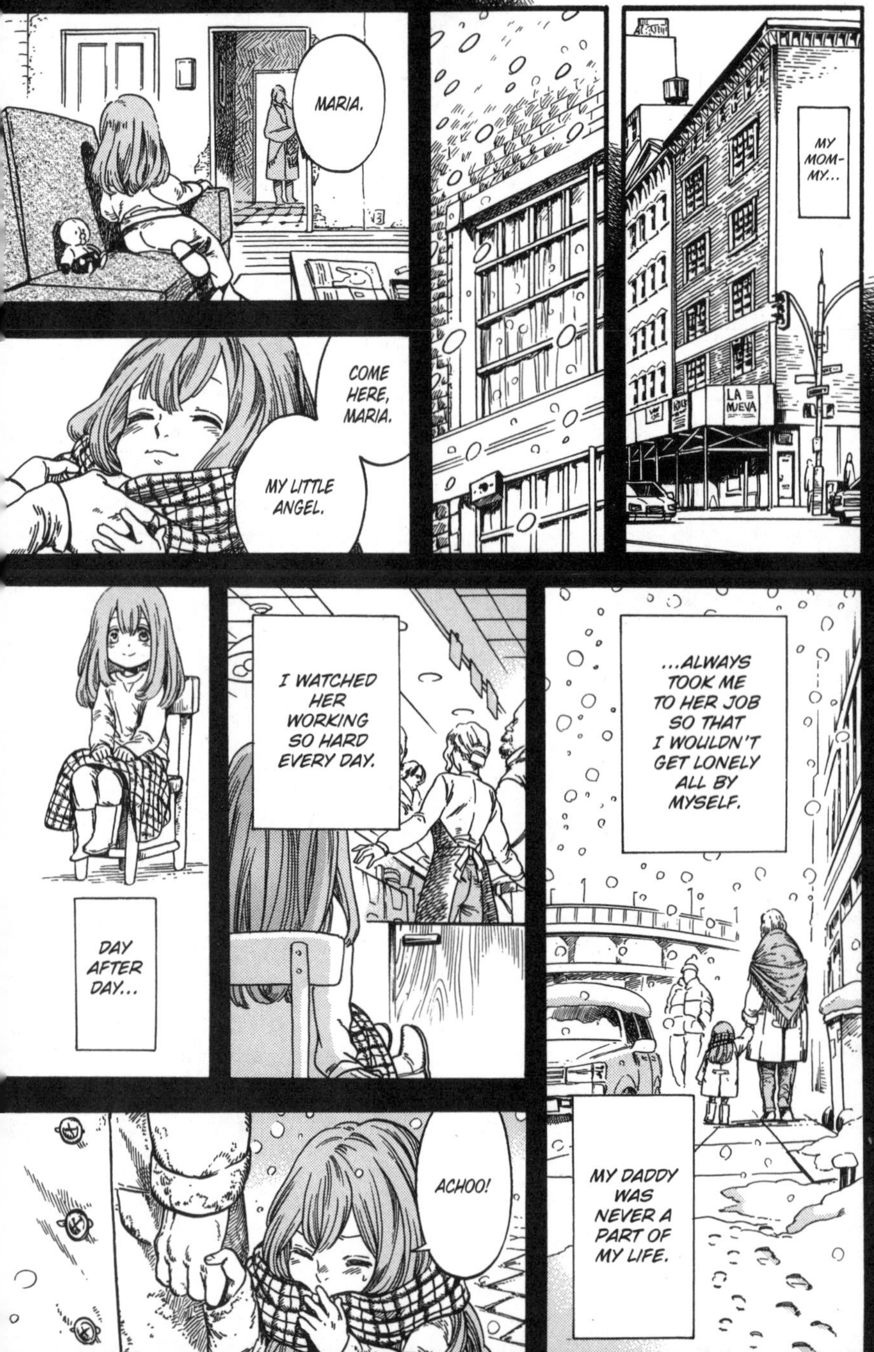
MY MOMMY...
MARIA.
COME HERE, MARIA.
MY LITTLE ANGEL.
...ALWAYS TOOK ME TO HER JOB SO THAT I WOULDN'T GET LONELY ALL BY MYSELF.
MY DADDY WAS NEVER A PART OF MY LIFE.
I WATCHED HER WORKING SO HARD EVERY DAY.
DAY AFTER DAY...
ACHOO!

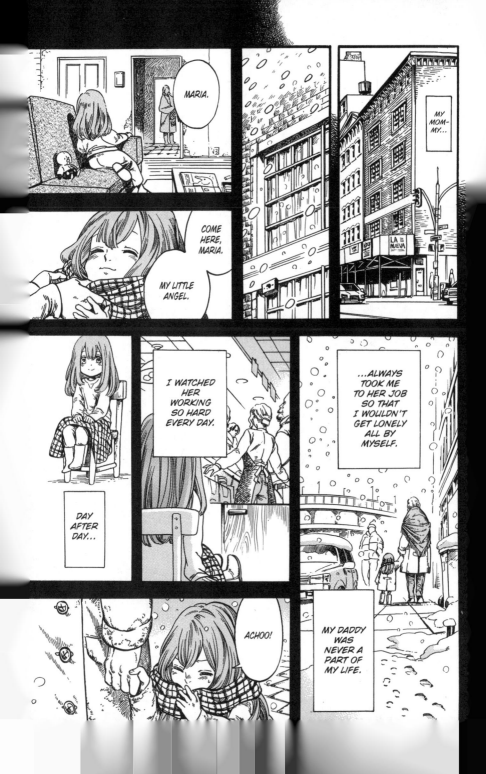

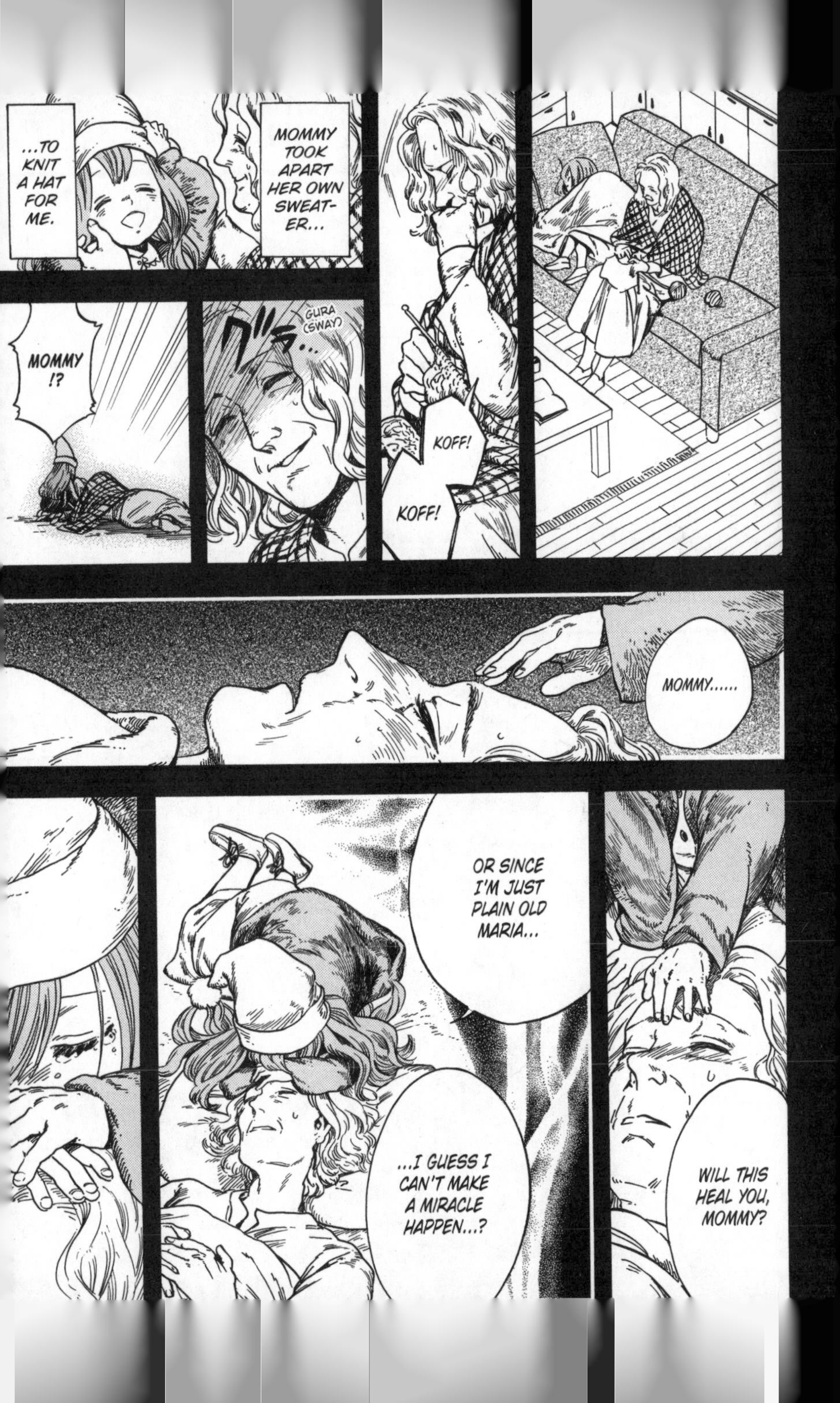
KOFF!
KOFF!
MOMMY TOOK APART HER OWN SWEATER...
...TO KNIT A HAT FOR ME.
GURA (SWAY)
MOMMY !?
MOMMY......
WILL THIS HEAL YOU, MOMMY?
OR SINCE I'M JUST PLAIN OLD MARIA...
...I GUESS I CAN'T MAKE A MIRACLE HAPPEN...?

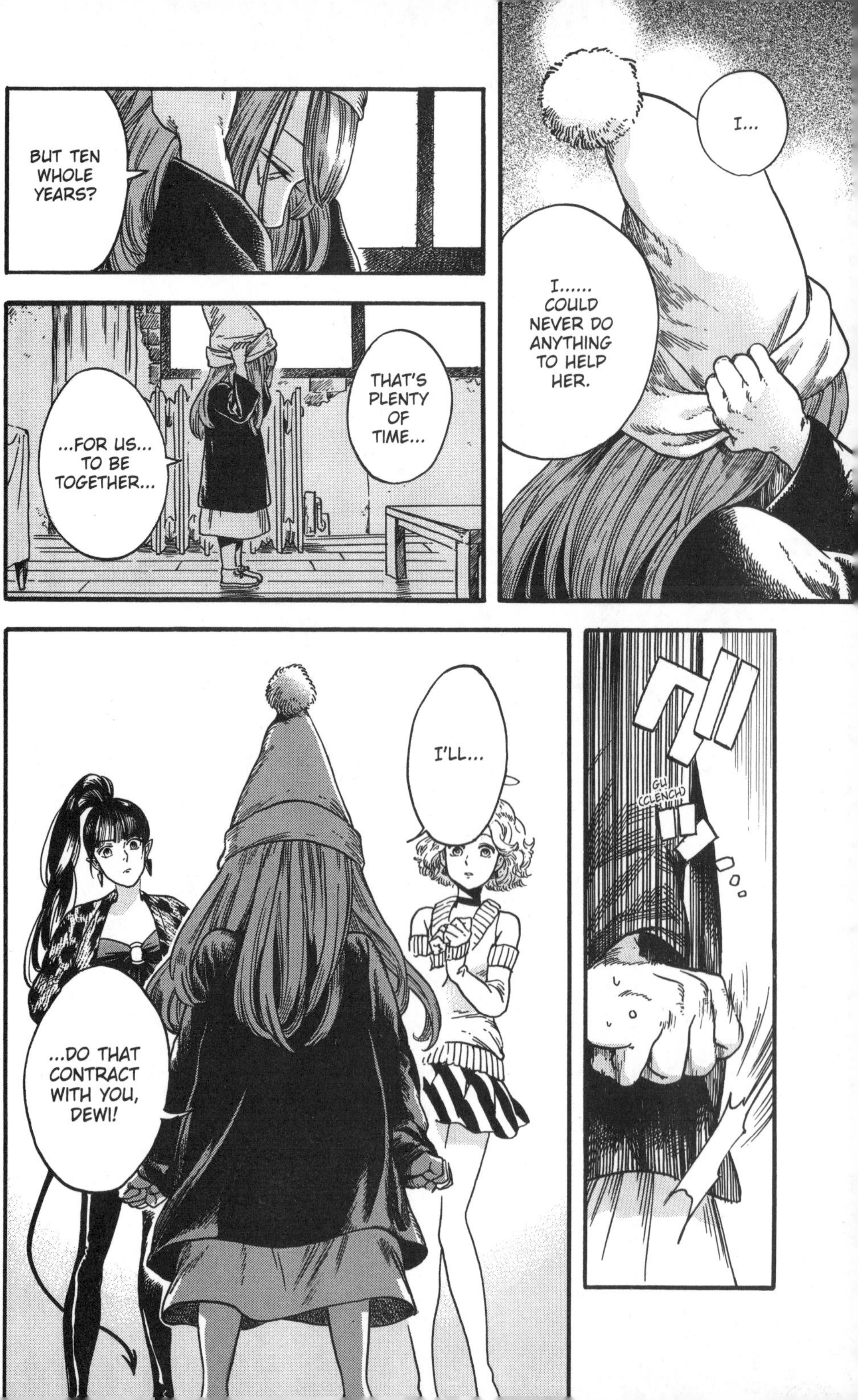
I...
I...... COULD NEVER DO ANYTHING TO HELP HER.
BUT TEN WHOLE YEARS?
THAT'S PLENTY OF TIME...
...FOR US... TO BE TOGETHER...
GU (CLENCH)
I'LL...
...DO THAT CONTRACT WITH YOU, DEWI!

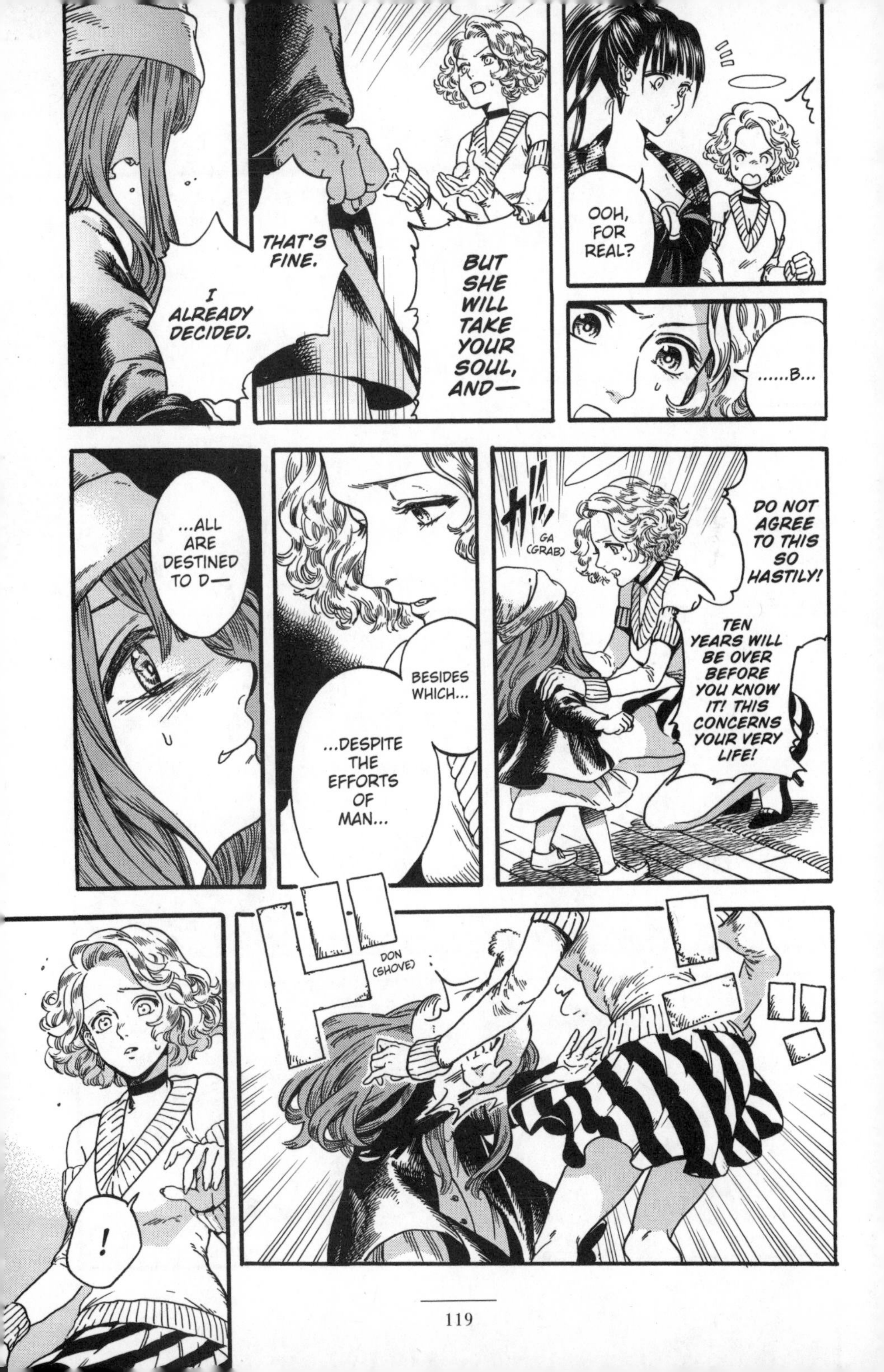
OOH, FOR REAL?
......B...
BUT SHE WILL TAKE YOUR SOUL, AND—
THAT'S FINE.
I ALREADY DECIDED.
GA (GRAB)
DO NOT AGREE TO THIS SO HASTILY!
TEN YEARS WILL BE OVER BEFORE YOU KNOW IT! THIS CONCERNS YOUR VERY LIFE!
BESIDES WHICH...
...DESPITE THE EFFORTS OF MAN...
...ALL ARE DESTINED TO D—
DON (SHOVE)
!

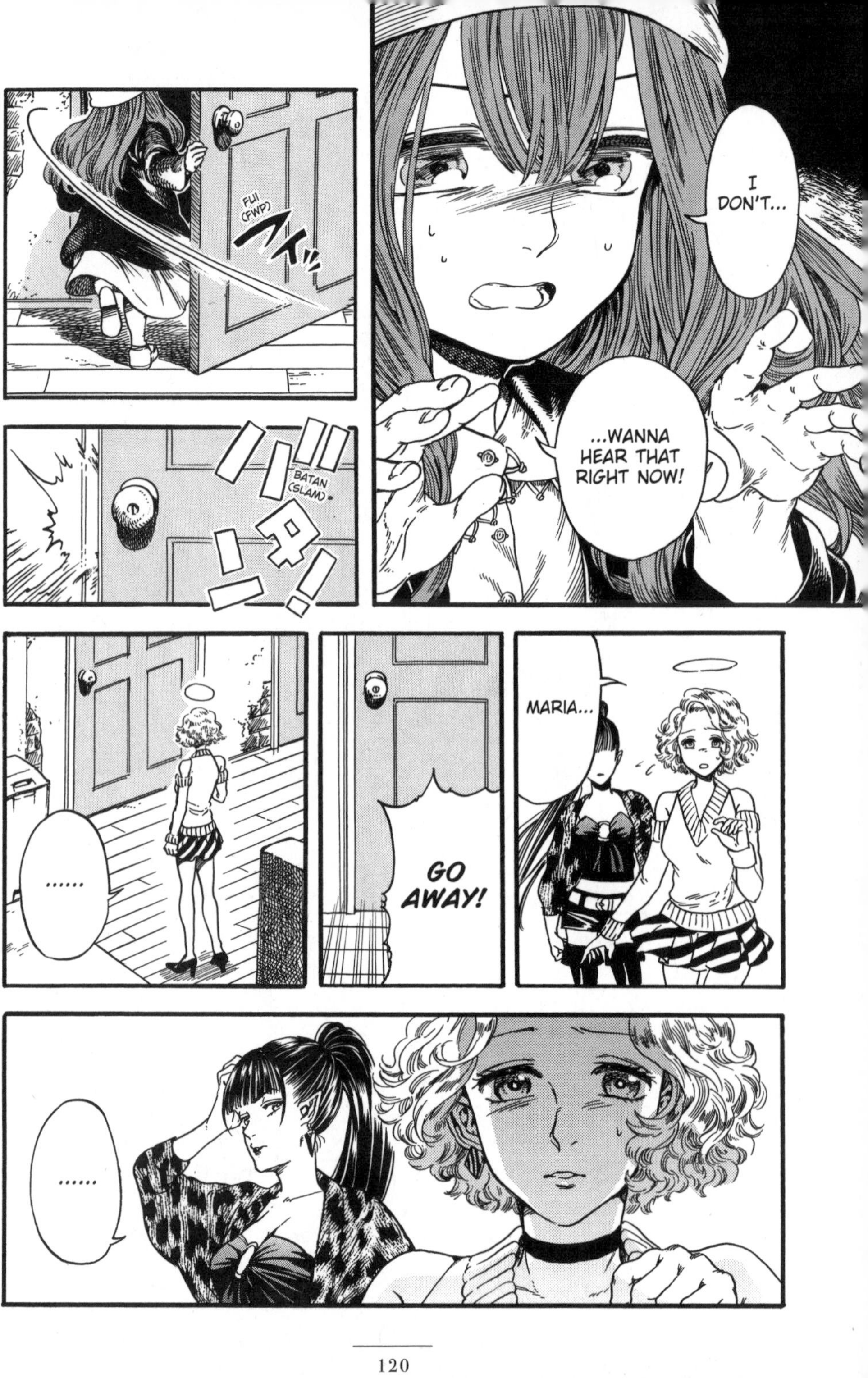
I DON'T...
...WANNA HEAR THAT RIGHT NOW!
FUI (FWP)
BATAN (SLAM)
MARIA...
GO AWAY!
......
......

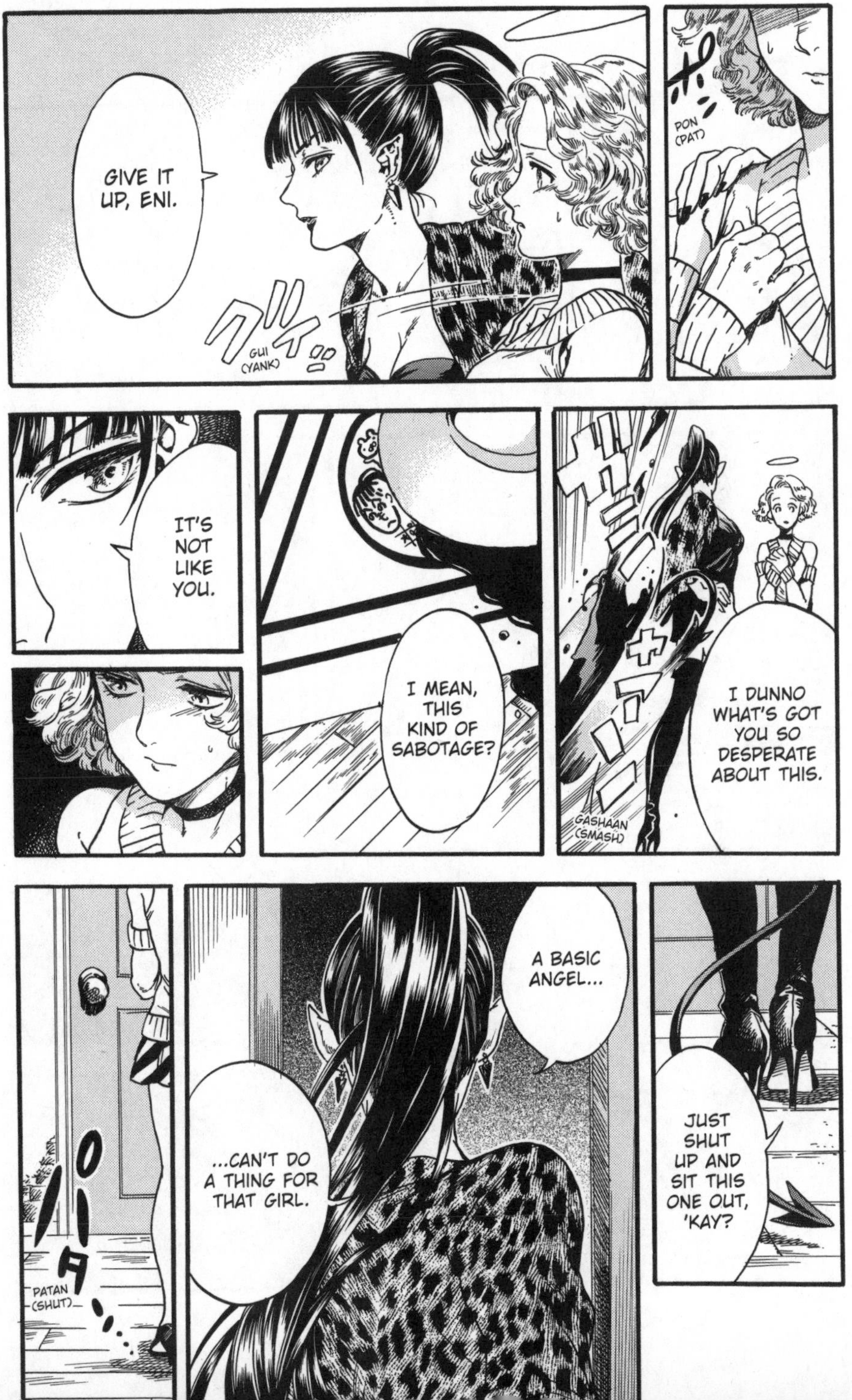
PON (PAT)
GIVE IT UP, ENI.
GUI (YANK)
GASHAAN (SMASH)
I DUNNO WHAT'S GOT YOU SO DESPERATE ABOUT THIS.
I MEAN, THIS KIND OF SABOTAGE?
IT'S NOT LIKE YOU.
JUST SHUT UP AND SIT THIS ONE OUT, 'KAY?
A BASIC ANGEL...
...CAN'T DO A THING FOR THAT GIRL.
PATAN (SHUT)

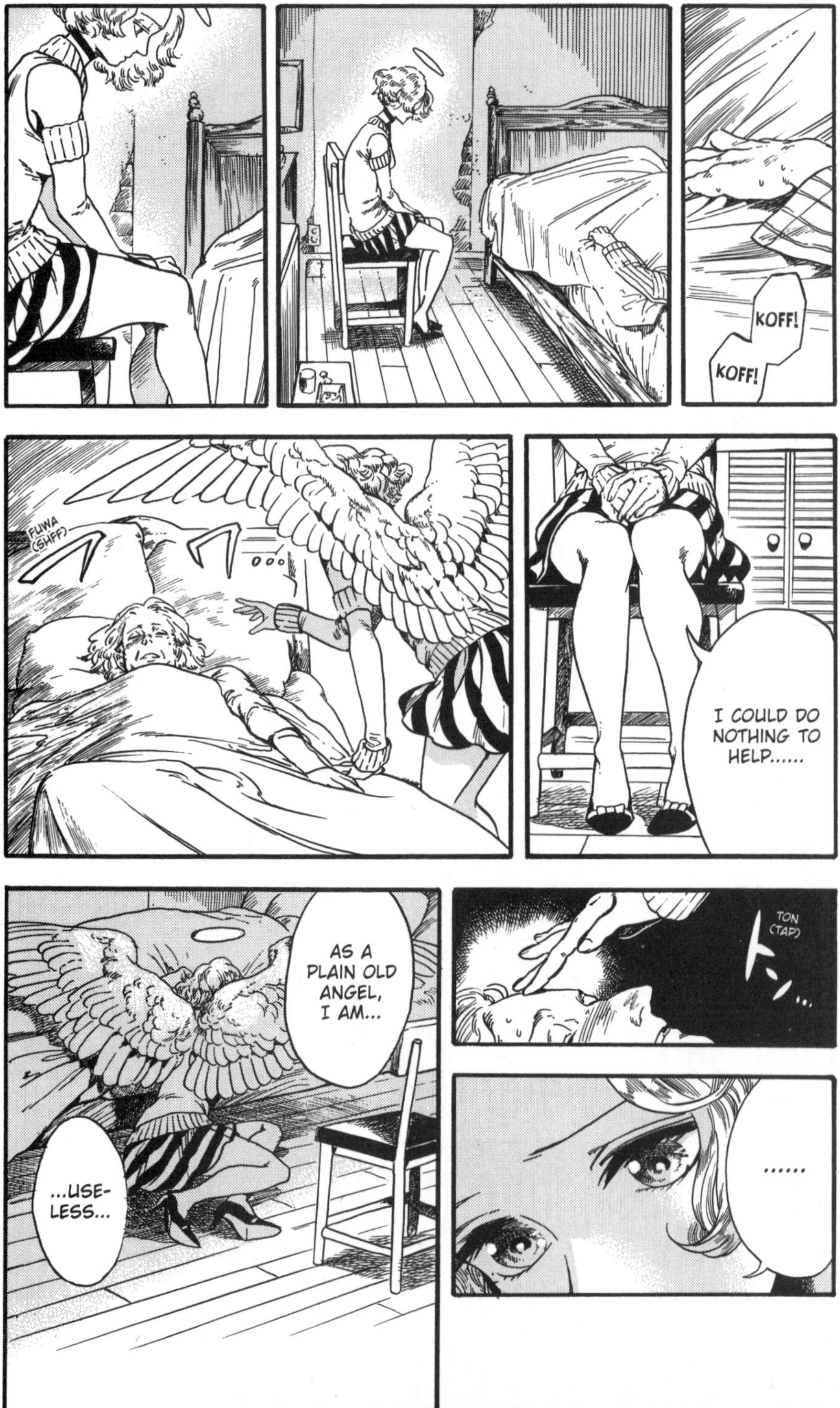
KOFF!
KOFF!
I COULD DO NOTHING TO HELP......
FUWA (SHFF)
TON (TAP)
......
AS A PLAIN OLD ANGEL, I AM...
...USE-LESS...

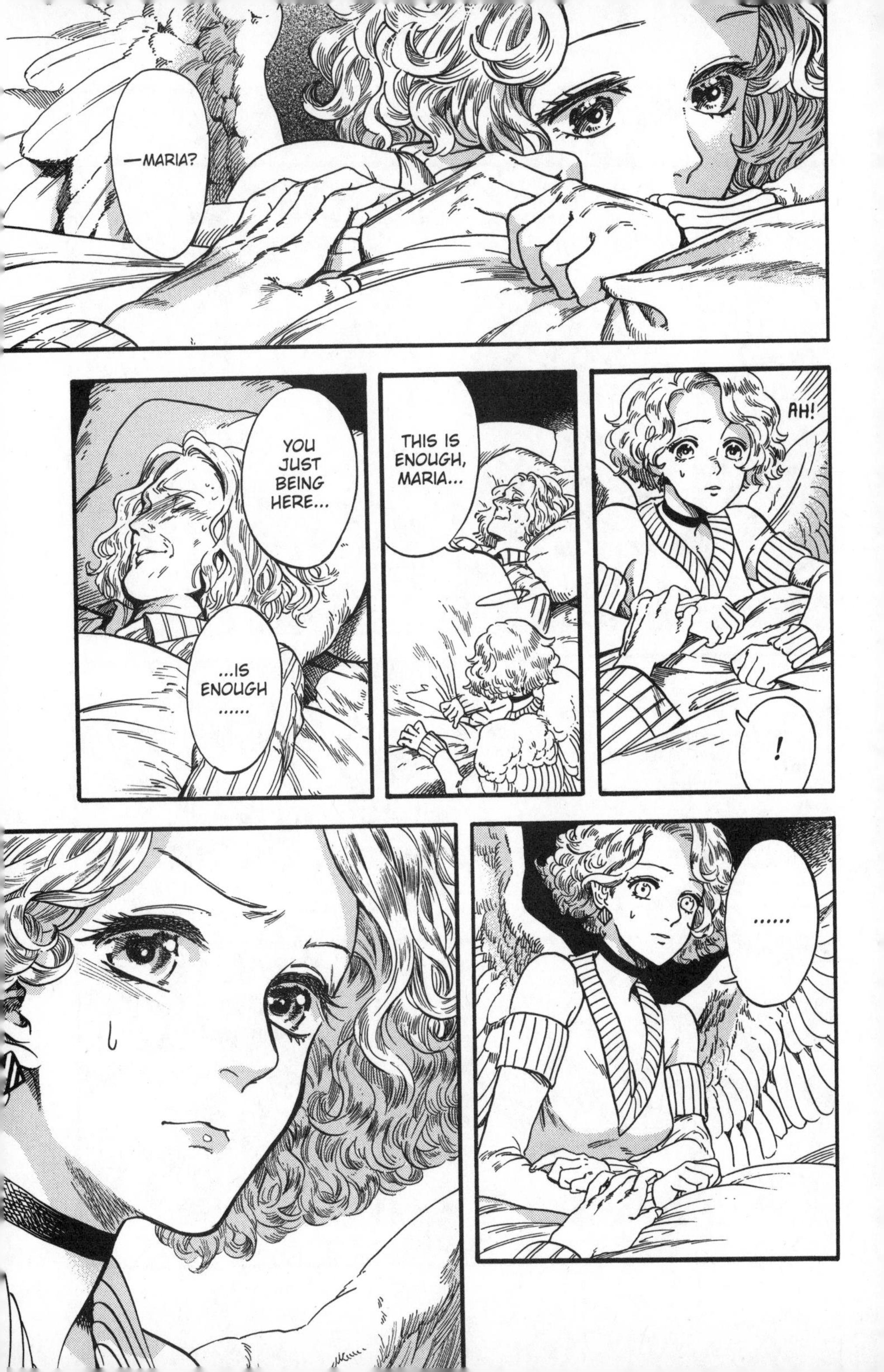
—MARIA?
AH!
!
THIS IS ENOUGH, MARIA...
YOU JUST BEING HERE...
...IS ENOUGH ......
......

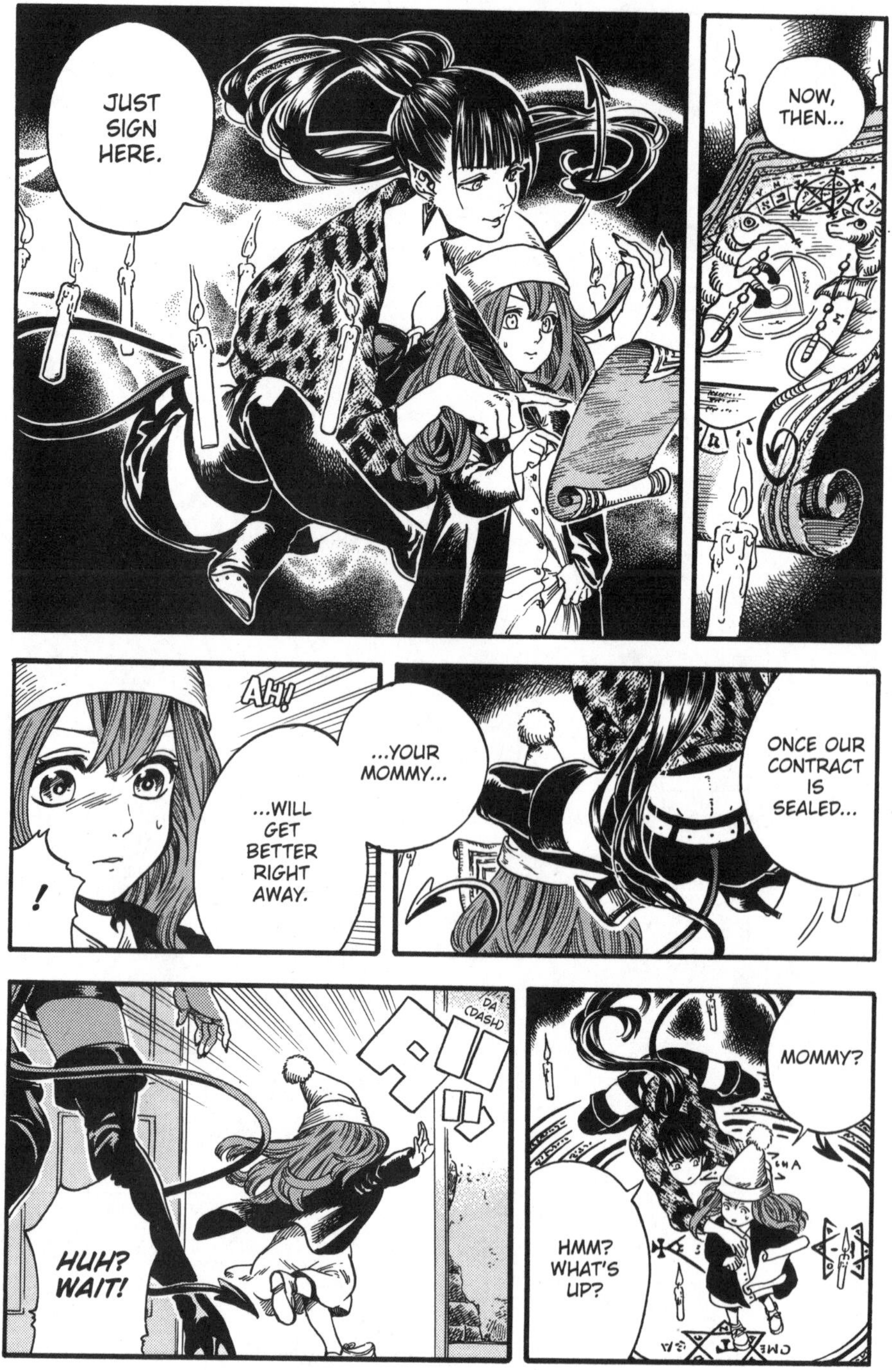
NOW, THEN...
JUST SIGN HERE.
ONCE OUR CONTRACT IS SEALED...
...YOUR MOMMY...
...WILL GET BETTER RIGHT AWAY.
AH!
!
MOMMY?
SHA
HMM? WHAT'S UP?
DA (DASH)
HUH? WAIT!

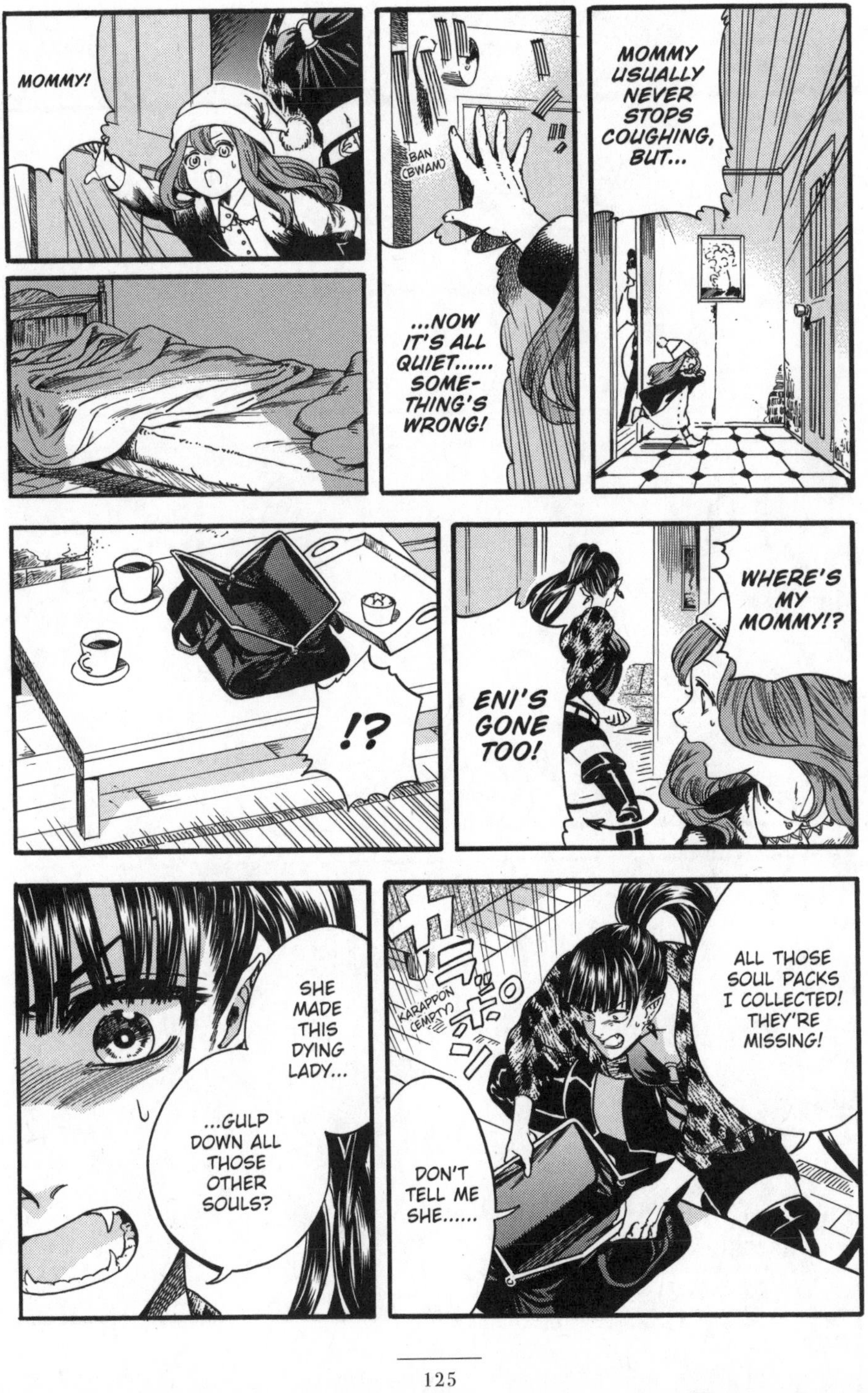
MOMMY USUALLY NEVER STOPS COUGHING, BUT...
BAN (BWAM)
...NOW IT'S ALL QUIET...... SOME-THING'S WRONG!
MOMMY!
WHERE'S MY MOMMY!?
ENI'S GONE TOO!
!?
ALL THOSE SOUL PACKS I COLLECTED! THEY'RE MISSING!
KARAPPON (EMPTY)
DON'T TELL ME SHE......
SHE MADE THIS DYING LADY...
...GULP DOWN ALL THOSE OTHER SOULS?

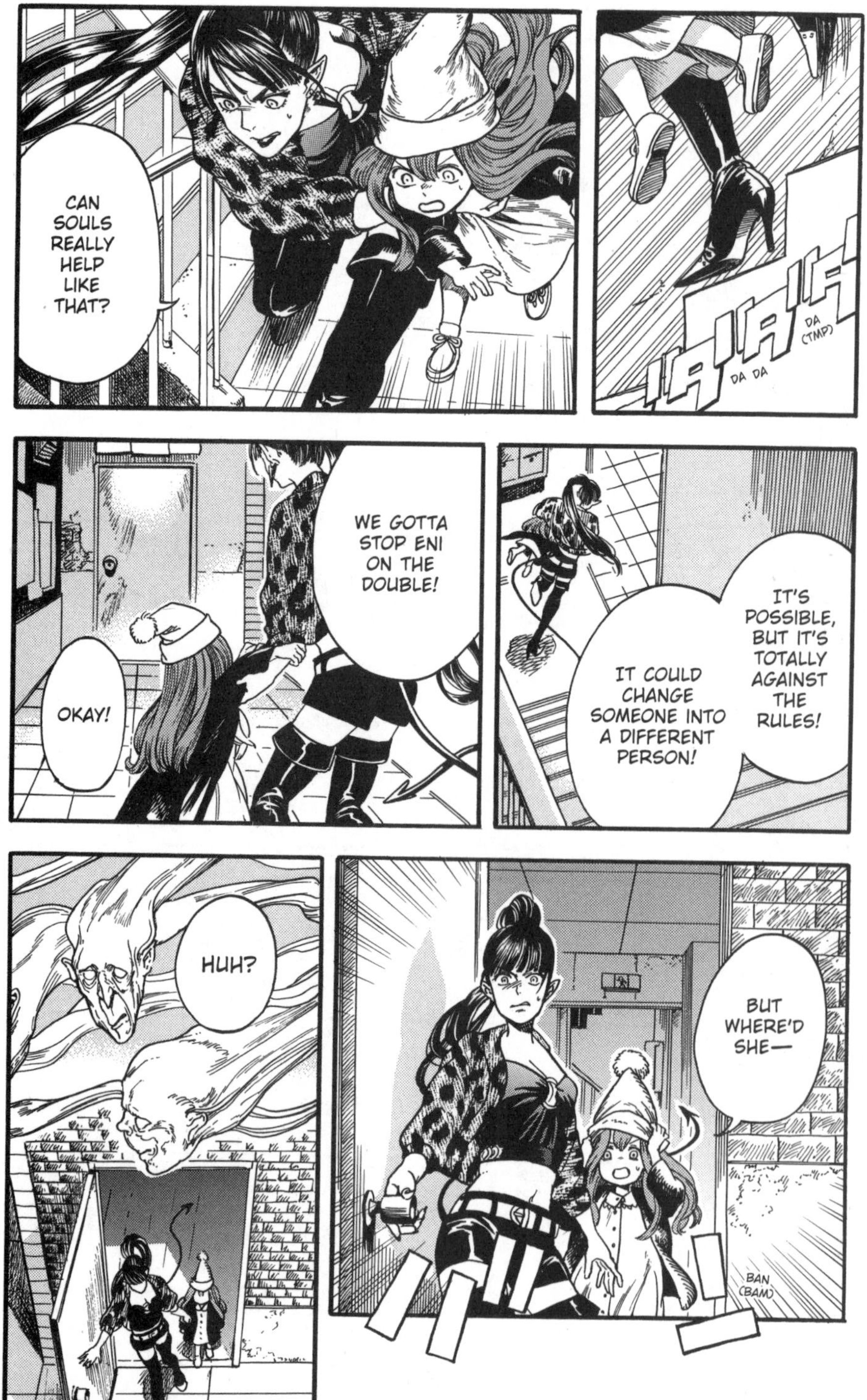
DA (TMP)
DA DA
CAN SOULS REALLY HELP LIKE THAT?
IT'S POSSIBLE, BUT IT'S TOTALLY AGAINST THE RULES!
IT COULD CHANGE SOMEONE INTO A DIFFERENT PERSON!
WE GOTTA STOP ENI ON THE DOUBLE!
OKAY!
BUT WHERE'D SHE—
BAN (BAM)
HUH?

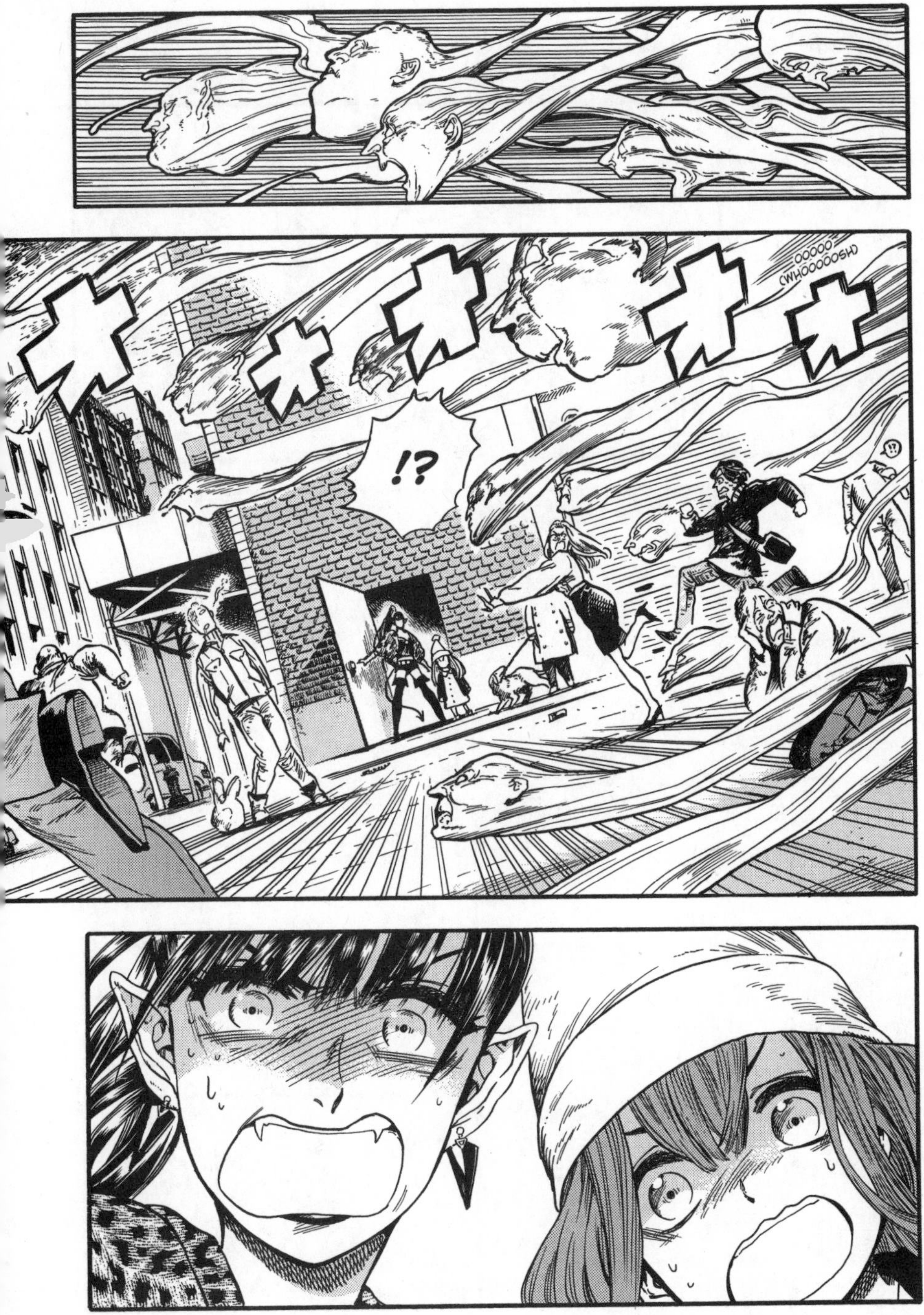

オオオオオ
OOOOO
(WHOOOOOOSH)
!?
!?

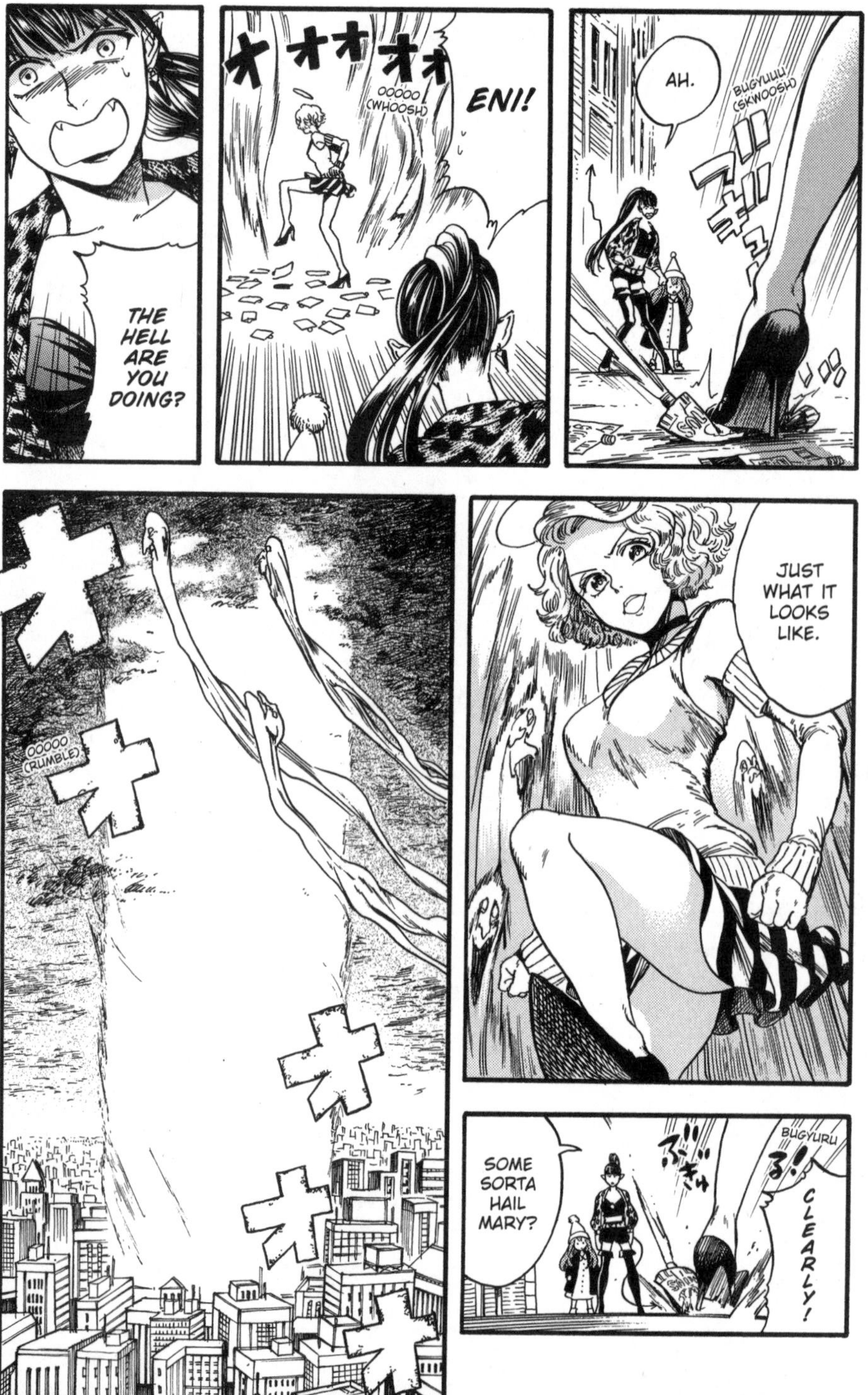
AH.
BUGYUUU (SKWOOSH)
OOOOO (WHOOSH)
ENI!
THE HELL ARE YOU DOING?
JUST WHAT IT LOOKS LIKE.
BUGYURU
SOME SORTA HAIL MARY?
CLEARLY!
OOOOO (RUMBLE)

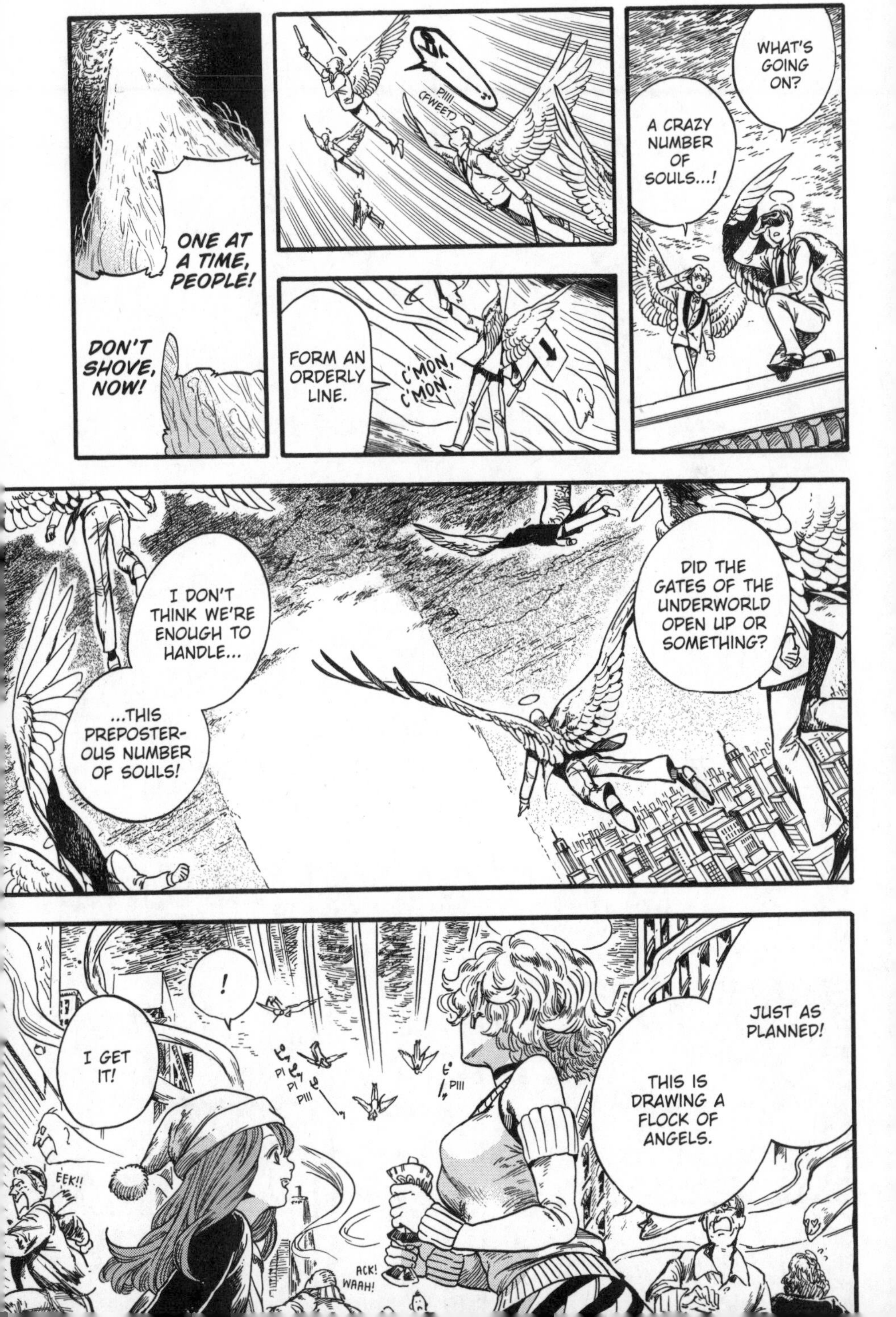

WHAT'S GOING ON?
A CRAZY NUMBER OF SOULS...!
PIIII (FWEET)
FORM AN ORDERLY LINE.
C'MON, C'MON.
ONE AT A TIME, PEOPLE!
DON'T SHOVE, NOW!
DID THE GATES OF THE UNDERWORLD OPEN UP OR SOMETHING?
I DON'T THINK WE'RE ENOUGH TO HANDLE...
...THIS PREPOSTER-OUS NUMBER OF SOULS!
JUST AS PLANNED!
THIS IS DRAWING A FLOCK OF ANGELS.
PIII
PI PI PIII
!
I GET IT!
EEK!!
ACK! WAAH!

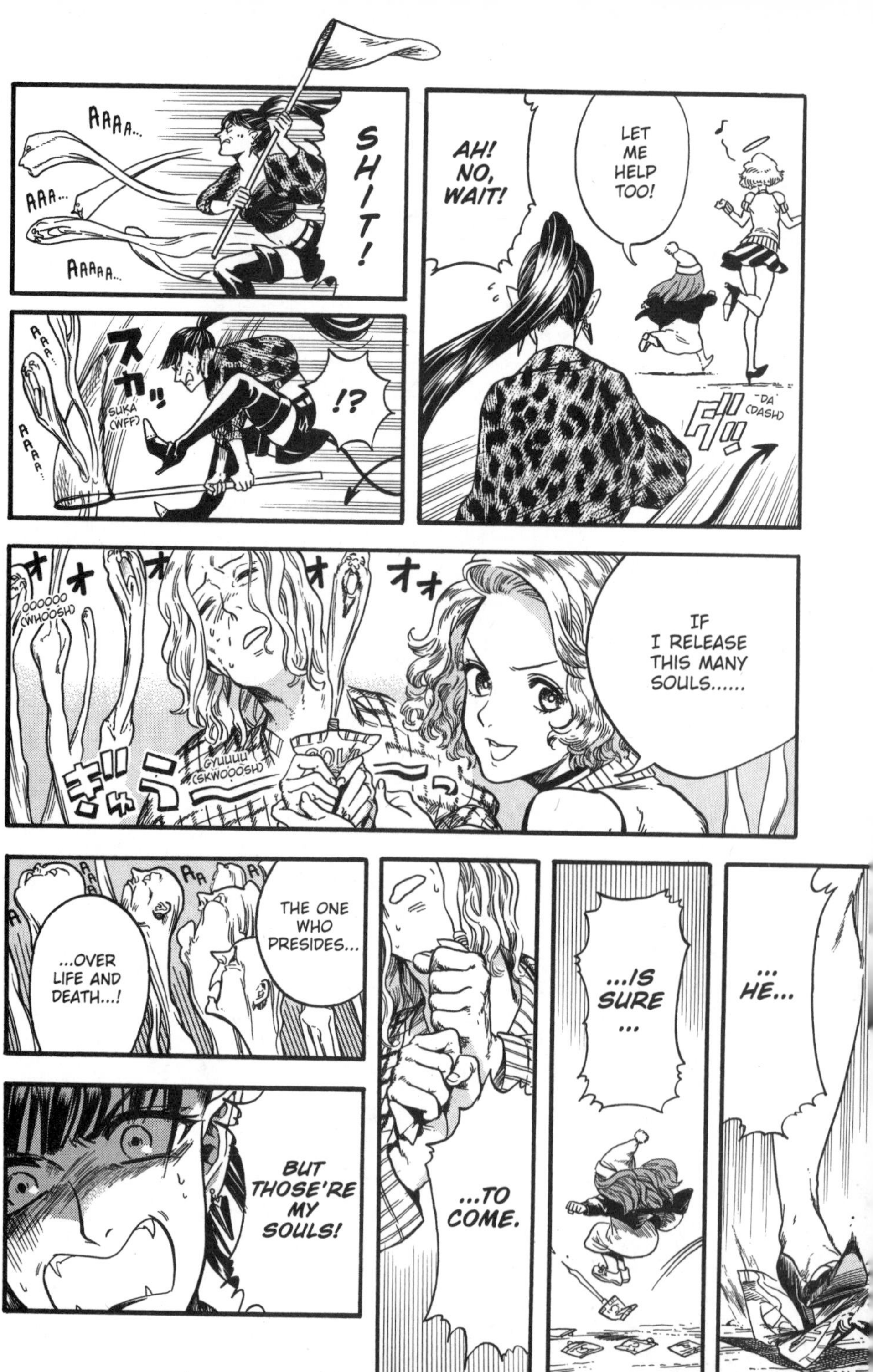

LET ME HELP TOO!
AH! NO, WAIT!
DA (DASH)
SHIT!
AAAA...
AAA...
AAAAA...
!?
AAA...
SUKA (WFF)
AAAA...
IF I RELEASE THIS MANY SOULS......
OOOOOO (WHOOSH)
GYUUUU (SKWOOSH)
... HE...
...IS SURE ...
...TO COME.
THE ONE WHO PRESIDES...
...OVER LIFE AND DEATH...!
BUT THOSE'RE MY SOULS!

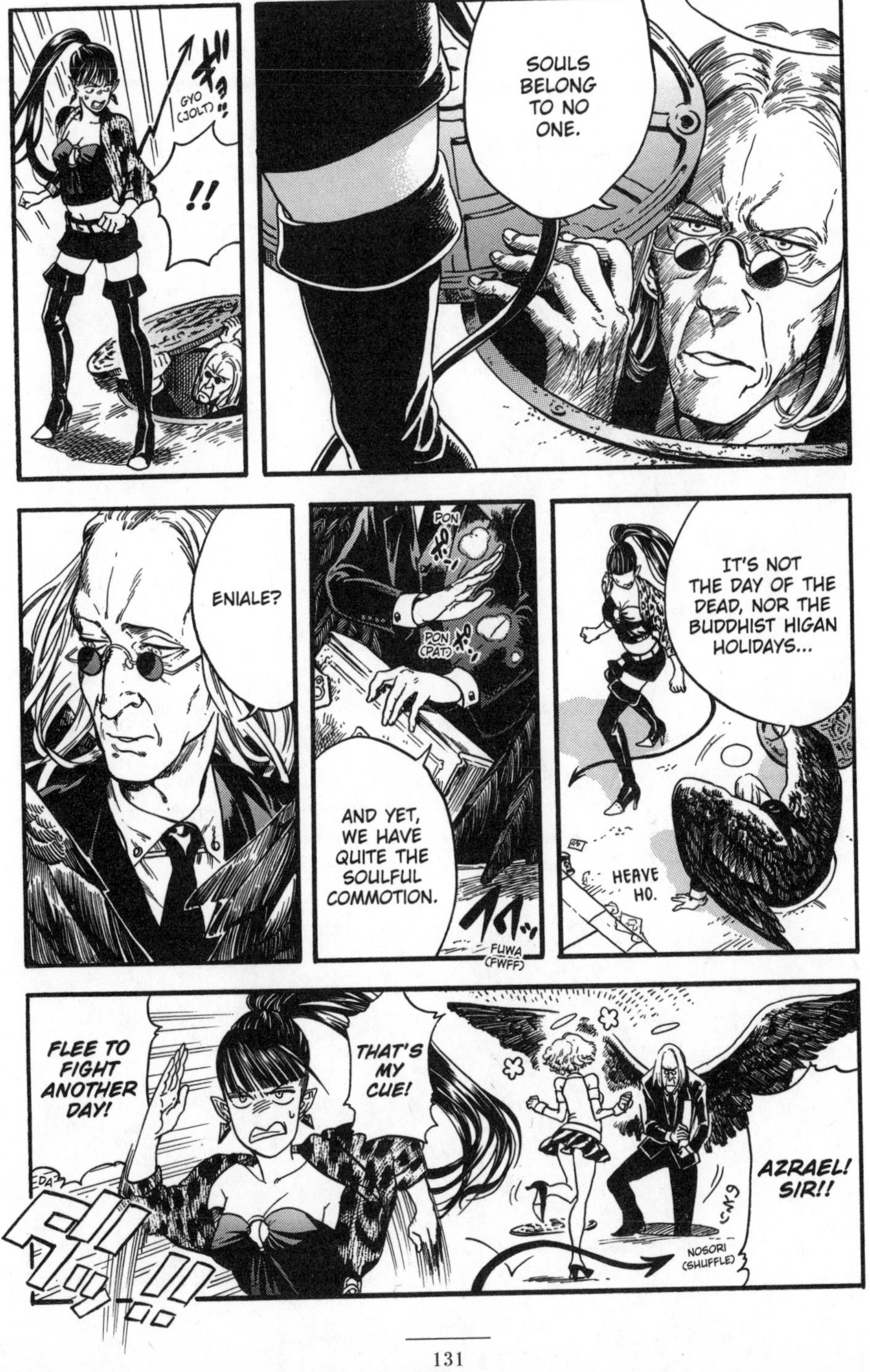
SOULS BELONG TO NO ONE.
GYO (JOLT)
!!
IT'S NOT THE DAY OF THE DEAD, NOR THE BUDDHIST HIGAN HOLIDAYS...
HEAVE HO.
PON
PON (PAT)
AND YET, WE HAVE QUITE THE SOULFUL COMMOTION.
FUWA (FWFF)
ENIALE?
AZRAEL! SIR!!
NOSORI (SHUFFLE)
THAT'S MY CUE!
FLEE TO FIGHT ANOTHER DAY!
DA

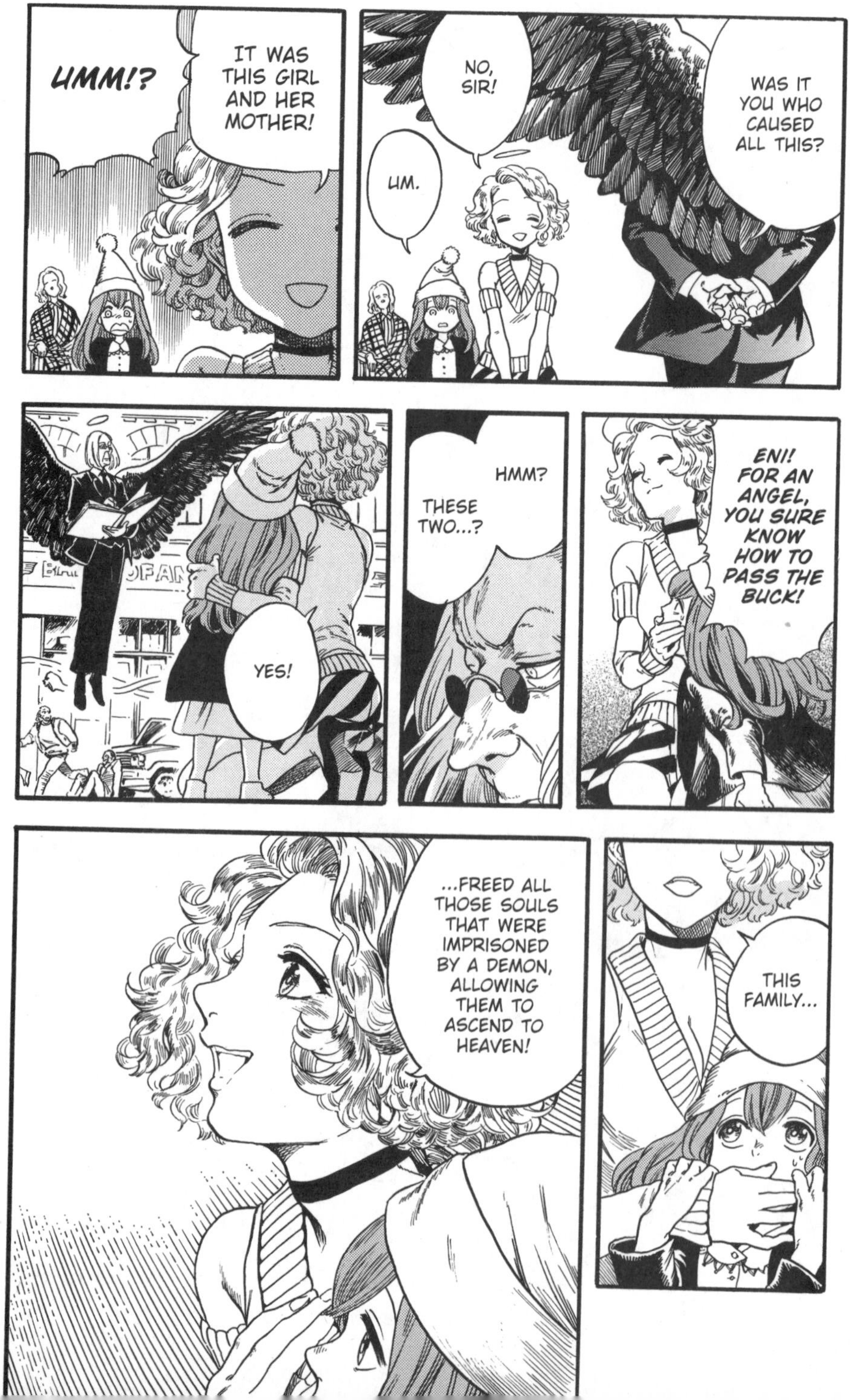
WAS IT YOU WHO CAUSED ALL THIS?
NO, SIR!
UM.
IT WAS THIS GIRL AND HER MOTHER!
UMM!?
ENI! FOR AN ANGEL, YOU SURE KNOW HOW TO PASS THE BUCK!
HMM?
THESE TWO...?
YES!
THIS FAMILY...
...FREED ALL THOSE SOULS THAT WERE IMPRISONED BY A DEMON, ALLOWING THEM TO ASCEND TO HEAVEN!

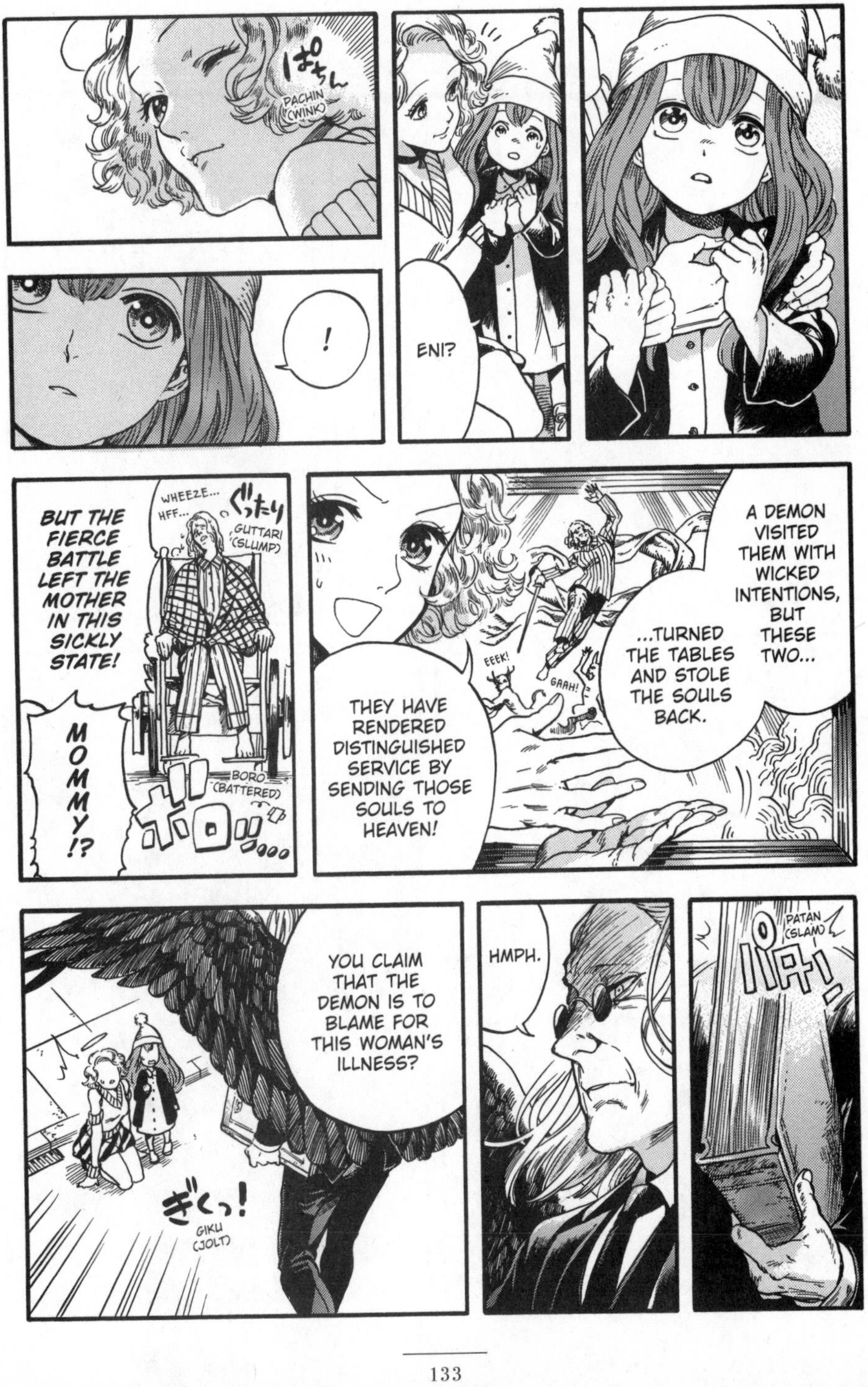
ENI?
ぱちん
PACHIN (WINK)
!
A DEMON VISITED THEM WITH WICKED INTENTIONS, BUT THESE TWO...
...TURNED THE TABLES AND STOLE THE SOULS BACK.
EEEK!
GAAH!
THEY HAVE RENDERED DISTINGUISHED SERVICE BY SENDING THOSE SOULS TO HEAVEN!
WHEEZE... HFF...
ぐったり
GUTTARI (SLUMP)
BUT THE FIERCE BATTLE LEFT THE MOTHER IN THIS SICKLY STATE!
MOMMY!?
ボロッ
BORO (BATTERED)
パタン
PATAN (SLAM)
HMPH.
YOU CLAIM THAT THE DEMON IS TO BLAME FOR THIS WOMAN'S ILLNESS?
ぎくっ!
GIKU (JOLT)

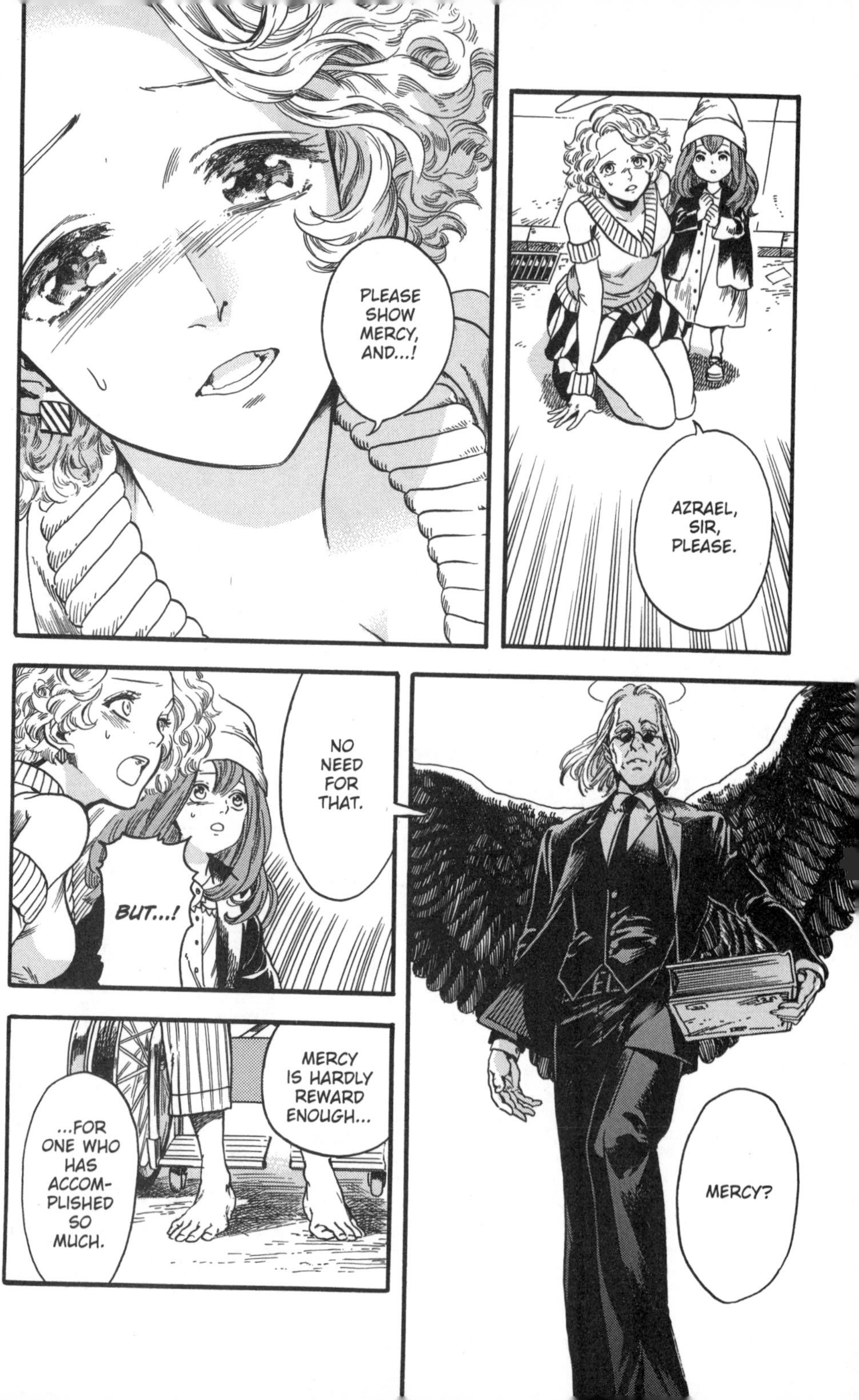
AZRAEL, SIR, PLEASE.
PLEASE SHOW MERCY, AND...!
MERCY?
NO NEED FOR THAT.
BUT...!
MERCY IS HARDLY REWARD ENOUGH...
...FOR ONE WHO HAS ACCOM-PLISHED SO MUCH.

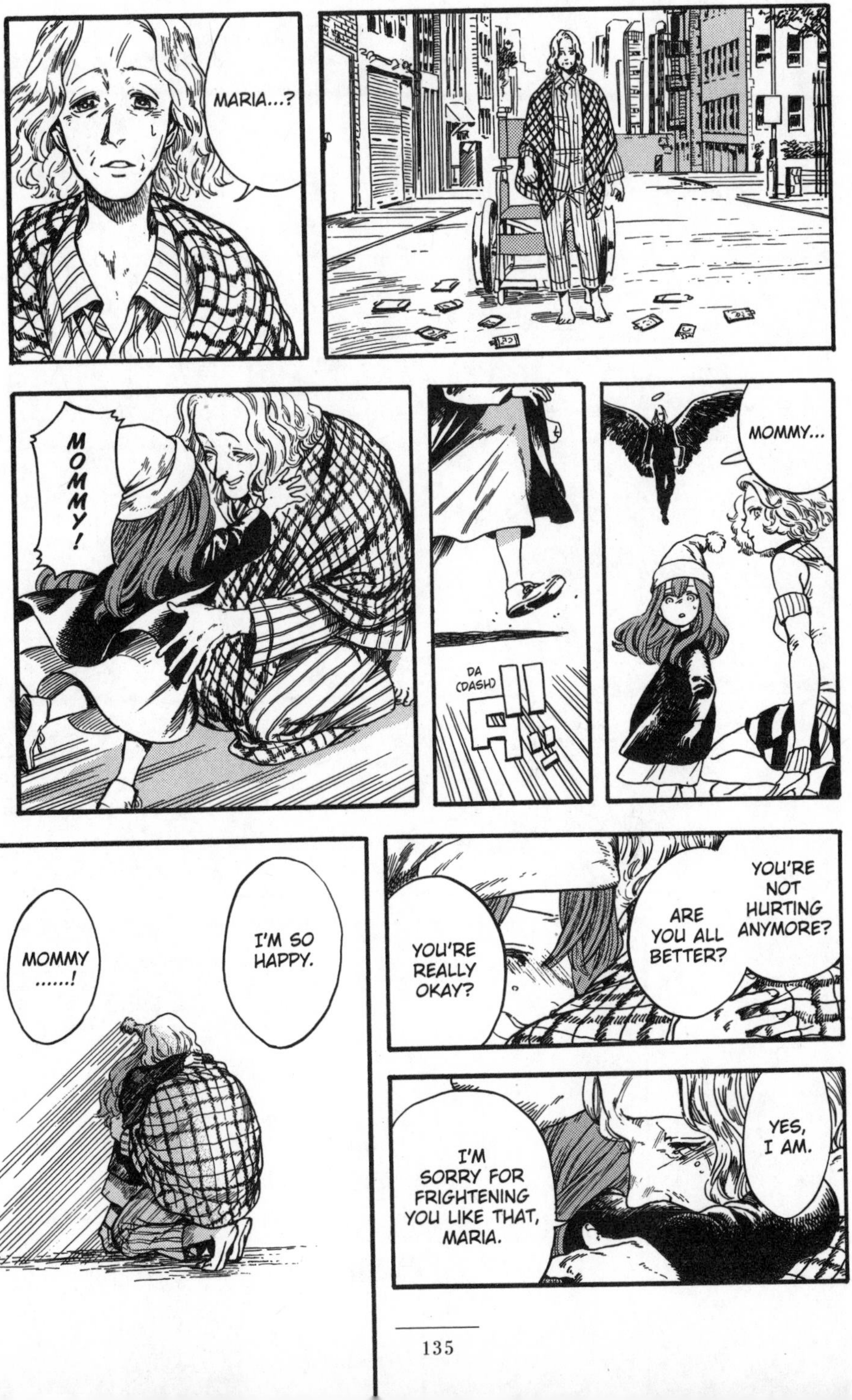
MARIA...?
MOMMY...
DA (DASH)
MOMMY!
YOU'RE NOT HURTING ANYMORE?
ARE YOU ALL BETTER?
YOU'RE REALLY OKAY?
YES, I AM.
I'M SORRY FOR FRIGHTENING YOU LIKE THAT, MARIA.
I'M SO HAPPY.
MOMMY ......!

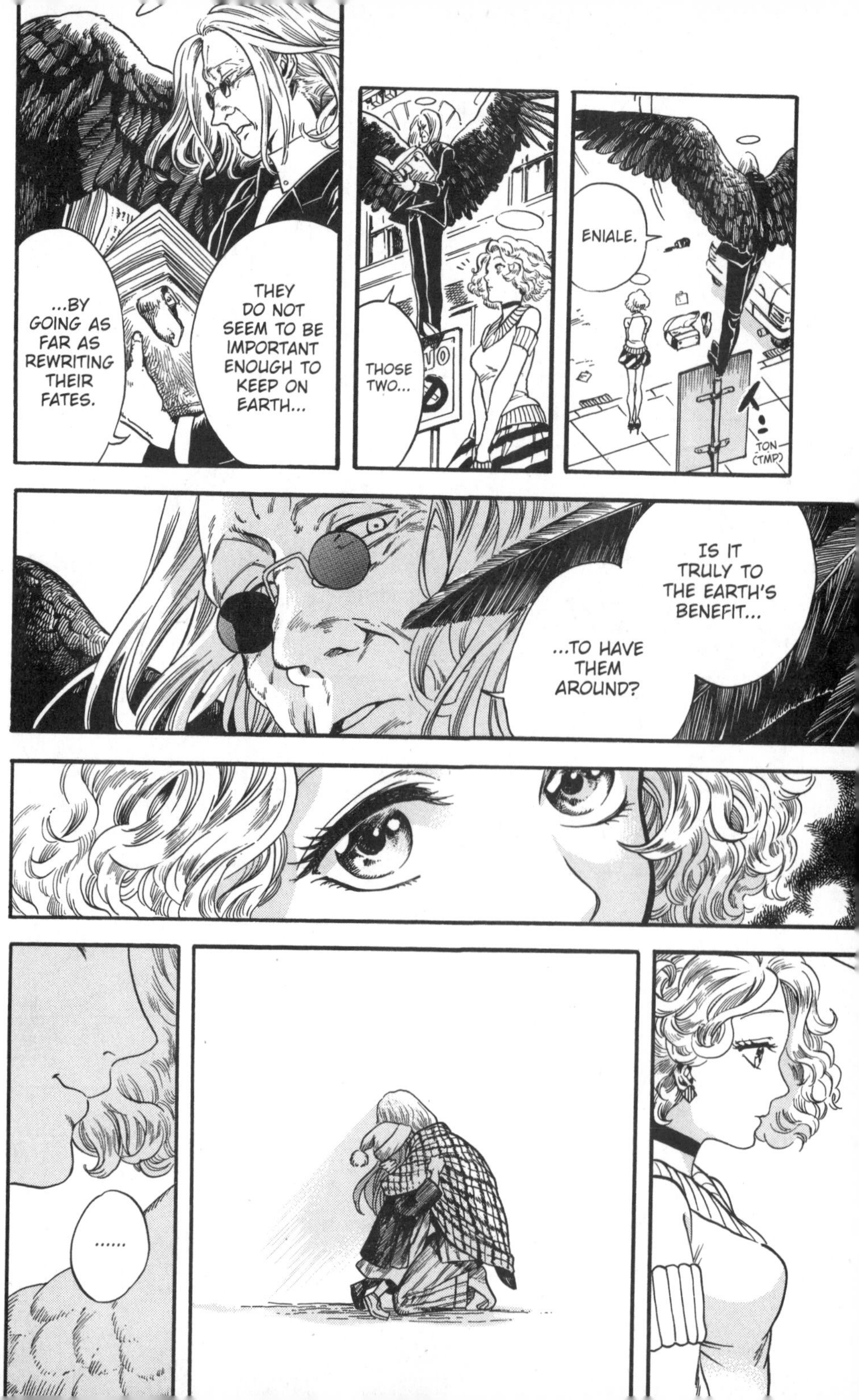
ENIALE.
TON (TMP)
THOSE TWO...
THEY DO NOT SEEM TO BE IMPORTANT ENOUGH TO KEEP ON EARTH...
...BY GOING AS FAR AS REWRITING THEIR FATES.
IS IT TRULY TO THE EARTH'S BENEFIT...
...TO HAVE THEM AROUND?
......

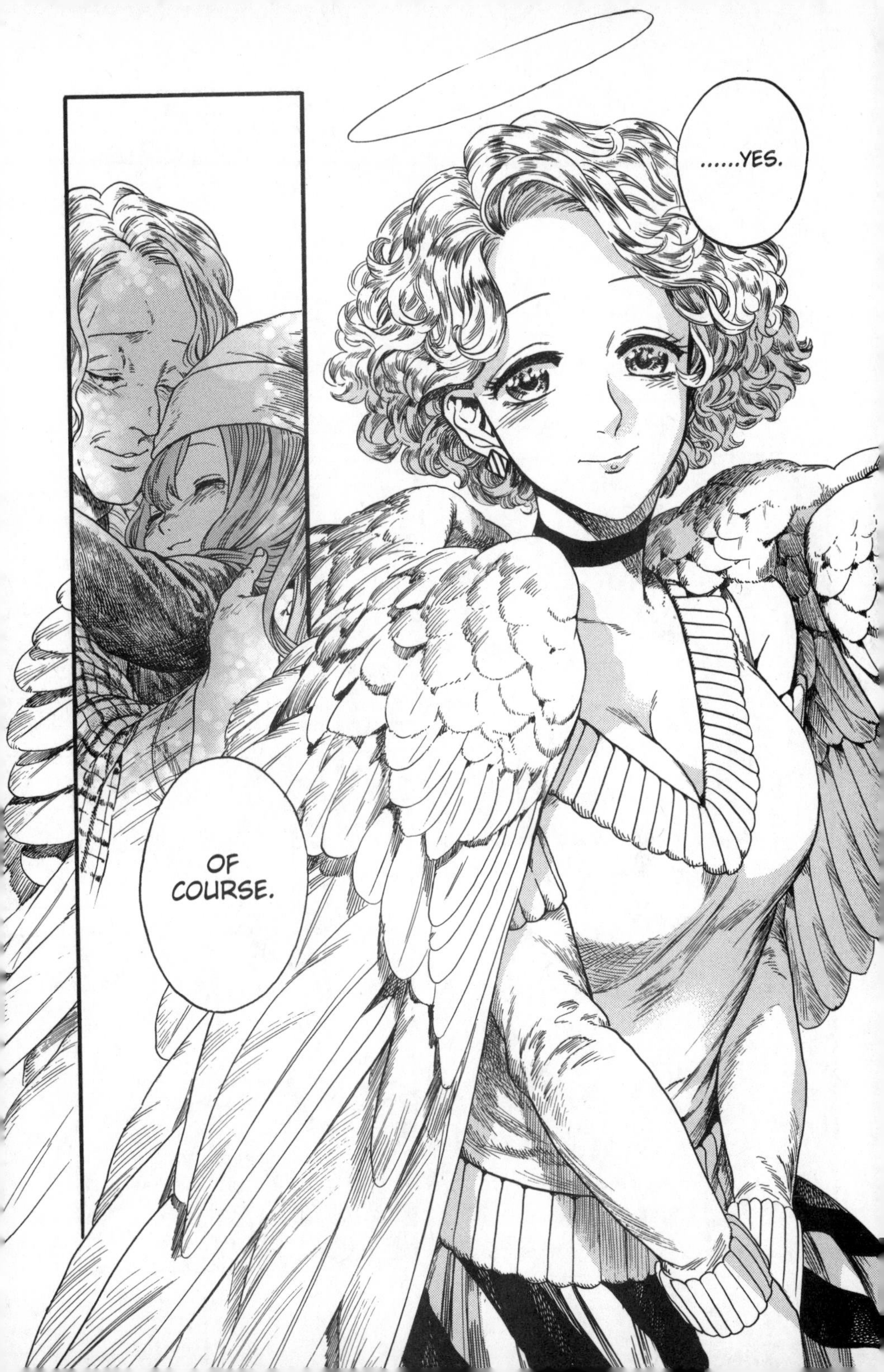

......YES.
OF COURSE.

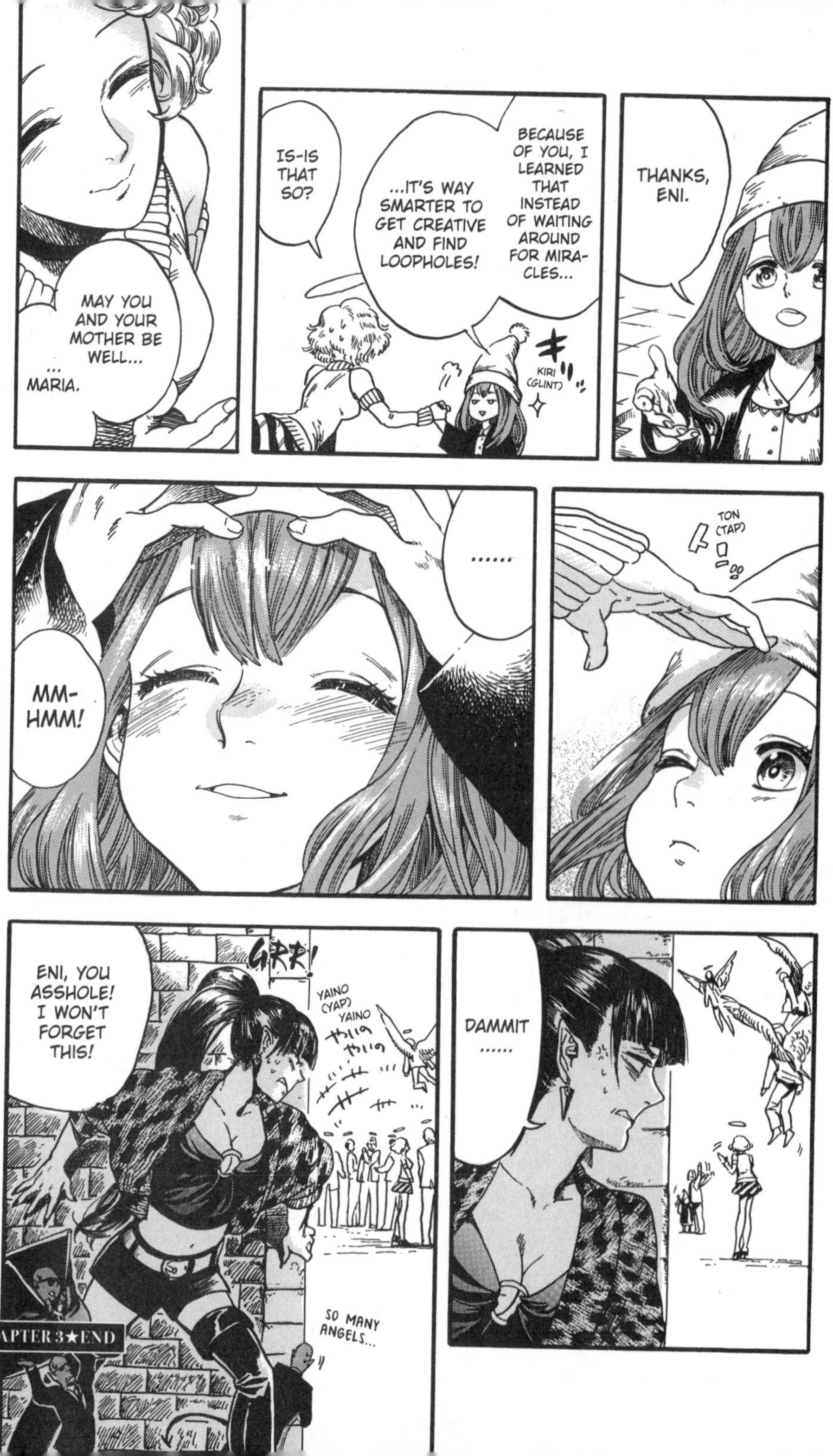
THANKS, ENI.
BECAUSE OF YOU, I LEARNED THAT INSTEAD OF WAITING AROUND FOR MIRA-CLES...
...IT'S WAY SMARTER TO GET CREATIVE AND FIND LOOPHOLES!
KIRI (GLINT)
IS-IS THAT SO?
MAY YOU AND YOUR MOTHER BE WELL...
... MARIA.
TON (TAP)
......
MM-HMM!
DAMMIT ......
GRR!
ENI, YOU ASSHOLE! I WON'T FORGET THIS!
YAINO (YAP) YAINO
やいの やいの
SO MANY ANGELS...
CHAPTER 3★END

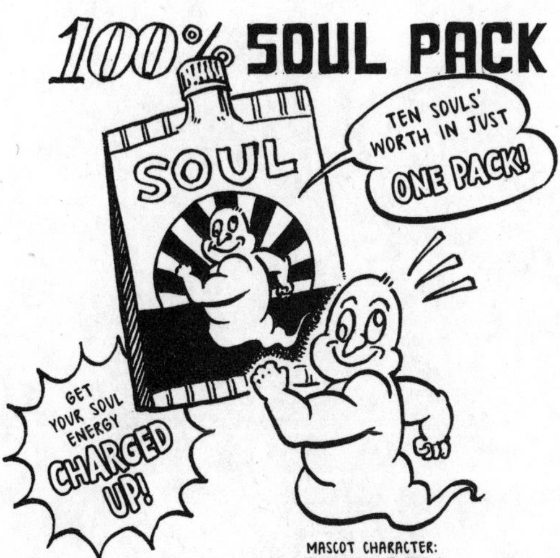
100% SOUL PACK
SOUL
TEN SOULS' WORTH IN JUST ONE PACK!
GET YOUR SOUL ENERGY CHARGED UP!
MASCOT CHARACTER:
SOULSBY

ENIALE & DEWIELA

1

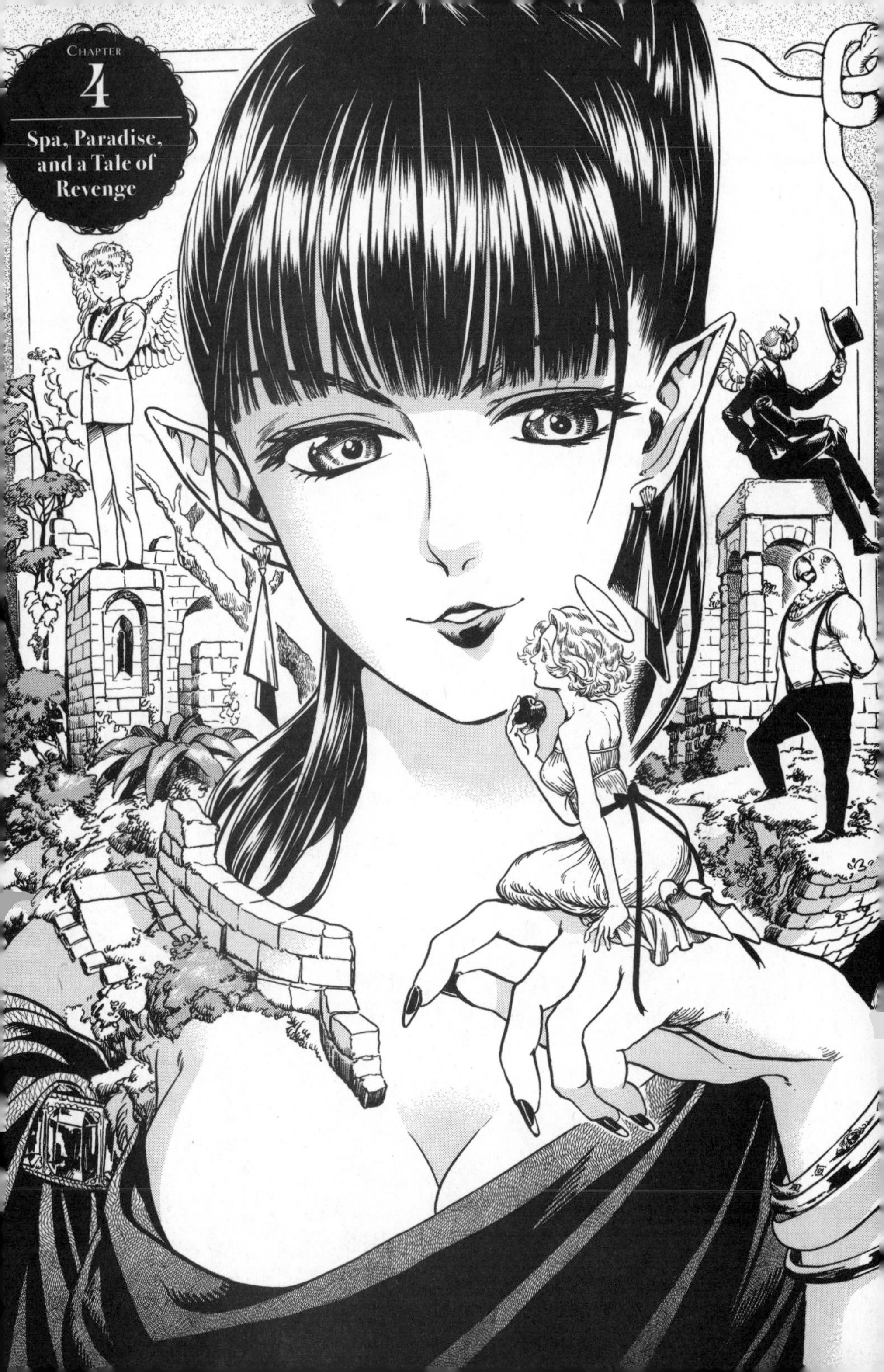
Chapter
4
Spa, Paradise, and a Tale of Revenge

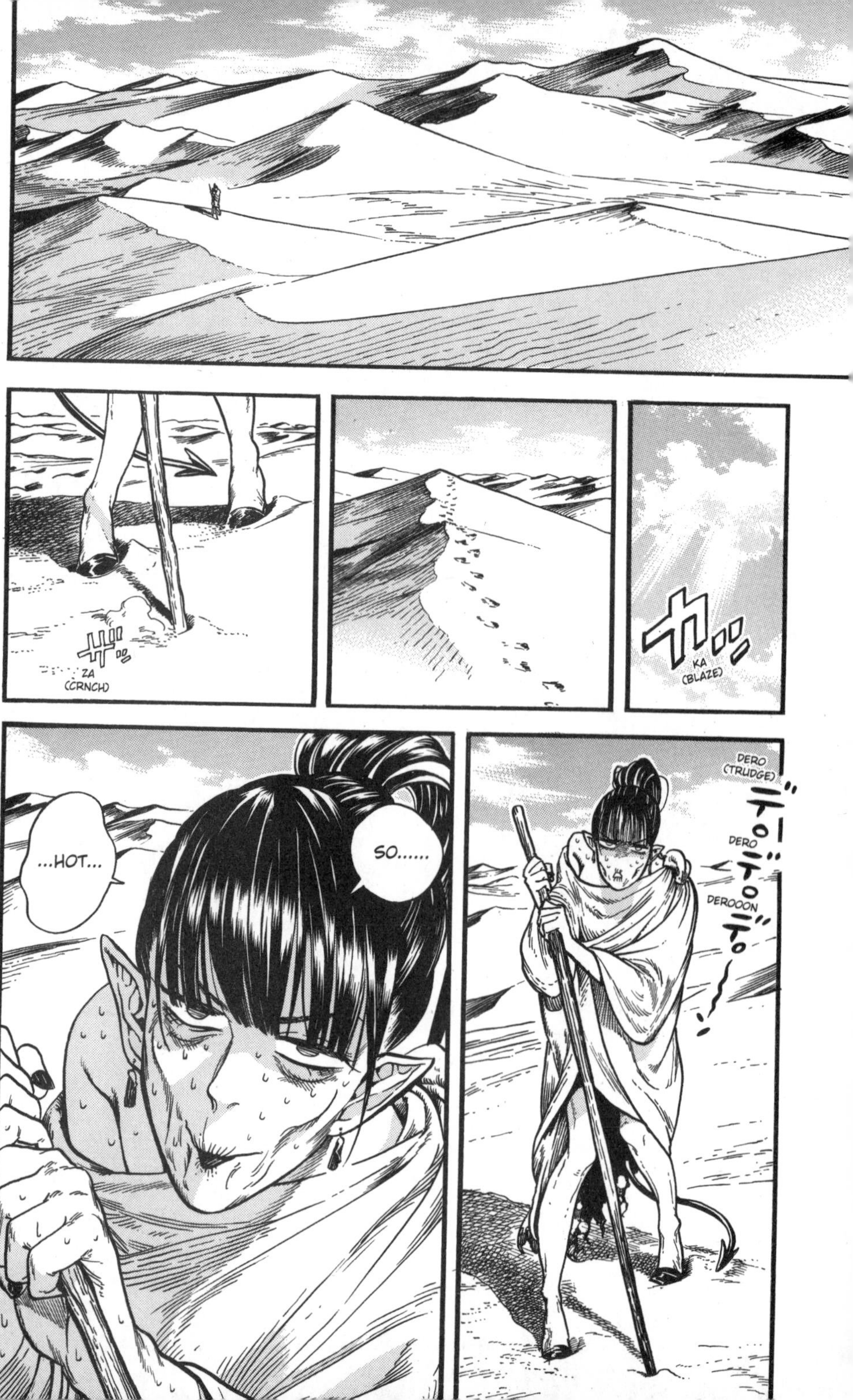
カッ
KA
(BLAZE)
ザッ
ZA
(CRNCH)
デロ
DERO
(TRUDGE)
デロ
DERO
デロ〜ン
DEROOON
SO......
...HOT...

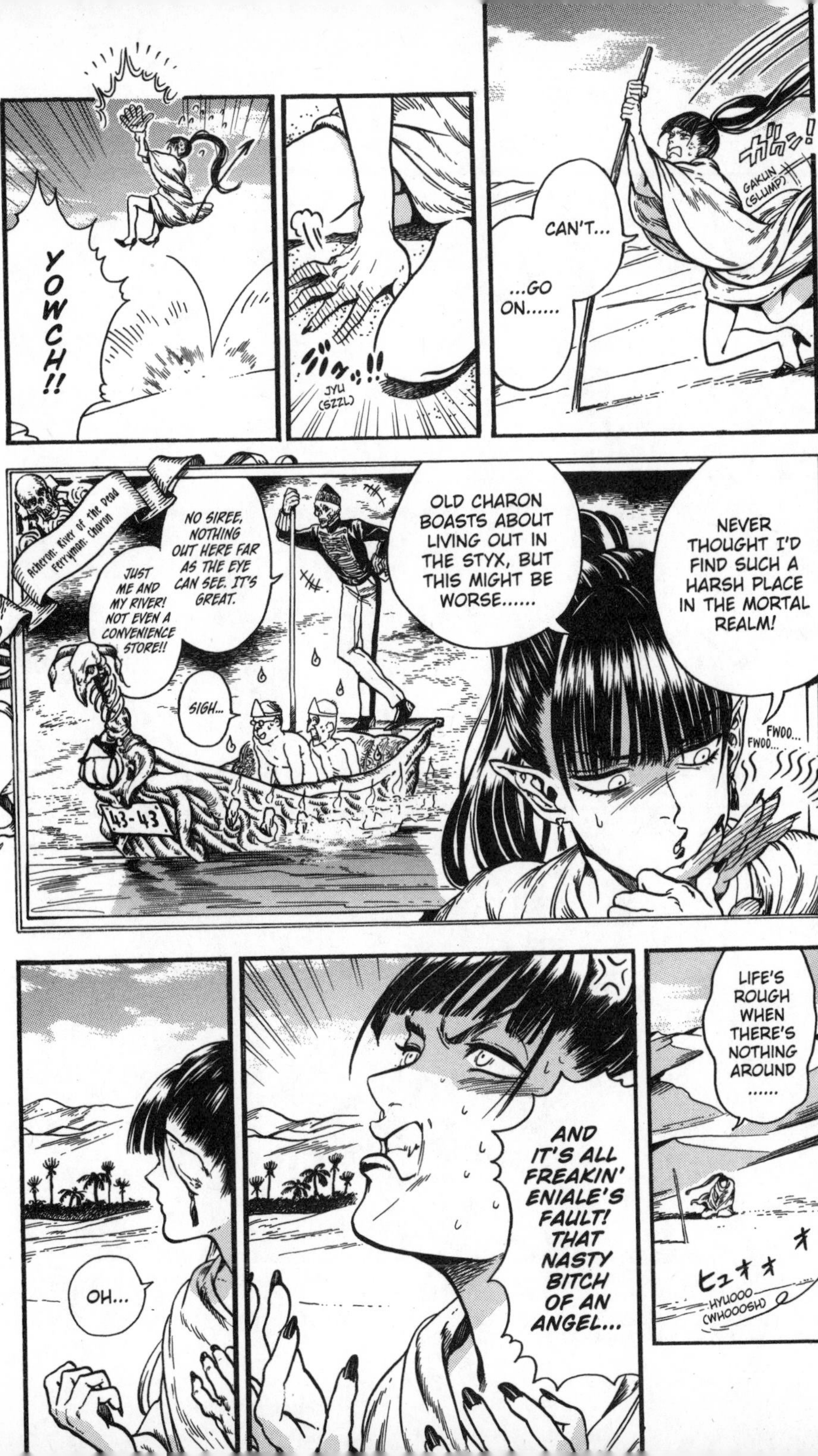
ガクッ!
GAKUN (SLUMP)
CAN'T...
...GO ON......
ジュッ!!
JYU (SZZL)
YOWCH!!
NEVER THOUGHT I'D FIND SUCH A HARSH PLACE IN THE MORTAL REALM!
FWOO... FWOO...
OLD CHARON BOASTS ABOUT LIVING OUT IN THE STYX, BUT THIS MIGHT BE WORSE......
NO SIREE, NOTHING OUT HERE FAR AS THE EYE CAN SEE. IT'S GREAT.
JUST ME AND MY RIVER! NOT EVEN A CONVENIENCE STORE!!
SIGH...
Acheron: River of the Dead
Ferryman: Charon
43-43
LIFE'S ROUGH WHEN THERE'S NOTHING AROUND ......
ヒュオオオ
HYUOOO (WHOOOSH)
AND IT'S ALL FREAKIN' ENIALE'S FAULT! THAT NASTY BITCH OF AN ANGEL...
OH...

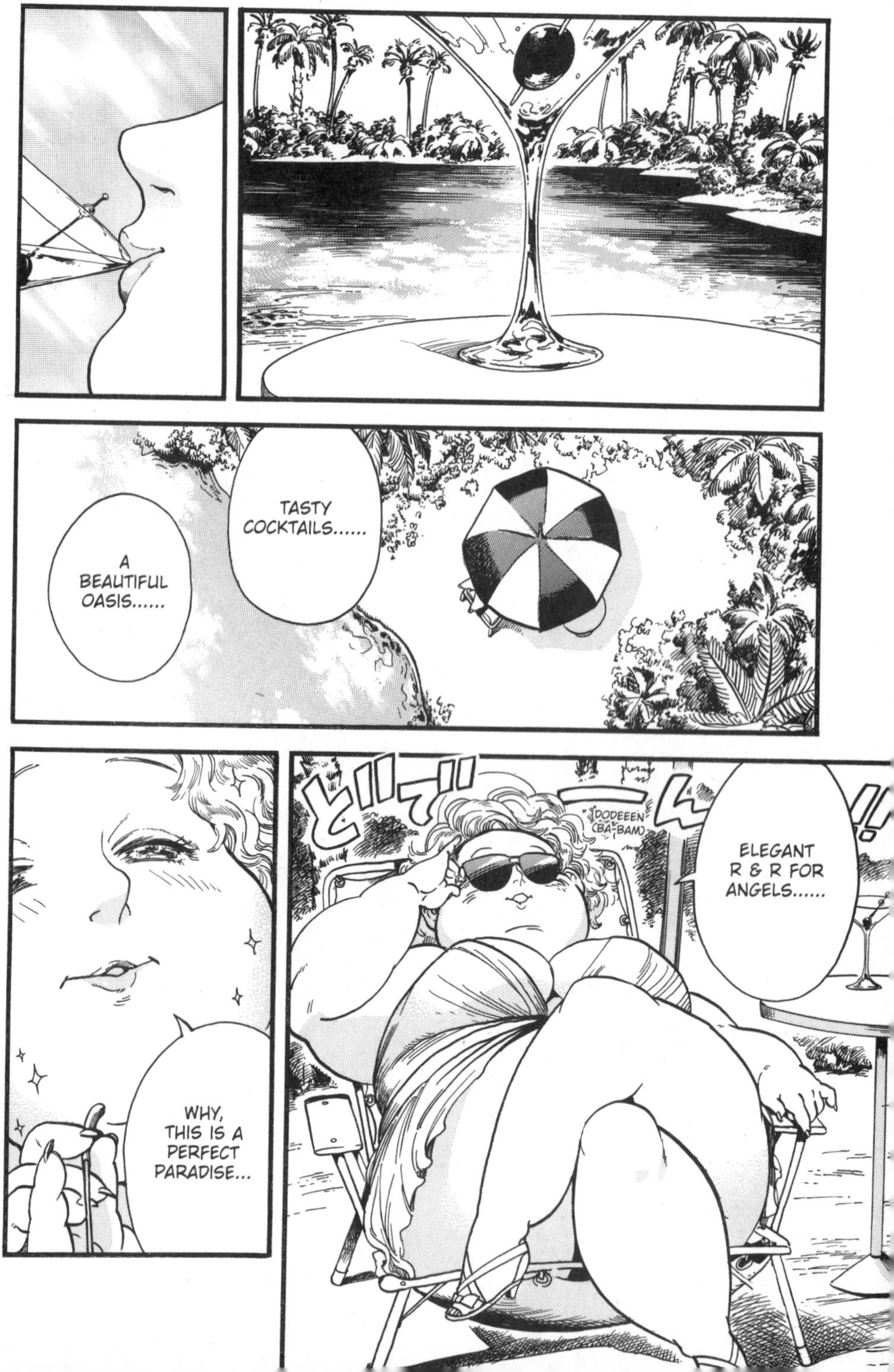
TASTY COCKTAILS......
A BEAUTIFUL OASIS......
ELEGANT R & R FOR ANGELS......
DODEEEN (BA-BAM)
WHY, THIS IS A PERFECT PARADISE...

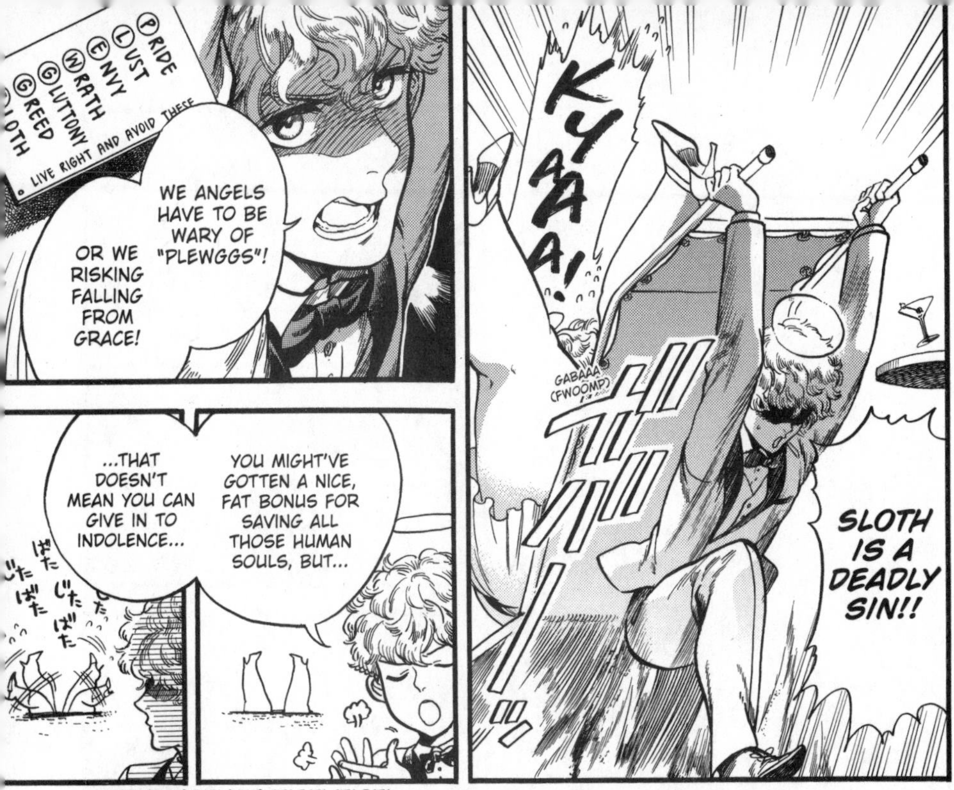
KYAAAA!
GABAAA (FWOOMP)
SLOTH IS A DEADLY SIN!!
PRIDE
LUST
ENVY
WRATH
GLUTTONY
GREED
SLOTH
LIVE RIGHT AND AVOID THESE
WE ANGELS HAVE TO BE WARY OF "PLEWGGS"!
OR WE RISKING FALLING FROM GRACE!
YOU MIGHT'VE GOTTEN A NICE, FAT BONUS FOR SAVING ALL THOSE HUMAN SOULS, BUT...
...THAT DOESN'T MEAN YOU CAN GIVE IN TO INDOLENCE...
じた ばた じた ばた

SFX: JITA (FLAIL) BATA (KICK) JITA BATA JITA BATA

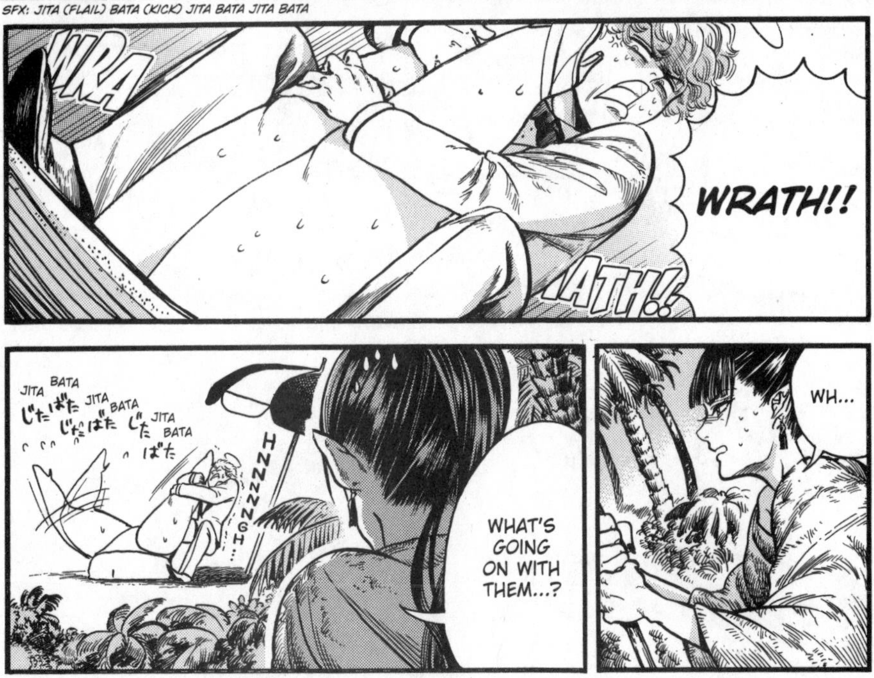
WRA
WRATH!!
ATH!!
WH...
WHAT'S GOING ON WITH THEM...?
HNNNNNGH...
JITA BATA じたばた
JITA BATA じたばた
JITA BATA じたばた

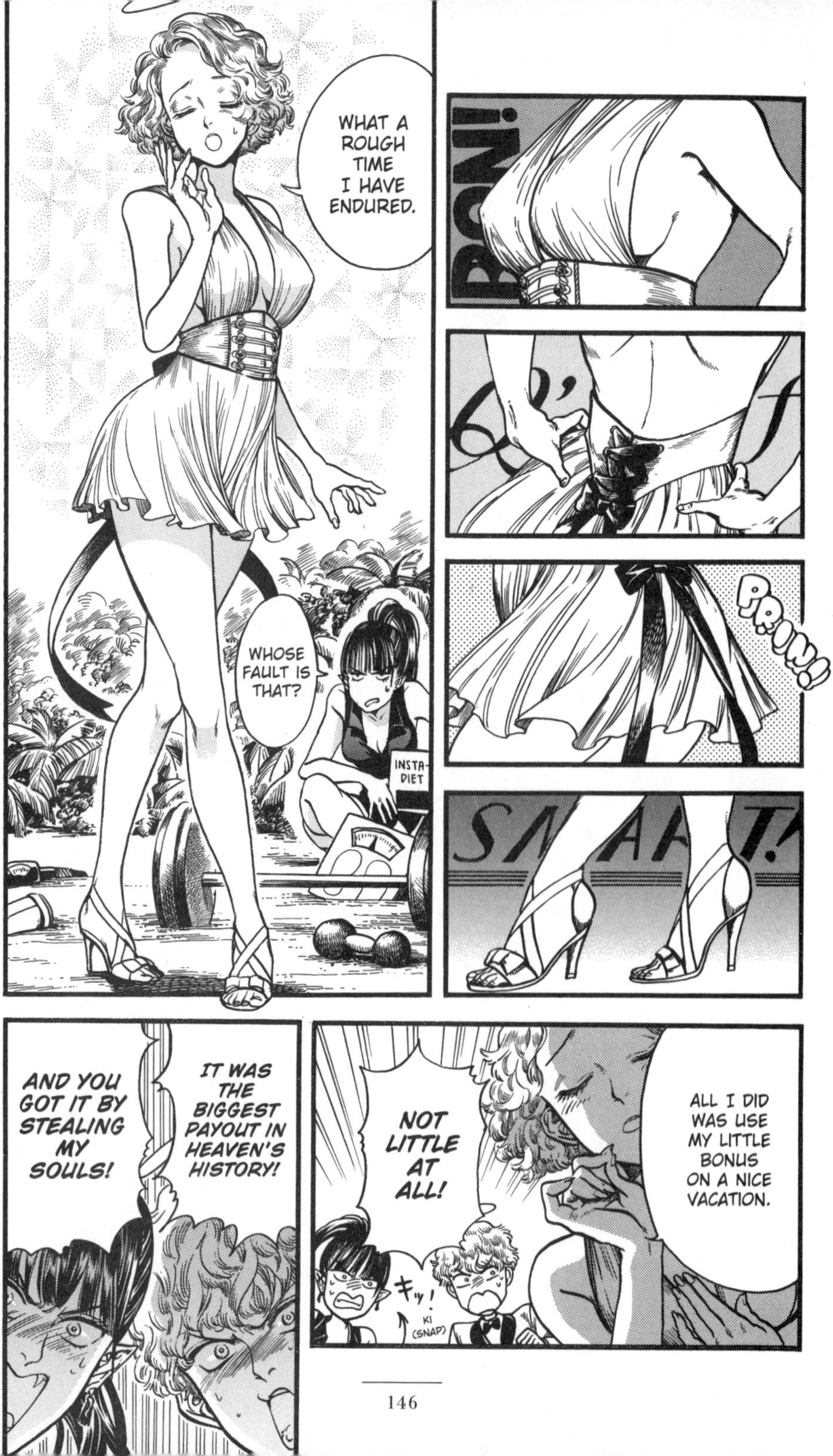
BON!
PRIN!
WHAT A ROUGH TIME I HAVE ENDURED.
WHOSE FAULT IS THAT?
INSTA-DIET
ALL I DID WAS USE MY LITTLE BONUS ON A NICE VACATION.
NOT LITTLE AT ALL!
キッ!
KI (SNAP)
IT WAS THE BIGGEST PAYOUT IN HEAVEN'S HISTORY!
AND YOU GOT IT BY STEALING MY SOULS!

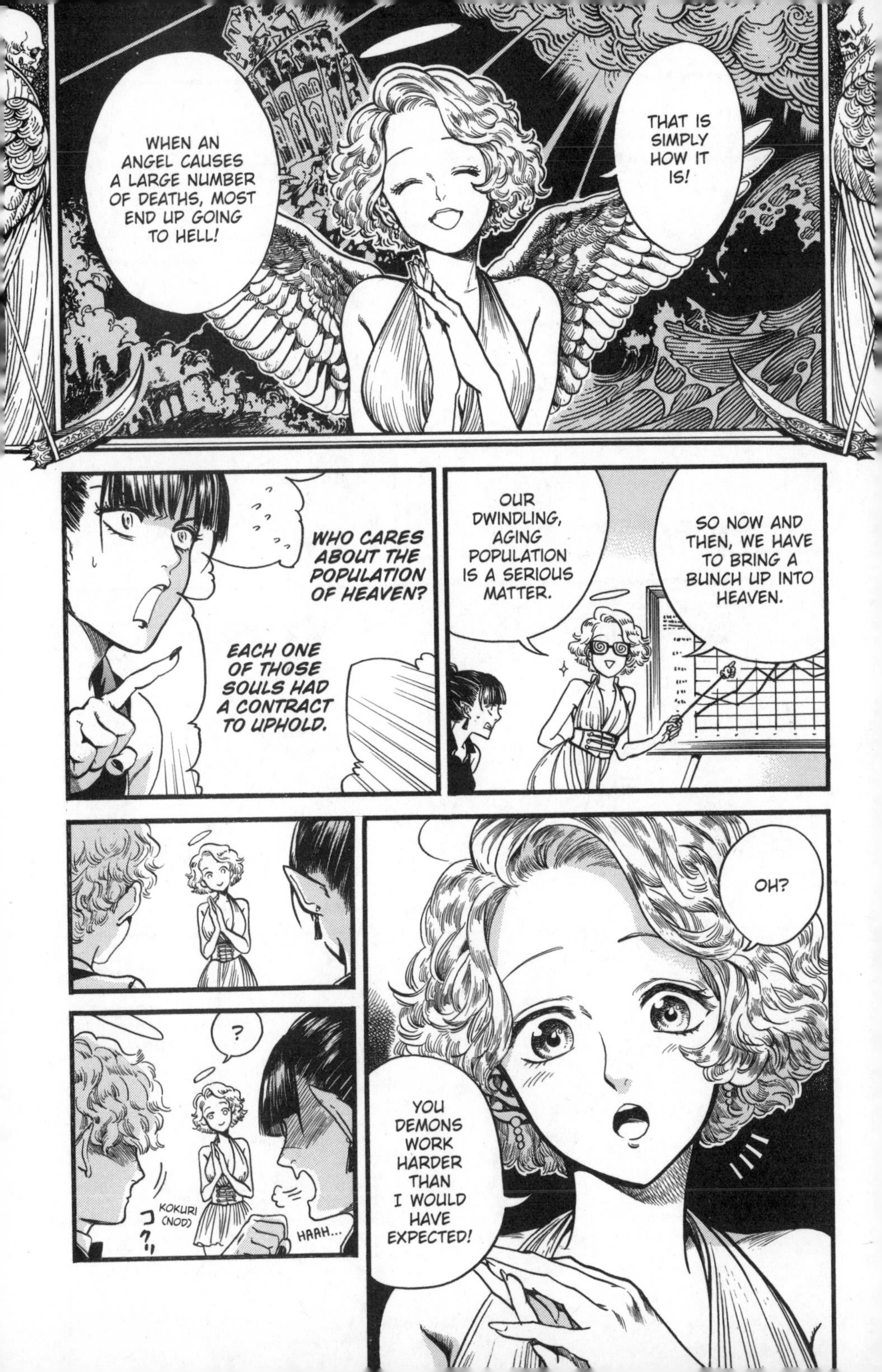
THAT IS SIMPLY HOW IT IS!
WHEN AN ANGEL CAUSES A LARGE NUMBER OF DEATHS, MOST END UP GOING TO HELL!
SO NOW AND THEN, WE HAVE TO BRING A BUNCH UP INTO HEAVEN.
OUR DWINDLING, AGING POPULATION IS A SERIOUS MATTER.
WHO CARES ABOUT THE POPULATION OF HEAVEN?
EACH ONE OF THOSE SOULS HAD A CONTRACT TO UPHOLD.
OH?
YOU DEMONS WORK HARDER THAN I WOULD HAVE EXPECTED!
?
KOKURI (NOD)
HAAH...

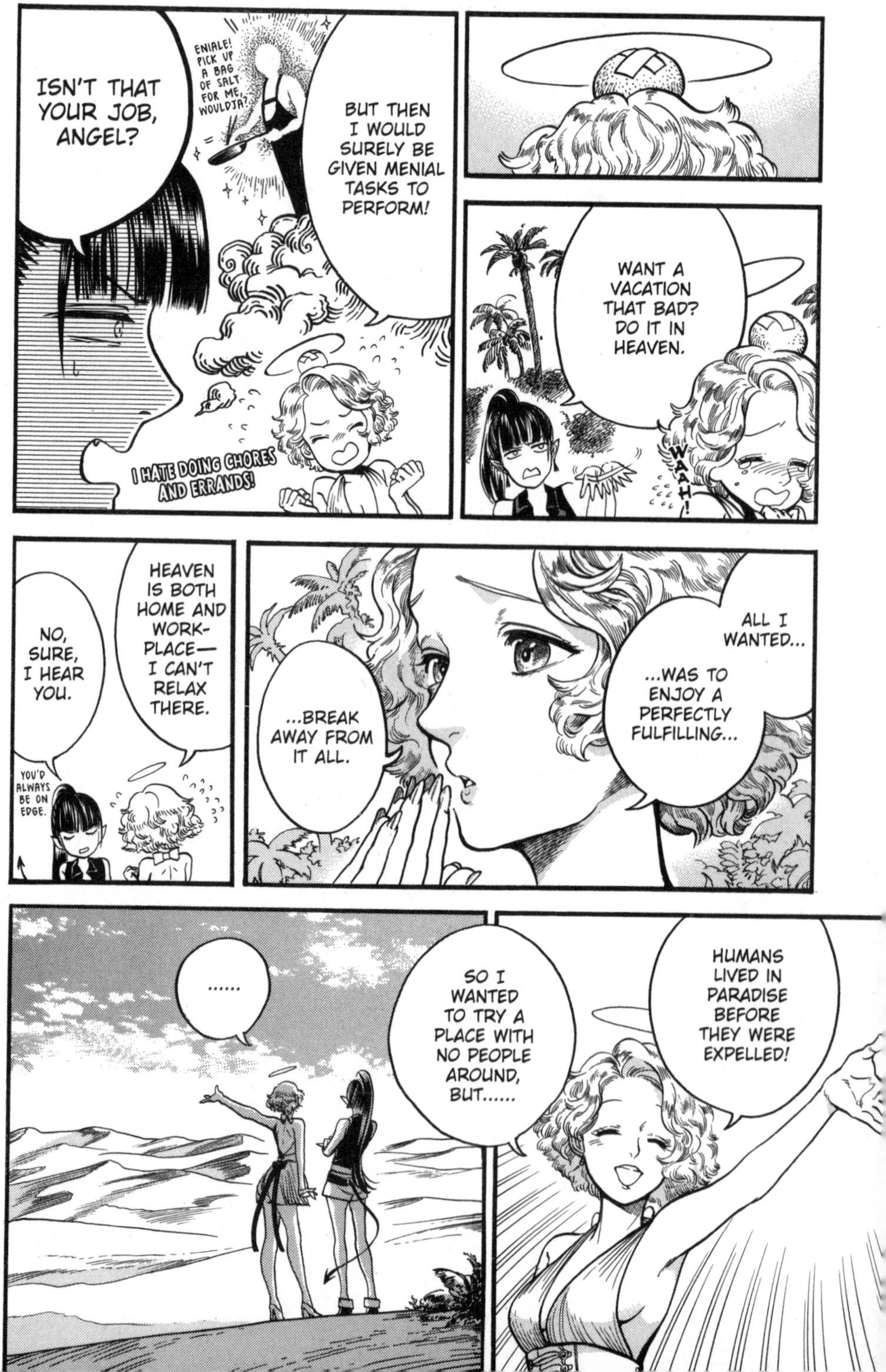
WANT A VACATION THAT BAD? DO IT IN HEAVEN.
WAAH!
BUT THEN I WOULD SURELY BE GIVEN MENIAL TASKS TO PERFORM!
ENIALE! PICK UP A BAG OF SALT FOR ME, WOULDJA?
ISN'T THAT YOUR JOB, ANGEL?
I HATE DOING CHORES AND ERRANDS!
ALL I WANTED...
...WAS TO ENJOY A PERFECTLY FULFILLING...
...BREAK AWAY FROM IT ALL.
HEAVEN IS BOTH HOME AND WORK-PLACE— I CAN'T RELAX THERE.
NO, SURE, I HEAR YOU.
YOU'D ALWAYS BE ON EDGE.
HUMANS LIVED IN PARADISE BEFORE THEY WERE EXPELLED!
SO I WANTED TO TRY A PLACE WITH NO PEOPLE AROUND, BUT......
......

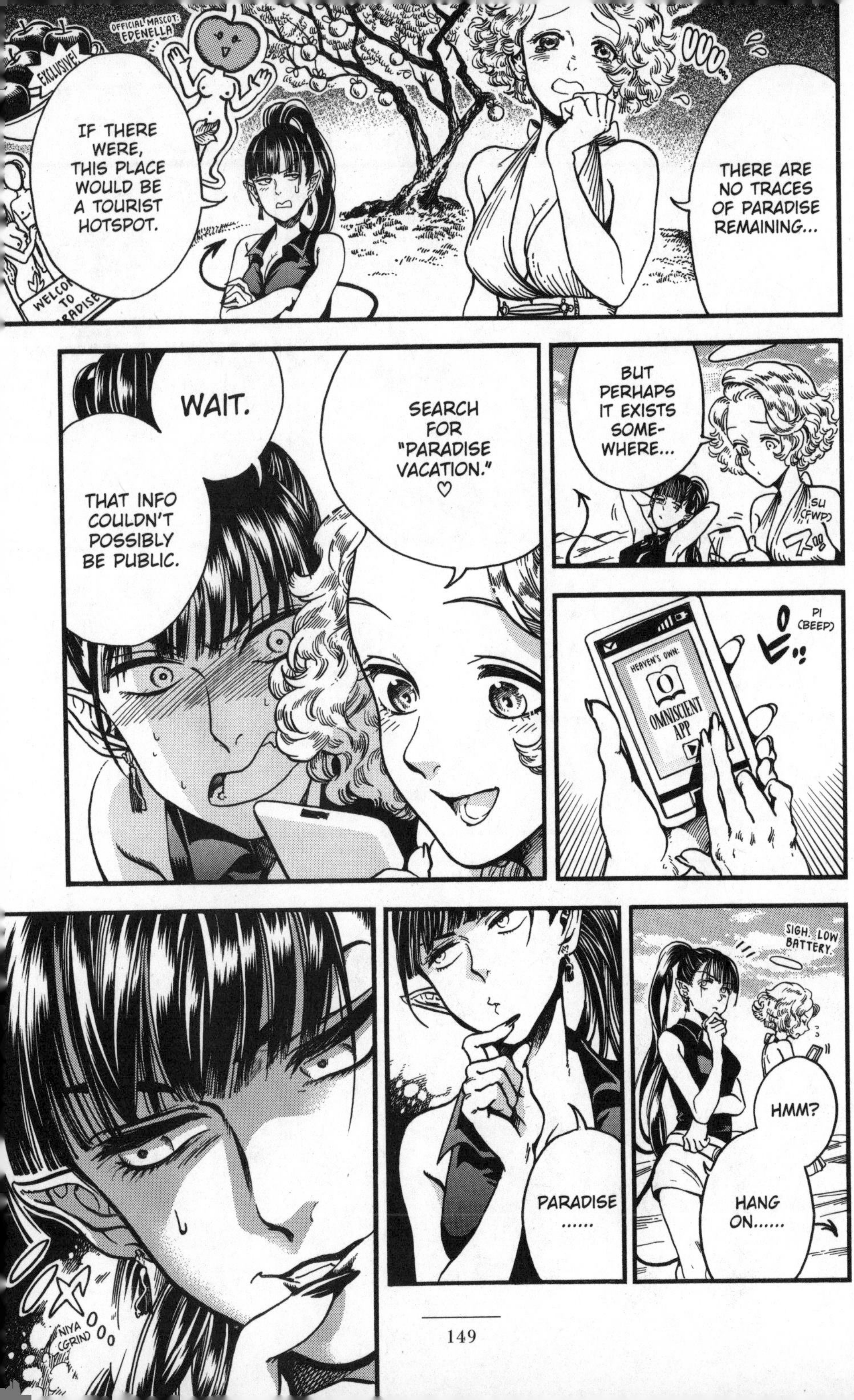
OFFICIAL MASCOT: EDENELLA
EXCLUSIVE!
UUU
THERE ARE NO TRACES OF PARADISE REMAINING...
IF THERE WERE, THIS PLACE WOULD BE A TOURIST HOTSPOT.
BUT PERHAPS IT EXISTS SOME-WHERE...
SU (FWP)
PI (BEEP)
HEAVEN'S OWN:
OMNISCIENT APP
SEARCH FOR "PARADISE VACATION." ♡
WAIT.
THAT INFO COULDN'T POSSIBLY BE PUBLIC.
SIGH. LOW BATTERY.
HMM?
HANG ON......
PARADISE ......
NIYA (GRIN)

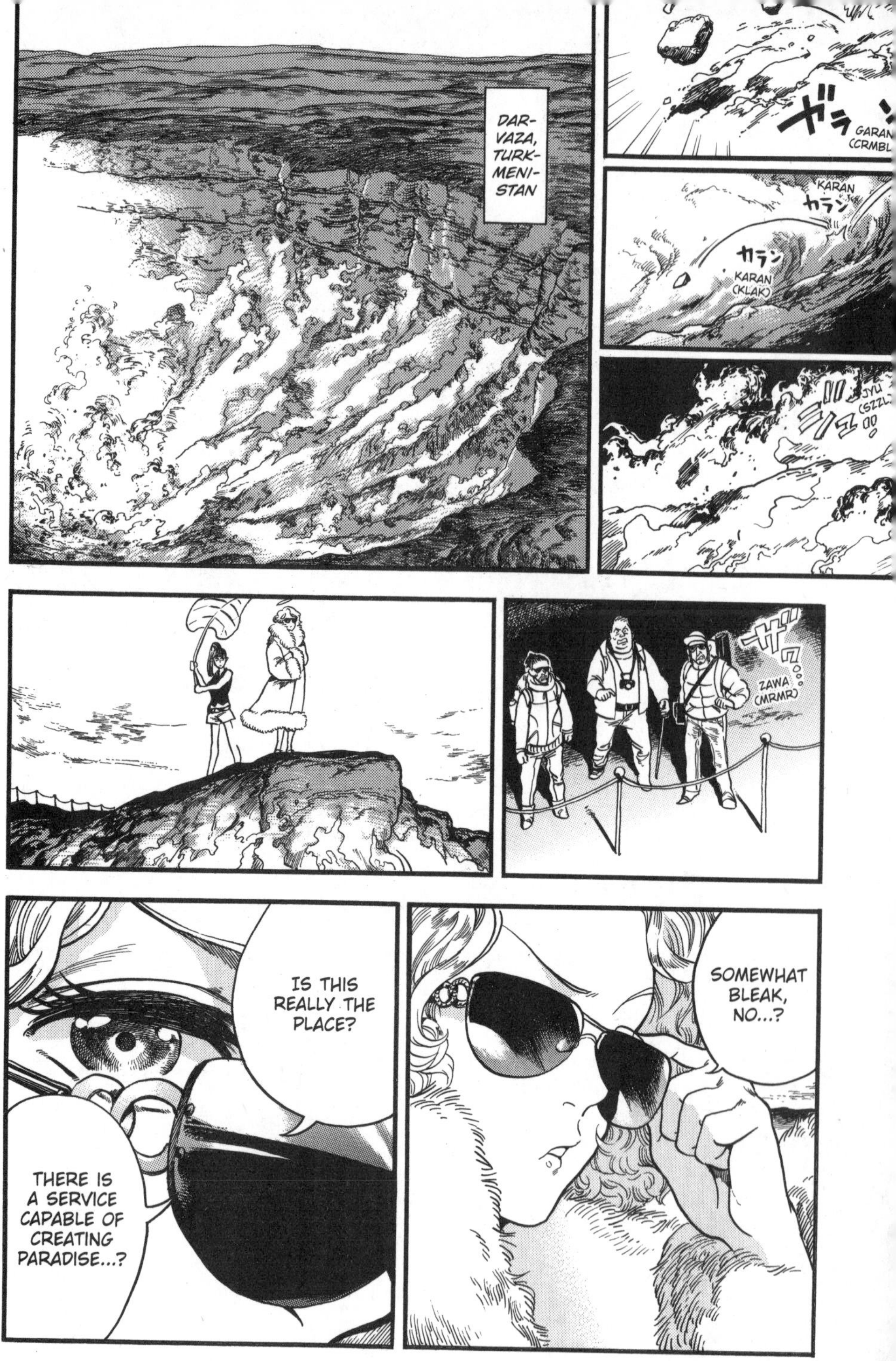

ガラ
GARAN
(CRMBL
KARAN
カラン
カラン
KARAN (KLAK)
JYU (SZZL)
ジュ!!
DAR-VAZA, TURK-MENI-STAN
ザワ...
ZAWA (MRMR)
SOMEWHAT BLEAK, NO...?
IS THIS REALLY THE PLACE?
THERE IS A SERVICE CAPABLE OF CREATING PARADISE...?

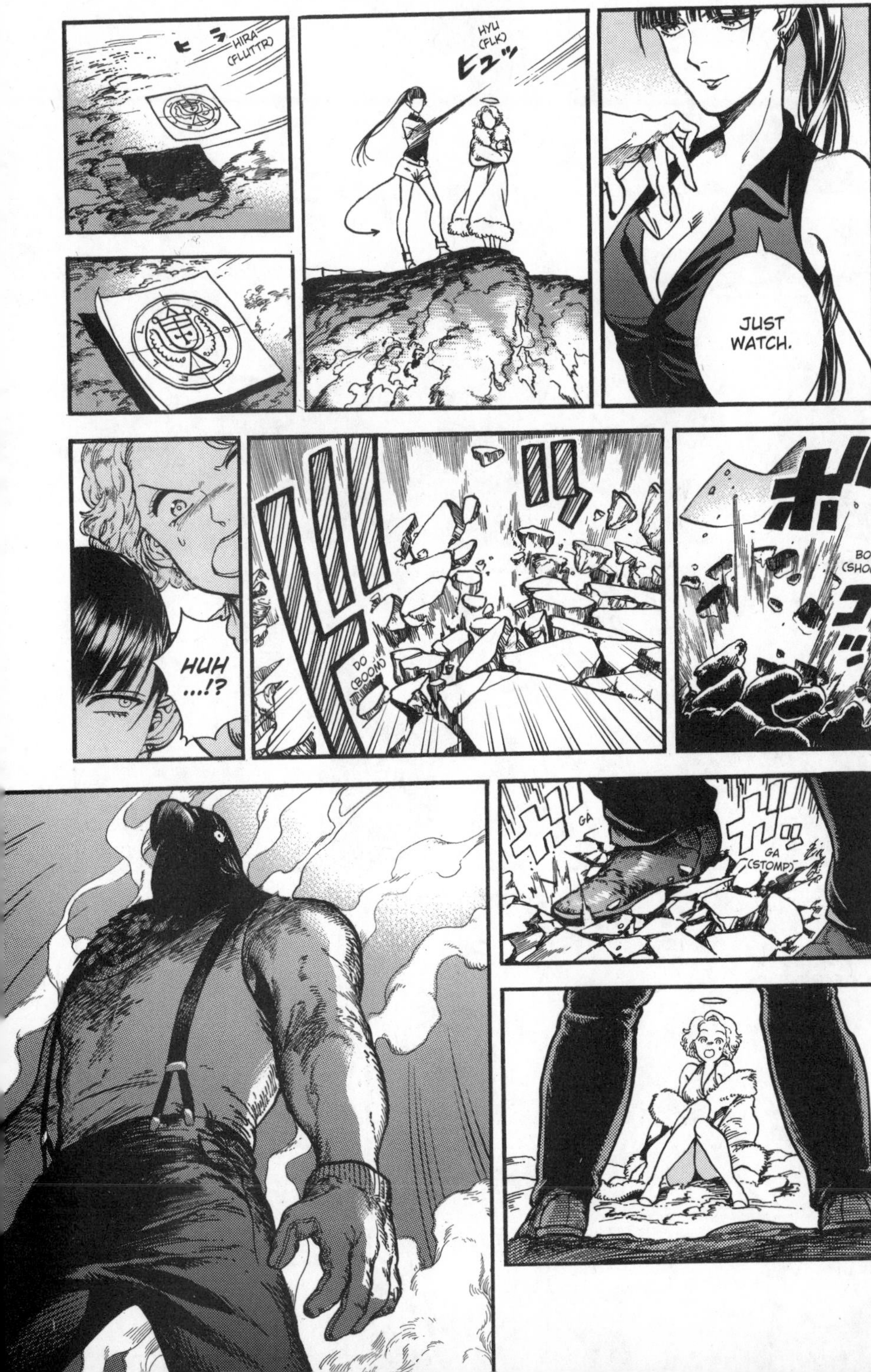

JUST WATCH.
ヒュッ
HYU (FLK)
ヒラ
HIRA (FLUTTR)
BOKO (SHOONK)
DO (BOOM)
HUH ...!?
GA
GA (STOMP)

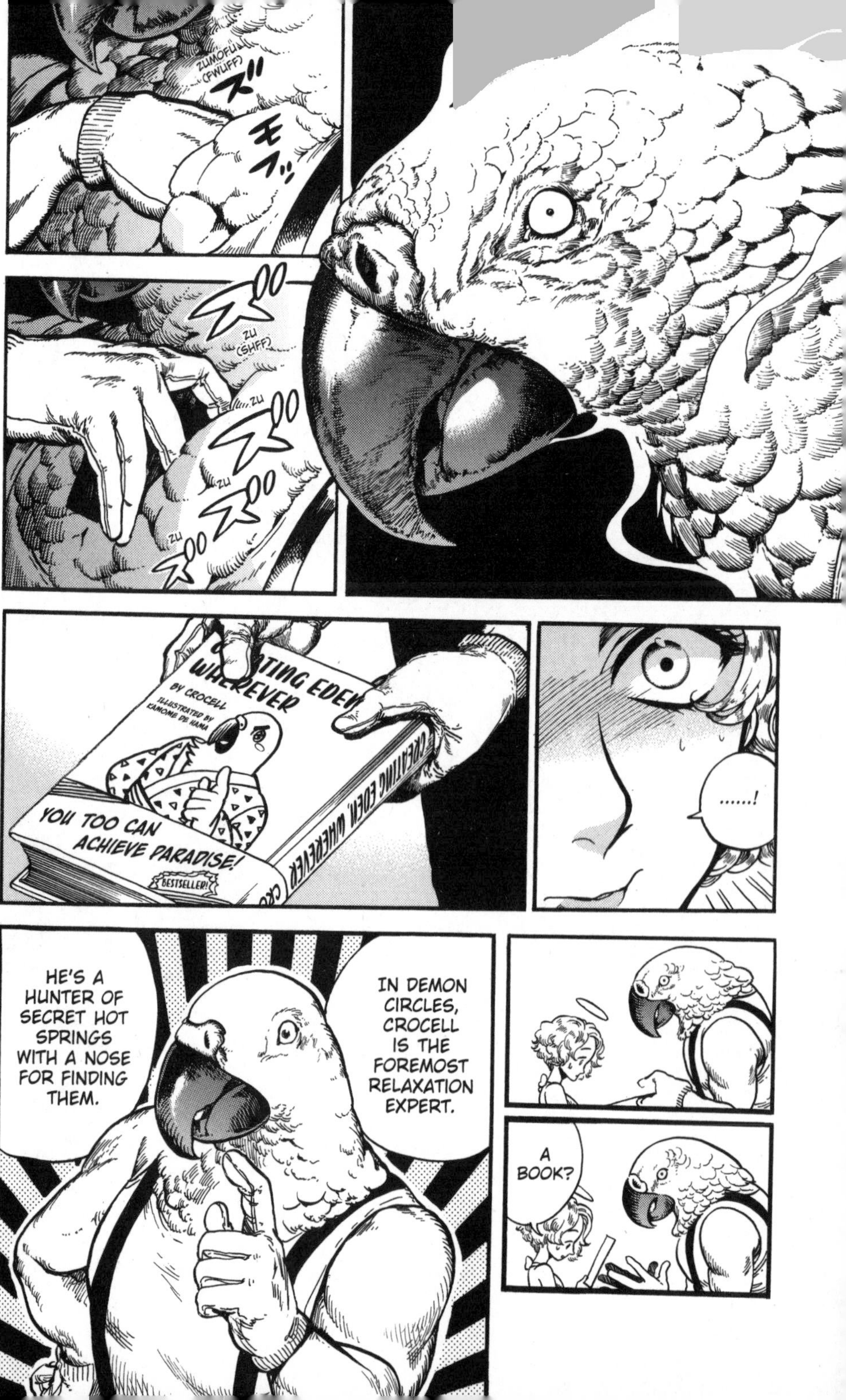
ZUMOFU (FWUFF)
ZU (SHFF)
ZU
ZU
ZU
......!
CREATING EDEN WHEREVER
BY CROCELL
ILLUSTRATED BY KAMOME DE HAMA
YOU TOO CAN ACHIEVE PARADISE!
BESTSELLER!
CREATING EDEN, WHEREVER
A BOOK?
IN DEMON CIRCLES, CROCELL IS THE FOREMOST RELAXATION EXPERT.
HE'S A HUNTER OF SECRET HOT SPRINGS WITH A NOSE FOR FINDING THEM.

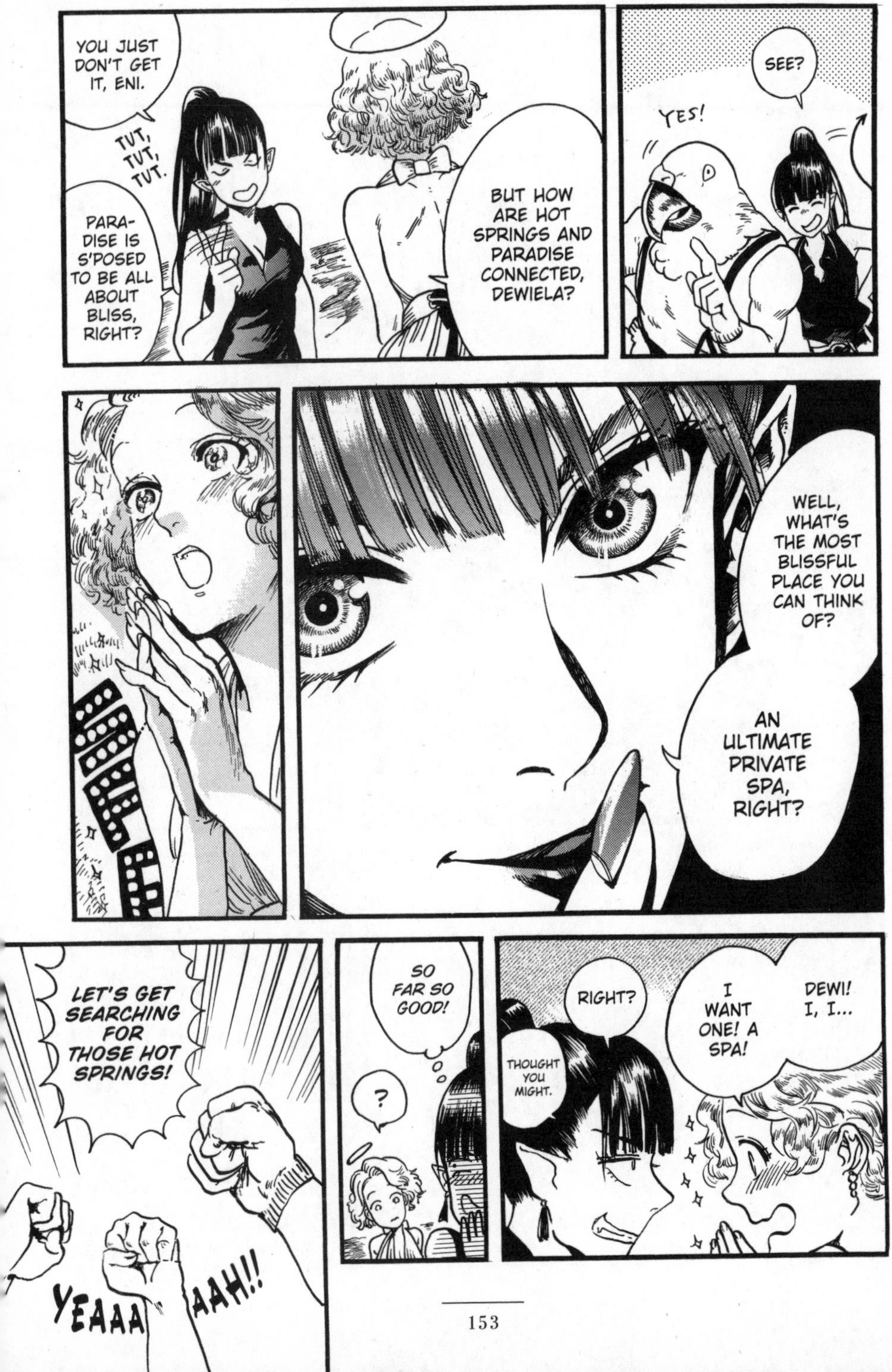
SEE?
YES!
BUT HOW ARE HOT SPRINGS AND PARADISE CONNECTED, DEWIELA?
YOU JUST DON'T GET IT, ENI.
TUT, TUT, TUT.
PARA-DISE IS S'POSED TO BE ALL ABOUT BLISS, RIGHT?
WELL, WHAT'S THE MOST BLISSFUL PLACE YOU CAN THINK OF?
AN ULTIMATE PRIVATE SPA, RIGHT?
DEWI! I, I...
I WANT ONE! A SPA!
RIGHT?
THOUGHT YOU MIGHT.
SO FAR SO GOOD!
?
LET'S GET SEARCHING FOR THOSE HOT SPRINGS!
YEAAAAAH!!

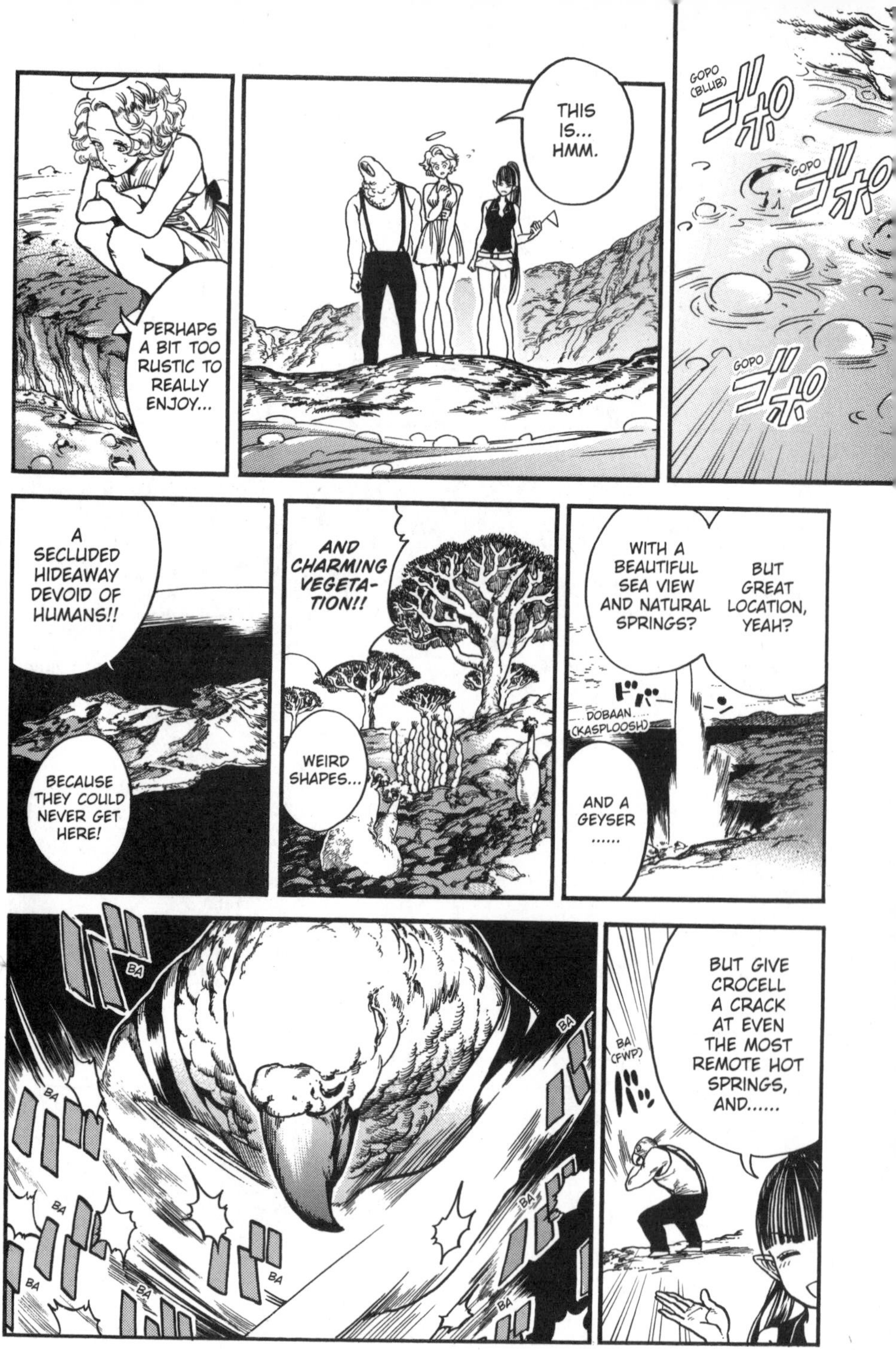
GOPO (BLUB)
ゴポ
GOPO
ゴポ
GOPO
ゴポ
THIS IS... HMM.
PERHAPS A BIT TOO RUSTIC TO REALLY ENJOY...
BUT GREAT LOCATION, YEAH?
WITH A BEAUTIFUL SEA VIEW AND NATURAL SPRINGS?
ドバーン
DOBAAN (KASPLOOSH)
AND A GEYSER ......
AND CHARMING VEGETATION!!
WEIRD SHAPES...
A SECLUDED HIDEAWAY DEVOID OF HUMANS!!
BECAUSE THEY COULD NEVER GET HERE!
BUT GIVE CROCELL A CRACK AT EVEN THE MOST REMOTE HOT SPRINGS, AND......
BA (FWP)
バッ
BA
BA
BA
BA
BA
BA
BA
BA
BA

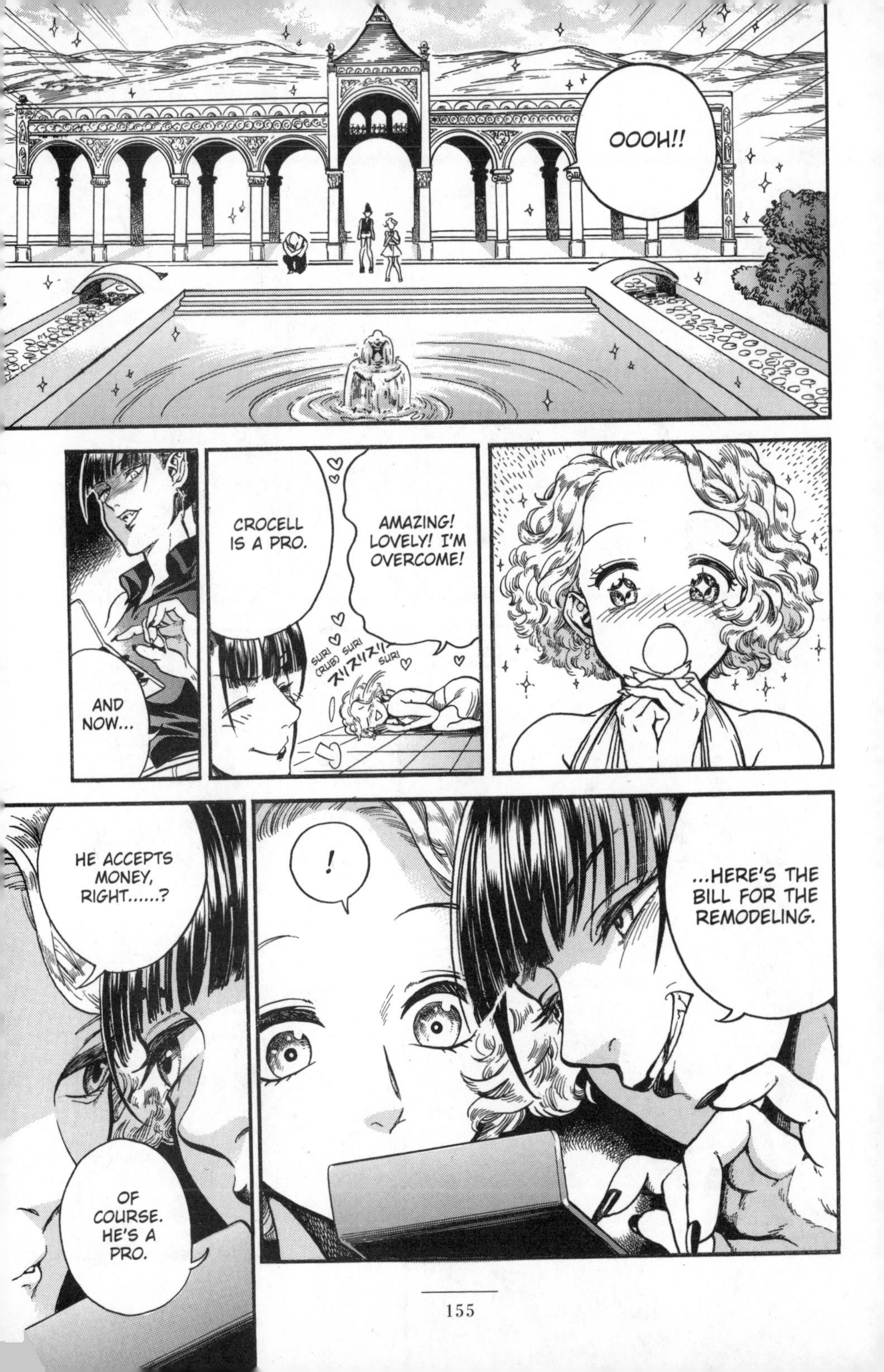
OOOH!!
AMAZING! LOVELY! I'M OVERCOME!
CROCELL IS A PRO.
SURI (RUB) SURI スリスリスリ SURI
AND NOW...
...HERE'S THE BILL FOR THE REMODELING.
!
HE ACCEPTS MONEY, RIGHT......?
OF COURSE. HE'S A PRO.

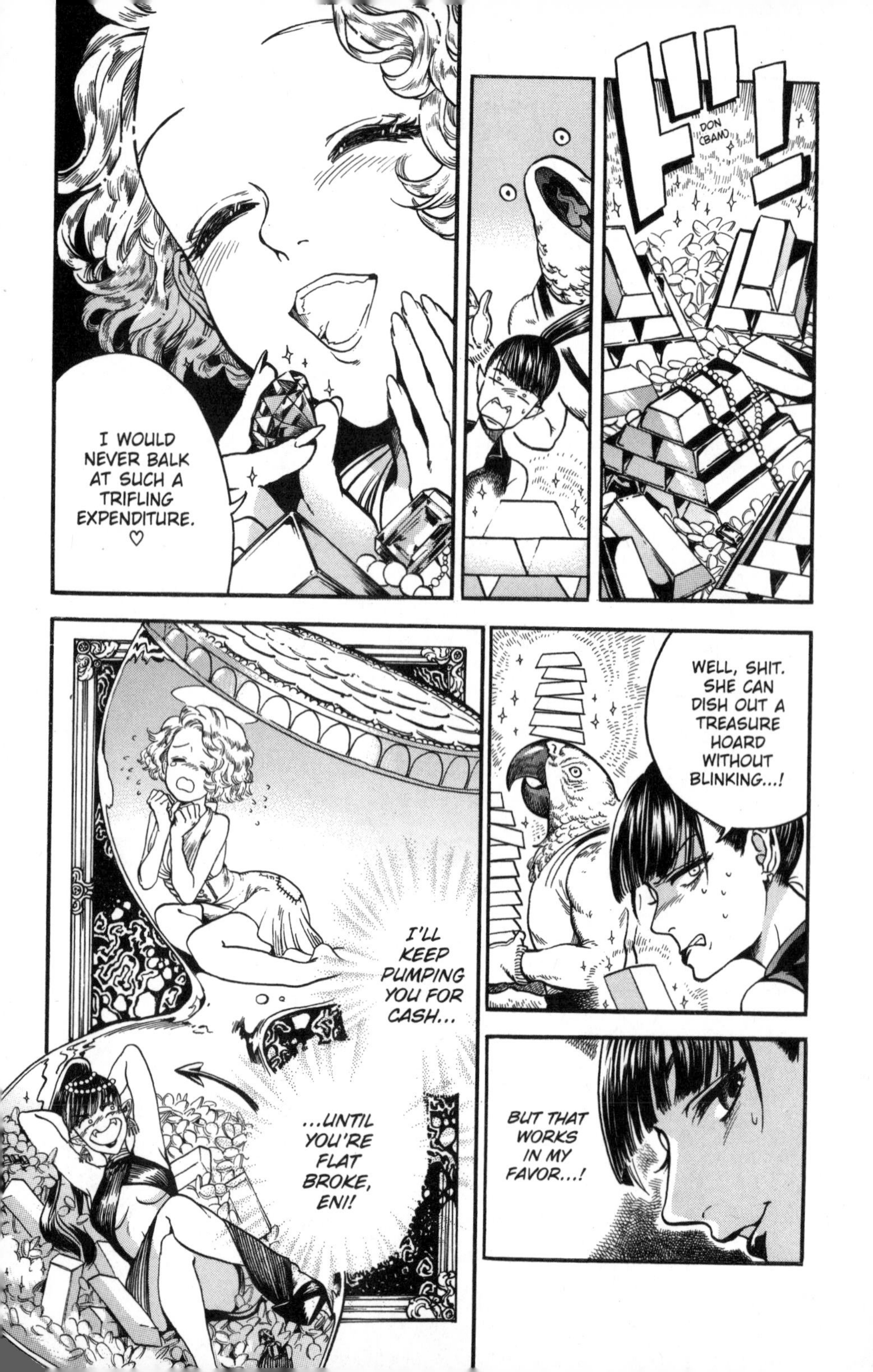
DON (BAM)
I WOULD NEVER BALK AT SUCH A TRIFLING EXPENDITURE. ♡
WELL, SHIT. SHE CAN DISH OUT A TREASURE HOARD WITHOUT BLINKING...!
BUT THAT WORKS IN MY FAVOR...!
I'LL KEEP PUMPING YOU FOR CASH...
...UNTIL YOU'RE FLAT BROKE, ENI!

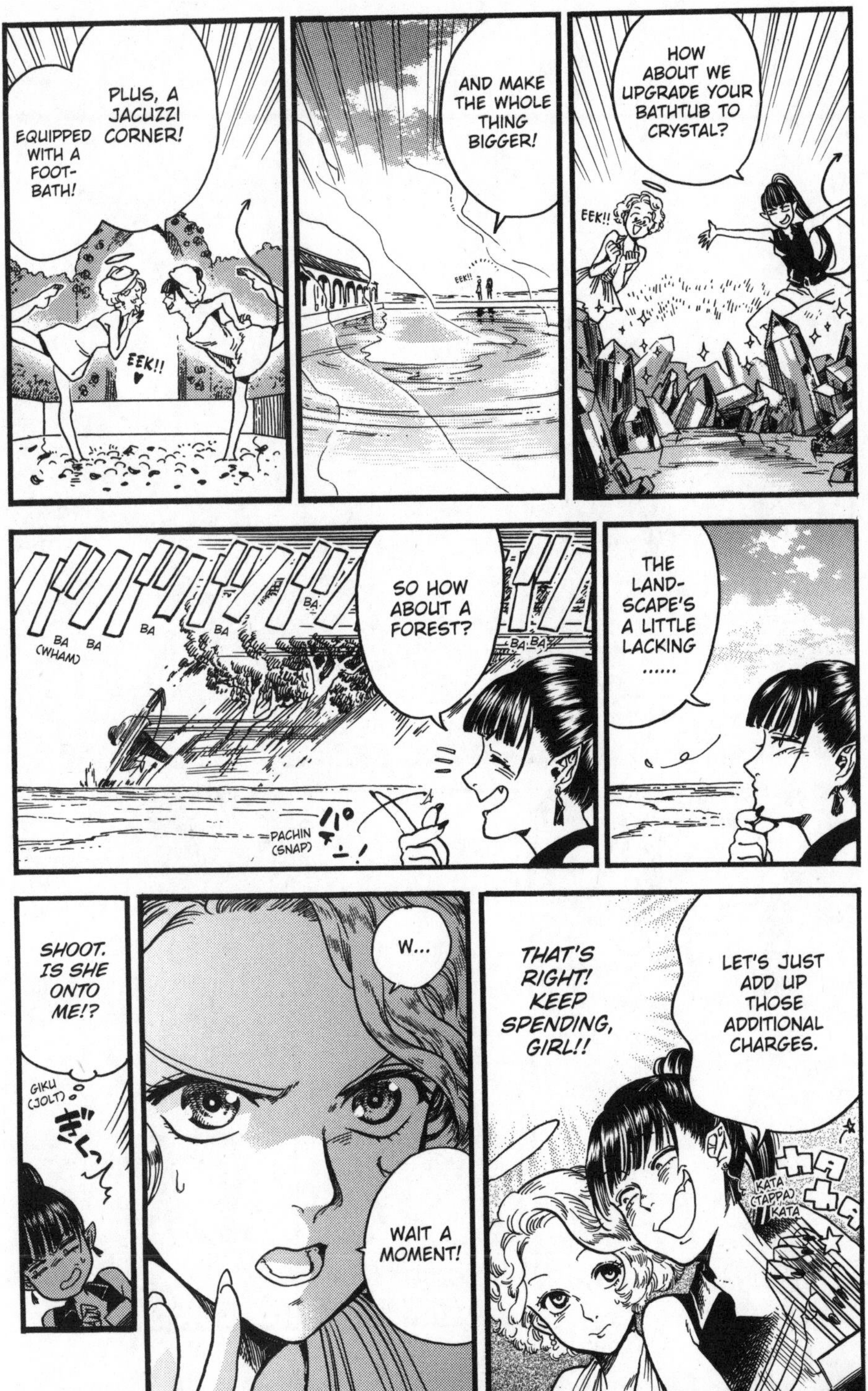
HOW ABOUT WE UPGRADE YOUR BATHTUB TO CRYSTAL?
EEK!!
AND MAKE THE WHOLE THING BIGGER!
EEK!!
PLUS, A JACUZZI CORNER!
EQUIPPED WITH A FOOT-BATH!
EEK!!
THE LAND-SCAPE'S A LITTLE LACKING ......
SO HOW ABOUT A FOREST?
BA BA
BA BA BA BA
BA BA (WHAM)
PACHIN (SNAP)
LET'S JUST ADD UP THOSE ADDITIONAL CHARGES.
THAT'S RIGHT! KEEP SPENDING, GIRL!!
KATA (TAPPA) KATA
W...
WAIT A MOMENT!
SHOOT. IS SHE ONTO ME!?
GIKU (JOLT)

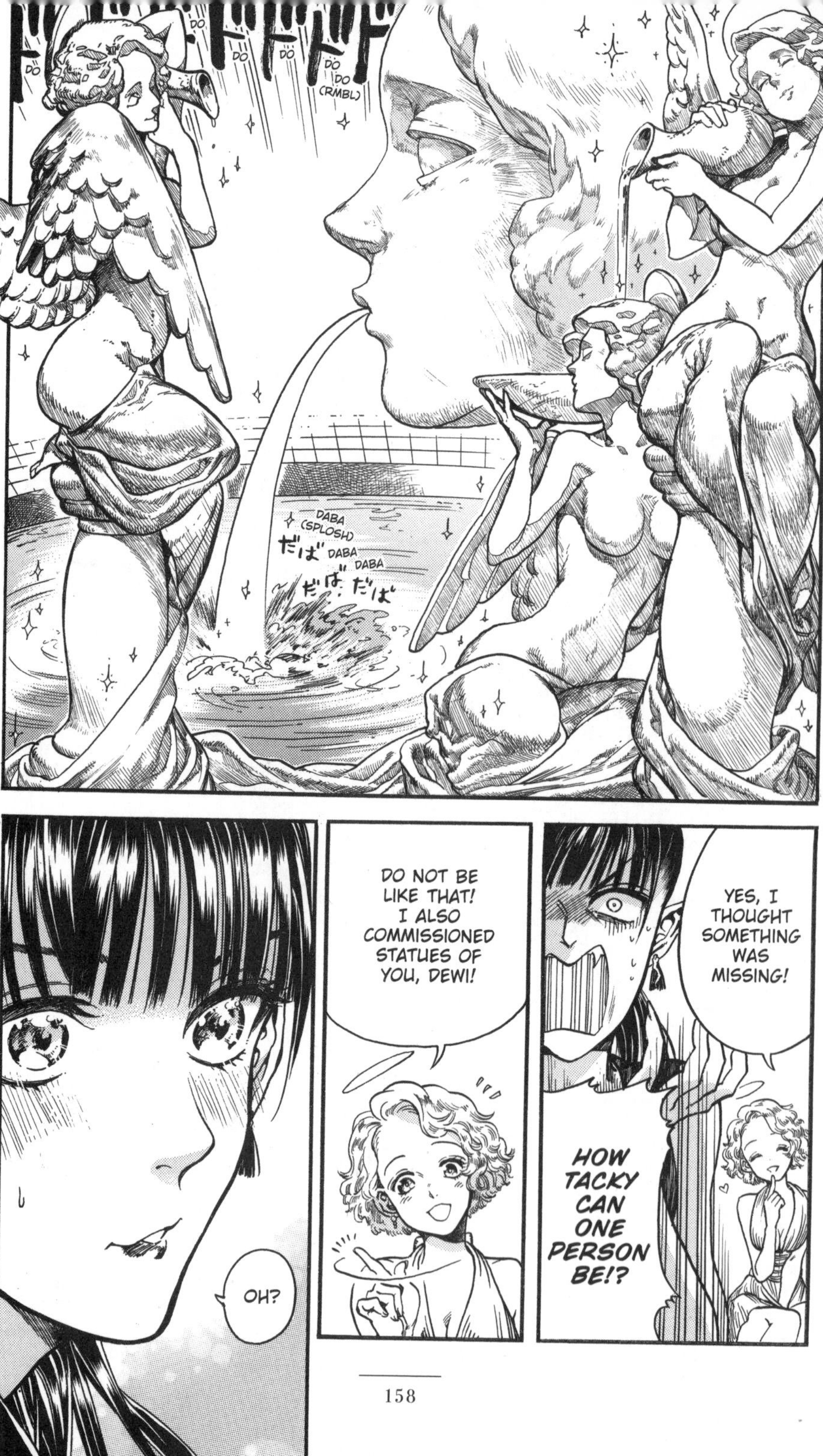
DO DO DO DO DO DO
(RMBL)
DABA (SPLOSH)
だば DABA DABA
だばだば
YES, I THOUGHT SOMETHING WAS MISSING!
HOW TACKY CAN ONE PERSON BE!?
DO NOT BE LIKE THAT! I ALSO COMMISSIONED STATUES OF YOU, DEWI!
OH?

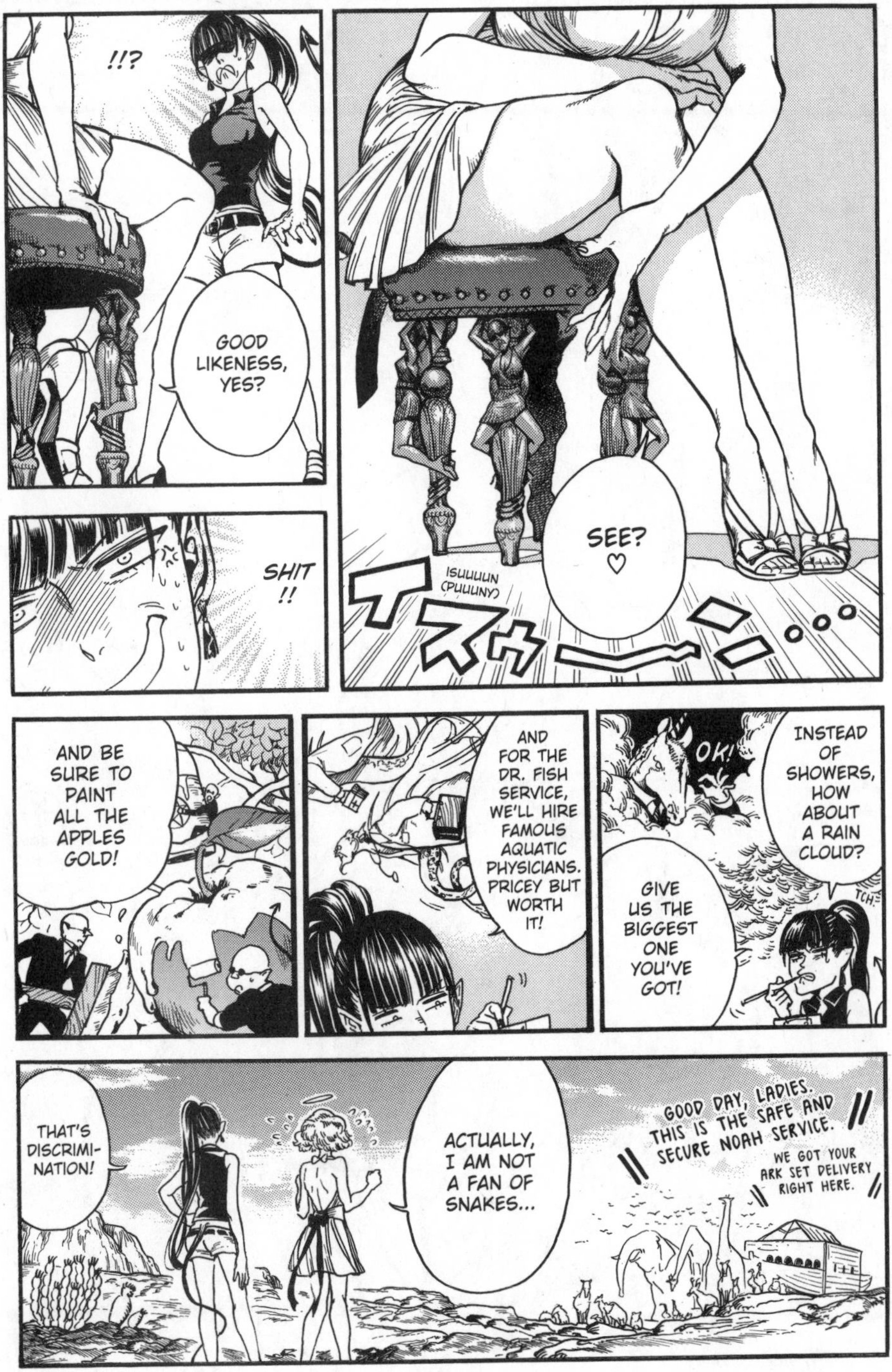
SEE? ♡
ISUUUUN (PUUUNY)
!!?
GOOD LIKENESS, YES?
SHIT !!
INSTEAD OF SHOWERS, HOW ABOUT A RAIN CLOUD?
OK!
GIVE US THE BIGGEST ONE YOU'VE GOT!
TCH.
AND FOR THE DR. FISH SERVICE, WE'LL HIRE FAMOUS AQUATIC PHYSICIANS. PRICEY BUT WORTH IT!
AND BE SURE TO PAINT ALL THE APPLES GOLD!
GOOD DAY, LADIES. THIS IS THE SAFE AND SECURE NOAH SERVICE.
WE GOT YOUR ARK SET DELIVERY RIGHT HERE.
ACTUALLY, I AM NOT A FAN OF SNAKES...
THAT'S DISCRIMINATION!

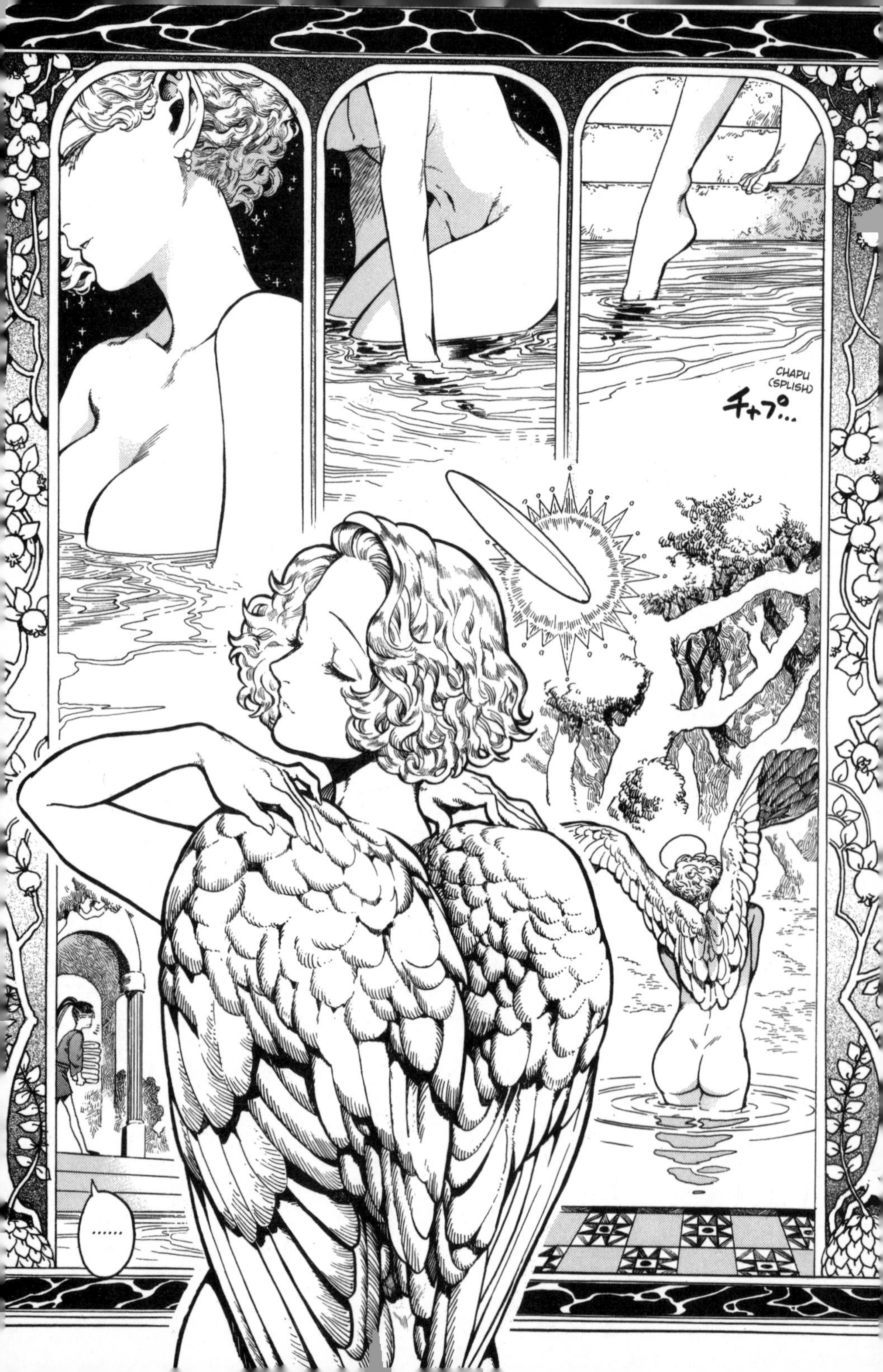
CHAPU (SPLISH)
チャプ…
……

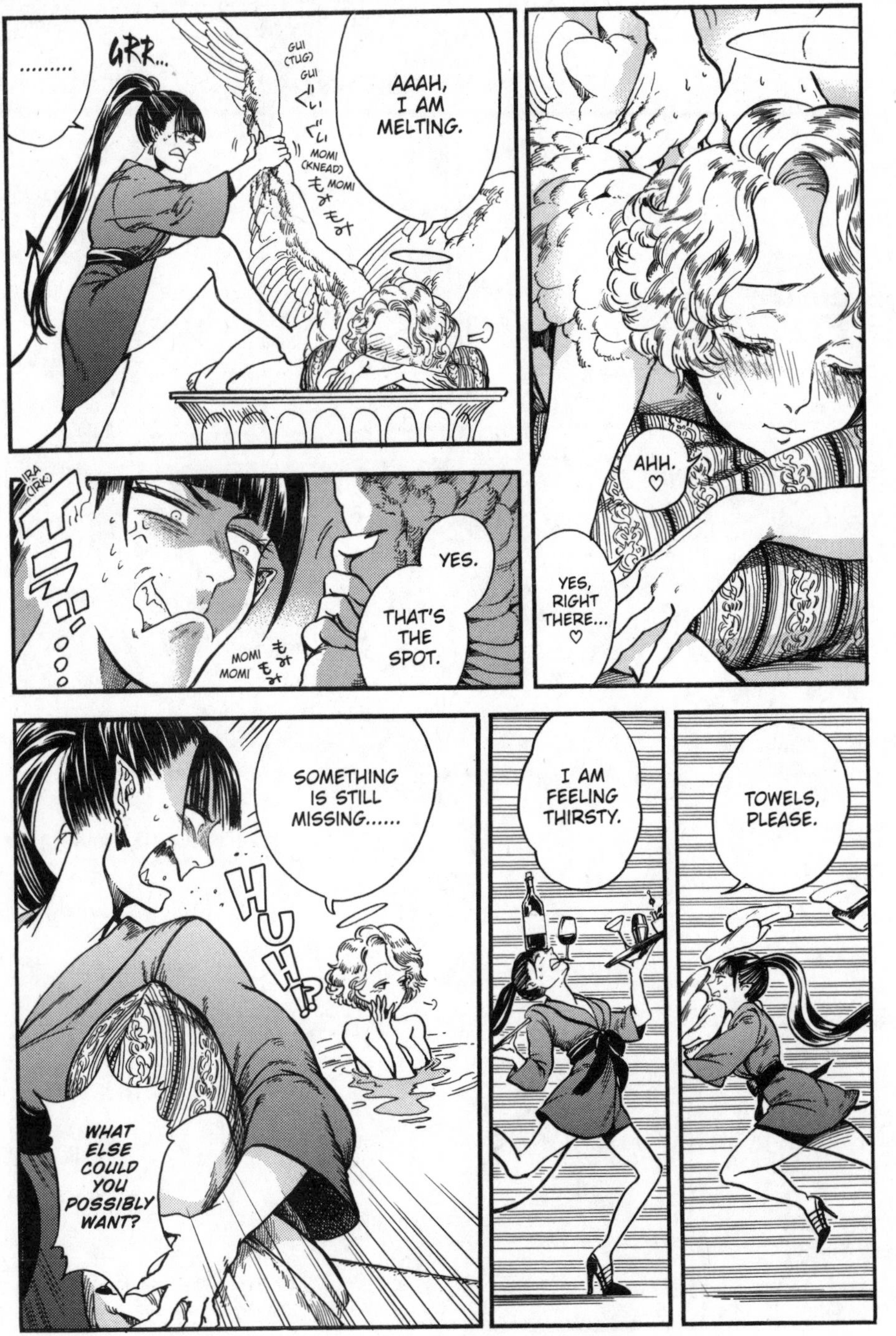
AHH. ♡
YES, RIGHT THERE... ♡
AAAH, I AM MELTING.
GUI (TUG) GUI
MOMI (KNEAD) MOMI
GRR...
....
YES.
THAT'S THE SPOT.
MOMI MOMI
IRA (IRK)
TOWELS, PLEASE.
I AM FEELING THIRSTY.
SOMETHING IS STILL MISSING......
HUH?!
WHAT ELSE COULD YOU POSSIBLY WANT?

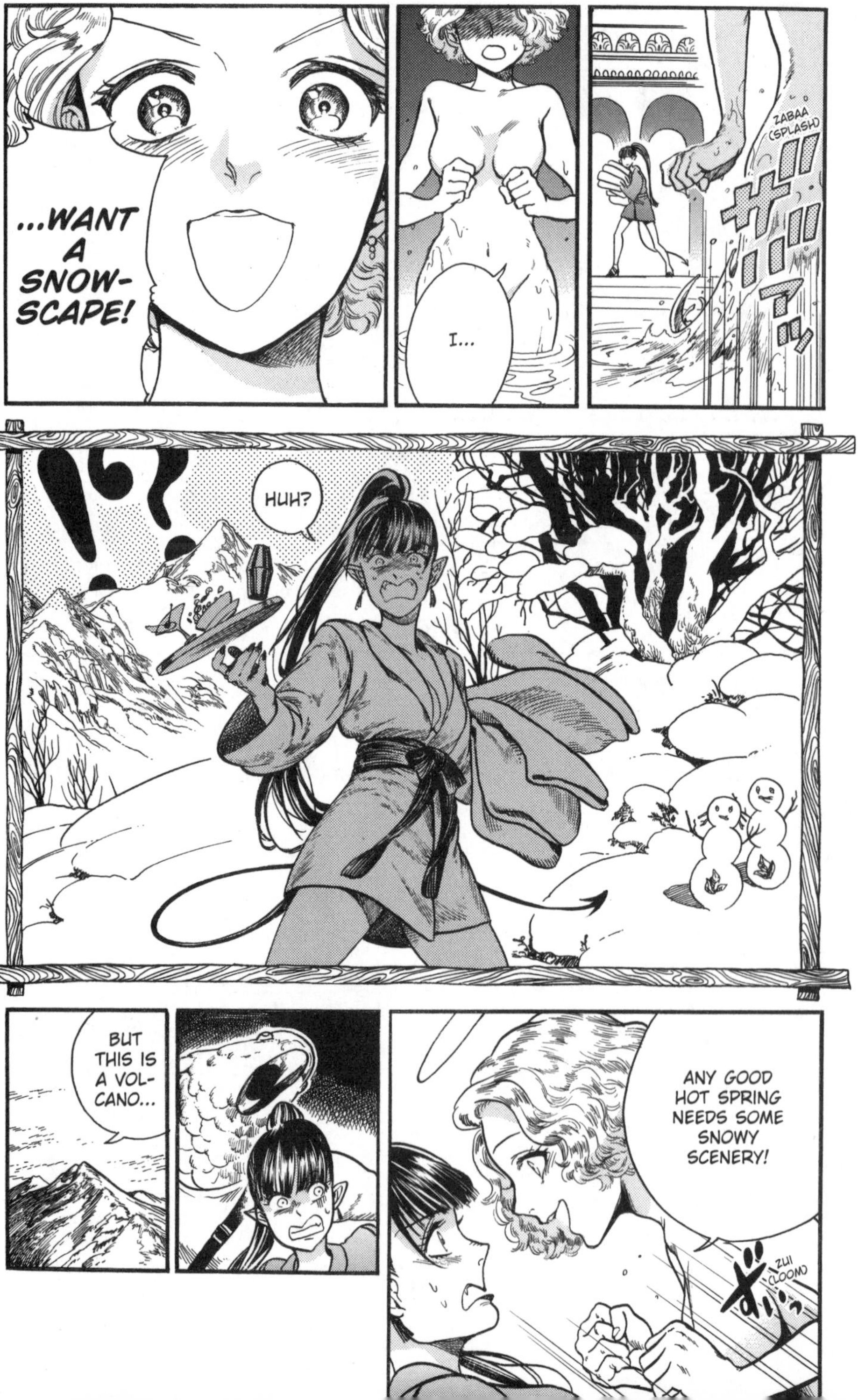
ZABAA (SPLASH)
I...
...WANT A SNOW-SCAPE!
HUH?
!?
ANY GOOD HOT SPRING NEEDS SOME SNOWY SCENERY!
ZUI (LOOM)
BUT THIS IS A VOL-CANO...

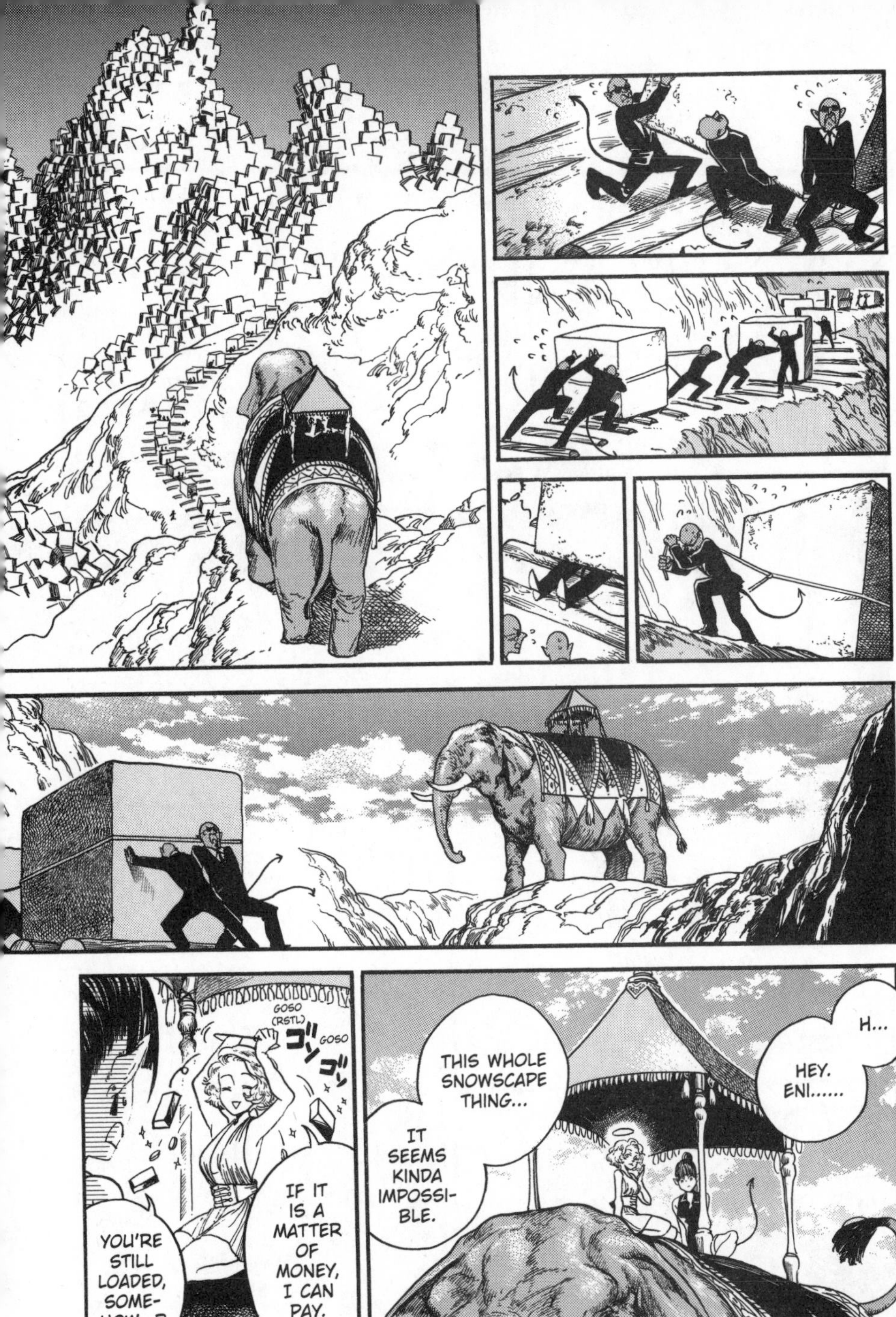
H...
HEY. ENI......
THIS WHOLE SNOWSCAPE THING...
IT SEEMS KINDA IMPOSSI-BLE.
GOSO (RSTL)
ゴソ
GOSO
ゴソ
IF IT IS A MATTER OF MONEY, I CAN PAY.
YOU'RE STILL LOADED, SOME-HOW...?

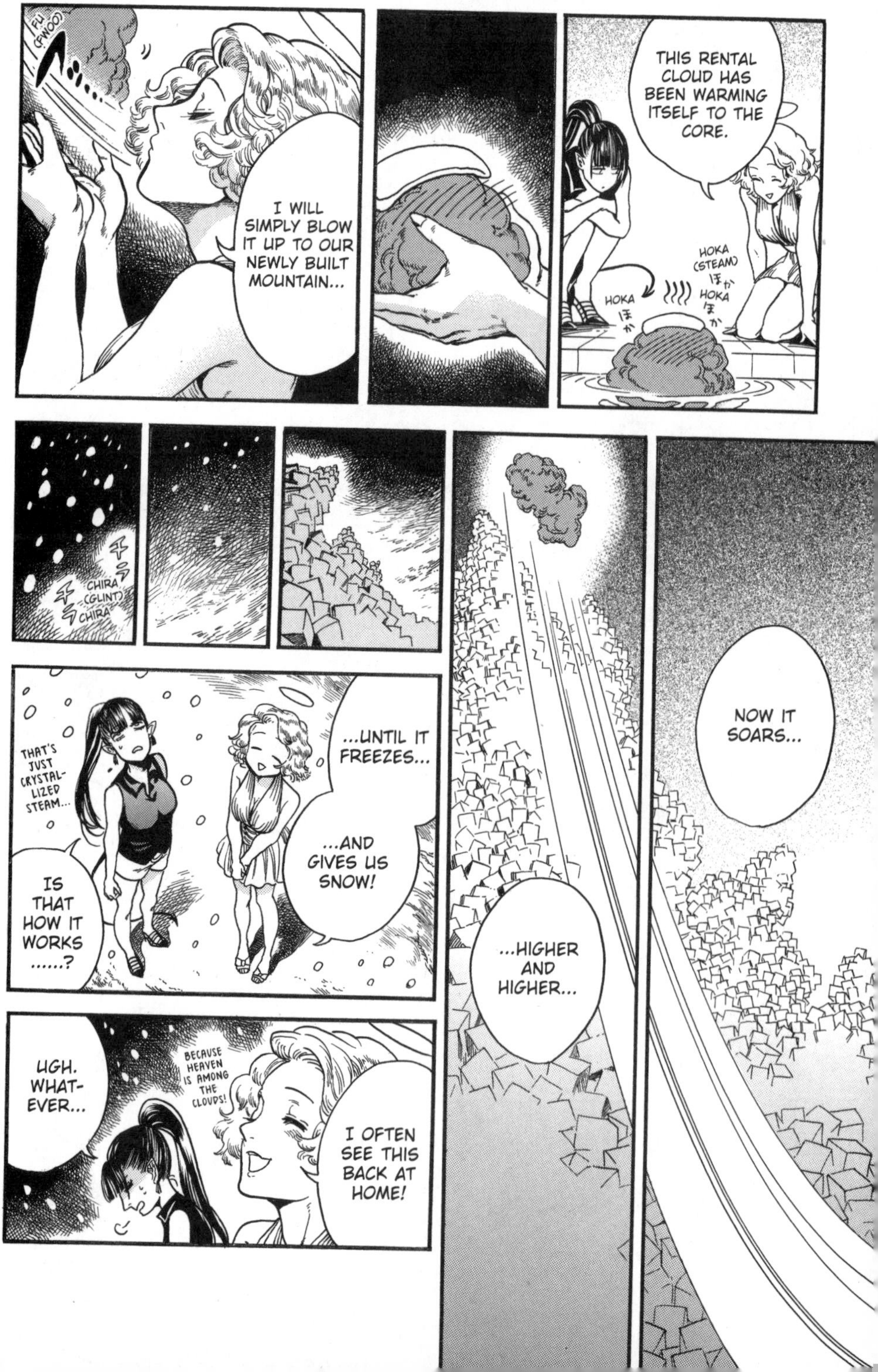
THIS RENTAL CLOUD HAS BEEN WARMING ITSELF TO THE CORE.
HOKA (STEAM) ほか HOKA ほか
HOKA ほか
I WILL SIMPLY BLOW IT UP TO OUR NEWLY BUILT MOUNTAIN...
FU (FWOO)
NOW IT SOARS...
...HIGHER AND HIGHER...
CHIRA (GLINT) CHIRA
...UNTIL IT FREEZES...
...AND GIVES US SNOW!
THAT'S JUST CRYSTALLIZED STEAM...
IS THAT HOW IT WORKS ......?
I OFTEN SEE THIS BACK AT HOME!
BECAUSE HEAVEN IS AMONG THE CLOUDS!
UGH. WHATEVER...

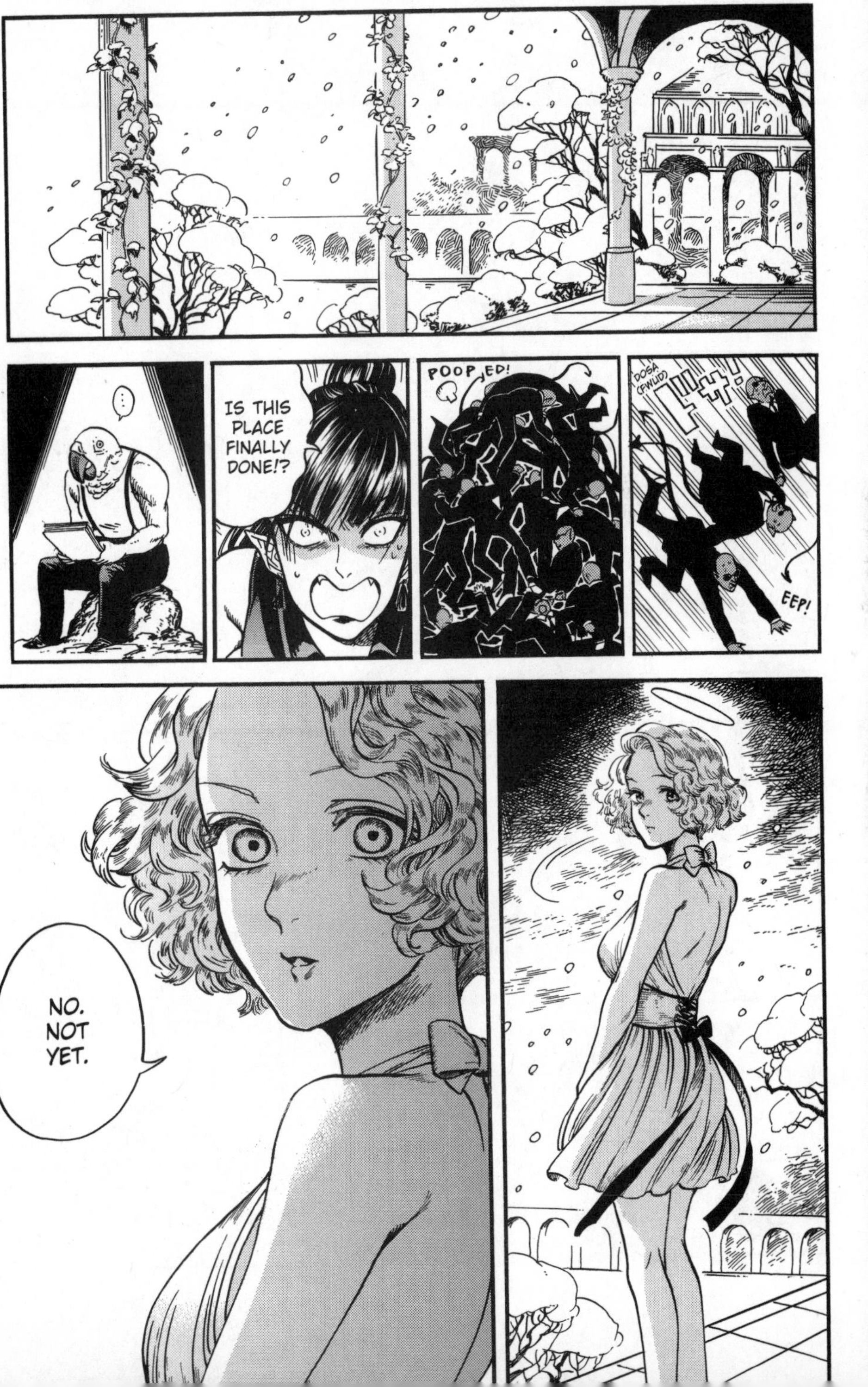
DOSA
(FWUD)
EEP!
POOP ED!
IS THIS PLACE FINALLY DONE!?
...
NO. NOT YET.

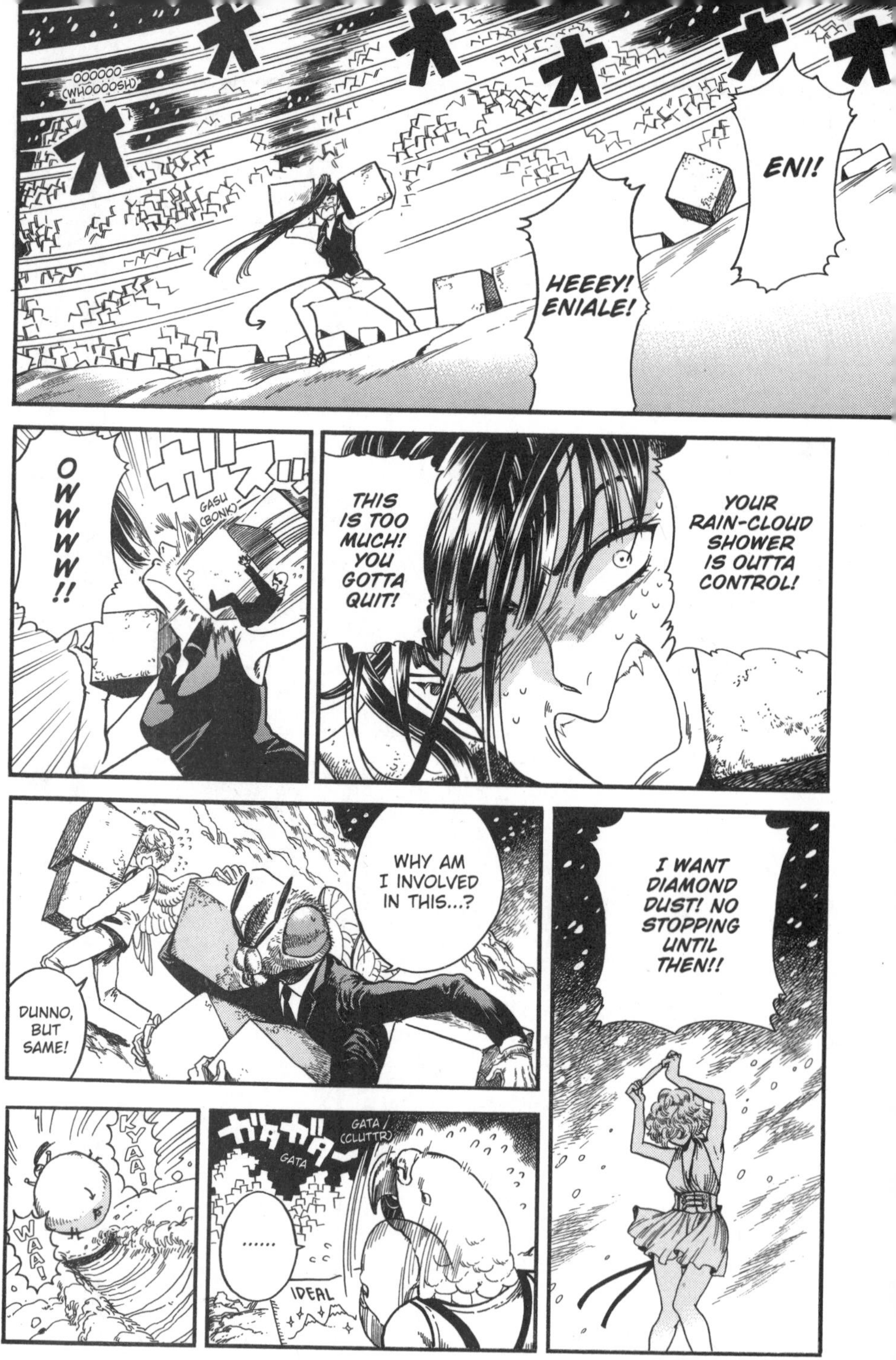
ENI!
HEEEY! ENIALE!
OOOOOO (WHOOOOSH)
YOUR RAIN-CLOUD SHOWER IS OUTTA CONTROL!
THIS IS TOO MUCH! YOU GOTTA QUIT!
GASU (BONK)
OWWWWW!!
I WANT DIAMOND DUST! NO STOPPING UNTIL THEN!!
WHY AM I INVOLVED IN THIS...?
DUNNO, BUT SAME!
GATA GATA (CLUTTR)
......
IDEAL
KYAA!
WAAA!

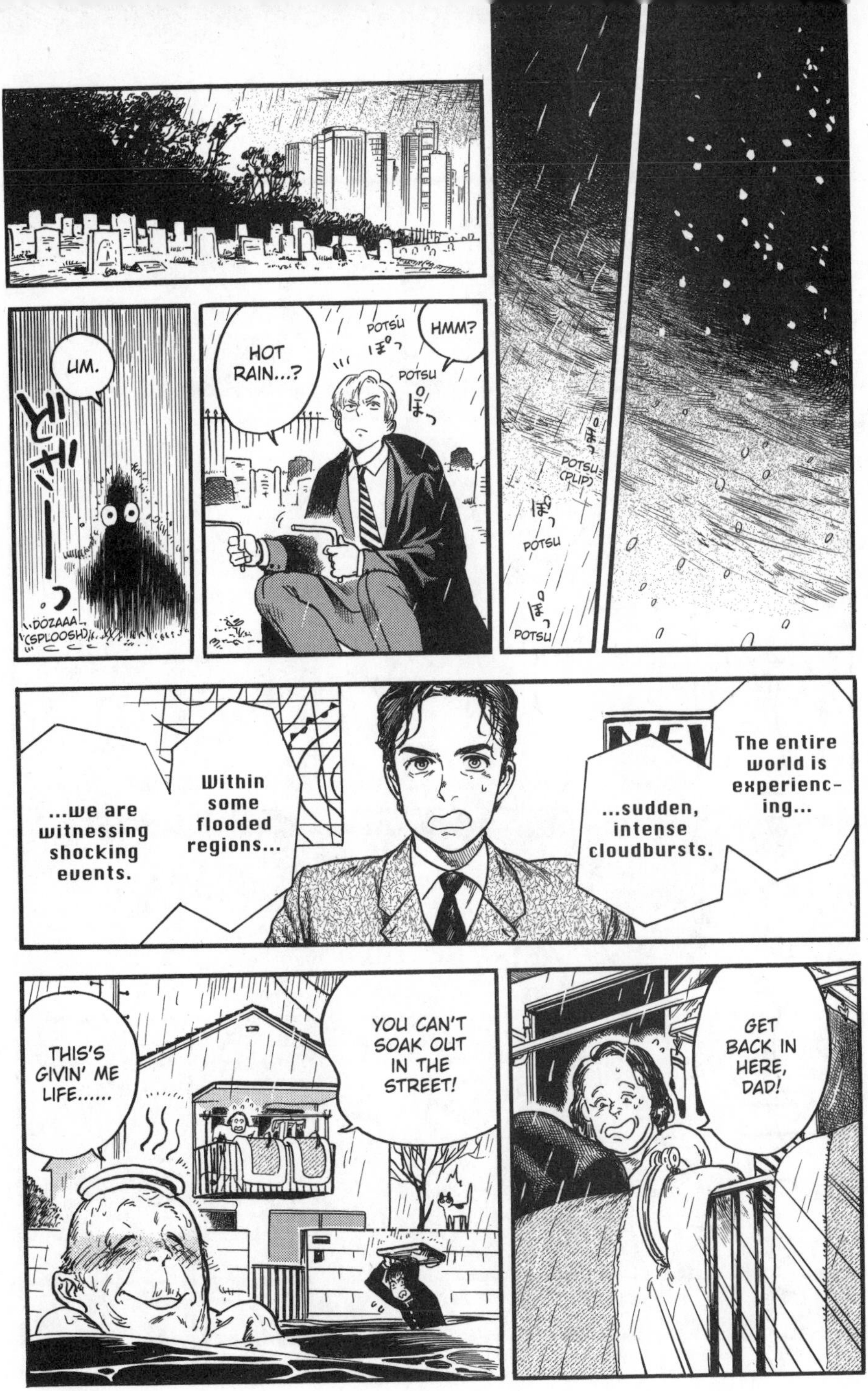
ぽっ
POTSU (PLIP)
ぽっ
POTSU
ぽっ
POTSU
HMM?
POTSU ぽっ
POTSU ぽっ
HOT RAIN...?
UM.
どざーっ
DOZAAA (SPLOOSH)
The entire world is experiencing...
...sudden, intense cloudbursts.
Within some flooded regions...
...we are witnessing shocking events.
GET BACK IN HERE, DAD!
YOU CAN'T SOAK OUT IN THE STREET!
THIS'S GIVIN' ME LIFE......

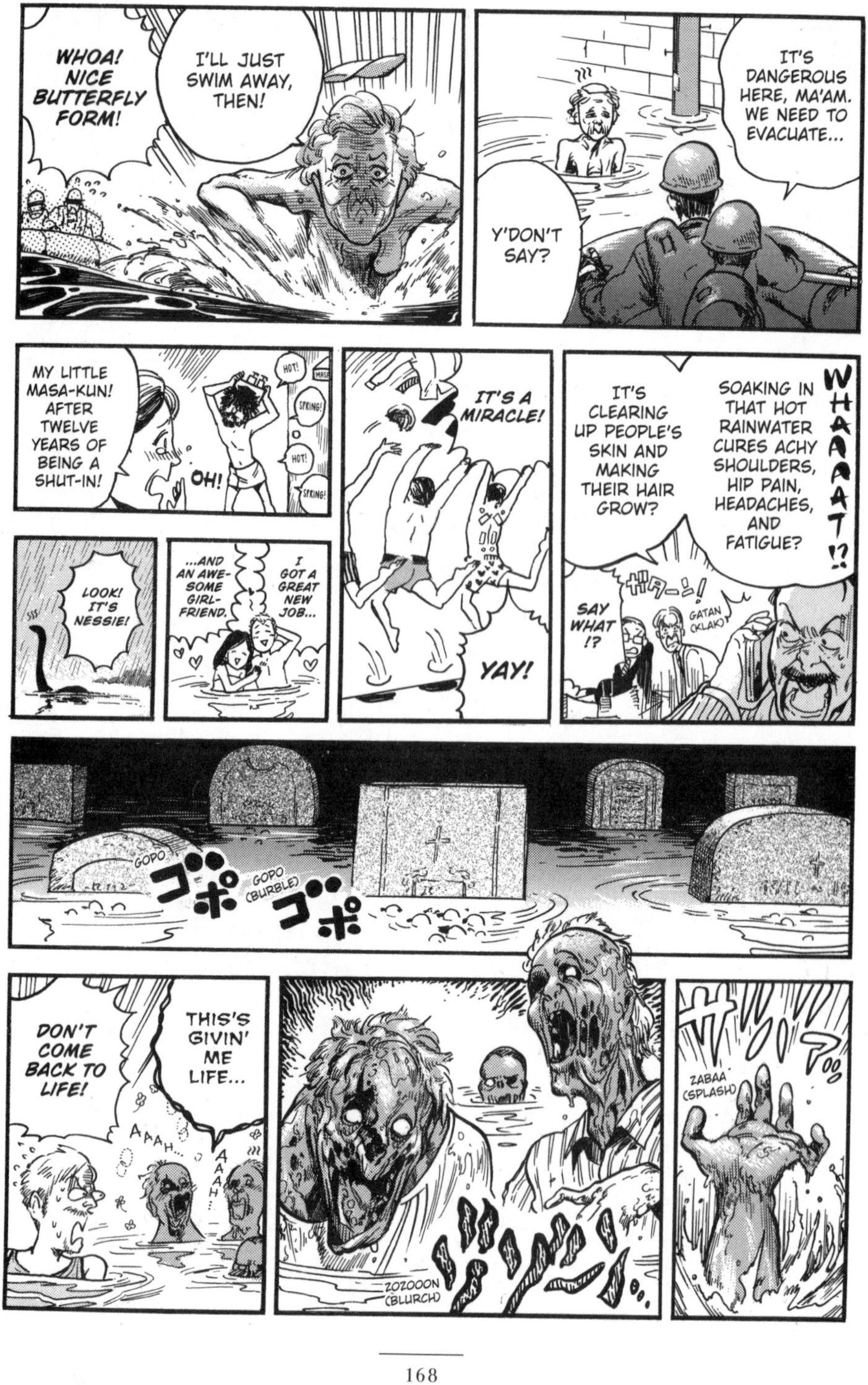
IT'S DANGEROUS HERE, MA'AM. WE NEED TO EVACUATE...
Y'DON'T SAY?
I'LL JUST SWIM AWAY, THEN!
WHOA! NICE BUTTERFLY FORM!
SOAKING IN THAT HOT RAINWATER CURES ACHY SHOULDERS, HIP PAIN, HEADACHES, AND FATIGUE?
IT'S CLEARING UP PEOPLE'S SKIN AND MAKING THEIR HAIR GROW?
WHAAAAT!?
GATAN (KLAK)
SAY WHAT!?
IT'S A MIRACLE!
YAY!
MY LITTLE MASA-KUN! AFTER TWELVE YEARS OF BEING A SHUT-IN!
HOT!
SPRING!
HOT!
SPRING!
OH!
I GOT A GREAT NEW JOB...
...AND AN AWESOME GIRL-FRIEND.
LOOK! IT'S NESSIE!
GOPO
GOPO (BURBLE)
ZABAA (SPLASH)
ZOZOOON (BLURCH)
THIS'S GIVIN' ME LIFE...
DON'T COME BACK TO LIFE!
AAAH...
AAAH...

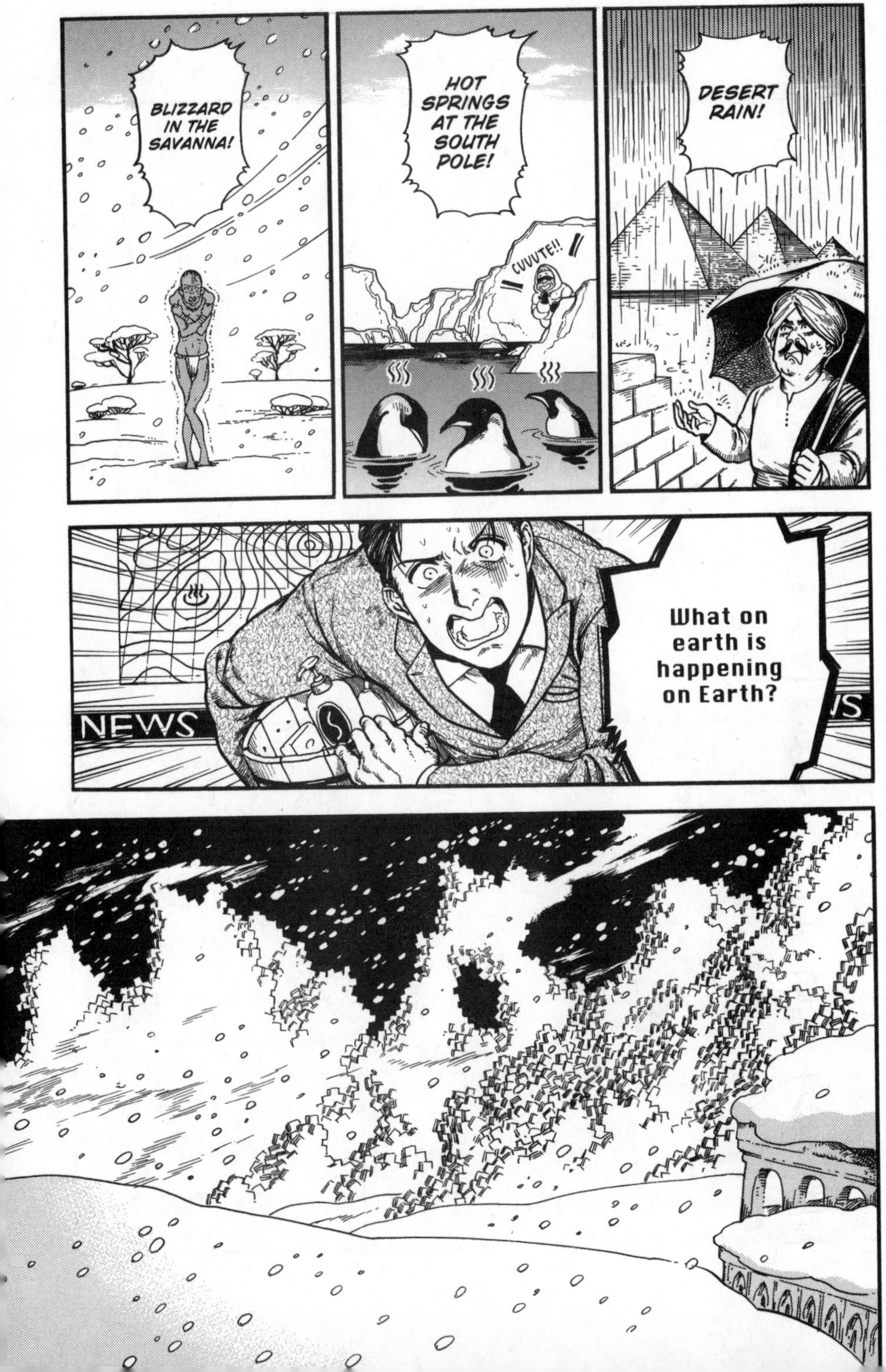
DESERT RAIN!
HOT SPRINGS AT THE SOUTH POLE!
CUUUTE!!
BLIZZARD IN THE SAVANNA!
What on earth is happening on Earth?
NEWS

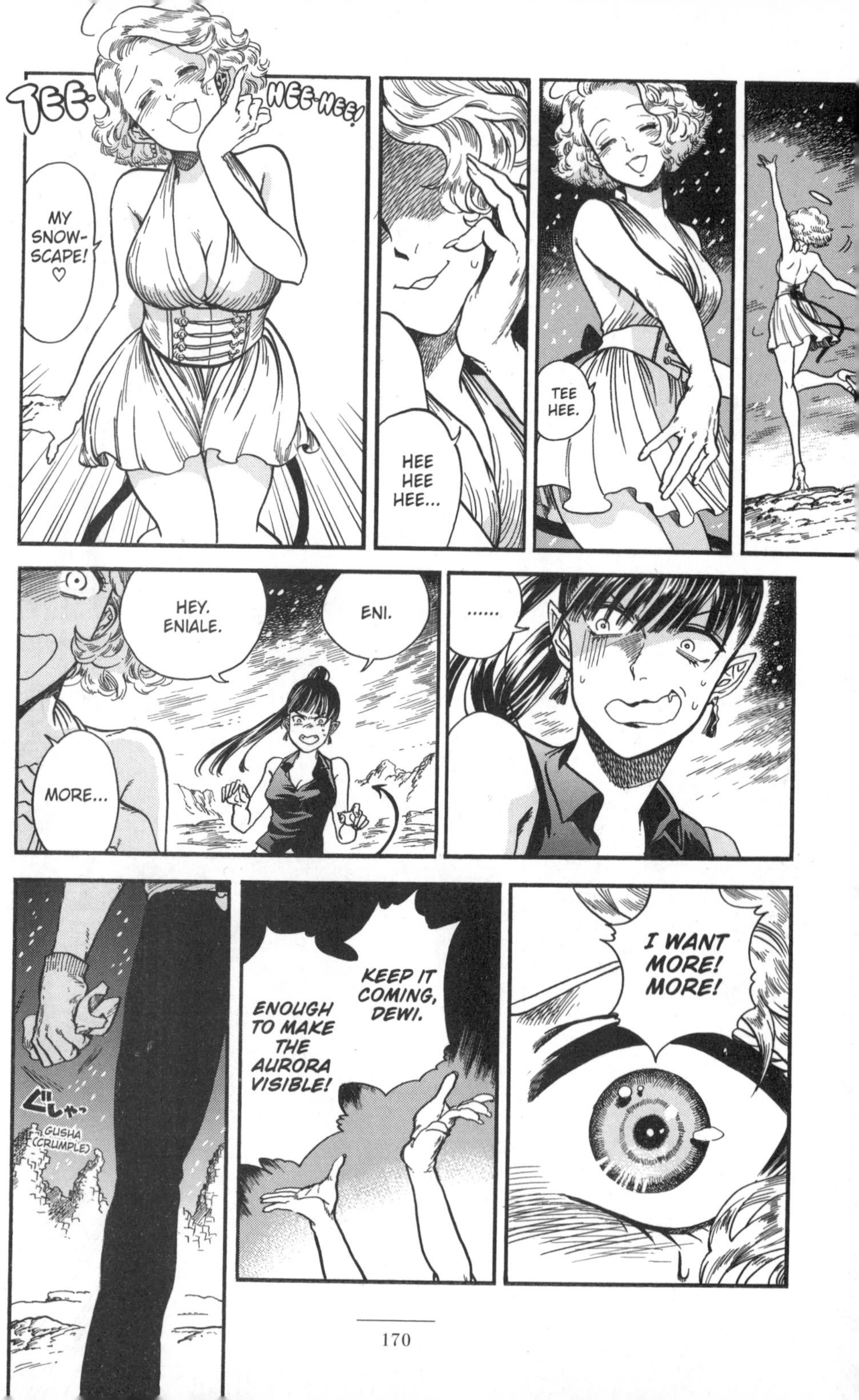
TEE HEE.
HEE HEE HEE...
TEE-HEE-HEE!
MY SNOW-SCAPE! ♡
......
ENI.
HEY. ENIALE.
MORE...
I WANT MORE! MORE!
KEEP IT COMING, DEWI.
ENOUGH TO MAKE THE AURORA VISIBLE!
ぐしゃっ
GUSHA (CRUMPLE)

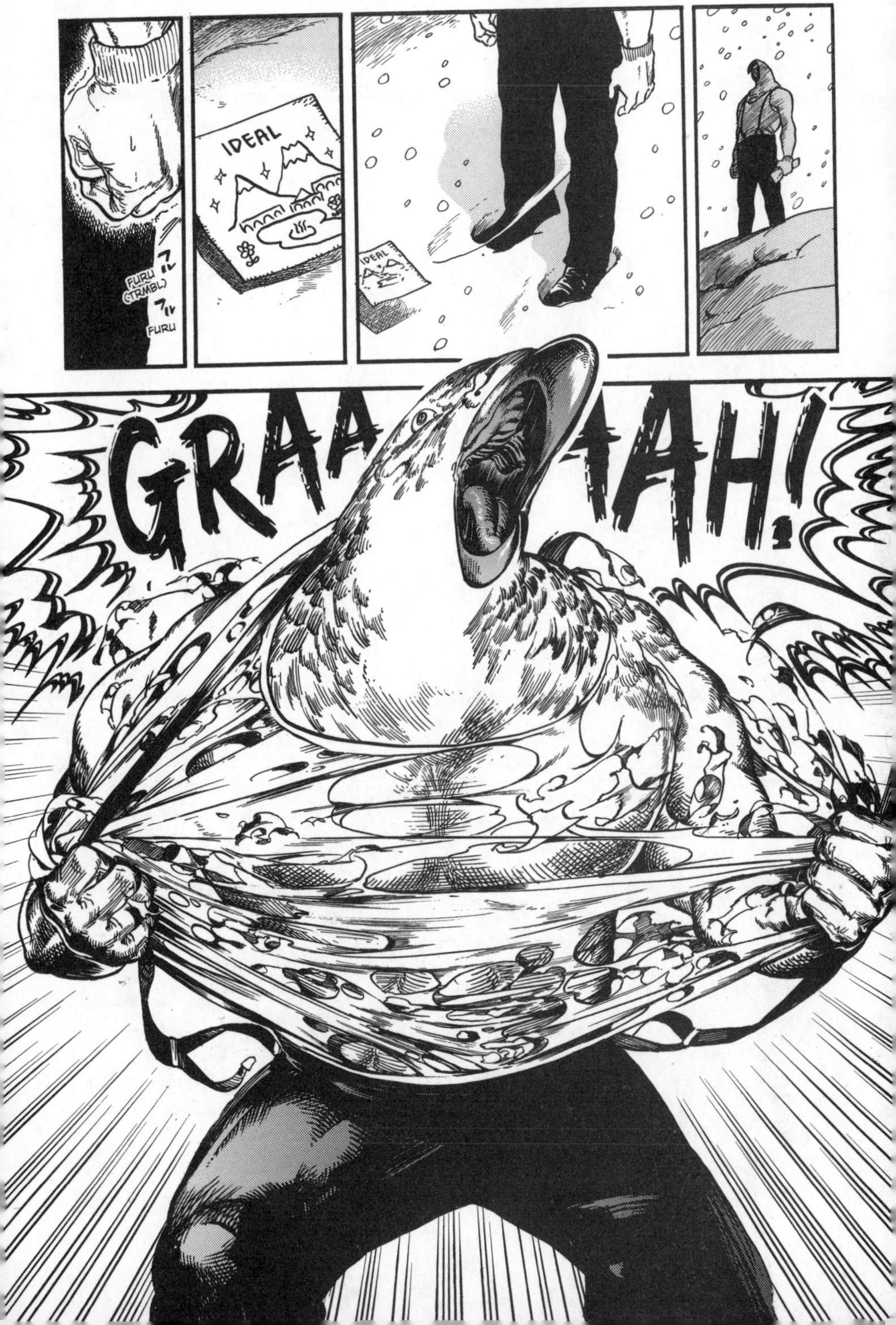
IDEAL
IDEAL
フル FURU (TRMBL)
フル FURU
GRAAAAH!

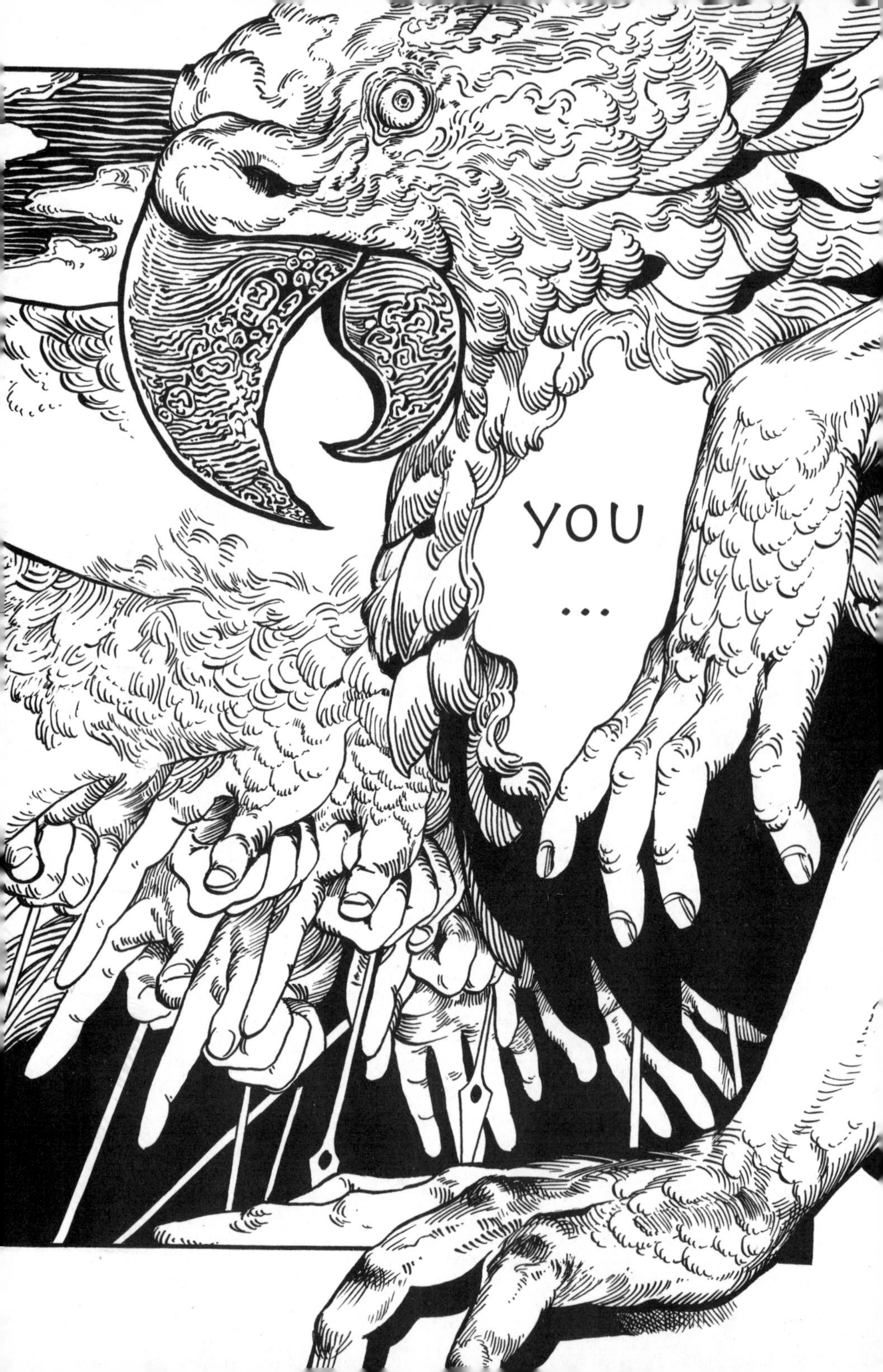
YOU
...

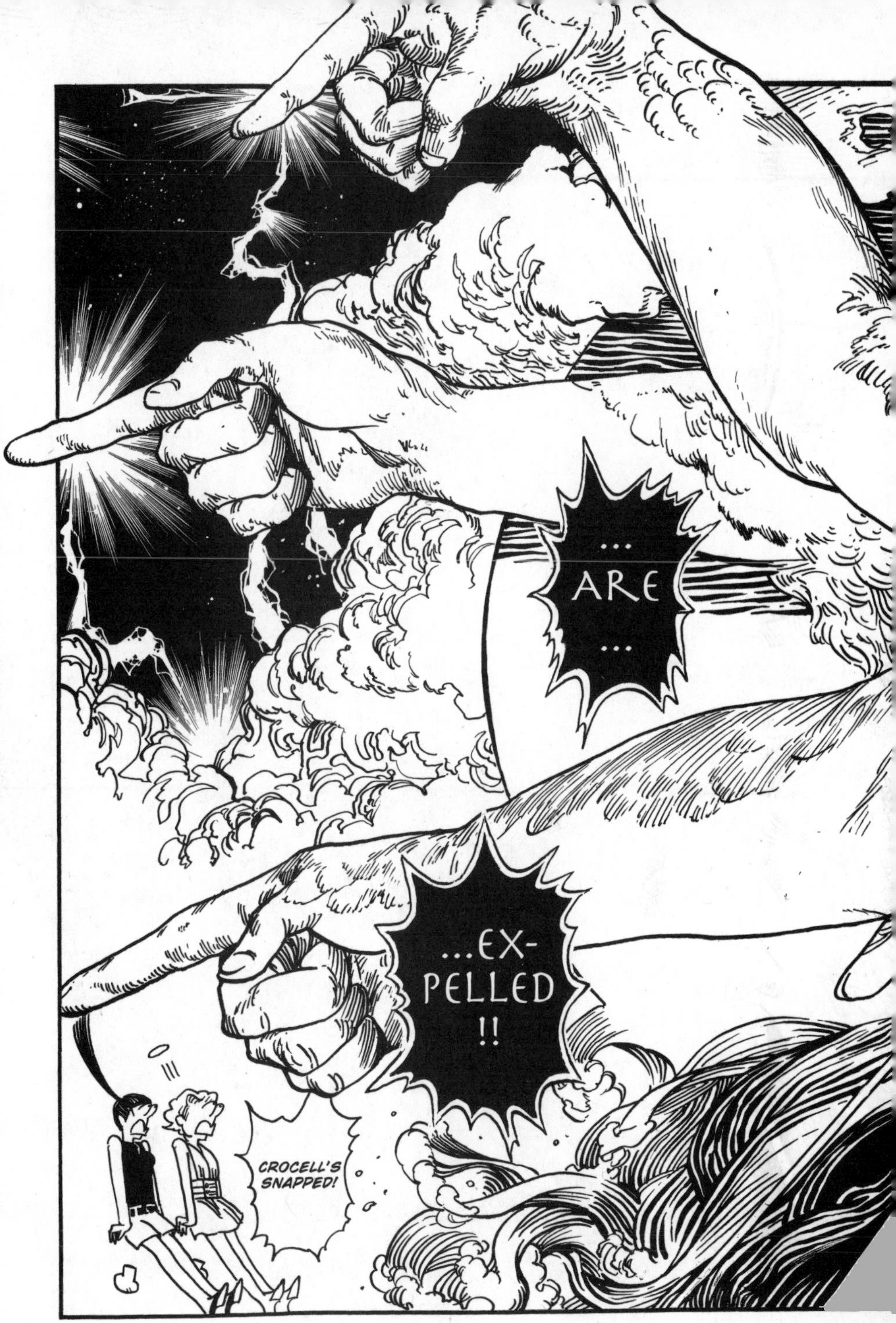
...ARE...
...EX-PELLED!!
CROCELL'S SNAPPED!

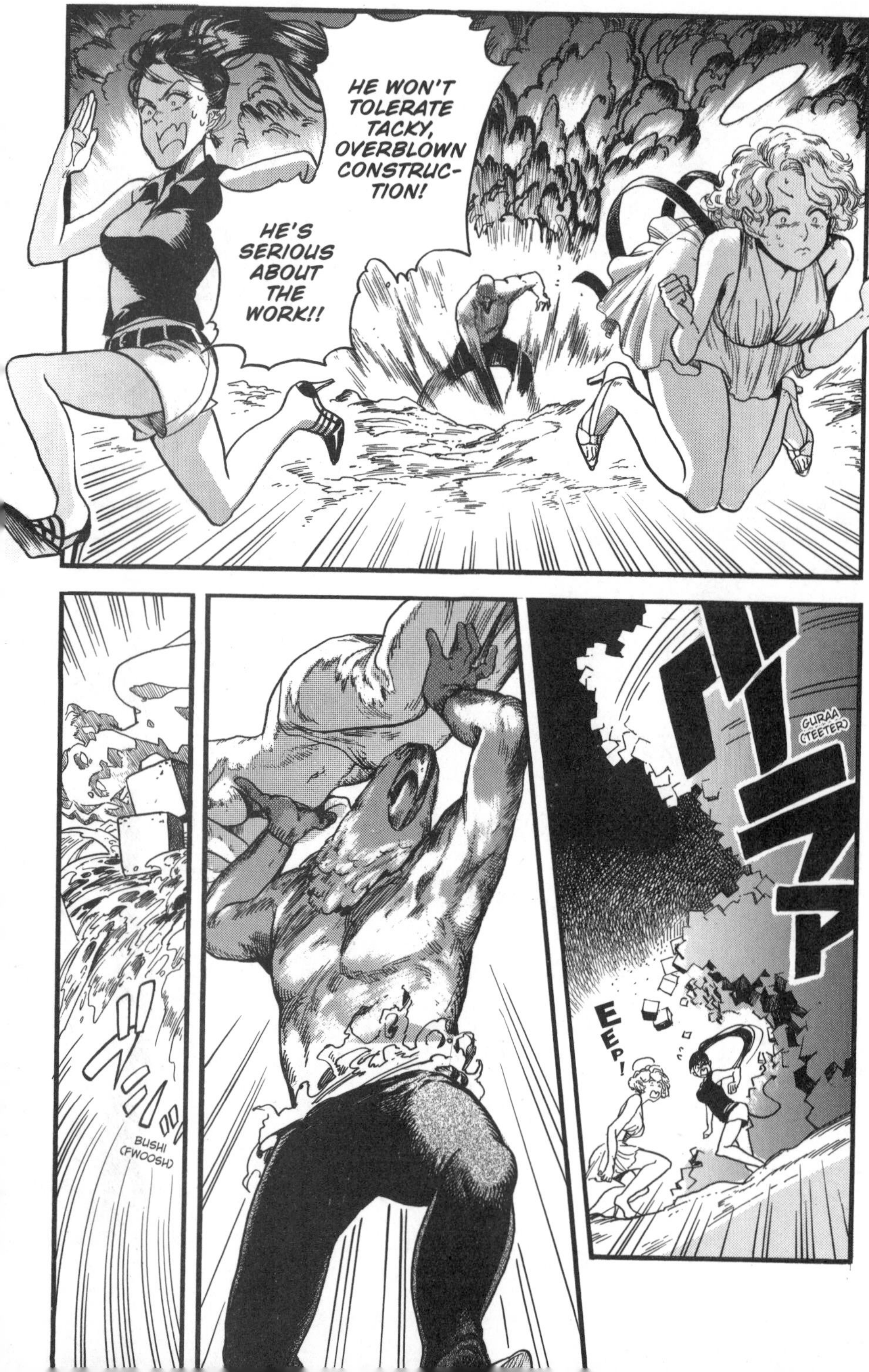
HE WON'T TOLERATE TACKY, OVERBLOWN CONSTRUCTION!
HE'S SERIOUS ABOUT THE WORK!!
GURAA (TEETER)
EEP!
BUSHI (FWOOSH)

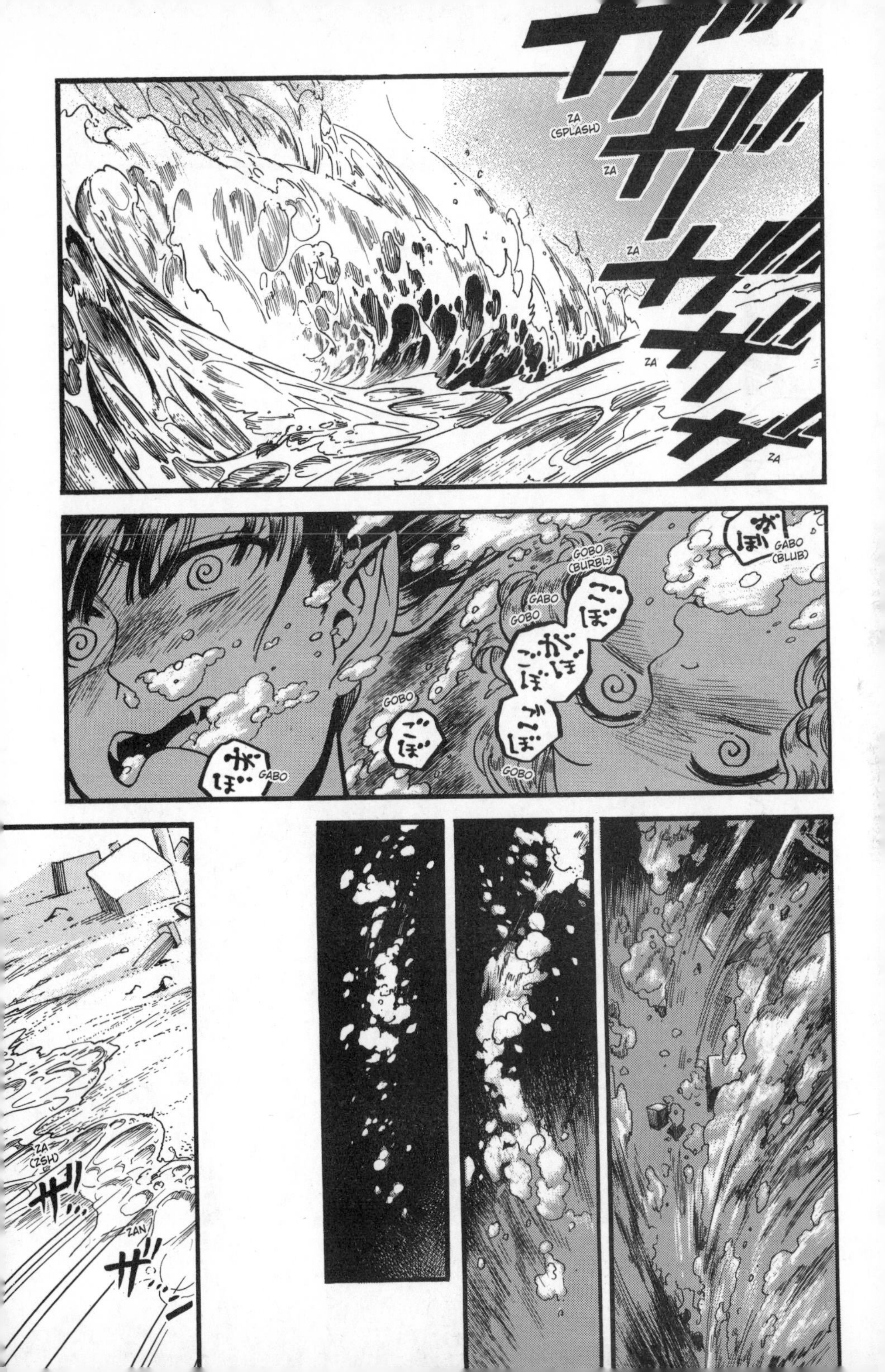

ZA (SPLASH)
ZA
ZA
ZA
ZA
がぼ
GABO (BLUB)
ごぼ
GOBO (BURBL)
がぼごぼ
GABO GOBO
ごぼ
GOBO
ごぼ
GOBO
がぼ
GABO
ZA (ZSH)
ZAN

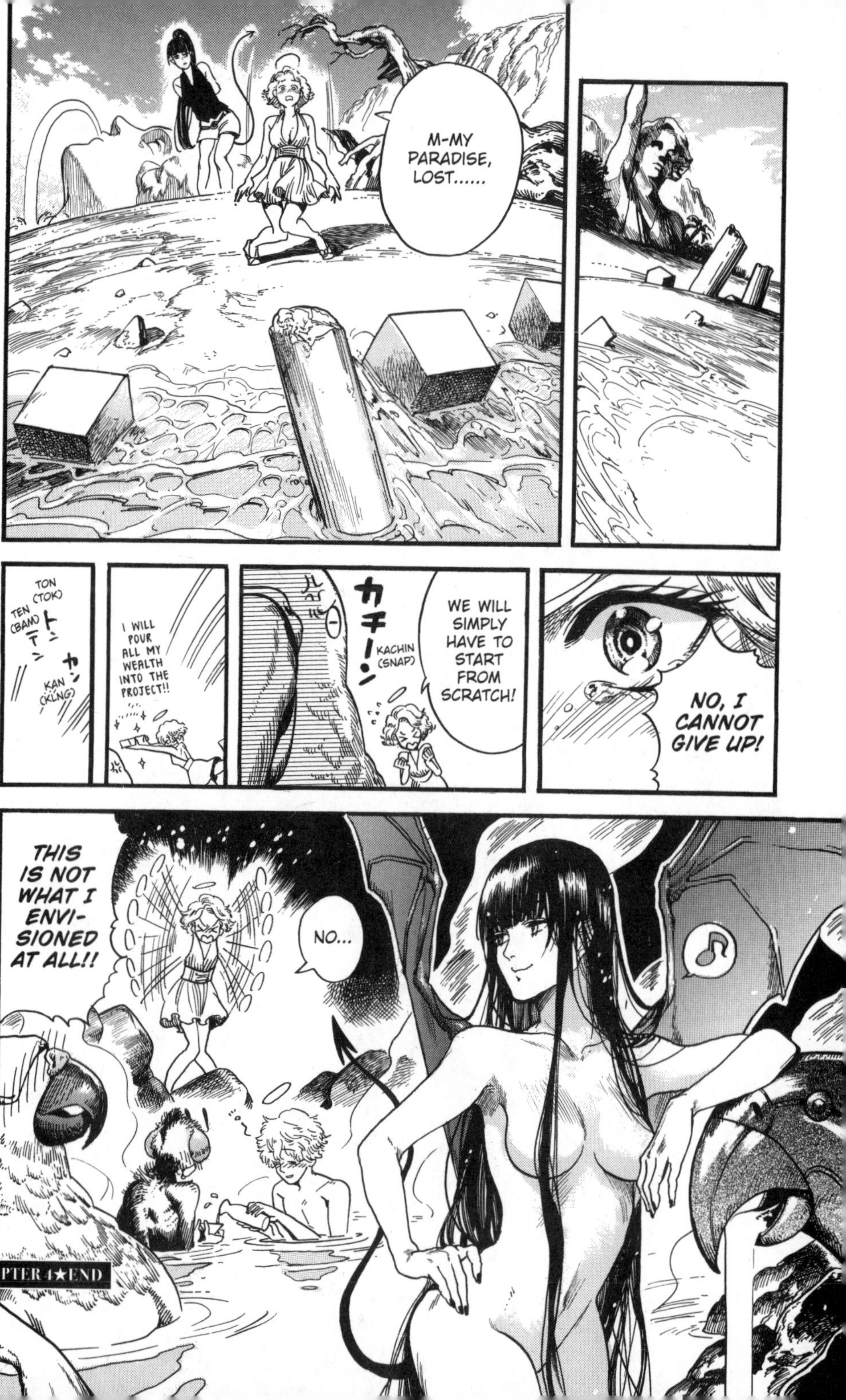
M-MY PARADISE, LOST......
NO, I CANNOT GIVE UP!
WE WILL SIMPLY HAVE TO START FROM SCRATCH!
カチーン
KACHIN (SNAP)
I WILL POUR ALL MY WEALTH INTO THE PROJECT!!
トン
TON (TOK)
テン
TEN (BAM)
カン
KAN (KLNG)
NO...
THIS IS NOT WHAT I ENVISIONED AT ALL!!
CHAPTER 4★END

Translation Notes

GENERAL
Many of the demons mentioned appear in various demonological grimoires, such as the *Pseudomonarchia Daemonum* and *The Lesser Key of Solomon*. Examples include Glasya-Labolas, Buer, Gaap, Eligos, Forneus, Furfur, and Crocell.

PAGE 55
"I spy the lights of Paris!" is a reference to the Japanese title of the 1957 film *The Spirit of St. Louis*, which is about Charles Lindbergh's historic transatlantic flight that started in Long Island and ended in Paris.

PAGE 131
Higan is a Buddhist holiday that takes place during the spring and autumnal equinoxes. It's a time to pay respects to departed ancestors (*higan* means "the other shore," referring to the Sanzu River, which separates the mortal world from the afterlife).

PAGE 143
In Greek and Roman mythological tradition, **Charon** is the ferryman who carries the dead across the Styx and Acheron rivers.

PAGE 150
Darvaza, Turkmenistan is the site of a natural gas field that collapsed into a crater known as the "Door to Hell." To avoid the spread of methane gas, geologists set it on fire in 1971, and it's still burning to this day.

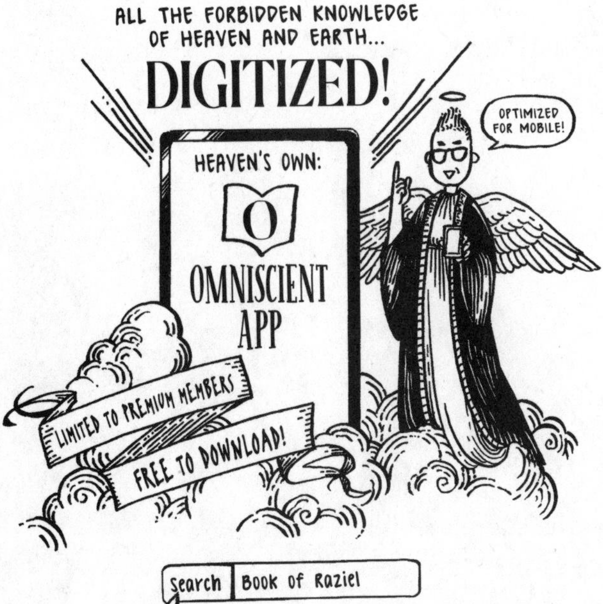
ALL THE FORBIDDEN KNOWLEDGE OF HEAVEN AND EARTH...
DIGITIZED!
OPTIMIZED FOR MOBILE!
HEAVEN'S OWN:
O
OMNISCIENT APP
LIMITED TO PREMIUM MEMBERS
FREE TO DOWNLOAD!
Search
Book of Raziel

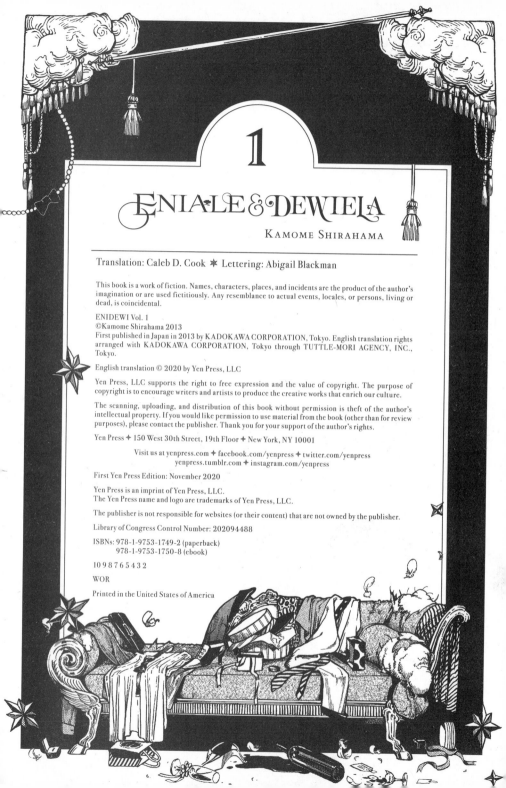

1

ENIALE & DEWIELA

KAMOME SHIRAHAMA

Translation: Caleb D. Cook ✸ Lettering: Abigail Blackman

ENIDEWI Vol. 1
©Kamome Shirahama 2013
First published in Japan in 2013 by KADOKAWA CORPORATION, Tokyo. English translation rights arranged with KADOKAWA CORPORATION, Tokyo through TUTTLE-MORI AGENCY, INC., Tokyo.

English translation © 2020 by Yen Press, LLC

Yen Press ✦ 150 West 30th Street, 19th Floor ✦ New York, NY 10001

Visit us at yenpress.com ✦ facebook.com/yenpress ✦ twitter.com/yenpress
yenpress.tumblr.com ✦ instagram.com/yenpress

First Yen Press Edition: November 2020

Yen Press is an imprint of Yen Press, LLC.
The Yen Press name and logo are trademarks of Yen Press, LLC.

The publisher is not responsible for websites (or their content) that are not owned by the publisher.

Library of Congress Control Number: 202094488

ISBNs: 978-1-9753-1749-2 (paperback)
       978-1-9753-1750-8 (ebook)

10 9 8 7 6 5 4 3 2

WOR

Printed in the United States of America